MSEA
12/82 IV.001973.

W9-CIK-418

Asia—The Winning of Independence

Macmillan International College Editions will bring to university, college, school and professional students, authoritative paperback books covering the history and cultures of the developing world, and the special aspects of its scientific, medical, technical, social and economic development. The International College programme contains many distinguished series in a wide range of disciplines, some titles being regionally biassed, others being more international. Library editions will usually be published simultaneously with the paperback editions. For full details of this list, please contact the publishers.

Macmillan Asian Histories Series:
D. G. E. Hall: A History of South-east Asia – 4th Edition
M. Ricklefs: A History of Modern Indonesia
J-P. Lehmann: The Roots of Modern Japan
B. W. Andaya and L. Y. Andaya: A History of Modern Malaysia

Related Titles:
J. M. van der Kroef: Communism in South-east Asia
H. Goulbourne (Ed): Politics and State in the Third World
A. Saich: China: Politics and Government

Jacket: Adapted from *People's Age*, Communist Party of India weekly newspaper, 23 March 1947, special number for the Inter-Asian Conference in New Delhi.

Asia—The Winning of Independence

Edited by
Robin Jeffrey

The Philippines
India
Indonesia
Vietnam
Malaya

(SOUTHEAST ASIAN REPRINT)

Editorial matter, Introduction and Chapter 2 © Robin Jeffrey 1981;
Chapter 1 © Alfred W. McCoy 1981; Chapter 3 © Anthony Reid
1981; Chapter 4 © David Marr 1981; Chapter 5 © Lee Kam Hing
1981; Conclusion © D. A. Low 1981.

All rights reserved. No part of this publication may be reproduced or
transmitted, in any form or by any means, without permission.

First published 1981 by
THE MACMILLAN PRESS LTD
London and Basingstoke
Associated companies throughout the world.

Southeast Asian Reprint 1982

Typeset by
Reproduction Drawings Ltd, Sutton, Surrey

Printed in Hong Kong

ISBN 0-333-27856-9
ISBN 0-333-27857-7 Pbk

The paperback edition of this book is sold subject to the condition that it
shall not, by way of trade or otherwise, be lent, re-sold, hired out, or otherwise
circulated without the publisher's prior consent in any form of binding other
than that in which it is published and without a similar condition including
this condition being imposed on the subsequent purchaser.

Contents

List of Maps and Tables

List of Illustrations

Preface

Humility must be the first word of this book. The events we describe touched the lives of hundreds of millions of people; the subtleties and nuances have engrossed hundreds of fine scholars for more than thirty years. We keenly appreciate the apparent arrogance of attempting to explain five major nationalist stories in just 75,000 words. We believe, however, that the book represents a co-operative and comparative venture worth attempting. We feel that it fills a gap—that there is no other book quite like it.

The book is intended as an introduction to that momentous period of Asian history from which emerged many conditions that prevail today. Saigon, for example, has become Ho Chi Minh City; the Indonesian army of President Suharto wondrously took shape in 1945; Jawaharlal Nehru's daughter is India's most important politician; the United Malay National Organisation (UMNO) dominates politics in Malaysia; the United States has military bases in the Philippines.

We hope the book whets appetites for, and fires curiosity about, countries that are important, vast and fascinating. We hope, too, that it stimulates interest in comparative studies at a time when, particularly in Europe, North America and Australia, tariff barriers, introversion and tending one's own garden seem increasingly characteristic. We should not tend other people's gardens for them; but occasionally we should look up from our own to admire other flowers and note other crops.

There are fifteen pages of illustrations which seem to us to capture the feeling of particular moments better than many thousands of words and in the following chapters, whenever an illustration is especially apposite to the text, the reader's attention is drawn to it.

To foster comparative analysis, the Timelines on pages xii and xiii allow one to note at a glance some important events in all five countries and the world between 1870 and 1960.

Each chapter contains at least one map, and nine maps in all have been specially drawn for the book.

The Biographical notes include all major Asian leaders mentioned in the text.

The Guide to Further Reading contains nearly 400 items, most with a brief comment about their content. The Guide begins with a section on general studies and thereafter is arranged by country. Used in conjunction with the notes to each chapter, it provides a thorough introduction to recent scholarship.

The Contents page lists subheadings within each chapter, and these, together with the index, will make it easy, we hope, for readers to make the book work for them.

Each chapter is preceded by a glossary of words and abbreviations.

We wish to thank Traill College, Trent University, Peterborough, Ontario, Canada, the Research School of Pacific Studies, Australian National University, Canberra (particularly its cartographers) and Latrobe University, Melbourne (particularly the Graphics and Reprography sections and the Department of Politics) for help in preparing this project.

Robin Jeffrey
Melbourne

Year	International	Philippines	India
1870	70-1 Franco-Prussian War	72 Nationalist priests executed	
	85 Congress of Berlin divides Africa	92 Katipunan founded	85 Indian National Congress founded
	95 Sino-Japanese War	96 Revolt against Spain begins; Rizal executed	
	98 Spanish-American War	98 Aguinaldo proclaims independence; US defeats Spain	
1900	01 Queen Victoria dies	01 US captures Aguinaldo, overcomes nationalists	
	04-5 Russo-Japanese War		05 Bengal partitioned
			06 Muslim League founded
	07 Entente Cordiale	07 Lower house elections	09 Morley-Minto reforms
	11 Chinese empire overthrown		11 Bengal reunited
	14 First World War begins		15 Gandhi returns to India
	17 Russian revolution	16 Upper house elections	
	18 First World War ends		19 Jallianwalla Bagh massacre; Montagu-Chelmsford reforms
	19 4 May Incident in China; Treaty of Versailles		
1920		22 Quezon wins control of Nacionalista Party	20-2 Non-cooperation and Khilafat movement
	24 Lenin dies		25 Communist Party founded
	28 1st Soviet 5-Year Plan		
	29 Economic depression begins		
1930	31 Japan invades Manchuria	30 Communist Party formed	30-3 Civil disobedience movement
	33 Hitler to power in Germany		
	34-5 Mao's Long March in China	35 Commonwealth established; Quezon president	35 Govt of India Act
	37 Japan invades China		37 Congress wins provincial elections
	39 Second World War begins		39 Congress govts resign
1940	40 Nazis overrun Europe	41 Japanese invasion	
	41 Nazis invade USSR; Pacific war begins	43 Japanese-backed republic established	42 Quit India movement
	45 Second World War ends	45 US drives out Japanese	45-6 Congress & Muslim League win elections
		46 Roxas president; independence proclaimed; Huk revolt begins	46 Naval mutiny, Bombay; communal violence
	48 Berlin blockade; 'cold war' begins	47 Military-bases agreement with US	47 Independence for India & Pakistan
	49 Chinese communists win power		48 Gandhi assassinated; Jinnah dies
1950	50 Korean War begins		50 Republic of India proclaimed
	53 Korean War ends; Stalin dies	54 Huk revolt ends	51-2 1st general elections, India
	56 Khrushchev denounces Stalin; Soviet invasion of Hungary; Anglo-French invasion of Egypt		56 Pakistan's 1st constitution inaugurated
		57 President Magsaysay killed in air crash	57 2nd general elections, India
	57 Ghana independent in Africa		58 Military coup, Pakistan
1960			

Indonesia	Vietnam	Malaya	
	67 French control over Cochinchina		**1870**
73 Dutch begin conquest of Aceh	84 French control over Annam & Tonkin	74 British impose Residents on 3 sultans	
91 Dutch conquer -4 Lombok		88 British Resident for Pahang	
	97 Vietnamese resistance quelled by French		
00 'Ethical Policy'		02 Malay College, Kuala Kangsar, founded	**1900**
03 Dutch conquer -5 Sulawesi			
07 Dutch complete conquest of Aceh			
08 Budi Utomo founded		09 British advisers placed in 4 states	
12 Sarekat Islam and Muhammadiah			
14 Socialist Party (ISDP)		14 British adviser placed in Johore	
18 Volksraad	17 Formation of bourgeois Constitutionalist Party		
20 Communist Party (PKI)			**1920**
22 Taman Siswa school system begins	25 Cao Dai Church established	22 Sultan Idris Teachers' College founded	
26 Abortive -7 communist revolt	26 Student strikes -7		
27 Sukarno's PNI founded			
28 'Youth Oath' of Indonesian unity			
30 PNI disbanded; Partindo founded	30 Indochinese Communist Party formed	32 Malayan Communist Party	**1930**
31 Hatta's New PNI			
33 Sukarno to internal exile	30 Peasant uprisings -1		
34 Hatta & Sjahrir to internal exile	36 Indochina Congress movement		
37 MIAI Islamic federation established	38 20,000 in May Day march, Hanoi	38 Young Malay Union (KMM)	
	39 Hoa Hao sect; French suppress legal opposition		
	40 Japanese dominate Indochina		**1940**
42 Japanese conquest	41 Communist-led Viet Minh formed; Japanese troops in Cochinchina	42 Japanese conquest; MPAJA resistance formed	
43 Japanese train Indonesian army		45 Japanese surrender; Malayan Union proposed	
44 Japanese promise independence			
45 Independence proclaimed; war with Dutch	45 Japanese remove French; Democratic Republic	46 UMNO founded; Malayan Union withdrawn	
46 Linggajati agreement	46 1st Indochina War	48 Emergency proclaimed; Federation of Malaya Agreement	
47 1st Dutch offensive			
48 Communist revolt; 2nd Dutch offensive		49 Malayan Chinese Association founded	
49 Federal Republic internationally acknowledged	49 French-sponsored state in Vietnam	51 Communists murder British High Cmr; Malayans serve on Executive Council	**1950**
50 Unitary Republic established	54 French defeated; Geneva Agreement ends war; two Vietnams emerge	52 local-govt elections	
53 Revolt in Aceh	55 Diem president in south	54 UMNO calls for independence	
55 1st national elections	58 Agricultural -9 cooperatives in north	55 1st federal elections	
58 PRRI revolt (Sumatra & Sulawesi)	60 National Liberation Front to fight Diem & Americans	57 Independence	
59 'Guided Democracy'		59 People's Action Party, Singapore	
		60 Emergency withdrawn	**1960**

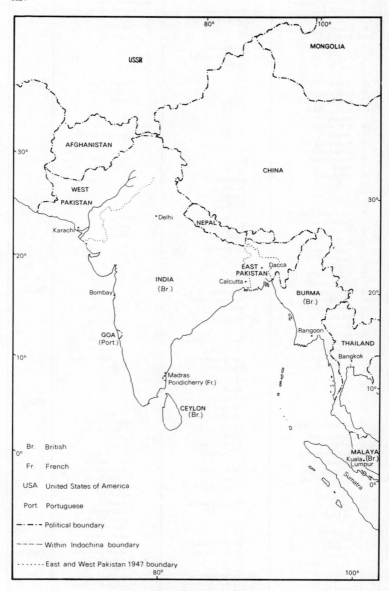

Asia before the Second World War

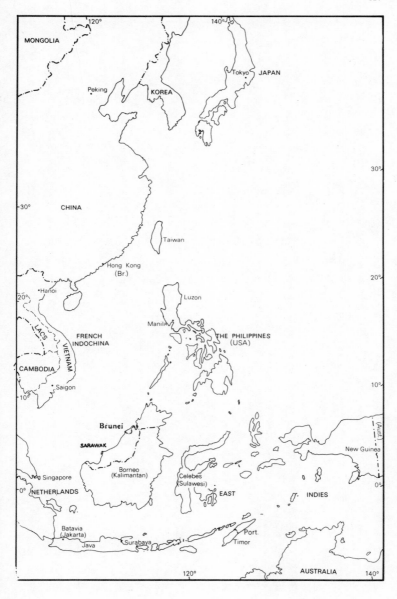

Introduction:
The Setting for
Independence

Robin Jeffrey

In the last months of 1945, Asia was in ferment. That much was clear even to readers of newspapers in countries far away, as items in the London *Times* showed:

CIVIL WAR THREAT IN PHILIPPINES. LUZON AN ARMED CAMP . . . clashes between the Filipino army and the Hukbalahaps, a powerful leftist independent guerilla movement. . . .

30 October 1945, p. 4.

BITTER CLASHES AT SAIGON. ANNAMITE ATTEMPT TO TAKE AIRFIELD. New French forces . . . forward positions . . . strong opposition. . . . 15 October 1945, p. 4.

FIGHTING IN SURABAYA. BRITISH FORCES ENGAGED. INDONESIANS WELL ARMED. British troops . . . principally 49th Indian Brigade . . . heaviest casualties to date. . . .

30 October 1945, p. 4.

LEFT-WING RALLY IN SINGAPORE. More than 5,000 Chinese . . . left-wing resistance groups. . . . 18 September 1945, p. 3.

ELECTION MOVES IN INDIA. VIGOROUS CAMPAIGN BY CONGRESS. 12 October 1945, p. 3.

MR. JINNAH ON DUTCH "IMPERIALISM". "Dutch dominion and imperialism", he said, "must come to an end, like any other foreign dominion and imperialism . . . or else this terrible war has been fought in vain." 13 October 1945, p. 3.

For the peoples of colonially ruled Asia the war with Japan that began in December 1941 brought dislocation, violence and starvation. Japan's defeat left tension, excitement, uncertainty; a readiness to take risks and seek changes. The mood crossed borders and language barriers. 'The psychological effect of revolts in French Indo-China and Indonesia' produced in India a situation that was, the Viceroy warned, 'more dangerous' than at any time for ninety years.[1] Even Britain's aloof, conservative *Times* conceded that 'the entire practice of the rule of one race by another' was now 'discredited'.[2]

Within a few years of the end of the war, the countries of colonially ruled Asia had become sovereign states: the Philippines in 1946, India and Pakistan in 1947, Ceylon and Burma in 1948, Indonesia (internationally acknowledged) in 1949. The French were driven out of Indochina in 1954; Malaya became independent in 1957. By 1960, only enclaves like Hongkong, Goa and Portuguese Timor, and the vast island of New Guinea (Irian), divided between Dutch and Australians, remained under non-Asian governments. By 1980, citizens of the Philippines, India, Pakistan and Bangladesh had experienced the traumas of more than thirty years of independence; Indonesia had been torn by, but survived, a bloody abortive coup in 1965; Vietnam had overcome the Americans as it had the French and found itself in conflict with China and embroiled in Kampuchea; Malaya — from 1963, the federation of Malaysia — had weathered strife between Chinese and Malays and, like Singapore, appeared to prosper more than most Asian or African countries.

In 1939 when the Second World War began, few would have predicted that the end of colonial rule was imminent. From Baluchis on the western frontiers of India to Tagalogs on Luzon and Bugis on Sulawesi in the eastern islands, only the Thais — and farther north, the Chinese and Japanese — had remained largely self-governing. Japan's conquest of Southeast Asia and assault on the eastern frontiers of India accelerated processes that might otherwise have taken generations. Yet these processes had already begun: the yeast was in the dough; Japan provided the heat that so suddenly made it rise.

GUIDEBOOKS AND LANDMARKS

This book may be regarded as a guidebook in that it attempts to point out and describe the forces that shaped independence movements and independent governments. Like a guidebook, it can only identify landmarks, attempt to spark the reader's interest with a provocative argument or intriguing detail and hope that the reader will thereby be induced to explore more widely.

The chapters attempt to trace the threads of independence movements into the nineteenth century. For governments aiming to instil new identities, and for anyone wishing to understand such governments and their goals, the past is crucial. An example perhaps will illustrate. In December 1921, a court in British India sentenced a sixty-year-old Indian to prison for political offences. His son later wrote: 'My daughter, aged four at the time, had her first experience of the dock during father's trial, as he held her in his arms throughout.'[3] The girl was Indira Gandhi.

Why should we consider these particular countries – the Philippines, India, Indonesia, Vietnam and Malaya – and why discuss them in a single book? Each is, we feel, important in its own right. The Philippines was the first colony to gain independence after the war. India was the second; but, more important, it was the greatest of all colonies, 'the jewel in the crown' of the British Empire.[4] Indonesia and Vietnam demonstrated that Asia's colonially ruled peoples would and could fight for their independence. Their example quickened the pace of change in the rest of Asia and Africa. Malaya provided a paradox: a powerful communist insurgency like Vietnam; a tangled communal problem like India; yet ultimately a non-revolutionary transfer of power amid remarkable interracial co-operation. In crude population terms, these areas in 1980 sustain (though in some cases, barely) more than 1000 million people.

Individually, then, each country is important in the modern world. Moreover, if one looks at them together, one begins to see more clearly the distinctive features of each independence movement and each independent nation. Comparison clarifies and dramatises. The final chapter of this book explores more systematically a few enticing, comparative themes. For now it is enough to ask, for example, whether, until one considers the partition of India, one can appreciate the importance that the relative absence of religious divisions has had for Indonesia and Vietnam. If independence fell to the Philippines almost like a ripe apple, the massacres of partition brought it to India and Pakistan as sour as a lemon. By placing apples beside lemons we begin to appreciate the differences.

Though one can argue strongly that colonial powers controlled

China and Thailand economically in the early twentieth century, we have not considered them in this book. Whatever the extent of their economic subjugation and resulting social dislocation, they did not feel the cultural yoke in the same way as Filipinos, Indians, Vietnamese, Indonesians and Malayans. The Philippines chapter in this book particularly emphasises the 'bi-nationalism' that the colonial experience engendered (see illustration p. 21). The consequences are neatly symbolised in a photograph of the President of India in 1980, pads strapped over traditional *churidar* pyjamas, batting in a parliamentary cricket match. A few months before he had declared: 'The Indian dream that anyone can become President has come true. I am a villager. I am a farmer.'[5] Can one, without a smile, visualise Mao keeping wicket? One may assume, too, that children in non-colonial countries did not have to study textbooks in foreign languages that told them, for example, that 'we Filipinos have . . . some very undesirable traits. . . . We still have much to learn.'[6] It was not simply European officials in gold braid and plumed hats that made the colonially ruled countries different from China, Japan and Thailand.

We have also not considered Burma, Sri Lanka, Kampuchea and Laos. This is not because their stories lack fascination or importance. Indeed, a reader of this book would, we hope, be primed to explore their modern history. We have, however, been aiming for contrasts and comparisons, not for comprehensiveness, and we have been influenced by the fact that Burma, Sri Lanka, Kampuchea and Laos came to independence as a result in many ways of events in their larger, dominant neighbours, India and Vietnam.

If this is a guidebook, what landmarks should readers be looking for? What roads should they expect to travel?

One may suggest that there are two broad roads, one signposted 'revolutionary', the other 'evolutionary'. On the former lie Indonesia and Vietnam where colonial institutions, and classes allied to the colonial powers, were violently overturned in the years after 1945. On the 'evolutionary' road lie the Philippines and India. There, colonial institutions – the civil service, business houses, the army – survived intact. To be sure, there was violence. Hundreds of thousands died during the partition into India and Pakistan in 1947; the Hukbalahap attempted armed rebellion against the Philippine government in the late 1940s. But in both instances, the governments to whom the colonial powers transferred authority withstood

TABLE I.1

Europeans in Asian colonies and proportion to total populations, 1930s

	Philippines	India	Indonesia	Vietnam	Malaya*
Total population	14 m	350 m	61 m	19 m	7 m
Europeans	9000	96,000	300,000	40,000	24,000
Europeans to total population	1:1550	1:3650	1:200	1:475	1:290

*Excludes Straits Settlements.

Sources: Theodore Friend, *Between Two Empires. The Ordeal of the Philippines, 1929-46* (New Haven: Yale University Press, 1965) p. 18; N. Mansergh and P. Moon (eds.), *The Transfer of Power, 1942-7*, vol. VIII (London: HMSO, 1979) p. 275.

the shocks. Malaya lies like a twisting path between the two roads, fascinating for the contrasts it shows with both. Like Indonesia and Vietnam, it had moved little towards independence by 1941; like them too, it produced a leftwing guerrilla movement during the war and offered the prospect of successful revolution after 1945. Indeed, it was 1960 before that prospect was largely removed. Yet Malaya produced an evolutionary transfer of power in which traditional Sultans and twentieth-century business interests were maintained.

What landmarks can one expect to find on each of the two broad roads? On the one marked 'evolutionary', one may suggest:

A long period of colonial rule that, however grudgingly, fostered education and participatory government.
A large Westernised elite, the product of generations familiar with, and sympathetic to, the existing structure of government.
A relatively small number of European residents (see table I.I).
A large, well-developed colonial bureaucracy and army, staffed by local people.
A colonial government ready, for various reasons, to release its grip.

On the road marked 'revolutionary', one might look for:

A relatively short period of colonial rule.
Little Western-style education.
No nationwide Westernised elite until well into the twentieth century.
Larger number of European residents (see table I.I).
Little participatory government.
A heavy colonial economic interest in the country.
A colonial power unwilling to leave.

Readers should keep an eye out for such landmarks in the chapters that follow. But they will also no doubt discover landmarks of their own that cast still longer shadows. A guidebook reflects the foibles of the guide.

THE ECONOMIC SETTING

HARRISONS AND CROSFIELD LIMITED. TEA AND RUBBER POSITION AND OUTLOOK. MR. H. ERIC MILLER'S REVIEW.
The Company has interests in the Netherlands East Indies,

Malaya, India, Ceylon and North Borneo. Mr. Miller was critical of events in the N.E.I. The foundations of good government, he said, could not be built "by shouting slogans and by letting irresponsible adolescents loose with firearms. Thorough eduction extending over several generations was needed . . ." He concluded, however, that "we are able to show substantially higher profits and feel justified in recommending an increased dividend on the Deferred Ordinary stock of 15 per cent".

The Times, London, 31 October 1945, p. 8.

Imperialism is based on advantage, profit and exploitation. European powers began their activities in Asia as traders. Though they transformed themselves into rulers in the late eighteenth and nineteenth centuries, and talked much of white men's burdens (not to mention white women's honours), profit remained the dominant concern of the majority. Indeed, the Pacific war had obvious economic causes. Japan's manufactured goods pushed into the Asian colonies in the 1920s and 1930s, squeezing out those from Europe and America. At the same time, Japan required assured supplies of oil, rice, rubber, tin and other goods from the region. Markets and raw materials have become old chestnuts in debates about what caused imperialism; but the Pacific war owed much to attempts by both the Japanese and the colonial powers to pull those chestnuts out of the other's fire. In spite of the interruption of the war, by the 1970s Japanese economic influence was paramount throughout much of ex-colonial Asia.

France and the Netherlands leaned heavily on their Asian colonies. The Dutch plaintively argued that they were running a vast tropical estate for the benefit of the world: of imports into Indonesia in 1939, only about a quarter came from the Netherlands; only about a seventh of exports went there.[7] But of the US $2000 million invested in Indonesia in the 1930s, 73 per cent was Dutch, and between 10 and 20 per cent of the Netherlands depended directly for its livelihood on the Indies (this book, p. 133).

Similarly, by 1939, the Bank of Indochina was one of the richest enterprises in France, owning 110 undertakings throughout the world (p. 165-7). Though any explanation of France's intransigence in Indochina in 1945-6 needs to include the desperate longing to re-establish French military prestige after the humiliations of the Second World War, one must also emphasise France's huge economic stake. By the late 1940s, to be sure, the Bank of Indochina was pulling out much of its capital; but that, of course, only made it easier to accept defeat in 1954: the economic interest had in some measure been removed. One can construct an enticing argument that France and Holland clung to their empires in Asia with such ferocity because their commercial connection was so important to so many of their people.

British interests in Malaya also remained great (see illustration, p. 209). Indeed, in the immediate aftermath of the war, Malaya was seen as one of Britain's marketable assets:

> MALAYAN TIN AND RUBBER. A correspondent calls for them to be used to overcome the dollar crisis Britain is experiencing as a result of the end of the lend-lease agreement with the United States. He points out that before the war the value of Malayan tin and rubber imported by the U.S. exceeded that of all its imports from the United Kingdom.
>
> *The Times*, London, 18 September 1945, p. 5.

The fact that the British retained such important interests in Malaya no doubt helped to explain their readiness to fight a protracted guerrilla war and their pains to foster a conservative and aristocratic successor government. Even in the Philippines, where the colony could scarcely be considered vital to the vast American economy, the United States secured the interests of its businessmen through the Bell Act of 1948 (p. 58 and illustration, p. 19).

In India, the strong links of private gain had weakened. By 1945, less than 20 per cent of India's imports were coming from British factories (in 1900: 69 per cent) and only about 28 per cent of Indian exports were going to Britain (in 1870: 53 per cent).[8] The British in 1945 had given up any idea of attempting to hold India by force. This stemmed partly from realism: after the war it would have been an almost impossible task and politically disastrous for any British government. Partly, too, however, the economic relationship had attenuated; fewer Britons derived economic benefit from India than Frenchmen did from Indochina, Dutch from the Indies or indeed, Britons from Malaya.

THE CONDITION OF THE PEOPLE

PROHIBITION OF OPIUM. BRITISH RULING FOR FAR EAST
TERRITORIES. The British military administration in Singapore
has announced a total prohibition of the sale of opium in Malaya
and all British-protected territories in the Far East. This takes the
place of the policy in Malaya before the war of gradually reducing
Government revenue from the opium monopoly with total prohibition as the ultimate object.

The Times, London, 10 October 1945, p. 3.

By 1945 the burden on the British in their eastern territories had
eased sufficiently to allow them to stop financing their rule through
the sale of dangerous drugs to their subjects and other peoples. But
opium had been a mainstay of Indian finance throughout the nineteenth century.[9]

Not surprisingly, the living conditions of the majority of subjects
worsened during colonial rule. In part, this resulted from rises in
population, the outcome of simple innovations in public health
(smallpox vaccination, for example). The population of India rose
from 305 million in 1921 to 389 million in 1941, an increase of
28 per cent in twenty years. In the period of 1911 to 1941, the
quantity of grain available annually for each Indian fell by 30 per
cent.[10] In Java by the 1930s, rice production was capable of providing each inhabitant with only 220 grams a day, less than half the
requirement for an adult (p. 119). The majority of colonial subjects
had less to eat than had their grandparents and great-grandparents.

The imperial powers, sometimes directly (as in the 'culture
system' in Indonesia), sometimes indirectly, induced peasants to
grow non-edible cash crops. 'Ironically,' Blyn writes, ' . . . the crops
which increased most rapidly . . . were the market oriented nonfood-
grains'.[11] Such crops were known throughout the world. To 'Manila
hemp', 'India rubber', 'Java' (coffee) and 'Makassar oil' (coconut
oil), one could add sugar and coconut from the Philippines, pepper,
tobacco, coconut and sugar from Indonesia, rubber and tea from
Malaya, rice (grown for export on vast estates) and rubber from
Vietnam. In India, peasants turned to coconut, cotton, tobacco,
sugarcane, oilseeds – and 'elite' foodgrains like wheat and rice intended for sale, in place of coarser grains consumed locally.

Extractive industries – oil in Indonesia, tin in Malaya, coal in

Vietnam — and commercial agriculture drove the disruptive elements of a cash economy deep into old societies. At the same time, the flexibility of local custom was replaced by the rigidity of codified, Western-style law. Village lands, often held in common in the past, became privately 'owned': often by accident when colonial officials sought to establish neat, familiar systems of private property; sometimes by design when sly government officials had lands registered in the names of relatives or patrons. The effect was worst perhaps in Vietnam (pp. 168), least in Malaya, but the phenomenon was to be found in every area. Societies were pulled apart. Families that had for generations tilled land in a locality became, if they were lucky, owners; if they were unlucky, tenants; or, unluckier still, simply labourers. The new legal system, with laws on debt and private property, was backed up by colonial police forces that were often corrupt and inefficient but invariably powerful enough to evict tax defaulters or foreclose on mortgages.

Yet the colonial administrations were limited and fragile. In India, the government was never able to prevent famine in the nineteenth century. Colonial power dissolved before the Japanese in 1942, and colonial administrations in India and Vietnam were totally unable to protect their subjects from starvation in the war years. Between one and two million died in the Vietnam famine of 1944-5; at least one-and-a-half million, by the government's admission, in Bengal in 1942-3.

ELITES AND LEADERS

Obituary
SIR N. N. SIRCAR. FORMER LAW MEMBER OF THE VICE-ROY'S COUNCIL. As became the grandson of Peary Churn Sircar, a noted pioneer of English education in Bengal, he was a man of scholarly attainments. . . . He was called to the Bar from Lincoln's Inn, having been first honours man in the Bar Final Examination of 1907. He was knighted in 1931 and Law Member of the Viceroy's Council from 1934-9. He married Nabanalim, only daughter of Durgadas Basu, and had eight sons.

The Times, London, 13 August 1945, p. 7.

The leaders of the independence movements did not come from the afflicted peasantries. They came, as one would expect, from classes educated in the ways of the West and experiencing the tension of two cultures warring within a single man or woman. Of the men who presided over their countries at independence, only Ho Chi Minh could in any way be described as having a non-elite background. Even Ho's father was a mandarin, though Ho himself seems to have roamed the streets of Hue as a child.[12] On the other hand, Manuel Roxas in the Philippines, Jawaharlal Nehru in India, M.A. Jinnah in Pakistan, Sukarno in Indonesia and Tunku Abdul Rahman in Malaya were all products of families that had enjoyed prestige and influence not only under the foreign rulers but in pre-colonial times as well. All five were raised in households where European languages were already known. Ho's father, in contrast, refused to learn French,[13] though he sent his son to a French-language school.

The size and extent of the Westernised elite varied with the length of colonial rule and the colonial power's commitment to education.

TABLE I.2

Literacy, 1930s

	Philippines	India	Indonesia	Vietnam	Malaya
Population	14 m	350 m	61 m	19 m	7 m
Literate	50 %	12 %	8 %	10 %	29 %

Source: Estimates based on census statistics.

India and the Philippines contrasted sharply with Indonesia, Vietnam and Malaya. The Philippines claimed the oldest universities in Asia, San Carlos in Cebu City (1595) and Santo Tomas in Manila (1611). India's first three universities were founded in 1857. By the 1920s, 3 million Indians knew English. The literacy rate in 1941 was only 12 per cent, yet in absolute numbers, this meant that 47 million people could read and write. In India in the 1930s, there were more than 100,000 university graduates; in Indonesia, 300. In the Philippines, perhaps a fifth of the population knew English and a half was literate.

Indonesia, Vietnam and Malaya, on the other hand, were under colonial rule for a much shorter period. The French and Dutch were still fighting 'pacifications' in Vietnam and Indonesia in the decade before the First World War, and the British established their authority over the Sultans of Kelantan and Trengganu only in 1909. Indonesia and Vietnam got permanent universities only towards the end of the First World War; Malaya and Singapore, in the 1950s. Western influence had less chance to pervade Vietnam, the outer islands of Indonesia and Malaya than it did India and the Philippines.

The larger Westernised elite grew in part from American and British ideas about the desirability of education. A logical extension was the desirability of participatory government. The Americans had created a national assembly in the Philippines by 1907; the India Act of 1919 gave real power in the provinces to Indian ministers who were responsible to an elected legislature. There was nothing comparable in Indonesia, Vietnam or Malaya.

Similarly, widespread education produced a bureaucracy overwhelmingly run by Filipinos and Indians. When India and Pakistan became independent in 1947, there were virtually no positions, except the Viceroyalty, that Indians had not already filled. An Indian had been appointed a provincial governor as early as 1920, and in the Philippines, 'by 1928 virtually the entire colonial government, from cabinet ministers down to postal clerks, was manned by Filipinos' (p. 43). In both India and the Philippines large classes grew up that were cognisant with, and sympathetic to, colonial institutions; such classes had an interest in preserving them.

ARMIES

INDIA'S FIGHTING FORCES. Four Indian V[ictoria] C[rosse]s and a representative group of other Indian soldiers . . . were entertained at tea by the Royal Empire Society [in London] yesterday.

The Times, London, 30 October 1945, p. 6.

At the same moment, British-led Indian troops were fighting Indonesian and Vietnamese nationalists in Surabaya and Saigon and re-establishing the British empire in Malaya. The Indian Army in 1945 stood as perhaps the largest, strongest institution in colonial Asia – 2 million men, with 15,740 Indian officers, more than forty at or above the rank of lieutenant-colonel. Composed entirely of volunteers, it had fought Britain's battles in North Africa and Italy and provided 70 per cent of the troops who defeated the Japanese in Burma.[14] The Indian officers, recruited at the rate of a few dozen a year from the 1920s, represented the cream of Westernised society from all parts of India. Although 25,000 prisoners-of-war in Malaya had enlisted in Subhash Chandra Bose's Indian National Army to fight alongside the Japanese, the Indian Army in 1945 was unpoliticised. Even after its division into Indian and Pakistan armies in 1947, it provided a stable – some would have said an alienated and reactionary – base on which a new government could rely without immediate fear of being overthrown or overruled. Pakistan's first military coup came only in 1958, eleven years after independence.

None of the other countries had pre-war colonial armies as large or as long-established as India's. Malaya had only two battalions of British-officered Malay troops in 1941; its unsuccessful defence against the Japanese was undertaken chiefly by British, Australian and Indian soldiers. Only the Philippines had a significant pre-war officer corps of local men. From the point of view of indigenous leftwing forces, this absence was an advantage. As Marr writes of the Indochinese Communist Party, 'the possibility of a bourgeois Vietnamese officer corps was chilling' (P. 183). Such men would have been far less obvious examples of foreign oppression than European or American officers, yet they could have been expected to defend their own elite's interests and the status quo. In Indonesia, the tiny group of Indonesian officers in the Dutch colonial army, plus those of the Japanese-inspired PETA, combined with the furious patriotism of the youth (the *pemuda*) to create the army of the Indonesian republic in the last months of 1945. A vital element in the revolution in Indonesian society, and the spearhead of the war against the Dutch, the army was inextricably involved in the political processes of the new republic. But its diverse origins – it had no equivalent of the Viet Minh at its source – and predominantly nationalist inspiration meant that it was inhospitable to communism. In Vietnam, French-officered Vietnamese troops were expected to keep order for the Japanese during the occupation, but such troops had long been suspicious of their French officers and had mutinied in the past. Though the French attempted to recruit a Vietnamese officer corps after 1949, such men came on the scene too late to influence events before the French defeat in 1954; their impact was to be felt far more after 1960.

COMMUNISTS

JAPANESE GIVE UP ARMS TO COMMUNISTS.
The Times, London, 13 August 1945, p. 4.

In 1941 communist parties in colonial Asia were illegal or virtually non-existent. The Indonesian Communist Party, the PKI, had been smashed and banned in the 1920s. The Indochinese Communist Party was constantly harassed by the French colonial police, and Ho Chi Minh had only recently managed to return from exile (see illustrations, pp. 158, 159). In India, the party had been banned since 1934, while in Malaya and the Philippines, though there was interest among intellectuals, communist parties had little influence among workers and peasants; they existed more on paper than in practice. All except the Indian communists had from the 1930s begun to look to China as their exemplars, even if the font of wisdom lay theoretically in Moscow. Japan's war on China from 1937 identified the Japanese as the potential enemy.

With Japan's conquest of Southeast Asia, communist parties found themselves in the frontline, custodians in many ways of national honour and decency, and allies, sometimes, of the former colonial masters. In the Philippines, communists became a powerful element of the anti-Japanese resistance movement, the Hukbalahap. In Malaya, the Malayan Communist Party, heavily Chinese, waged a troublesome guerrilla campaign. In both countries, the guerrillas received arms, which they retained after the war, from British and American air drops and submarines. In Vietnam, the Viet Minh led the struggle against the Japanese, who ruled through the compliant Vichy French until 1945. Even in Indonesia, where the communist party was perhaps weakest, it gained respect for its efforts at resistance. Only in India did the communists fail to enhance their strength and reputation during the war. Legalised in July 1942, the party had thrown its support behind the British war effort after the invasion of the Soviet Union. It denounced the Indian National Congress of Gandhi and Nehru, which opposed the war and launched the Quit India movement in August, as a 'fifth column' of the fascists. In countries the Japanese overran, it was all very well for communists to link arms with the ex-colonial masters to fight fascism. But in India, where British rule remained, the communist–imperialist alliance appeared to be directed as much against the Indian National Congress as Japan (see illustration, p. 68). Nor did the communists in India acquire arms, as they did elsewhere. Their position after the war left them open to denunciation as collaborators of the British and traitors to true nationalism. This contrasted dramatically with the situation in Vietnam, the Philippines, Malaya and Indonesia, where the communists emerged from the war with enhanced respect, arms and the real prospect of capturing power. The last chapter of this book looks at the comparisons and contrasts in greater detail.

'FROM ALLAHABAD TO JAKARTA'

'By air Batavia [Jakarta] can be reached in two days from Allahabad', Jawaharlal Nehru wrote to a colleague in October 1945, informing him of an invitation from Sukarno to come to view events in Indonesia, especially the use of Indian troops. 'I replied that if there is need for me there in the interest of Indonesian freedom I shall come'[15] (see illustration, p. 109).

An intense common interest and experience were growing among the colonially ruled peoples of Asia in the last months of 1945. The war had fostered this. To suit Japanese interests, men and women had moved, and been forced to move, throughout Asia: nationalist leaders, and would-be leaders, had been flown to Tokyo; labourers had been transported hundreds of miles to build roads and airfields; refugees and guerrillas had fled to wherever shelter was available. Wherever they ruled, the Japanese trumpeted their Greater East Asian Co-prosperity Sphere in the controlled press, and numerous conferences of journalists and politicians were held in Tokyo under its authority. Subhash Chandra Bose, who led the Indian National Army, drew recruits from prisoners-of-war in Malaya, saw his army fight in Burma, made a 'triumphal progress' through Japanese-occupied Asia including Manila and Saigon in November 1943, and died in a plane crash on Taiwan in August 1945.[16] The pace had truly quickened.

The returning colonial powers also contributed to the strengthening of Asian links. The expression 'Southeast Asia', widely used during the war,[17] implanted the notion of common problems, interests and characteristics in the minds of hundreds of thousands of newspaper readers and radio listeners. So, too, did the return of men and women who had been in exile abroad, the attempt by the colonial powers to co-ordinate their activities in the aftermath of the Japanese defeat, and the dramatic improvement in air transport and communications.

Loose connections had always existed. The ancient Hindu kingdoms had reached as far as Bali; trade routes had passed through the islands of Indonesia and the Philippines to link southwestern India and China. In the late nineteenth and twentieth centuries, members of colonial Asia's elites occasionally travelled or sought refuge in neighbouring countries or at least followed their political developments and were influenced by them. Jose Rizal, the Filipino patriot, worked at the India Office Library in London in the late 1880s. M. N. Roy, the Indian revolutionary, journeyed to Java in 1915 in the hope of acquiring German arms that could be used for rebellion in India. Rabindranath Tagore was lionised when he visited Java and Bali in 1927. In the same year, Jawaharlal Nehru met Mohammad Hatta of Indonesia at the Congress of Oppressed Nationalities in Brussels. Gandhi's portrait was displayed beside those of Marx, Lenin and Tan Malaka, the Indonesian communist, at a conference of the Indonesian Communist Party (PKI) in 1924. Vietnamese nationalists advocated a Gandhian non-violent movement in the late 1920s, and some, when imprisoned in 1936, went on protest fasts in imitation of Gandhi. Tan Malaka himself found refuge in Manila in the 1920s. In 1927, he was deported from there to Canton, a centre of Asian political fugitives in the 1920s. Numbers, too, journeyed to Moscow, where they met Asian neighbours and learned of conditions in other Asian countries. The coming of Philippine self-government in 1934 was thrown in the face of the Dutch by Indonesian nationalists who feted Manuel Quezon, the Philippine president, when he visited Java in 1935. The Dutch managed to have a second visit in 1939 called off.[18] All these were significant breaches in the 'mental frontiers' — not to mention the physical ones — 'colonialism imposed on Asia'.[19] But the shattering of the frontiers awaited the Japanese.

For a few heady years in the late 1940s, as they fought to win their political independence, the peoples of colonial Asia faced similar enemies, experienced common emotions and looked to each other for support and example. 'Even in the villages the peasants refer to the example of the Philippines', an American wrote from Vietnam in January 1946, and concluded that 'the demand for independence is widespread'.[20] To think that the people of Indochina would be 'content to settle for less than Indonesia has gained from the Dutch or India from the British', an American adviser wrote in 1949, 'is to underestimate the power of the forces that are sweeping Asia today'.[21]

As early as 1916, Rabindranath Tagore, travelling in Japan, spoke of the grand dream of 'a free China, Siam and, perhaps, in the ultimate course of things a free India. An associated Asia would be a powerful combination'.[22] In the late 1940s, such an association seemed at least a possibility. Once free of Western rule, however, countries began to follow their own narrower, national interests; differences began to outweigh similarities. In the 1980s, the non-alignment policy of Nehru, Nasser and Tito—'neutralism' to its detractors, 'independence' to its advocates—is one of the few survivors of the fellow-feeling of the 1940s and 1950s. Though institutionalised today as the 'non-aligned movement' of more than ninety countries, many would question its practical influence. Today, too, the hotly debated questions revolve around whether ex-colonial countries are independent economically or simply neo-colonies, whether their people are free, whether indeed political freedom is important or possible in the fight against grinding poverty. Why the countries of formerly colonial Asia should in 1980 differ so markedly—from military governments in Pakistan and Indonesia, through a suspended democracy in the Philippines, to working democracies in India and Malaya, to a communist Vietnam—can be satisfactorily explained only by examining the circumstances in which they won their political independence. The following chapters attempt to provide a clear, compact and occasionally provocative guide to that vast and exciting terrain.

NOTES

1. Wavell to Pethick-Lawrence, 28 Oct. 1945, in N. Mansergh and P. Moon (eds.), *The Transfer of Power, 1942-7*, vol. VI (London: HMSO, 1976) p. 418.
2. *The Times*, London, 18 Sept. 1945, p. 5.
3. Jawaharlal Nehru, *An Autobiography* (London: Bodley Head, 1953; 1st pubd 1936) p. 88.
4. Though it is unclear who first used the expression, it was long applied to India. Paul Scott took it as the title for a powerful novel set at the time of the Quit India movement in 1942, *The Jewel in the Crown* (London: Heinemann, 1966).

18   *Asia – The Winning of Independence*

5. *Overseas Hindustan Times*, 14 Feb. 1980, p. 1; *India Today*, 1–15 Sept. 1979, p. 18.

6. Conrado Benitez and Ramon S. Tirona, *Philippines Social Life and Progress* (Boston: Ginn & Co., 1937) pp. 53–9.

7. See the *Indonesia Handbook* for 1941.

8. R. L. Varshney, 'Foreign Trade', in V. B. Singh (ed.), *Economic History of India: 1857–1956* (Bombay: Allied, 1975; 1st pubd 1965) pp. 448, 467.

9. Amiya Kumar Bagchi, *Private Investment in India, 1900–39* (Madras: Orient Longman, 1975) p. 168; Bipin Chandra, *The Rise and Growth of Economic Nationalism in India* (New Delhi: People's Publishing House, 1966) p. 570n.

10. George Blyn, *Agricultural Trends in India, 1891–1947: Output, Availability and Productivity* (Philadelphia: University of Pennsylvania Press, 1966) pp. 242–3.

11. *Ibid.*, p. 248. For Indonesia and Vietnam, see this book, pp. 119–22, 167–8.

12. David Marr, *Vietnamese Anticolonialism, 1885–1925* (Berkeley: University of California Press, 1971) p. 254.

13. Jean Lacouture, *Ho Chi Minh* (Harmondsworth: Penguin, 1968) p. 15.

14. Philip Mason, *A Matter of Honour* (London: Cape, 1974) p. 511; War Cabinet Minutes, 5 Mar. 1945, in Mansergh and Moon (eds.), *Transfer of Power*, vol. III, p. 55.

15. Durga Das (ed.), *Sardar Patel's Correspondence, 1945–50*, vol. II (Ahmedabad: Navajivan, 1972) p. 6.

16. Hugh Toye, *Subhash Chandra Bose: The Springing Tiger* (Bombay: Jaico, 1966; 1st pubd 1962) p. 107.

17. D. G. E. Hall, *A History of South-East Asia* (London: Macmillan, 1976; 1st pubd 1955) p. 3.

18. Austin Coates, *Rizal. Philippine Nationalist and Martyr* (Hong Kong: Oxford University Press, 1968) pp. 155–6; J. P. Haithcox, *Nationalism and Communism in India* (Princeton: Princeton University Press, 1971) pp. 5–6; Stephen Hay, *Asian Ideas of East and West* (Bombay: Oxford University Press, 1970) pp. 322–3; S. Gopal, *Jawaharlal Nehru*, vol. I (Cambridge, Mass.: Harvard University Press, 1976) p. 101; Alexander Woodside, *Community and Revolution in Modern Vietnam* (Boston: Houghton Mifflin, 1976) p. 64; Theodore Friend, *Between Two Empires. The Ordeal of the Philippines, 1929–46* (New Haven: Yale University Press, 1965) p. 170.

19. Coates, *Rizal*, p. 351.

20. Memorandum, 30 Jan. 1946, by Richard L. Sharp, US State Dept, of conversation with Maj.-Gen. Philip Gallagher, head of US military mission in Indochina, in Gareth Porter (ed.), *Vietnam: A Definitive Documentation of Human Decisions*, vol. I (Stanfordville, N.Y.: Earl M. Colemann Enterprises, Inc., 1979) p. 93.

21. Memorandum by Raymond B. Fosdick, Consultant to the Secretary of State on Far Eastern Policy, for Ambassador-at-Large Philip Jessup, 4 Nov. 1949, in *ibid.*, p. 214.

22. Quoted in Hay, *Asian Ideas*, p. 67.

The Philippines:
Illustrations

Filipinos are suspicious of the strings attached to independence.

Philippines Free Press, 24 December 1932.

"QUO VADIS?"

Quezon and Osmena disagree over the terms of independence, while America, preoccupied with the great depression, turns its back and Japan looks on thoughtfully.

Philippines Free Press, 15 July 1932.

'Saluting the Flag.' Even after independence, Filipino children saluted two flags, those of the United States (flying higher) and the Philippines.

From Camilio Osias, *The Philippines Readers: Book Five* (Boston: Ginn & Co., 1947) pp. 272–4.

Glossary for Chapter 1

Huk

A shortened form of *Hukbo ng Bayan sa Hapon*, Tagalog for People's Anti-Japanese Army. During the Second World War, communist-front guerrilla forces in central Luzon used this title, but after the war it was retained as a popular term for anti-government insurgents.

Ilustrado

Spanish term meaning literally 'educated' or 'enlightened'. First used in the nineteenth century to describe non-Spaniards who gained a university education in Manila or Europe; later used more loosely for a whole class of educated Filipinos during the late nineteenth century.

Katipunan

Shortened form of the full title of the nationalist secret society, *Kataastaasan Kagalanggalang na Katipunan ng mga Anak ng Bayan*, Tagalog for the Highest and Most Respectable Society of the Sons of the People. Organised by Andres Bonifacio in 1892, it merged into the revolutionary army after his execution in 1897.

Mestizo

Spanish term meaning mixed blood and used to describe the offspring of unions between Malay-Filipinos and foreigners. Spanish *mestizos* were less numerous and received special privileges from the Spanish regime. Chinese *mestizo* communities developed in all major Philippine towns in the eighteenth and nineteenth centuries. American-Filipino unions were less common. Unless qualified, the term *mestizo* is used to refer to Chinese–Filipino racial mixture.

1 The Philippines: Independence without Decolonisation

Alfred W. McCoy

RAISING THE FLAG

Sometime after 4 o'clock on the afternoon of 12 June 1898 in a small town just south of Manila a 'motley crowd' gathered before the gothic-style, wooden home of General Emilio Aguinaldo, commander of the Philippine revolutionary forces, to witness the declaration of independence from a Spanish colonial regime that had ruled the islands or more than three centuries. Appearing stolid and martial with the close-cropped haircut that matched the squarish cast to his jaw, General Aguinaldo, still only twenty-nine years old, was proclaimed 'Dictator' and 'Supreme Chief of the Nation'. Following the reading of the Act of the Declaration of Independence from Spain, the new Philippine flag was raised officially for the first time, while a band played the *Marcha Nacional Filipina*. Aguinaldo's aide, General Artemio Ricarte, spoke to the crowd explaining the significance of the new flag's colours and markings. Featuring a stylised sun blazing in a triangle of white, the Philippine flag symbolised the nation's birth and unity – the sun itself was the emblem of the nationalist secret society that had launched the revolution in August 1896 and its eight rays represented the provinces that first rallied to the revolt[1] (see illustration, p. 21).

The flag-raising took place at a critical time. After two years of intermittent armed struggle, Philippine revolutionary armies were mobilising to clear the archipelago of Spanish colonial garrisons. The end of Spanish dominion was at hand. But anchored just offshore were five gunboats of a US Navy squadron under the command of Admiral George Dewey. Despite the Admiral's early promises of

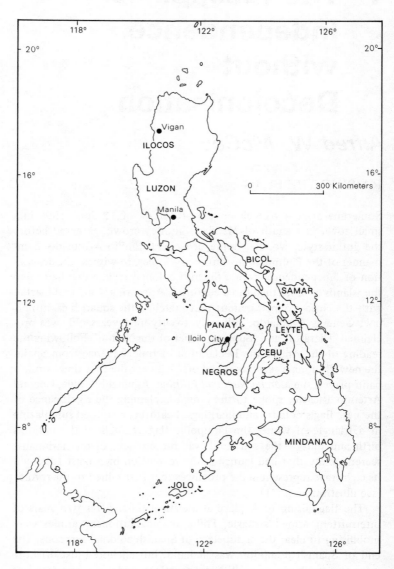

The Philipppines

support for the Philippine cause, US Army troops occupied Manila over General Aguinaldo's protests in August and American diplomats began quiet negotiations for the purchase of the islands.[2] After months of diplomatic wrangling, Spain finally ceded the Philippines for US $20 million, prompting a major American assault on the armies of the infant Republic. During four years of bitter fighting, the US Army slowly crushed the Philippine forces in a brutal pacification campaign, captured General Aguinaldo and established American colonial rule across the archipelago. American authorities initially banned the Philippine flag, and for three decades it enjoyed either a non-official or secondary status.

Thirty-four years after the last revolutionary general had surrendered to the US Army, there was another Philippine flag-raising ceremony, this time with American sponsorship. Under the terms of the ten-year transition process to full independence established by the US Congress in 1934, seventeen US senators, a legion of diplomatic representatives and half-a-million Filipinos gathered before the Legislative Building in downtown Manila at 7 o'clock in the morning of 15 November 1935, to witness the establishment of an autonomous Philippine Commonwealth and the inauguration of its president, Manuel Quezon, a former major in the revolutionary army. Although President Quezon's inauguration was hailed with only a nineteen-gun salute, two short of the twenty-one guns for a head of state, the Philippine flag was raised to precisely the same height as the American flag.[3] For the duration of the Commonwealth period, the Philippine and American flags were accorded equal status— Filipino soldiers swore loyalty to two flags, and Filipino school children pledged their allegiance every morning to two flags (see illustration, p. 21).

Eight years later, on the morning of 14 October 1943, another crowd gathered at the same spot before the Legislative Building in Manila to witness a third flag-raising ritual. Instead of American senators, the reviewing stand was filled with Japanese Army officers who had ruled the islands since their invasion in 1942. To the cheers of half-a-million Filipino spectators, the Japanese Army commander announced the termination of the military administration. A Filipino Catholic bishop gave the invocation: 'Bless this land O Lord . . . Bless our national flag, benign symbol of our dear Philippines.' As the orchestra played the national anthem and many in the crowd wept openly, an ageing General Emilio Aguinaldo, once commander of the

Philippine revolutionary army, and his former aide General Artemio
Ricarte, hoisted the national flag for the first time since the Japanese
landing. The Philippines was now proclaimed an independent republic, but its new president had been selected by the Japanese Army,
and it was recognised only by Japan and its client states.[4]

Only three years later, however, Manila was witness to a fourth
and final independence ceremony, this time under American sponsorship. Following a massive landing at Leyte Island in October 1944,
US Army divisions under the command of General Douglas MacArthur
defeated the Japanese military forces and once again raised the two
flags of the Philippine Commonwealth over Manila. Keeping precisely to the timetable prescribed by the US Congress ten years
earlier, a smaller crowd of dignitaries and spectators gathered in a
public park not far from the ruins of the war-ravaged Legislative
Building on 4 July 1946 to observe the inauguration of the Philippine
Republic. At a quarter past nine in the morning the US High
Commissioner lowered the American flag and Manuel Roxas, the
Republic's newly elected president, raised the Philippine flag on the
same white cord. In his inaugural speech, President Roxas expressed
a heartfelt gratitude, remarkable, at least at first glance, for the leader
of a nation emerging from a half century of colonial rule:[5]

The world cannot but have faith in America. For our part, we cannot
but place our trust in the good intentions of a nation which has been
our friend and protector for 48 years. To do otherwise would be to
forswear all faith in democracy, in our future, and in ourselves.

As we pursue our career as a nation, as we churn through treach-
erous waters, it is well to have a landfall, that we may know our
bearing and chart our course. Our safest course, and I firmly believe
it is true for the rest of the world as well, is in the glistening wake of
America whose sure advance with mighty prow breaks for small craft
the waves we fear.

Unique among the nations of Asia, the Philippines has raised its
flag to declare national independence not once, but four times—a
frequency which is but the most obvious sign of the complex and
often compromised struggle for Philippine national independence.
The experience has left a legacy of controversy which still surrounds
analysis of the Philippines' anti-colonial struggles.

Underlying this protracted history of anti-colonialism lies an irony
central to an understanding of Philippine nationalism – although the
Philippines launched one of Asia's first national revolutions, it has

been one of the last to sever the ties of dependence to its former colonial master. The United States granted formal political independence in 1946, but in certain significant areas relations have changed little since the establishment of the Commonwealth in 1935. The Philippines is a republic in name, but still retains much of the substance of Commonwealth ties in such crucial areas as national defence, international trade, internal government reforms and national culture. The United States still holds major military bases in the Philippines and remains responsible for its strategic defence – just as it did in 1935. America has remained the Philippines' major trading partner since independence, the US Agency for International Development (AID) plays a role in fostering major administrative reforms, and English is still the dominant official language.

These close ties survive because they serve the interests of the ruling Filipino elite. Many are bound to the United States through export trading relationships or joint ventures with American multinational firms, and most remain comfortable with the bi-national, Phil–American cultural identity implanted during the half-century of US colonial rule. Reflecting the highly articulated class divisions within Philippine society, there have emerged over the past century, two kinds of nationalism – the compromised, bi-national identity of the elite and the more profound, almost religious nationalism of the peasantry. For much of the elite, the Philippine flag has been a negotiable bit of bunting to be raised or lowered as suits the needs of business or the political exigencies of the moment. For the peasantry, untainted by foreign ties, the flag remains an almost mystical symbol of national aspirations. Its blazing sun heralds the hope of national redemption, and its stylised rays evoke the similarly shaped halo above the head of Christ crucified as he appears on the altars of Philippine churches.[6] Since the elite has been the prime architect of Philippine nationalism, both its growth and compromise, any explanation of the failure of decolonisation in the Philippines must focus on the Filipino elite's origins, character and response to colonial rule.

Over the past century armed peasant movements have been consistently crushed, leaving the elite free to fashion an official nationalism in its own image. Viewed from the perspective of the elite, the dominant theme in the history of Philippine nationalism is the development of divided, 'bi-national' loyalties to both the Philippines and the United States. Bi-nationalism first appeared in the latter half of the nineteenth century as the early elite nationalists articulated a strong sense of pride in the Filipino *race* which co-existed, ironically, with a genuine loyalty to the Spanish *nation*. Educated in Spanish, the Filipino elite gained access to European literature which inspired nationalist agitation, but was simultaneously left with an abiding affection for Spain and her culture. As the renowned Filipino poet Flavio Zaragoza Cano put it in his poetic tribute 'To the Spanish Race' written in 1933: 'I love my country more than the sun's rays/ But my purest love is not for her alone/For as a patriot I am a Malay/But as a poet my soul is Spanish.'[7] After an initial period of adjustment, most of the elite, unlike the Hispanophile poet Cano, transferred its bi-national loyalty from Spain to America after 1900. Under a more tolerant American colonial rule, the nineteenth century distinction between *race* and *nation* disappeared and the bi-national elite now advocated 'immediate, unconditional' independence under an American protectorate. Influenced by colonial education and its growing economic ties to America, the elite worked for fulfilment of its national aspirations within the context of a permanent protectorate relationship with the United States. Within the history of Philippine nationalism there are also important undercurrents of a more militant peasant ideology, exemplified by the post-war *Huk* revolt. Moreover, a number of elite politicians, like Senator Claro Recto, dissented vigorously from the pro-American censensus of their day. Overwhelmed, however, by the reality of economic dependence and the popular mandate for America, their voices have only rarely been heard above the whisper of a chiding conscience.

THE BACKGROUND OF NATIONALISM

While there may be some grounds to argue that the Filipino elite has been more open to *political* compromise with colonial powers than some of its Southeast Asian counterparts, it would be a misreading of Philippine history to conclude that Philippine nationalism is therefore 'weak' or 'undeveloped'. As products of a maritime trading society and direct descendants of a mercantile elite that emerged in the late eighteenth century, Philippine leaders have usually given precedence to issues of *economic* nationalism over those of simple *political* nationalism. Throughout the century which spanned the first nationalist crisis of 1872 to the declaration of martial law in

1972, Filipino leaders have consistently demonstrated a strong concern for the *economic* implications of any *political* decision. What good is a Philippine flag, they have argued, flying over a nation free of colonial dominion but full of impoverished and under-nourished citizens?

The Filipino elite's emphasis on 'economic nationalism' is a product of the country's history. From at least the fourteenth century onwards, social and economic developments in the sparsely settled archipelago fashioned a society, or more precisely a number of widely scattered societies, whose economic skills were far in advance of their expertise in the field of statecraft. Typically in many Malay states across the expanse of island Southeast Asia, political authority usually did not extend far beyond the village level and in no place covered more than a small island or the fraction of a larger island. There are no lost cities, massive monuments, traditional kingdoms or great empires in the Philippine past, and hence nothing like Vietnam's Confucian bureaucrats or Indonesia's traditional aristocracy to lay the foundation for a modern Philippine political, or bureaucratic, elite. Fragmented into warring microstates and scattered across 1700 km of ocean, the Philippine archipelago fell easy victim to a handful of Spanish *conquistadores* and missionaries who crossed the Pacific Ocean in the 1560s and laid claim to the islands in the name of their king.

The economic skills of the Philippine microstates, called *barangays*, were far in advance of their statecraft. Instead of decaying temples and ruined palaces, the pre-Hispanic Philippines has left an archaeological harvest of trade pottery, Ming and Siamese porcelains, so rich that today the fields in some regions seem almost sown with fragments of Chinese plates and jars. Judging from early Spanish accounts of Luzon and the Visayas, most *barangays* were involved in an elaborate interisland and international trade, and their folk technology was equal, if not superior, to that found in the villages of sixteenth-century Europe.[8]

The impact of three centuries of Spanish colonial rule accentuated this imbalance between economic and political skills. While Spanish colonials, often suspicious to the point of a collective paranoia, restricted Filipino political activity to municipal elections, they initially ignored and later encouraged economic activities. Unlike the Dutch in Java or the French in Vietnam, the Spanish administration of the Philippines was only secondarily concerned with trade and profit. Regarding the Philippines—with a population of only 500,000 in 1600 and 6 million in 1900, and no easily exploitable gold or silver mines—as a remote and unprofitable portion of its rich Latin American empire, the Spanish Crown made missionary work its main priority in the archipelago.

During the 300 years before the rapid growth of export agriculture tied the Philippines to the world economy in the late nineteenth century, Spanish colonials ignored local commerce and concentrated themselves in Manila where they speculated in a trans-Pacific galleon trade based on the exchange of Mexican silver for Chinese luxury goods, usually porcelains and silks. Every Manila Spaniard had a share in the China commerce, but it was the Spanish religious orders that dominated the galleon trade. Although their profits were considerable, the Spanish missions – unlike the British and Dutch East India companies – did not remit their surpluses to Spain but instead kept them in Manila to finance local charities and the evangelisation of eastern Asia, later enabling them to make a major contribution to the growth of export agriculture in the nineteenth century. Indicative of their importance in the initial growth of commercial farming, the Spanish religious and charitable orders purchased half the capital stock in the Bank of the Philippine Islands when it was established in 1851 – the first modern bank in Asia and the most important single source of capital for commercial agriculture until the 1920s.[9]

Absorbed in the easy profits of the trans-Pacific galleon trade, the Spanish colony abandoned provincial trade to Chinese, Filipino and half-caste entrepreneurs until the latter half of the nineteenth century. Profiting from their dominance of local and regional economies, prosperous native entrepreneurs first appeared in the late eighteenth century and their descendants later exploited the quickening pace of economic growth in the mid-nineteenth century to acquire large landed and commercial interests – gaining in the process many of the characteristics of the modern Philippine elite.

The changing economic activity from the late eighteenth century to the end of Spanish rule in 1898 had a major impact on the emerging nationalist elite. It is possible to divide developments into three distinct periods.[10] The first phase of accelerated economic growth began in the 1780s with a series of projects launched by the innovative reformer, Governor Jose Basco y Vargas. Seeking to substitute agricultural profits for declining galleon revenues, the Spanish administration promoted a variety of local economic ventures.[11]

Most importantly, the latter decades of the eighteenth century saw the emergence of the Chinese *mestizos*, descendants of unions between Chinese men and Filipina women, as the dominant group in provincial and regional trade. Following the explusion of all Chinese from the islands in 1765 as punishment for their collaboration with the enemy during the British occupation of Manila, the Chinese *mestizos*, spared expulsion because they had adopted the culture and Catholicism of their Filipina mothers, established trading networks radiating outwards from the cities where they resided — Cebu, Iloilo, Sorsogon, Manila and Vigan.[12]

Beginning with the end of the galleon trade in 1820 and the establishment of American merchant houses in Manila, the second phase of economic development was characterised by a substantial growth of export agriculture. But the overall pace of export development across the archipelago did not accelerate dramatically until the opening of provincial ports to direct foreign trade after 1855, an event which marks the third phase of economic growth. By 1870 so much capital and labour was being devoted to the production of sugar cane that the Philippines was no longer able to feed itself and was forced to begin regular rice imports. Again, the Chinese *mestizos* became the prime beneficiaries of these changes. Pressed by Chinese merchants who returned to the Philippines in the 1840s, wealthy Chinese *mestizo* traders began to abandon the cities and take up residence in the provincial towns. There they acquired substantial land holdings and merged into the local Filipino elite. By 1898 the Philippines was a major export producer of several tropical commodities and the large Filipino landholders had acquired wealth exceptional by the standards of their grandfathers' generation.[13]

It is one of the truisms of Philippine historiography that the economic changes of the late nineteenth century had a strongly positive influence on the growth of Philippine nationalism. Prosperity from export-crop production allowed provincial landowners to educate their sons in Manila and Europe, and many young men returned home to spread anti-colonial propaganda. Unified through their mutual command of Spanish and friendships formed in college, so goes the standard account, the educated elite, called *ilustrados*, from disparate areas of the archipelago joined together to launch reform movements. Aggrieved because the Spanish refused to allow them political authority commensurate with their education and wealth, the *ilustrados* led the revolt against Spain and later the

war against the United States.[14] Like the five fingers of a hand
drawn together in the raised fist of revolution, the different classes
and regions of the archipelago were pulled together by the process
of socioeconomic change to form a unified nationalist movement.

Recent research into Philippine provincial and local history
indicates that the process of social change that produced the revolution of 1896–8 was far more complex and uneven than previously
imagined. Perhaps the single most important political consequence
of the rise in agricultural exports during the late nineteenth century
was the transformation of the Chinese *mestizos* from ghetto merchants into a national elite. But the path from urban ghetto to
national revolution was a complex one, and the Chinese *mestizos*
appear to have passed through several states of intermediate consciousness before they began to think of themselves as 'Filipinos'.

Spanish colonial policy was responsible, directly and indirectly,
for the initial formation of *mestizo* communities and their ultimate
identification with the mass of the Filipino population. Spanish
colonials administered the *mestizos* through racially exclusive ghetto
councils and used the colonial law to preserve their distinctiveness.
Although they comprised less than 5 per cent of the archipelago's
population, the Chinese *mestizos* merited special attention in a
confidential Spanish report which advised in 1842 that *mestizos*
and the Malay-Filipinos should be held 'separate and at odds so
they can never form one mass nor have a common public spirit'.[15]
Such measures preserved the *mestizos*' sense of separateness; other
colonial policies pushed them into confrontation with the Spanish
regime – a process which first forced an intermediate group identity,
what might be called '*mestizo* consciousness', upon the urban ghetto
communities.

The transition from parochial to national identity took place in
the latter half of the nineteenth century. As the *mestizos* moved
from the urban ghettos to take up land in the agricultural hinterland,
they merged with the local communities and were now identified as
members of the native (*indio*) municipal elite. Prospering from the
rapid growth of agricultural exports in the late nineteenth century.
Filipino landholders began sending their children to Manila and
Europe for tertiary education where they were influenced by the
currents of anti-Spanish propaganda that grew in the three decades
following 1870.

By the 1870s the Chinese *mestizos* had begun to merge into a developing Filipino national elite. On the eve of the 1896 revolution there was already, then, a self-conscious 'Filipino' elite with identifiable characteristics. Although its ethnic orgins were mixed, the elite shared a common culture – an orthodox Roman Catholic faith, mastery of written and spoken Spanish and a sense of itself as the rightful leader of its society. Although it was highly Hispanicised, the elite had a strong racially based identity which made it feel like a society apart from Spanish colonial circles. Its political skills were still not commensurate with its economic influence, and most of the elite had no experience outside of the elections for municipal mayors.

While economic change contributed to the growth of national unity, the rise in agricultural exports also retarded the growth of nationalism in certain important respects. Instead of linking the disparate archipelago into a single network of credit and markets focussed on Manila, the growth of export agriculture divided the Philippines into distinct regions oriented towards separate international markets for their special commodities. Multilingual *ilustrados* involved in export crops like sugar thought of themselves as citizens of the world first and Filipinos second – their ultimate loyalties lay with the foreign sugar factors, the New York and London sugar markets, and their crop-loan mortgages.

The growth of cash-crop farming laid the base for a conflict of interests among the various regions. Rice farmers in the eight Tagalog-speaking provinces ringing Manila leased their lands from the Spanish religious corporations and had everything to gain from a successful revolt against Spain. As owners of vast sugar plantations protected from labour unrest by the patrols of the Spanish *Guardia Civil*, the planters of the Western Visayas region, in contrast, had every reason to support the maintenance of Spanish colonial rule. Sugar planters obtained credit from foreign export houses by mortgaging their plantations to guarantee delivery of the next crop, and were strongly opposed to any insurgency which might threaten the harvest of standing cane or deny them access to foreign markets.

Common to most areas of Luzon and the Visayas was a growing gap between the new elite and the mass of the Filipino peasantry. The social and economic transformation of the nineteenth century created an upper social stratum culturally distinct from the peasantry. Urbane and Spanish-educated, the new elite practised an orthodox Catholicism, debated the principles of European liberalism, and had a bi-national image of itself as members of the Filipino *race* and the Spanish *nation*. In contrast, the more traditional peasantry wrote and thought exclusively in the indigenous languages, conceived of politics in terms of folk religions, and held a much clearer vision of the Philippines as a nation apart from Spain.[16]

The process of export development fostered economic conflicts between the elite and the peasantry. In regions where cash-crop farming expanded rapidly, the conditions of peasant life declined in rough proportion to the rising wealth of the landholding elite. The integration of the Philippines into international trade networks produced a sudden collapse of village weaving along the Ilocos coast of north-western Luzon and Panay Island in the Western Visayas. Denied the cash income that the women's weaving provided, the overcrowded villages of both regions experienced an out-migration of unprecedented proportions to nearby agricultural frontiers.

Once peasant pioneers had completed the arduous task of clearing the land, *mestizos* used their legal skills and colonial contacts to gain title to vast holdings, totalling up to 14,000 hectares, through a variety of methods—court procedures marked by bribery and false swearing, crop loans at impossible rates of interest and the use of armed mercenaries to terrorise the peasants off the land. As the elite acquired legal title to prime frontier land, the peasants were reduced progressively to a status of tenants and wage labourers on Spanish and *mestizo*-owned plantations. While there was some spectacular elite landgrabbing, it was the structure of interest rates on crop loans that gradually forced most of the peasantry into a position of economic dependence. A European sugar factor might extend an annual crop loan of ₱20,000 to a substantial Chinese *mestizo* planter at 6–9 per cent interest, while the planter made loans of less than ₱50 to peasants at interest in excess of 100 per cent per annum. As victims of elite landgrabbing and financial legerdemain, the peasantry grew increasingly hostile to the large landholders who they began to see as an exploitive class.[17]

THE NATIONALIST MOVEMENT

Members of the emerging elite moved to translate their new wealth and education into political influence; but they found themselves blocked by an aggressively conservative colonialism determined to frustrate their aspirations—a policy which precipitated the emergence of a nationalist movement. The changing character of the nineteenth-century nationalist movement can best be seen in the careers of three key leaders — Fr Jose Burgos, Dr Jose Rizal and Andres Bonifacio. A Spanish *mestizo* who identified himself with all the colony's non-Spanish ethnic groups, Fr Burgos responded to colonial criticisms of the native clergy in the 1860s with an avid defence of his race, becoming the first to articulate the concept of the 'Filipino' as a racial-cum-national indentity. Fr Burgos himself was still bound to Spain by strong bi-national loyalties and his reform movement was easily crushed, a repression that culminated in his execution in 1872. Spanish pressure stifled the movement for almost two decades, and Fr Burgos's successor did not emerge until the late 1880s. A Chinese *mestizo* who, like many of the new elite, sought advanced professional training at European universities in the 1880s, Dr Rizal refined Fr Burgos's rudimentary concept of the 'Filipino' into a national credo and demanded a comprehensive reform of Spanish policy beyond the narrow ecclesiastical concerns of clerical reformers of the 1860s. Ultimately, however, Rizal could not sanction a violent break with Spain and in the end chose exile over revolution. Unlike Rizal and the elite reformers who were restrained by property interests and bi-national loyalties to Spain, Andres Bonifacio, a self-educated Manila worker, realised that revolution was the only road to national independence. Inspired by the nationalist writings of Rizal and other elite propagandists, Bonifacio formed a nationalist secret society in the slums of Manila and launched the national revolution of August 1896.

As the most important institution affecting the daily lives of the islands' people, the Church was the first target of *mestizo* aspirations and the initial point of conflict between early nationalists and the colonial regime. Barred from many positions in the colonial civil service in the late eighteenth and early nineteenth centuries, educated Filipinos, predominantly Chinese and Spanish *mestizos*, sought vocations in the Church. The first Filipino priest was not ordained until 1720, but by 1750 native clergy occupied 142 of the archipelago's 569 parishes.

Promotion of Filipino secular priests remained official policy until Spain lost its Latin American empire in the revolutions of 1810–20 and became concerned that the Philippines too might rise in revolt. Mexican and Peruvian priests had played key roles in their national revolutions; Spain was determined that history should not repeat itself. In 1826 the Spanish court ordered that all parishes taken from Spanish friar missionaries in the eighteenth century must be returned to them. The transfer of the parishes to Spanish friars proceeded slowly until the arrival of a new group of Spanish Jesuit missionaries in 1859 forced the colonial regime to accelerate the process. Within a few years many Filipino secular priests, largely in central Luzon, were expelled from their parishes and replaced with Spanish friars, a change that sparked the colony's first nationalist agitation.

The transfer of parishes generated an intense political controversy in both Manila and Madrid. In defence of their expulsion of native clergy, Spanish religious orders and their conservative allies published a number of articles in the Madrid press accusing the Filipino priests of sedition, ignorance and racial inferiority. At the height of the controversy in 1864, the Madrid newspaper *La Verdad* printed an article which read:

The Filipino by his nature, by his character, by the influence of the climate on the race, is not food for undertaking lofty offices . . . The Filipino who is consecrated to the service of the altar ordinarily carries out well the discharge of the routine offices in a church, but he never succeeds in excelling when he is found possessing the presthood . . . Nor can [Filipinos] carry out the office because of the circumstance that their intelligence is not equal to the lofty office of the pastor of souls.[18]

Fr Burgos, then 27, responded to the attack in an anonymous manifesto signed as 'Los Filipinos'. He argued that there was no scientific basis for a racial theory of intelligence and catalogued the numerous achievements of Filipinos in the fields of linguistics, theology, law and science. Burgos then attacked the Spanish friars for abuse of authority in the parishes and maladministration of their vast landed estates.[19]

Although Fr Burgos was the first to articulate a strong pride in the qualities of the Filipino *race*, he affirmed his loyalty to the Spanish *nation*. Denying the friars' assertion that their presence in the parishes was the best defence against Filipino sedition, Fr Burgos extolled Spain's generous contributions to Philippine life, strong evidence of his own bi-national loyalties:

For we know and understand very well that away from the Spanish name and from the flag which waves over us, we will be nothing and perhaps worse than nothing. For we are not ignorant that once emancipated from the magnanimous and generous Spanish nation, this country would be handed over to the most complete anarchy or would be a slave of the harsh rule of a foreigner . . . It is to our own interest to maintain Spanish rule, sheltering ourselves under its great shadow, a source of protection and of highest culture.[20]

Fr Burgos demanded reform — expulsion of the religious orders and confiscation of their vast estates encircling Manila — as a means of ending the 'abuses' which had sparked minor revolts in years past.[21]

Throughout his distinguished pastoral and academic careers in the 1860s, Fr Burgos remained active as a nationalist defender of the Filipino priest and became a natural target of friar antagonism during the brief period of reformist agitation from 1868 to 1872. Following the revolution of September 1868 which dethroned the conservative Spanish monarch Isabela II, Madrid despatched the liberal Carlos de la Torre to Manila as Governor-General. Lending his qualified support to a local reformist group largely comprised of distinguished Spanish *mestizos*, de la Torre presided over a brief period of public debate and open reformist agitation. Paralleling the liberal reform movement among secular priests and Spanish *mestizo* professionals, law students at the University began to agitate for internal reforms under three leaders of Chinese *mestizo* descent who later gained considerable prominence—Paciano Rizal, elder brother of the national martyr Jose Rizal; Gregorio Sancianco, later known as a critic of Spanish taxation policy; and Felipe Buencamino, Sr, an influential political leader during the first decade of American colonial rule.[22]

Repression fell first upon the students, and in late 1869 Buencamino was imprisoned for four months as punishment for his role as a nationalist instigator. Although de la Torre and his successor Rafael de Izquierdo were both liberals who had supported the anti-monarchist cause in Spain, they acted more conservatively in the Philippines and supported the friars as necessary for the maintenance of Spanish rule. Even their qualified liberalism ended after a twenty-four-hour revolt by some 200 Filipino troops at the Cavite barracks, just south of Manila, in January 1872. Although the revolt was the result of purely local grievances such as unpaid wages, the friars falsely accused the Filipino reformers of instigating the revolt and used the allegations to crush the reform movement. After a hasty, secret trial whose transcript was never released, Fr Burgos and two other secular priests were executed by garrotte in a public park on 17 February 1872 for the crime of trying 'to separate this archipelago from the mother country'. An instrument of slow and painful death, the garrotte gradually breaks the spinal cord at the neck with each measured twist of the heavy, iron screw. In addition to the spectacular brutality of the public executions, nine Filipino priests and thirteen laymen were sentenced to a year's exile in the Marianas Islands.

While the harsh repression of the Filipino liberal movement stifled political discussion in Manila for several decades, a younger generation of Filipino students studying in Europe during the 1880s formed the 'propaganda movement' to agitate for reforms. Led by the same class of wealthy Chinese and Spanish *mestizos* involved in the earlier liberal movement, the Propagandists devoted most of their efforts to the publication of manifestos, newspapers and novels exposing the abuses of the Spanish colonial regime. Like Fr Burgos in his 1864 manifesto, the Propagandists concentrated their fire on the friars and demanded major reforms in Spanish policies, but stopped short of advocating independence or revolution.[23]

The most influential of the Propagandists was a young medical student, Jose Rizal, whose statue today stands in the plaza of almost every Philippine municipality as a tribute to his martyrdom for the nationalist cause. Born in the town of Calamba, southeast of Manila, Rizal was descended from Chinese *mestizos* on both sides of his family. Like many Luzon *mestizos*, Rizal's family had left Manila and become affluent farmers by leasing a large block of land on a sprawling Spanish religious estate. Although Rizal was only ten when Fr Burgos was executed in 1872, the events of the early 1870s made a lasting impression on him and other nationalist leaders of his generation. He was shocked by the garrotting of the three priests, and gained insight into the political struggles through his elder brother Paciano, a student under Fr Burgos at the University of Santo Tomas.[24]

After quitting the medical course at the University of Santo Tomas in 1882, Rizal travelled to Europe where he spent the next decade completing his medical studies at the University of Madrid and leading the Propaganda Movement. Together with other nationalists among the Filipino student community, Rizal produced pamphlets and newspaper articles strongly critical of Spanish colonial abuses and calling for reforms. His most important work, the novel *Noli Me Tangere*, was set in a central Luzon municipality and depicted the evil influence of the local parish priest, a Spanish friar. Although Rizal's works constituted a brilliant critique of Spanish colonialism and extolled the culture of the pre-Hispanic Philippines, neither he nor any of his fellow Propagandists demanded separation from Spain. Even the editor of the nationalist newspaper *La Solidaridad*, Marcelo H. del Pilar, known for his radicalism, favoured reform, not revolution. Writing in the introduction to a Spanish–Tagalog dictionary, del Pilar said: 'The diffusion of the Spanish language will unite the Philippines more closely to Spain, being as it is a part of Spain . . . it should be Spanish in its language as it is in its government, Spanish in its religion, in its sentiments, in its habits, in its aspirations.'[25]

Returning to Manila in June 1892, Rizal immediately launched himself into a campaign for reforms. Meeting with a number of prominent Filipinos in the Manila suburb of Tondo, Rizal formed a reformist mutal aid society, *La Liga Filipina*. Despite the society's moderate aims, the Spanish Governor-General found Rizal's activities subversive and, only four days after its formation, ordered him banished to a small town in northern Mindanao.[26]

Rizal's arrest and the Spanish government's refusal to grant any concessions soon led to the collapse of the elite reformist movement. With the arrest of Rizal, leadership of the nationalist movement passed to a poor Manila worker, Andres Bonifacio. Born in November 1863, two years later than Rizal, Bonifacio was a Malay–Filipino and a member of the Manila working class. Although poorly educated and employed as a lowly clerk–messenger by several foreign commercial houses, Bonifacio was a man of keen intellect who devoted his spare time to reading.[27]

Well known and evidently respected in Tondo, Manila's crowded *indio* quarter, Bonifacio was not an altogether illogical successor to Rizal as a nationalist leader. Within hours of Rizal's arrest in July 1892, Bonifacio and a small number of lower-class Tondo residents met to form the *Katipunan*, a secret society dedicated to winning national independence through revolution. The *Katipunan* grew slowly to a society of only 300 members until early 1896 when it acquired a small printing press and began publishing the nationalist prose and poetry of Emilio Jacinto, a brilliant young Tagalog propagandist also born in Tondo to a poor Malay–Filipino family. As the

Katipunan's Tagalog-language tabloid sheet *Kalayaan* (Liberty) began circulating secretly in Manila and the surrounding towns, the society's membership suddenly swelled from 300 to 30,000 within the space of a few months, winning the secret society a whole new class of supporters. While most of its Tondo membership was drawn from the urban working class and lower rungs of the Filipino intelligentsia, its branches in the towns ringing Manila comprised the local land-holding elite. Embittered towards the Spanish religious orders for their arbitrary management of the vast Church estates, comprising up to 85 per cent of arable land in the provinces near Manila, the leading farmers in the capital region had everything to gain from the expulsion of the friars and the confiscation of their estates.

By 1896, then, the nationalist movement had expanded its political base to include both urban workers and Tagalog landholders, but had lost its original support among the wealthy Manila *mestizos* still bound to Spain by bi-national loyalties. Immediately following the outbreak of the *Katipunan* revolt in 1896, for example, Felipe Buencamino, imprisoned in 1870 for his role as a student leader, issued a loyalist manifesto: 'One would have to be blind or bereft of reason not to recognize the blessings that we enjoy under the beneficent shadow of the Spanish flag. Death to the traitors who disturb our peace and tranquillity! Death to the ignoble and cowardly authors of those libels and anonymous writings'.[28]

THE REVOLUTION

Although Andres Bonifacio had moved the ideology of the nationalist movement from reform to revolution, neither he nor his followers was really ready for the revolt when it came. The *Katipunan* began collecting arms in June 1896, but on 19 August one of its members exposed the society and its revolutionary aims during confession to the Spanish parish priest of Tondo. As the Spanish troops began ransacking Tondo in search of *Katipunan* members, Bonifacio and his followers fled Manila leaving behind forged letters implicating wealthy Filipinos as *Katipunan* members, a subtle way of securing *ilustrado* support. Finally on 29 August a thousand poorly armed *Katipunan* members met on the outskirts of Manila and agreed to launch a revolt against Spanish rule.[29]

Simultaneously, Emilio Aguinaldo, the local *Katipunan* leader for

Kawit, Cavite Province, planned a parallel uprising. Demonstrating an obvious flair for military leadership, Aguinaldo, a young Chinese *mestizo* landowner then serving as mayor of his home town, launched a successful attack on the local Spanish militia garrison and cleared the province of colonial troops in a matter of days. After his troops won several battles in November 1896, Aguinaldo emerged as the man of the hour and the Spanish began to panic. In an arbitrary act of vengeance, Spanish colonial authorities tried Jose Rizal for treason and ordered his execution. Demonstrating the dramatic calm of Christ crucified as performed in Easter passion plays on the town plazas of central Luzon, Rizal died a martyr's death by firing squad before a crowd of thousands in December 1896.

Successfully repulsing further Spanish military advances in the first half of 1897, Aguinaldo emerged as the unchallenged military leader of the revolution and in May consolidated his control with the execution of *Katipunan* leader Andres Bonifacio. As Spanish pressure on his lines mounted, Aguinaldo's forces later retreated to Biak-na-Bato in the mountains of Bulacan to the north of Manila. Stalemated and lacking arms, Aguinaldo, negotiating with the Spanish through intermediaries, agreed to surrender his arms and go into exile in exchange for a grant of ₱1.4 million. After accepting an inital payment of ₱400,000, he and his staff sailed for Hong Kong on 27 December while the Spanish colony celebrated its victory with masses in the Manila Cathedral.[30]

While Aguinaldo remained in exile during the first five months of 1898, the revolution, suffering only a temporary setback from his surrender, revived itself and began to spread beyond its central Luzon heartland to the rest of Luzon and the Visayas. During its initial phase, support for the revolution had been concentrated largely in the Tagalog-speaking provinces ringing Manila where the vast Church estates were concentrated. Lacking any parallel economic incentive to revolt, the elite in outlying regions like the Ilocos, Bicol, Cebu and the Western Visayas remained loyal to Spain and equipped several battalions of Loyal Volunteers, all Filipinos, to fight *with* the Spanish *against* Aguinaldo. Shortly after news of the *Katipunan* revolt reached the Western Visayas in August 1896, the municipal council of Jaro, comprising the region's wealthiest sugar planters, passed the following resolution typical of loyalist sentiments: 'These acts of rebellion undertaken in the Capital of the Archipelago have vitally wounded the undeniable patriotism of this town ... This uprising will find no echo in the noble hearts of Jaro's citizens, who do not forget their immense gratitude toward Spain which raised us to a life of civilisation and progress from a state of the most abject savagery and barbarism. As we were born Spaniards, we want to live and die Spaniards – with honor!' When American intervention in May 1898 made Spain's eventual defeat inevitable, revolutionary committees began organising in the loyalist regions, even in the town of Jaro, and by the time Spain ceded the archipelago to America in December, only the sugar districts of Negros Island remained openly hostile towards the revolution.[31]

Following his return from exile in May 1898, Aguinaldo moved quickly to establish a national government with the support of a number of wealthy Manila *ilustrados* – Felipe Buencamino, the Spanish *mestizo* intellectual Dr T. H. Pardo de Tavera and others. The Republic's chances for an orderly administration were short-lived, however. US Army troops began pushing north from Manila through Philippine lines in February 1899 and by November occupied the settled areas of the central Luxon plain, forcing Aguinaldo to retreat into northern Luzon and abandon regular military operations for guerrilla warfare. In a bold coup, a US Army colonel leading a party of Filipino mercenaries captured Aguinaldo in March 1901, and little more than a year later President Theodore Roosevelt issued a formal declaration terminating hostilities. Although sporadic guerrilla activity continued in some areas until 1907, most revolutionary leaders surrendered in early 1901 after the re-election of US President William McKinley, author of America's policy of imperial expansion, made it clear that there was no further hope of playing upon internal political divisions in the United States. Pressed by the increasingly harsh pacification measures adopted by the US Army, revolutionary armies marched out of the hills, swore an oath of loyalty to the United States and, like Aguinaldo, returned to their homes.[32]

AMERICAN COLONIAL RULE

Although the Philippine Republic had lost the war against the United States, it had won the battle for the loyalties of the great mass of the Filipino people. The glory of the revolution's victories over Spain, the martyrdom of Dr Jose Rizal and the agony of the Republic's ultimate subjugation established the ideal of national independence as the ultimate political aspiration of the Philippine working class. Although Filipino political leaders gave serious consideration to some sort of permanent protectorate status under the United States, the ideal of national independence was so strong that advocacy of anything less was an act of almost certain political suicide.

Complementing the Philippine pursuit of national independence, the United States quickly decided that it was not really interested in making the islands a permanent possession. Unlike Britain, Holland and Spain, who required territorial empires to augment the meagre resources found within their narrow confines, the United States was preoccupied with settling a vast and bountiful continent. The United States lacked sufficient domestic capital for the development of its own resources and had few investors seriously interested in speculating in remote tropical enterprises. America's main aim in acquiring overseas territories at the century's turn was strategic — the Panama Canal Zone, Guantanamo Naval Base in Cuba, Pearl Harbour in Hawaii and Guam Island in the Western Pacific. While Manila Bay was ideally placed for commercial and naval access to the China coast, it brought with it 6 million brown Filipinos whose colour made them unacceptable to white Americans as subjects for assimilation.

Unwilling, in the final analysis, to contemplate the naturalisation of 6 million Filipinos, the United States established a tutelary colonialism aimed at preparing the Filipinos for the governance of an independent nation. There was, then, a progressive extension of political power to Filipinos during the four decades of American colonial rule—municipal elections in 1901, provincial government elections in 1902, lower-house legislative elections in 1907, upper-house elections in 1916 and election of a Commonwealth president in 1935. Paralleling the growth of elective offices was a gradual transfer of bureaucratic positions from Americans to Filipinos. In 1903 Filipinos held 49 per cent of US colonial appointments, mainly at the bottom of the bureaucracy; by 1913 they held 71 per cent; by 1920 there were 12,561 Filipinos employed against 582 Americans; and by 1928 virtually the entire colonial government, from cabinet ministers down to postal clerks, was manned by Filipinos. Although more racist in their personal dealings with Filipinos than the Spanish, American colonials still achieved a fair success in preparing the archipelago for independence.[33] More enlightened American officials sponsored promising Filipino political leaders at the national and provincial levels, and shiploads of American educators tried to mould mass social values through public education. Ignoring the issue of economic dependence which troubled some Filipino leaders, the American colonial regime laid the basis for a prosperous export economy through various infrastructure projects and financial reforms.

Filipinos responded positively to the American penchant for social engineering. Unlike the confrontation between an authoritarian colonialism and suppressed nationalism in Vietnam or Indonesia, Philippine colonial politics developed a mutual dependence between American officials and Filipino leaders. To defend itself against rival political parties, the dominant Nacionalista Party needed patronage in the form of jobs and infrastructure projects that only the American officials could dispense in the early decades of US colonial rule. Having conceded the Filipinos a measure of legislative authority, American officials depended upon the active support of Filipino political leaders to make the government function smoothly, thereby assuring the success of their colonial careers.

To raise the Philippines out of the economic depression which accompanied the turmoil of the revolution, American colonial officials secured free access to US markets for Philippine products in 1913, sparking a sudden increase in sugar, coconut and tobacco production. By 1920 Philippine–American trade dominated the archipelago's economy and the booming sugar industry, which experienced a massive expansion during the First World War, was completely dependent upon access to the American market for its survival. Unlike Indonesia where European colonials monopolised commercial agriculture, the sudden growth of Philippine exports was largely the work of established Filipino landholders, new Philippine institutions like the Philippine National Bank or Spanish creole corporations with a permanent commitment to the archipelago, most notably the Bank of the Philippine Islands. As the export economy boomed and Filipino national entrepreneurs prospered, there developed a growing contradiction between the demands of an established *political* nationalism and the needs of an emerging *economic* nationalism. Faced with economic disaster and a possible strategic threat from Japan if they broke with the United States, Filipino political leaders became firmly convinced of the necessity of a permanent protectorate relationship with America during the 1920s and 1930s — an idea complemented by the divided, or bi-national, loyalties taught in the colonial school curriculum.

The conflicting demands of continued economic growth and the political ideal of national independence forced Filipino leaders into an almost schizophrenic political posture. Privately, Filipino leaders developed amiable, sometimes intimate, working relationships with American colonial officials and expressed strong doubts, even fears, of the perils of full and complete national independence. Publicly, the emotional legacy of the revolution forced Filipino politicians to attack American colonialism and demand immediate national independence. While much of the elite may have been comfortable in the growing bi-national loyalty to America, the mass of Filipino workers and peasants, less influenced by the socialising experience of colonial education, remained faithful to the ideals of Philippine nationalism fashioned in the battles of the revolution. Torn between the reality of economic dependence and the political demands of nationalism, Filipino political leaders pushed forward reluctantly towards national independence, in the process willingly conceding much of its substance to preserve what they saw as essential economic and military ties to America.

COLONIAL POLITICS

The history of Filipino politics under American colonial rule is dominated by two rival parties — the Federalista Party, which initially favoured US statehood for the Philippines, and the Nacionalista Party, which advocated immediate independence. Although the two parties took conflicting positions on the independence question during the first years of American colonial rule, they gradually blurred into indistinguishable contenders for power identifiable only by their leaders and not by their policies. In power until 1907, the Federalista Party, led by wealthy *ilustrados* who had wanted a lasting union with Spain, was favoured with American patronage and advocated a permanent union with the United States. Out of power until its ultimate dissolution in 1932, the Federalista Party and its successor parties, the Progresista and later Democrata, tried to win votes by attacking the Nacionalista Party for its collaboration with the American regime. Out of power until 1907, the Nacionalista Party gained electoral strength by attacking the Federalistas for their pro-American stance. In power from 1907 until 1941, the Nacionalista Party leaders monopolised American political patronage and pushed forward on the independence question with a growing sense of regret, hoping privately for a lasting 'special relationship' with America. Although often attacking American colonial officials for partisan advantage, Filipino political leaders worked amicably with their American patrons during the years of colonial rule, fought with America against Japan during the Second World War and traded much of the substance of national independence for a 'special' Philippine–American relationship in post-war years.[34]

Convinced that the Filipinos were unprepared for self-government, America's first Governor-General, William Howard Taft, initially fashioned a colonial civil service dominated by Americans and kept the reins of power firmly in his grasp. From the day he landed at Manila in June 1900, Taft, later President of the United States, formed a low opinion of Filipino capabilities. In his letters he described the peasants as 'superstitious and ignorant' and 'in many respects nothing but grown up children'. The wealthy *ilustrados* were 'glib and superficial', and the Filipinos as a whole would require 'the training of fifty or a hundred years before they shall even realize what Anglo-Saxon liberty is'. Taft none the less felt that America should tutor the Filipinos in the craft of governance and progressively transfer power as their capabilities improved.[35]

Given his aristocratic mien and low opinion of ordinary Filipinos, Taft naturally found his clients among the wealthy *ilustrados* who formed the Federalista Party. The Filipino for whom Taft had greatest respect was Dr Trindad H. Pardo de Tavera, a Spanish *mestizo* bibliophile who dominated colonial politics during Taft's five years in the islands. Following the American capture of Manila in August and the collapse of Spanish rule, he was appointed Secretary of Foreign Affairs in Aguinaldo's cabinet. Convinced, however, that the future of the Philippines lay with the United States, Pardo de Tavera resigned after only a month in office and founded a daily newspaper, *La Democracia*, to advocate acceptance of American rule.

In December 1900, a month after President McKinley's re-election affirmed the permanency of America's occupation, Pardo de Tavera organised the Federalista Party together with Dr Frank S. Bourns, a senior American intelligence agent, and a number of prominent Filipino *ilustrados*, among them Felipe Buencamino. Already a confidant of the new American governor, Taft, Pardo de Tavera travelled widely during 1900 campaigning for the surrender of revolutionary commanders and the restoration of peace under American rule. Convinced by his scholarly studies that the Philippines was 'a worn out and incomplete civilisation', Pardo de Tavera explained that the ultimate aim of the Federalista Party was 'the Americanization of the Filipinos and the spread of the English language . Complementing this 'unconditional adoption of American civilisation , the Philippines should join the United States as a new state after an adequate period of preparation. In recognition of their services, Taft appointed Pardo de Tavera and two other Federalista Party leaders to the government's highest executive body, the Philippine Commission, in September 1901.[36]

Despite its initial monopoly of American political patronage, Federalista influence was relatively short-lived. As American political repression slackened, nationalists mounted an effective attack on the Federalista Party for its advocacy of American statehood. Increasingly embarrassed, the Federalista Party rescinded its statehood policy in June 1904 and advocated instead progressive Filipino control of the colonial government leading to eventual independence. During a visit to the United States in 1904, Pardo de Tavera and other Federal Party leaders discovered to their dismay that few American leaders were willing to consider US statehood for the Philippines. Identified with a statehood policy acceptable to neither Americans nor Filipinos, the Federalista Party began to lose influence rapidly after Taft returned to the United States in 1904. Finding that the Party's utility was waning, Luke E. Wright, Taft's successor, began to seek new bases of Filipino support beyond the Federalistas. Further antagonised by new taxes which hit directly at the business interests of leading party members, Pardo de Tavera launched a concerted political attack on Wright's government in 1905 and petitioned his former patron, Taft, for Wright's recall. Taft, now serving as Secretary of War, ordered Wright home in late 1906 and arranged a face-saving appointment for him as the first United States Ambassador to Japan. Several other anti-Federalista officials were also removed, leaving W. Cameron Forbes, a millionaire Boston financier, the only senior American to survive Pardo de Tavera's subtle intrigues.[37]

The Federalista victory was largely pyrrhic, and within two years their enemies had combined to cast them out of power into permanent opposition. Finding himself at a hopeless impasse with the Federalistas, W. Cameron Forbes, Secretary of Commerce and

Police (1904-9) and later Governor (1909-13), sought new Filipino allies and found them, logically enough, in the ranks of the independence movement. Although he formed a lasting alliance with the leaders of the Nacionalista Party, both he and they were ambivalent towards the independence issue and felt the real problem was not political but economic—the development of roads, harbours and efficient business institutions.

Convinced that the nationalists were more interested in defeating their rivals than in winning freedom, Forbes set about locating promising clients in their ranks to serve him, just as Taft had allied himself with the Federalistas. Forbes' sense of timing was excellent, for a new kind of nationalist politician was emerging from the provinces in 1906-7 as he began his search for allies. The first nationalist parties were formed in January 1906, and the following year coalesced into a single party, the Partido Nacionalista, to challenge the Federalistas in the first elections for the new National Assembly to be held in July 1907.[38] Although the electorate, only 100,000 voters out of a total population of 6 million, was restricted to the landed and educated who were expected to favour the pro-American Federalista Party, now called the Progresista Party, the Nacionalistas scored an overwhelming triumph that laid the basis for an unbroken monopoly on political power that lasted until the end of colonial rule in 1946. Having won 72 per cent of the Assembly seats, the Nationalista Party took firm control of the new legislature and elected two of its most influential leaders, Sergio Osmeña and Manuel Quezon, as Speaker and Floor Leader respectively.[39]

The Nacionalistas won their spectacular victory with a patriotic rhetoric that would have aroused outrage among Dutch or French colonials. Yet immediately after, Cameron Forbes wrote in his diary: 'Osmeña was elected, as I expected, and will be Speaker. It means I shall have great power with the Assembly.' Osmeña and Quezon were in fact the very clients Forbes had been cultivating, and their victory, to a considerable extent, was the result of patronage he and other American colonials had provided. Although their provincial origins and ideals distinguished them from Federalistas like Pardo de Tavera, Osmeña and Quezon shared his willingness to play the colonial game.

Although Quezon and Osmeña presented themselves as strong nationalists, their initial rise to power was, like Pardo de Tavera's, due to American patronage. Only nineteen when the revolution began, Osmeña, a Chinese *mestizo* from Cebu, remained loyal to Spain until the end. Shortly after the US occupation began, Osmeña established a Spanish-language newspaper in Cebu which espoused nationalistic sentiments, while he cultivated close relationships with American officials. With the support of American colonials, Osmeña was elected governor of Cebu Province and had emerged as its most influential politician by 1905.[40] Impressed with Osmeña's administration, Forbes began courting the young governor in 1906.[41]

Born in a small town on Luzon's rugged Pacific coast, Manuel Quezon was the son of two Spanish *mestizo* schoolteachers. Graduating from San Juan de Letran College in Manila with highest honours in 1894, Quezon enrolled in the law course at the University of Santo Tomas and, like his classmate Osmeña, remained loyal to Spain until her defeat in 1898. Soon after the outbreak of the Philippine–American War, Quezon enlisted in the Philippine Army as a lieutenant and rose to the rank of major by the time he surrendered to the US Army.[42] Imprisoned for some six months, Quezon certainly had little reason to love the American government. But he quickly found that individual Americans were invaluable political patrons. After joining the Bar in 1903, Quezon returned home to Tayabas Province where he soon attracted the attention of the local Constabulary commander, Colonel Harry H. Bandholtz, who was instrumental in Quezon's rapid rise from obscurity to provincial governor in only two years.

During their two-year transition from provincial dominance to national prominence between 1905 and 1907, both Quezon and Osmeña drew upon diverse sources of American patronage, most importantly that of Bandholtz and his superior, Secretary for Commerce and Police, Cameron Forbes. Both Bandholtz and Forbes worked actively for the advancement of Quezon and Osmeña throughout 1906, and were instrumental in forging a formal political alliance between the two three months before the 1907 Assembly elections. After their election, Quezon and Osmeña paid their political debts by supporting Forbes in his rise to the Governorship and assisting his administration by delivering whatever legislation he needed from the National Assembly.[43]

Although a great deal has been written about the turns and twists of colonial politics between the first Assembly elections in 1907 and the establishment of the Philippine Commonwealth in 1935, one central fact emerges from the mass of detail—there was a remarkable lack of change in leaders, policies or the pattern of colonial politics. The Nacionalista Party never came close to losing control of the legislature and its leaders, Quezon and Osmeña, dominated colonial politics almost until the end of American rule in 1946. Demonstrating a remarkable mastery of parliamentary tactics, Osmeña retained control of the party in and out of the Assembly until Quezon launched a successful challenge to his leadership in 1922. Excepting only a momentary break with Quezon over proposed independence legislation in 1933–4, Osmeña served him loyally as the Party's second leader from 1922 to 1933 and as his Commonwealth vice-president from 1935 to 1944. When Quezon died in the United States while heading a wartime government-in-exile, Osmeña ascended to the office and remained in power until he lost the 1946 presidential elections only months before the end of US colonial rule.

There was a similar ebb-and-flow to their relations with senior American colonial officials. Although their relations with Cameron Forbes cooled during his last years in office, Quezon and Osmeña found his successor, Francis Burton Harrison (Governor, 1913–22), the ideal partner in colonialism. Somewhat uncritical in his supervision of various Filipino activities, Harrison failed to check excesses in the management of the Philippine National Bank which brought it, and the colony's economy, to the point of near collapse. Determined that such disasters would not occur under his adminsitration, Harrison's successor, Leonard Wood (Governor, 1921–7), reduced the autonomy of action Filipino officials had enjoyed under Harrison and provoked a major political confrontation with the Nacionalista Party. The succeeding governor, Henry Stimson (1927–8), restored amicable working relations with Quezon and healed the breach. Stimson was the last American governor forced to play an active public role in Philippine politics, and his successors retired to their offices leaving public leadership to Quezon and Osmeña.

EDUCATION AND BI-NATIONALISM

While American patronage drew the Filipino political elite into a web of exchange relationships with colonial officials, the colonial education system fostered a complementary ideology of a lasting 'special relationship' between the Philippines and the United States. American colonial education did not deny Philippine nationalism — as did the Dutch in Indonesia and the French in Vietnam — but, in fact, studied and encouraged it. American colonial education defined a total world view for the Filipino child and drilled it in with song, lesson and story. Through texts on history, civics, reading and music developed especially for the Philippines, the colonial education system covered every area of human social experience — individual, family, community and nation — and presented lessons in a manner consistently complementary to a protectorate relationship with America. There was considerable debate among the early American directors about the goals of Philippine education, but all agreed that its ultimate aim was the transmission of new American-style values not just simple facts and technical skills.[44] The lessons of bi-nationalism had the greatest impact on middle and upper-class children who remained in school longest, and probably had less influence on peasant children who usually left school after only four years of primary education.

History texts rewrote the Philippine–American War to make it seem complementary to Phil–American friendship. One text, published in the Commonwealth period, handled the defeat of the 1896 revolution in a way that made it seem the fulfilment of Philippine nationalism:

The capture of Aguinaldo at Palanan on March 23, 1901, broke the military morale of the Filipinos. Subdued by main force, they gave up their armed struggle for national independence. America's policy of attraction, together with her strength, had broken Filipino resistance. The people saw by America's policy in the Philippines that their national aspiration could be attained with the aid of the United States. The revolutionary leaders themselves, having proved that their people knew how to give the utmost sacrifice when their country called, were now willing to sacrifice their military pride and heed the call of their countrymen who had accepted peace and were beginning a new type of struggle within the bounds of law and order.[45]

The primary readers were even less subtle in their indoctrination of bi-national values. Written by a distinguished Filipino educator and reprinted five times between 1919 and 1947, *The Philippine*

Reader contains an illustrated lesson, titled 'Saluting the Flag', which begins:

When boys and girls salute the flag, they do not merely express their pride that it is a flag honored over the world. They ought to remember that the flag represents the country to which there are duties every hour of their lives. All the time they are receiving blessings from that country, and all the time they have duties to that country.

The large illustration accompanying the lesson in the 1947 edition, published the year *after* independence, shows four Filipino primary schoolchildren saluting *two* flags – the American flag in the place of honour at the top of the pole and the Filipino flag in the secondary spot lower down the pole [46] (see illustration, p. 21).

The subordination of the Filipino flag to the American flag implicit in the Book Five lesson, was explained in a civics lesson in the 1940 Primer Series, Book Three:

The Flags

1) When the Flags are raised or lowered, or when they pass in front of you, stand straight and be very quiet. If you are a boy, take off your hat and hold it over your heart.
2) Never allow the flags to touch the ground.
3) The Filipino Flag should be at the left of the American Flag or below it.[47]

While the readers inculcated the rituals of bi-national flag reverence among primary pupils, civics and social life tests prepared for high-school students contained extensive critiques of Philippine society, depicting it as immature and incomplete. A text titled *Philippine Social Life and Progress*, published by two Filipino educators during the Commonwealth era, had damning things to say about Filipinos, but portrayed the Philippine–American relationship as a strongly positive influence for reform:

American-Filipino Co-operation. 1. (a) In what way did Americans and Filipinos co-operate against Spain in the war of 1898? (b) Why did they fight each other in 1899? (c) Had Americans and Filipinos known about each other better, would they have fought the Philippine–American war?
2. (a) Mention the different ways by which the United States tried

to co-operate in the promotion of Filipino social progress after peace was established between America and the Philippines. (b) Had there been no co-operation between America and the Philippines, would so much progress have been attained?
3. (a) In what way is the establishment of the Commonwealth a form of co-operation between Americans and Filipinos? (b) How is the United States helping us in our national-defense program?
4. (a) Should the United States decide to retain naval bases in the Philippines at the end of the Commonwealth period, as provided in the Independence Law, would such retention mean the end or the continuance of American–Filipino co-operation?
5. After independence is declared what American institutions or influences will be left in the Philippines to maintain and foster American–Filipino co-operation?[48]

Among the most tenacious survivors in the colonial curriculum was the *Philippine Progressive Music Series* compiled by Noberto Romauldez, Supreme Court Justice and uncle of the Philippines' first lady, Mrs Imelda Romauldez Marcos. The book was printed seven times – 1914, 1920, 1924, 1929, 1932, 1941, 1949 – and remained in use in some areas of the Philippines until the 1960s. The 1949, post-independence edition contained the following song, 'Heaven Watch the Philippines', dedicated to General Douglas MacArthur 'in commemoration of his liberation of the Philippines':[49]

> Heaven watch the Philippines,
> Keep her safe from harm.
> Guard her sons and their precious ones
> In the city and on the farm.
> Friendly with America
> Let her always be.

Not only were these colonial texts used for at least a decade after independence, but their lessons were replicated in many of the new school books prepared by Filipino educators after 1946. A basic primary reader prepared in 1951 as a part of an innovative vernacular education programme contained the following lesson in civic flag reverence: 'To you, flag of my nation, I offer my life, heart and strength'. The accompanying half-page illustration showed four Filipino pupils at the gate of their schoolyard saluting two flags— Philippine and American—flying side-by-side just as they had in Commonwealth texts.[50]

THE COMMONWEALTH AND THE SECOND WORLD WAR

Although American colonials and Nacionalista Party leaders were generally happy with the state of Philippine–American relations in the early 1930s, larger political pressures moved the Philippines towards Commonwealth status and eventual independence. While nationalistic Filipino voters continued to demand progress towards independence, the US Congress was at last eager to consider a concrete programme for granting the islands their freedom. American motives were a combination of idealism and self-interest.

With the onset of the depression in 1929, American interest groups demanded import restrictions, and the Philippines became the target of several lobbies—the US dairy industry wanted to cut imports of Philippine coconut oil; western beet-sugar farmers and Cuban sugar interests, financed by New York banks, wanted to reduce sugar supplies; and racist West Coast labour lobbies demanded an end to Philippine immigration (see illustration, p. 20). The combination of American lobbyists and a Filipino independence delegation led by Sergio Osmeña had its effect, and in 1933 the US Congress passed a law establishing an autonomous Commonwealth as the first step in a ten-year transition to independence.

Determined that his rival Osmeña should not have the glory of winning the independence bill, Quezon himself arrived in Washington, DC to seek major revisions to the legislation. At a meeting with key US senators, Quezon sought to explain the reasons for his opposition but was interrupted by the US Senate Majority Leader: 'Why don't you come clean and be frank? We believe you don't want independence. If so, why don't you say so?'[51] Unable to influence the US Congress, Quezon had the independence bill rejected by the Philippine Assembly and then returned to Washington where he secured passage of almost identical legislation. Having crushed Osmeña once again, Quezon, with a characteristic flair, then selected him as his vice-presidential running mate in the 1935 Commonwealth elections. Together the two rivals scored an overwhelming electoral victory, and Quezon took office as Commonwealth president in November.

At the height of his political powers and free from any serious opposition, Quezon turned his attention to the defence and development of the Philippine Commonwealth. To build a Philippine army capable of resisting a possible Japanese invasion, Quezon retained

General Douglas MacArthur, who had already served three tours of duty in the Philippines, as overall commander of the Commonwealth's armed forces. Alone among the major American public figures of this century, MacArthur identified his destiny with the colony's future. Retiring as Chief of Staff of the US Army in 1935, MacArthur came to Manila as adviser to his close friend Quezon and less than a year later was promoted to Field Marshal of Philippine armed forces, a rank created for him.[52] MacArthur rejected established US military doctrines which deemed the archipelago indefensible, and devised a mobilisation scheme based on the Swiss citizen army which, he argued, would make the Philippines impregnable. Assisted by Colonel Dwight D. Eisenhower, MacArthur launched an ambitious programme to build an independent Philippine army of 400,000 reserves but was far less than half way when the Japanese invasion came in December 1941.

Instead of meeting the Japanese on the beaches as he had planned, MacArthur declared Manila an 'open city' and ordered his Luzon forces to retreat into fortified positions on Bataan Peninsula and Corregidor Island at the mouth of Manila Bay. Although the rapid Japanese advance into Southeast Asia and the Pacific made it impossible for MacArthur to expect reinforcements, Philippine–American forces fought together bravely for five months despite declining food and material supplies which made their conditions desperate. The end came gradually. In February 1942 Quezon and Osmeña left Corregidor Island for Australia and from there went on to Washington, DC where they formed a government-in-exile. A few weeks later MacArthur abandoned his command with the histrionic pledge, 'I shall return', and fled to Australia where he established his new headquarters. Although Corregidor fell in May 1942 marking the end of American resistance, many Filipino troops retreated into the mountains and began a prolonged campaign of guerrilla warfare against the Japanese occupation forces.[53]

The Japanese Army found its occupation of the Philippines an especially difficult one. While Java's political leaders hailed Japanese troops as liberators and collaborated closely to win their support for Indonesian independence, most Filipinos viewed the Japanese as enemies and supported the guerrilla resistance. The Filipino decision to remain loyal to the United States was a unique combination of rational calculation and bi-national patriotism. Calculating that America's industrial might would make her the ultimate victor in the Pacific War, most Filipino leaders maintained their pro-American loyalties and only collaborated with the Japanese to survive until MacArthur returned. Compounding this rational military assessment, Filipino leaders knew Japan lacked the capacity to absorb the archipelago's most important export, sugar, and felt their economic future more secure under American protection. Many middle and upper-class Filipinos had prospered from contact with Americans, most commonly through the education system, and felt a residual sense of loyalty to their colonisers. In a memorandum in April 1945 typifying the pro-American attitudes of the Filipino elite, the wartime Chief Justice in the Japanese-sponsored government, Jose Yulo, explained his action:

Am I a pro-Japanese?
   My first words of English I learned on the lap of Sergeant Lewis, a kindly non-commissioned officer of blessed memory, who frequented my home in the little town of Bago, Negros Occidental, during the first days of the American occupation. I am an exclusive product of the public schools from the primary to the high school grades. I took my law course in the University of the Philippines . . . Since January, 1915, however, I secured employment in the law office of Bruce and Reed, one of the leading firms in Manila specializing in corporation law practice . . . To these firms . . . and to the two American lawyers who so generously gave me their fundamentals of coporate practice, I owe in large measure the little success that I had during my law practice and in later life while serving my people.

Yulo went on to explain that he, like the guerrillas, had remained confident that America 'would eventually come to redeem us' and claimed that he was only guilty of 'technical collaboration which by force of circumstance I may of [sic] had to render'.[54]
   The Second World War was one of the most difficult periods in modern Philippine history, exceeding even the revolutionary era in its violence and destruction. Finding that 'liberal' policies epitomised by their grant of national independence in November 1943 could not win the loyalties of most Filipinos, the Japanese military launched a series of bloody 'punitive expeditions' that led to the slaughter of 12,000 civilians on one island and countless atrocities across the archipelago. The Japanese pacification campaign only added to the popular longing for America's return—a sentiment carefully culti-

vated by MacArthur's staff. Submarines arriving from Australia with arms for the guerrillas carried millions of chocolate bars, match books, soap wrappers and leaflets, all carrying the same slogan—'"*I shall Return*", signed, General Douglas MacArthur.'

MacArthur's motto struck a deeply responsive chord in a Filipino folk-Catholicism animated by a belief in the immediacy of Christ's second coming. MacArthur's landing at Leyte Island at the head of a vast US Navy armada in October 1944 was hailed by many Filipinos as the 'redemption' of their nation. Striding through the surf at Leyte with President Sergio Osmeña, successor to the recently deceased Quezon, MacArthur himself evoked the messianic qualities of the event in his speech on the beach:

I have returned. By the grace of Almighty God our forces stand again on Philippine soil – soil consecrated by the blood of our two peoples . . .

The hour of your redemption is here. Your patriots have demonstrated an unswerving and resolute devotion to the principles of freedom that challenges the best that is written in the pages of human history . . .

Rally to me. Let the indomitable spirit of Bataan and Corregidor lead on . . . Let no heart be faint. Let every arm be steeled. The guidance of divine God points the way. Follow in His name to the Holy Grail of righteous victory.[55]

After securing their beachhead with a spectacular victory in the Battle of Leyte Gulf, MacArthur's forces swept towards Manila, liberating the capital in February 1945. The fighting left Manila the world's most heavily damaged major city after Warsaw and reduced the archipelago's economy to chaos. But the war years and their destruction served to consecrate the Philippine–American relationship with blood and fire. The lessons of the bi-national flag ritual taught in the pre-war school texts were, as evidenced by the massive pro-American majority in the post-war Constitutional referendum, accepted by most Filipinos regardless of class.

Almost from the moment the fighting ended in September 1945, however, the emotional rhetoric of Phil–American comradeship began to fade and many Filipinos were forced to realise that their 'friend', America, did not share their sense of mutual obligation. MacArthur himself went off to seek greater glories as head of the Allied occupation government for Japan. Instead of simply paying for the vast amount of war damages as the Filipinos had been promised, the US Congress tied relief payments to controversial legislation, the Bell Trade Act, which was passed on the eve of Philippine independence and re-imposed many Commonwealth controls. The Bell Act tied the Philippine peso to the US dollar; granted US citizens the same 'parity' with Filipinos in the economy that they had enjoyed under the Commonwealth; and re-established 'free trade' between the Philippines and the United States. Desperate for US rehabilitation funds of US $620 million to restore the war-ravaged economy, President Roxas and almost all major Filipino politicians campaigned in favour of a constitutional amendment to allow Americans economic 'parity' with Filipinos as required by the Bell Act. Although the constitutional amendment required a substantial concession of national independence to American businessmen, over 89 per cent of the voters approved the measure – presented to them as a vote of faith in America.[56]

Following hard upon approval of the Parity Amendment, American and Filipino leaders moved to restore the substance of Commonwealth ties in a variety of fields. The Military Bases Agreement (1947) affirmed America's continued responsibility for the stategic defence of the Philippines; the Military Assistance Agreement (1947) extended the US Army's role in training the Philippine armed forces begun under the Commonwealth; the Quirino–Foster Agreement (1950) initiated the US aid programmes which have given American officials a key role in many Philippine government reforms; and the Laurel–Langley Trade Agreement (1954) perpetuated the 'free trade' relationship which bound Philippine exports to the American market.[57] Despite two decades of nominal independence, the United States, under these and other treaties, still exercised considerable influence in the Philippines. In the mid-1960s the Philippine–American relationship was similar, in certain significant respects, to that under the Commonwealth of the 1930s.

POST-COLONIAL NATIONALIST MOVEMENTS

Not all Filipino political leaders were happy with the restoration of Commonwealth ties to the United States. Nationalist opposition gathered at two poles in the society – the *Hukbalahap*, or *Huk* guerrilla movement and the elite nationalist movement focussed around Senator Claro Recto.

The most serious challenge to the post-war political order came from communist-led guerrilla units based in central Luzon. Initially supportive of MacArthur and willing to play politics by the rules of the game, the communist *Huk* units were forced into armed rebellion as a defence against repressive measures adopted by Philippine–American conservatives. Immediately after the liberation of central Luzon in January 1945, US Army Counter-Intelligence Corps began disarming *Huk* units supporting the American advance on Manila and later approved the summary executions of *Huk* troops. When six leftist Congressmen were elected in the *Huk* heartland of central Luzon, during the April 1946 elections, the conservative majority refused to seat them. Strongly opposed to the neo-colonial relationship developing with the United States, the six central Luzon Congressmen were barred because their opposition to the Parity Amendment would have blocked passage of the enabling legislation. In mid-1946 newly-elected President Manuel Roxas, whose wife was a major central Luzon landowner, ordered a massive anti-*Huk* campaign by constabulary units, and in August a prominent peasant leader, Juan Feleo, disappeared en route to Manila for a meeting with the Secretary of Interior while passing near Roxas' plantation. Several weeks later his decapitated body was found floating in a nearby river, and it was widely believed that Roxas himself had ordered the murder. Five days after Feleo's disappearance, Luis Taruc, elected to Congress from central Luzon in April, slipped out of Manila to become the overall leader of the *Huk* guerrilla forces. Although *Huk* guerrillas held most of central Luzon for eight years and at one point seemed poised for a successful assault on Manila, they failed to expand out of their Luzon homeland and were ultimately defeated through the joint efforts of the Philippine army and the US Central Intelligence Agency. By 1954 most of the main *Huk* units had been broken up, and Taruc himself, feeling that the rebellion had failed, surrendered to the government.[58]

As the *Huk* movement's armed challenge to the conservative order faded in the early 1950s, Senator Recto's elite nationalist movement gathered strength. A leading colonial politician and pre-war Quezon supporter, Recto chaired the 1935 Constitutional Convention and served as Foreign Minister in the Japanese-sponsored wartime Republic. Most collaborators escaped arrest, but Recto remained before the courts for three years after the war and was forced to mount a costly legal defence to salvage his political reputation.

Elected to the Philippine Senate in the 1949 elections, he launched a nationalist campaign that lasted until his death in 1960. Recto's anti-Americanism was a combination of commonsense nationalism, anger at the years of harassment he suffered for his wartime collaboration, and an abiding allegiance to Hispano–Philippine culture. Spanish-educated like many of his generation, Recto gained a considerable reputation as a poet in Spanish and cultivated a lifelong love of Spain, exemplified by his enthusiastic support of the pro-Franco fascist movement among Manila's Spanish colony during the Spanish Civil War. Although more than competent in English, Recto never developed any affection for the language and, unlike most of the elite, refused to transfer his bi-national loyalties from Spain to America. Throughout the 1950s, Recto was a constant nationalist gadfly, attacking the continued dependence on the United States. Initially something of a lone prophet, Recto attracted a wide following among students, intellectuals and nationalist entrepreneurs who were then buying out American investments and establishing new industries. Recto himself, however, was far less than a perfect practitioner of his own doctrines. As a corporate lawyer for Luzon Stevedoring Corporation, one of the largest American corporations in the Philippines, he defended its controversial policies which denied Filipino workers millions of pesos in wages and the government substantial foreign-exchange earnings. Recto attacked American neo-colonialism while simultaneously serving one of its prime examples.[59]

After a brief lull in the early 1960s, the nationalist movement revived itself among students in the Manila university belt. Combining the elite nationalist ideals of Recto with the radical tactics of the *Huk*, student leaders formed *Kabataang Makabayan*, or Nationalist Youth, in the mid-1960s and launched a movement which revived the anti-American rhetoric of the colonial era. Following a bitter break with the old Moscow-line communist party in 1967–8, the leaders of Nationalist Youth formed a Peking-line communist party and withdrew to the countryside to launch a Maoist-style peasant revolt. Despite the movement's formal adoption of Marxism–Leninism, it is clear from the writings of its leader, Jose Ma. Sison, that nationalist questions involving US military bases, American investment and parity concessions were paramount. In one of history's ironies, a major revolutionary movement was launched a full quarter-century after formal independence with the nationalist rhetoric of a colonised people.[60]

CONCLUSION

There are no villains and heroes in this chronicle of bi-nationalism. If the barter relationship with American colonials worked to the advantage of the Filipino elite, it was essentially a compromising experience. The rise of bi-nationalism among Filipinos clouded their emerging national identity and eroded their capacities for development. Tied closely to the American 'free trade' and defence relationships, Filipino leaders refused to chart their own course for national development. Lacking a vision and plan for development, the Philippine economy moved forward slowly, tied to traditional exports and markets, while wasting valuable time, entrepreneurial talent and considerable natural endowments.

As the first generation born and raised in an independent nation matured in the 1960s, the old patterns of nationalist loyalties began to break down, producing a partial reversal of traditional positions. Throughout the half-century lasting until the mid-1950s, the elite had held bi-national loyalties, epitomised by the dual-flag ceremonies of the Commonwealth era, and the peasants retained a more radical nationalism. After the collapse of the *Huk* rebellion in the mid-1950s, the once unified and militant villages of central Luzon fragmented into competing factions as peasant families became absorbed in the difficult task of surviving in a region that could no longer sustain its dense population. For the peasants, the period of armed revolt had been sustained disaster, an experience they were not inclined to repeat. Paralleling the decline of peasant interest in radical nationalism, anti-colonial ideals gained influence rapidly among students, largely children of the elite, in Manila's university belt during the 1960s. Expropriating the old symbols of past peasant nationalists, the student leaders, particularly Jose Ma. Sison, came to advocate the Maoist doctrine of capturing Manila through an armed peasant revolt. Sison and his followers launched their revolt in 1968-9, but after more than a decade in the field failed to win significant peasant support. Although an active minority of young elite adopted the militancy of the new nationalism, the reversal in ideological stances between elite and peasant was by no means complete – the great bulk of the elite was still comfortable with its bi-national loyalties. In the months preceding the declaration of Martial Law in 1972, for example, the 'Philippine Statehood Movement' recruited some 7 million dues-paying members attracted to its goal of making the Philippines the fifty-first American state.

As the Philippines moved through its fourth decade of independence, emotional and material ties to America, although attenuated, had survived. Traditional nationalism, by contrast, was at an impasse. While the heroes and symbols of the 1896 revolution aroused stronger emotions than ever before, their romance was now a part of the past and no longer directly relevant to the complex lives of either peasant or elite in modern society.

NOTES

1. Teodoro A. Agoncillo, *Malolos: The Crisis of the Republic* (Quezon City: University of the Philippines, 1960) pp. 224–7; General Jose Alejandrino, *The Price of Freedom: Episodes and Anecdotes of Our Struggles for Freedom* (Manila: M. Colcol, 1949) pp. 91–4.
2. James A. Le Roy, *The Americans in the Philippines: A History of the Conquest and First Years of Occupation with an Introductory Account of the Spanish Rule*, Vol. I (Boston: Houghton Mifflin, 1914) pp. 156–71; Teodoro M. Kalaw, *The Philippine Revolution* (Manila: Manila Book Co., 1925) pp. 92–4, 102–3, 106–7.
3. Carlos Quirino, *Quezon: Paladin of Philippine Freedom* (Manila: Community Publishers, 1971) pp. 285–7; Theodore Friend, *Between Two Empires: The Ordeal of the Philippines, 1929–1946* (New Haven: Yale University Press, 1965) pp. 184–6.
4. Teodoro A. Agoncillo, *The Fateful Years: Japan's Adventure in the Philippines, 1941–5*, Vol. I (Quezon City: R. P. Garcia, 1965) pp. 392–7.
5. Friend, *Between Two Empires*, pp. 261–2; Hernando Abaya, *Betrayal in the Philippines* (New York: A. A. Wyn, 1946) pp. 280–1.
6. Brian Fegan, 'Continuities in Central Luzon Peasant Movements' (Ms., 1979); Reynaldo C. Ileto, '*Pasion* and the Interpretation of Change in Tagalog Society' (Cornell University, PhD dissertation, 1975).
7. Flavio Zaragoza Cano, *Cantos A España* (Iloilo: Lix Publishing, 1936) pp. 125–6
8. Francisco Alcina, SJ, 'Historia de las Islas e Indios de Bisayas' (Ms., 1668).
9. William L. Schurz, *The Manila Galleon* (New York: E. P. Dutton, 1939) pp. 154–215; Bank of the Philippine Islands, *Souvenir of the First Bank Established in the Far East* (Manila, 1928) pp. 3–11.
10. H. de la Costa, SJ, *Asia and the Philippines* (Manila: Solidaridad, 1967) pp. 66–80.
11. Nicholas P. Cushner, SJ, *Spain in the Philippines* (Quezon City: Institute of Philippine Culture, Ateneo de Manila University, 1971) pp. 3–41, 127–52.
12. Edgar Wickberg, *The Chinese in Philippine Life, 1850–1898* (New Haven: Yale University Press, 1965) pp. 3–41.
13. Benito Legarda, Jr, 'Foreign Trade, Economic Change, and Entrepreneurship in the Nineteenth Century Philippines' (Harvard University, PhD dissertation, 1955).
14. Cushner, *Spain in the Philippines*, pp. 197–222.
15. Tomas de Comyn, *State of the Philippines in 1870* (Manila: Filipiniana

Book Guild, 1969) pp. 144–5; Sinabaldo de Mas, *Report on the Conditions of the Philippines* (Manila: Historical Conservation Society, 1963) p. 163; Michael Cullinane, 'The Changing Nature of the Cebu Urban Elite in the 19th Century', in Alfred W. McCoy and Edilberto de Jesus (eds.), *Studies in Philippine Social History* (Ms., 1980, forthcoming), pp. 15, 18–28.

16. Alfred W. McCoy, *'Muy Noble y Muy Leal*: Revolution and Counter-revolution in the Western Visayas, Philippines, 1896–1907' (Sydney: 2nd Annual Asian Studies Association of Australia Conference, 1978).

17. Alfred W. McCoy, 'Yloilo: Factional Conflict in a Colonial Economy, Iloilo Province, Philippines, 1937–1955' (Yale University, PhD dissertation, 1977) pp. 12–142; Brian Fegan, 'Folk Capitalism: Economic Strategies of Peasants in a Philippines Wet Rice Village. (Yale University, PhD dissertation, 1979) pp. 8–95; Marshall McLennan, 'Peasant and Hacendero in Nueva Ecija: The Socio-Economic Origins of a Philippine Commercial Rice-Growing Region' (University of California at Berkeley, PhD dissertation, 1973).

18. John N. Schumacher, *Father Jose Burgos: Priest and Nationalist* (Manila: Ateneo de Manila University Press, 1972) pp. 2–15, 69.

19. *Ibid.*, p. 93.

20. *Ibid.*

21. *Ibid.*, pp. 95, 47, 115; Fidel Villaroel, OP, *Father Jose Burgos: University Student* (Manila: University of Santo Tomas, 1971), pp. 1–6, 61–93.

22. Villaroel, *Father Jose Burgos*, pp. 93–106.

23. John Schumacher, *The Propaganda Movement: 1880–1895* (Manila: Solidaridad, 1973) pp. 5–16, 267–78.

24. Cushner, *Spain in the Philippines*, pp. 222–9; Jacques Amyot, *The Manila Chinese: Familism in the Philippine Environment* (Manila: Institute of Philippine Culture, Ateneo de Manila University Press, 1973) fig. 15; Schumacher, *Father Jose Burgos*, p. 1.

25. Cushner, *Spain in the Philippines*, pp. 222–5; Teodoro A. Agoncillo, *The Revolt of the Masses: The Story of Bonifacio and the Katipunan* (Quezon City: University of the Philippines Press, 1956) pp. 26–31; Horacio de la Costa, *The Background of Nationalism and Other Essays* (Manila: Solidaridad, 1965) pp. 31–41.

26. Agoncillo, *Revolt of the Masses*, pp. 36–8.

27. Epifanio de los Santos, *The Revolutionists: Aguinaldo, Bonifacio, Jacinto* (Manila: National Historical Commission, 1973) pp. 85–97; Agoncillo, *Revolt of the Masses*, pp. 63–71.

28. Agoncillo, *Revolt of the Masses*, pp. 43–6, 76–97, 101–2.

29. *Ibid.*, pp. 128–43.

30. Kalaw, *The Philippine Revolution*, pp. 67–80; Cushner, *Spain in the Philippines*, pp. 227–8; de los Santos, *The Revolutionists*, pp. 13–15.

31. McCoy, *'Muy Noble y Muy Leal'*; McCoy, 'Yloilo', pp. 92–102.

32. McCoy, *'Muy Noble y Muy Leal'*; Milagros C. Guerrero, 'Luzon at War: Contradictions in Philippine Society, 1898–1902' (University of Michigan, PhD dissertation, 1977).

33. Peter W. Stanley, *A Nation in the Making: The Philippines and the United States, 1899–1921* (Cambridge: Harvard University Press, 1974), pp. 164, 207, 253; Glenn A. May, 'America in the Philippines: The Shaping of Colonial Policy, 1898–1913' (Yale University, PhD dissertation, 1975) pp. 119–20.

34. Quirino, *Quezon*, pp. 175–6; Stanley, *Nation in the Making*, pp. 179–80, 260–1; Friend, *Between Two Empires*, pp. 42–4, 48–59.

35. May, 'America in the Philippines'. pp. 64, 71–2, 87.

64   *Asia – The Winning of Independence*

36. E. Arsenio Manuel, *Dictionary of Philippine Biography*, vol. I (Quezon City: Filipiniana Publications, 1955) pp. 313–47; Stanley, *Nation in the Making*, pp. 68–73.
37. Stanley, *Nation in the Making*, pp. 73, 115–16, 117–27.
38. *Ibid.*, pp. 99–103.
39. Dapen Liang, *Philippine Parties and Politics: A Historical Study of National Experience in Democracy* (San Francisco: Gladstone, 1971) pp. 59–69.
40. Cullinane, 'The Changing Nature of the Cebu Urban Elite in the 19th Century', pp. 62–3.
41. Stanley, *Nation in the Making*, pp. 134–5.
42. Quirino, *Quezon*, pp. 34, 15–31, 49–58.
43. Michael Cullinane, 'Quezon and Bandholtz: The Origins of the Special Relationship' (Los Angeles: Asian Studies Association, Annual Meeting, 1979); Michael Cullinane, 'American-Made *Caciques*?: The Rise to Political Prominence of Manuel Quezon and the Emergence of the *Partido Nacionalista*, 1898–1907 (Ms., 1978).
44. May, 'America in the Philippines', pp. 91–173.
45. Conrado Benitez, *History of the Philippines* (Boston: Ginn & Co., 1940) p. 380.
46. Camilio Osias, *The Philippine Readers: Book Five* (Boston: Ginn & Co., 1947) pp. 272–5.
47. Eleanor G. Riss *et al.*, *Philippine Public School Readers: Book Three* (Manila: Bureau of Printing, 1940) pp. 4–5.
48. Conrado Benitez and Ramon S. Tirona, *Philippine Social Life and Progress* (Boston: Ginn & Co., 1937) pp. 53–9, 484–850.
49. Norberto Romauldez *et al.*, *The Philippine Progressive Music Series* (New York: Silver Burdett Co., 1949) pp. 5–6.
50. Rosa C. Preiser *et al.*, *Si Pepe Kag Pilar Nagdu-aw sa Dakbanua* (Iloilo: Iloilo Division of Schools, 1951) pp. 122–3.
51. Friend, *Between Two Empires*, p. 111.
52. *Ibid.*, pp. 79, 160–4.
53. *Ibid.*, pp. 161–8; David J. Steinberg, *Philippine Collaboration in World War II* (Ann Arbor: University of Michigan, 1967) pp. 25–6.
54. Statement of Jose Yulo, 24 April 1945, File: Collaboration, Roxas Papers, National Library, Manila.
55. Agoncillo, *The Fateful Years*, Vol. II, pp. 850–1.
56. Milton W. Meyer, *A Diplomatic History of the Philippine Republic* (Honolulu: University of Hawaii Press, 1965) pp. 48–53; Ronald K. Edgerton, 'The Politics of Reconstruction in the Philippines: 1945–1948' (University of Michigan, PhD dissertation, 1975) pp. 338–89.
57. Claude A. Buss, *The United States and the Philippines: Background for Policy* (Stanford: Hoover Institute Studies, 1977) pp. 19–22, 24–6; Mamerto S. Ventura, *United States-Philippine Cooperation and Cross Purposes: Philippine Post War Recovery and Reform* (Quezon City: Filipiniana Publications, 1974) pp. 100–1, 190–6, 221–6; George E. Taylor, 'The Challenge of Mutual Security', in Frank Golay (ed.), *Philippine American Relations* (Manila: Solidaridad, 1966) pp. 67–72.
58. Benedict J. Kerkvliet, *The Huk Rebellion: A Study of Peasant Revolt in the Philippines* (Berkeley: University of California Press, 1977) pp. 110–14, 143–55.
59. Renato Constantino, *The Making of a Filipino: A Story of Philippine Colonial Politics* (Quezon City: Malaya Books, 1969); *Eustaquio Maranon, et*

al., vs. *Luzon Stevedoring Corporation*, Iloilo Court of First Instance, Case nos. 3375, 3405, 3424, 3505.

60. Amado Guerrero [Jose Ma. Sison], *Philippine Society and Revolution* (Hong Kong: Ta King Pao, 1971) pp. 63–80, 113–59; William J. Pomeroy, *An American Made Tragedy: Neo-Colonialism and Dictatorship in the Philippines* (New York: International Publishers, 1974) pp. 84–5, 129–40; Philippino Constabulary, *So the People May Know* (Quezon City: Philippine Constabulary, Office of Civil Affairs, 1970) pp. 13–80; Eduardo Lachica *The Huks: Philippine Agrarian Society in Revolt* (New York: Praeger, 1971) pp. 204–68; Maj.-Gen. Edward G. Lansdale, *In the Midst of Wars: An American's Mission to Southeast Asia* (New York: Harper and Row, 1972) pp. 4–6, 9–10.

India:
Illustrations

LORD WILLINGDON'S DILEMMA

Willingdon, the Viceroy, imprisons Gandhi during the civil disobedience movement in May 1930, but is shaken to find thousands of other 'Gandhis' ready to go to jail.

IN INDIA, SIX MONTHS HENCE

Churchill's British government, unwilling to make constitutional concessions to win Indian co-operation in its war effort, is forced to imprison demonstrators when the Indian National Congress launches Gandhi's 'individual *satyagraha*' in November 1940.

To fight the British ...

... or the Japanese?

The Indian National Congress embarked on the 'Quit India' campaign on 8 August 1942. The Communist Party of India, bound by Moscow's directive to support the 'people's war' against German and Japanese fascism, risked appearing 'anti-national'. The CPI tried to put the best face on its dilemma by insisting that the Indian people could overcome both the British and the Japanese.

People's War, 16 August 1942.

Glossary for Chapter 2

ahimsa	Non-violence.
ashram	A retreat wherein a community lives a religiously oriented life.
charkha	Spinning wheel.
hartal	Closure of shops and businesses as a protest.
ICS	Indian Civil Service
khadi	Homespun cloth.
lathi	A stave, often bound with brass, favoured as a weapon in rural India and by the police.
maulvi	Muslim religious teacher.
satyagraha	'Soul-force', 'truth-force'; non-violent resistance to laws or actions deemed unjust.
swadeshi	Nationally made.
swaraj	Self-rule.
varna	'Caste' when referring to the four major divisions of classical Hinduism: Brahmin, Kshatriya, Vaisya, Sudra; contrast with *jati*, which refers to localised, endogamous, commensal groups, numbering thousands; *jatis* locate themselves within a *varna* category.

2 India: Independence and the Rich Peasant

Robin Jeffrey

THE SON OF A PEASANT

'I am the son of a peasant.'

Vallabhbhai Patel gloried in the words. 'I am not a leader; I am a soldier,' he told a meeting of the Indian National Congress in 1922, urging it to hold fast to its boycott of the legislatures created by the British. 'I am the son of a peasant and do not believe that we can gain independence by merely talking.' Two months before his death in 1950, the words were still on his lips: 'I am only a peasant and a humble soldier of the Congress. I am happy that I have taught the kisans [peasants] to take pride in themselves.'[1] By October 1950, however, Patel was much more than a peasant. He was deputy prime minister of independent India, the 'strong man' and boss of the Congress Party, second only to Jawaharlal Nehru, the prime minister.

Vallabhbhai Patel was the son of a Gujarati peasant who controlled ten acres of land, knew no English and was said to have fought in the army of the Rani of Jhansi when she joined the revolt against the British in 1857. By caste, they were Patidars, respectable in status, yet not wearers of the sacred thread and sometimes dismissed by outsiders as Sudras, the lowest of the four *varnas* of classical Hinduism (Brahmins, Kshatriyas, Vaisyas, Sudras). They lived in the fertile Charotar tract of Gujarat in western India, where from the 1860s men like themselves had begun to produce tobacco, fruit and dairy products for sale, as well as grain to eat themselves.

In later years, Vallabhbhai stressed his rural origins. Biographers claimed that as a boy, he learned to plough and sow and to work with cattle. This may have been exaggerated; the family may have been more lordly than Vallabhbhai and his admirers cared to admit. But in emphasising his peasant roots, he was testifying to the change that by the 1940s had taken place in Indian politics. No longer was

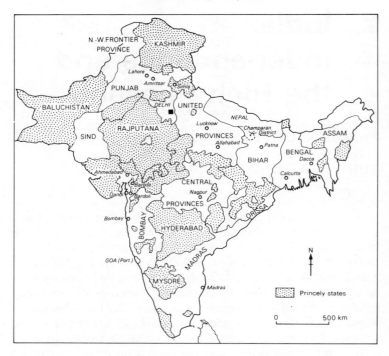

India, 1937

it an advantage to claim noble birth. The wealthy peasant—not the great, aristocratic landlords—had come to occupy a key position in the Congress Party and ultimately in the post-independence government.

Who were these 'rich peasants'? To generalise about India is foolhardy, particularly where the nature of the peasantry is concerned. The population in the 1930s was 338 million, speaking more than a dozen major languages and spread over 1.8 million square miles, about half the area of the United States. The patterns of landholding, and the types of tenure, varied widely among eleven provinces and 580 princely states. Yet, having emphasised the dangers, one may suggest that if there were 500,000 villages in India in the 1930s, each may have had on average four or five richpeasant families of between five and ten members. They would have totalled perhaps 25 million people, or roughly 8–10 per cent of the rural population. Each family held between 10 and 100 acres of land, which they cultivated partly perhaps by their own labour, but also with labourers and sharecroppers working under their supervision. Collectively, such families would have controlled—basing the estimate on statistics compiled for India in 1953—at least 50 per cent of all cultivated land. Above them stood the great landlords, less than 1 per cent of the rural population, but controlling huge estates totalling perhaps 25 per cent of the land. The remainder of the population in the countryside – 80–90 per cent consisted of smallholders, tenants and the landless, controlling less than 25 per cent of the land.[2]

These rich peasants usually belonged to the middle castes; in many cases, they had stood at the centre of village affairs even in pre-British times; and under the British, they had often begun to grow cash-crops.[3] Such men knew the countryside: they were part of it. But by the 1890s, drawn by commercial agriculture and the lure of litigation over land in the British-constituted law courts, they were increasingly straddling the rural–urban divide and sending their sons for high-school education in neighbouring towns.

Numbering millions, these men by themselves were to constitute a considerable force in the electoral politics, based on property qualifications, of twentieth-century British India. Given that each family had influence over dozens of inferiors and dependents, one can see how the role of the rich peasant in democratic politics came to be pivotal: as candidates, voters and mobilisers of the vote. Such men had a limited vision of 'revolution': removal of the British and agrarian reform directed against the great landlords. Vallabhbhai Patel expressed their views when he addressed a meeting in Calcutta in January 1950: 'Today you see no English face among our policemen. British governors have left only their statu[e?]s behind. What else is revolution if not this?'[4]

Whatever the depth of Vallabhbhai Patel's association with the land, the rural metaphor stayed with him all his life. 'You cannot obtain butter by churning water', he said dismissively of prolonged constitutional negotiations with the British government in 1942. He first attended school in his native village and began to learn English only at the age of thirteen. Later, he went to high school in a nearby town and matriculated at the advanced age of twenty-two. He became a small-town lawyer, kept his links with his village (his old neighbours brought their cases to him) and by 1905 had saved enough money to finance his elder brother's legal studies in Britain. In 1910, Vallabhbhai went to Britain and was called to the bar from the Middle Temple in 1913. He returned to India, one biographer wrote, with 'stylish suits and hats, a taste for cognac and the habit of chain-smoking'.

In 1917, however, he met M. K. Gandhi, recently returned from South Africa and just beginning to organise *satyagraha*—non-violent resistance—campaigns against the injustices of British rule. At first, Patel was unmoved. When Gandhi came to speak at the Gujarat Club in Ahmedabad, Patel is said to have ignored him and gone on playing bridge. But he soon succumbed to Gandhi's appeal: its emphasis on simplicity, Hinduism and things Indian. 'He . . . cast off his foreign dress . . . [and] lived with the workers sharing the plain food of the ashram . . . , sleeping on the ground, doing . . . the daily washing of his clothes and walking long distances in the villages.'[5]

Vallabhbhai Patel was to become perhaps the most successful practitioner of *satyagraha* against the British government. His brother, Vithalbhai Patel, on the other hand, was active even in 1917 in the British-sponsored legislatures and was to become president of the Central Legislative Assembly in New Delhi from 1925 to 1929. The brothers illustrate two crucial aspects of the struggle for Indian independence: the growing involvement from the time of the First World War of thousands of rich peasants, men whose roots lay deep in the small towns and villages; and the two dominant methods of political activity — membership of British–created legislatures or non-co-operation with the British government.

THE FIRST WORLD WAR

In India, as elsewhere, the First World War accelerated political and social changes that might otherwise have taken generations. The war stimulated Indian commerce and industry, because a certain measure of self-reliance for once suited British interests. More than a million men joined the army and travelled throughout India and the world. They came back to their villages with 'a new awareness of their plight and grumbles of their own about unfulfilled recruiting promises'.[6] The involvement of Turkey as an enemy of Britain provoked wide-spread Muslim mistrust of the British, for the Sultan of Turkey was recognised as the spiritual head of Islam. The rise in prices brought about by the war touched nearly every man and woman in India; nationwide economic grievances provided national issues. Finally, the rhetoric of Britain and her allies — Woodrow Wilson's emphasis on self-determination and making the world 'safe for democracy' — led Indian leaders to insist that India's reward for its sacrifices should be a large measure of constitutional progress towards self-government.

Who were these leaders? Until the First World War, those Indians involved in formal political activity were products of English education and institutions. They represented a Westernised elite that was tiny in proportion to India's total population: 315 million in 1911, of which 5.9 per cent was literate and fewer than 2 million knew English. Yet the elite was expanding rapidly; it outnumbered by many times the British rulers in India. In the 1830s when British officials had decided to implant an English-style education system, they had believed that the outcome would be 'a class of persons, Indian in blood and colour, but English in taste, in opinions, in morals and in intellect'.[7] Instead, by the 1890s, British governments found themselves confronted by a growing number of Indians who, though influenced by the West, sought to proclaim the superiority of their own traditions and attacked British rule and its values.

British officials, and later historians, saw the growth of educated unemployment as the key to 'Indian unrest'. The first three universities (Bombay, Calcutta and Madras) were founded in 1857, and until the 1890s, most young men who graduated could find the coveted government job. However, from the colleges came a torrent of graduates: 4700 between 1888 and 1892; 4200 in 1911 alone; 8400 in 1916; 9100 in 1921; 14,800 in 1931. What became increasingly evident, moreover, was the wastage of the system: those who studied but did not pass.[8]

The Indian National Congress, founded in 1885, embodied the anglicised elite. Indeed, its moving spirit in the early years was a European, A. O. Hume, a disillusioned ex-member of the Indian Civil Service. Congress meetings were held annually in the cool weather of December when the courts were in recess and the schools on holiday. These speech-making conventions, modelled on English public meetings, attracted a few hundred delegates who concerned themselves with issues that reflected their own interests. They continually passed resolutions emphasising the need to hold the examinations for the famed Indian Civil Service in India as well as

Britain and thus give Indian youths a better chance of success; to have more elected members on the legislative councils of the Viceroy and the provincial governors; and to reduce the military expenditure of the Government of India. There were no attempts to discuss the problems of peasants, and until 1906, no demand for self-government. More than a third of the delegates before 1914 were lawyers, and of eighty-six regular speakers at sessions in that period, sixty were lawyers and thirty-eight Brahmins, men of the highest caste. In short, the early Congress was English-educated, high-caste, city-based, well-off and genteel.[9]

The Congress tapestry, however, did not contain all the political threads. By the 1890s, terrorism, inspired by the Hindu religious revival in Bengal and Maharashtra, had begun to trouble the British. In 1897 a Maratha Brahmin murdered two British officials conducting heavy-handed public-health measures during a plague epidemic in Poona. B. G. Tilak, a Maratha Brahmin writer and politician who propagated a new and belligerent Hindu attitude towards the British and Muslims, justified the murders in his Marathi newspaper. He was convicted of incitement to sedition and sentenced to eighteen months' imprisonment. In the same year, the first serious riots between Muslims and Hindus occurred in the city of Calcutta.[10] Both terrorism, which usually involved members of the English-educated elite, and religious antagonism, which caught up the poor and less educated as its shock troops, were to grow in intensity and importance.

Within the Congress, divisions emerged between 'moderates' and 'extremists'. 'Moderates', like G. K. Gokhale, Tilak's rival in Maharashtra, contended that constitutional politics would bring from British governments constitutional reforms. They were confident that the Liberal Party in Britain, in power for less than three years between 1885 and 1906, would grant increased responsibility to Indians. 'Extremists' ridiculed such confidence. They addressed their followers in more Hindu-oriented terms and were often prepared to justify violence, as Tilak had done, in the cause of Mother India.

In 1906, this growing militance and tension within the Congress produced a resolution which for the first time called for 'self-government' as 'the only and chief remedy' for India's problems. This resolution, strong by the standards of the old Congress, delayed a split in the organisation for a year. But in 1907 the Congress session broke up in 'the brandishing of sticks and the unrolling of turbans, the breaking of chairs and bruising of heads; the crowning humiliation occurred when the police came and cleared the hall.' 'Moderates' and 'extremists' did not meet on the same Congress platform again until 1916.[11]

British officials regarded the Congress, even in its early form, as a threat to their rule and delighted in its disarray. George Nathaniel Curzon, Viceroy from 1899–1905, was eager, he wrote, to 'assist [the Congress] to a peaceful demise'.[12] To weaken the anglicised Hindu elite in its major bastion Calcutta, Curzon's government in October 1905 divided the huge province of Bengal, Bihar and Orissa (population 80 million) into two. In public, Curzon justified the partition for reasons of administrative efficiency; but privately, officials noted that one of the 'main objects' was 'to split up and thereby weaken a solid body of opponents to our rule'. The government concluded that 'Bengal united is a power. Bengal divided will pull several different ways'.[13] Bengali Hindus saw the partition as a plot to divide and rule: to create a Muslim-majority province in the eastern part of Bengal as a counterpoise to the Hindu-majority west. Waves of protest rolled across Bengal. British goods were boycotted; all patriots were urged to use only Indian-made— *swadeshi*—products. Attempts were made to start independent, 'national' schools, free of British influence. The campaign against the partition lasted well into 1908, and though it scarcely involved the countryside, it touched thousands of men and women and reached into smaller towns as no movement hitherto had.[14]

The partition was revoked in 1911 as a boon granted by the new King-Emperor, George V, on his visit to India, and as an attempt to mollify the Hindu elite. The 'moderate'-controlled Congress passed a resolution supporting Britain's war effort at its annual meeting in December 1914.

The Irish example, however, was widely known: England's difficulty could also be *India's* opportunity. Although plans for rebellion using German arms aborted in 1915,[15] in the following year, Tilak and Annie Besant, an Irishwoman resident in India from 1893, founded Home Rule Leagues on the Irish model to campaign for 'Home Rule for India'. At their peak early in 1918, the Leagues had close to 60,000 members and 400 branches. Their journals and public meetings commanded the attention of tens of thousands of people in urban India. 'The politicians of India,' the Secretary of State wrote, 'have found out how to agitate.'[16]

But the war also sent ripples into the countryside. Barriers between country and towns, between the urban elites and the rural well-to-do, were increasingly breached. The army, for example, needed men, and the best recruits in British eyes came from the 'sturdy peasant castes'. In Punjab, recruiting campaigns often involved a ruthless coercion that provoked men to question British rule. In Gujarat, on the other hand, government won the support of M. K. Gandhi who 'trudge[d] about 20 miles a day' from village to village to urge men to enlist in the army. After initial reluctance on the part of young peasants, his recruiting efforts bore fruit and 'quite a number of names were registered'.[17]

CONSTITUTION-MAKING

Having supported Britain's war effort to such an extent, Indian politicians considered themselves justified in expecting a large measure of self-government as their 'reward' after the war. Constitution-making was one of their crucial concerns for the next thirty years.

Constitutionalism and the notion of voting had been embedded in India since the Crown replaced the East India Company in 1858. The Indian Councils Act of 1861 provided for the appointment of Indians to the imperial and provincial legislative councils, where they were entitled to vote on bills presented by the government. By the 1870s, the right of taxpayers to elect members of municipal councils and local boards was widespread, and in 1882, Ripon, the Liberal Viceroy, carried resolutions calling on provincial governments to hold elections for local bodies wherever possible. By 1884, for example, the United Provinces (the UP) had more than 1200 elected members on its local boards and the municipalities. In 1892, the Indian Councils Act, intended, as was so much constitutional legislation, to take 'the wind out of the sails of the Congress'[18] expanded the legislative councils and allowed some indirect election of members.

The Morley–Minto reforms of 1909 (after John Morley, the Secretary of State, and Minto, the Viceroy) grew out of the partition-of-Bengal agitation and the election of a Liberal government in Britain in 1906. The imperial and provincial legislative councils were expanded, and the provincial councils were given non-official majorities with members elected by district boards, municipalites, universities and other bodies. The electorate was tiny: in the whole of Bengal in 1912 there were only 9200 voters.[19] In the Imperial Legislative Council, greater freedom was granted to ask questions and discuss the budget, but the councils were only advisory and real power lay with the executive.

The most important element in the reforms of 1909 was the provision of separate electorates and a guaranteed proportion of the seats for Muslims. The Muslim League, formed by aristocratic Muslims in 1906 to support the partition of Bengal, had lobbied for such 'safeguards' as the only way of preventing Muslims from being swamped by the Hindu majority. The consequences for the future were to be vast.

In December 1916, Hindu and Muslim leaders, including 'moderates' and 'extremists', held a joint meeting of the Congress and the Muslim League at Lucknow. The outcome was the Lucknow Pact, an agreement on the constitutional arrangements that elite nationalists would regard as acceptable after the war. The Congress agreed that Muslims should retain the separate electorates and guaranteed representation that had been granted in 1909. In five of the seven provincial legislatures, Muslims were to get a larger share of the seats than their population entitled them to, though they would still not have a majority. In return, in the Muslim-majority provinces of Punjab and Bengal, non-Muslims were to have a slender majority.[20]

The British response to this display of unity among the Indian elite came in August 1917 with the war in Europe threatening to bleed Britain white. Edwin Montagu, a Liberal, the Secretary of State for India, announced that the aim of British policy was 'the progressive realisation of responsible government in India as an integral part of the British Empire'. To Indian nationalists, this immediately suggested self-government on the lines of Australia, Canada, New Zealand and South Africa.

Upon this followed the Montagu–Chelmsford reforms of 1919 which enshrined the principle of direct election to the legislatures. In a country in which high-caste birth traditionally meant high social status and often material comfort, the principle of voting—the idea that a low-caste man who had numbers on his side could exercise power over high-caste men who had not — was revolutionary. The reforms enfranchised 7 million people, about 3 per cent of the population, who had the requisite property or educational qualifications. In the new provincial legislative councils, moreover, the so-called 'nation-building' departments – health, agriculture, public works, local government, etc. – were put in the hands of ministers who would be responsible to the legislature in the British parliamentary way. British officials, however, retained control of key departments like finance and police. The Central Legislative Assembly, however, did not enjoy even these concessions and remained purely advisory. The new system, known as 'dyarchy', was a long way from the responsible government of the 'white Dominions', yet it offered ambitious politicians real opportunities to wield money-spending, project-implementing powers.

An electorate of 7 million meant that politicians now needed 'not only zeal and a good record but organisation and discipline, ... money for local publicity and canvassing ... a leader who could appeal to the wider electorate; and they needed to respect the symbols and terms of the new mass politics.'[21] The new constitution in itself was helping to cast the net of institutional politics more widely, to lead ambitious politicians to try to gather larger numbers than ever before into formal political processes.

'AND THEN GANDHI CAME'

'And the Gandhi came.' The words are Jawaharlal Nehru's, and they suggest too magical a change. Indeed, one could argue, in paraphrase of Voltaire, that if Gandhi had not existed in 1919, it would have been necessary to invent him. His ideas, and his way of expressing them, answered a deep craving in the minds and hearts of millions of Indians. His appeal went far beyond the Westernised elites of the great cities. 'He did not descend from the top,' Nehru wrote, 'he seemed to emerge from the millions of India, speaking their language.'[22] Wherever Indians chafed at the indignities of British rule and yearned for bold affirmation that Indian culture was equal or superior to that of the West, there Gandhi found a passionate response. Yet he did not create the conditions that made men and women so ready to accept his leadership. Those conditions resulted from the interplay between Hindu culture and the consequences of British rule – racial arrogance and Western education; revolutionised communications and commercialised agriculture; English law and Christian missionaries. Unlike earlier elite politicians, Gandhi declared that Indian ways were excellent ways and that the attitude of Indians should be one of pride, not apology. He affirmed his message in his daily life. At a conference called by the Viceroy in 1918, for example, he insisted on speaking simple Hindi (sometimes called Hindustani), the *lingua franca* of north India. It was, his friends told him, 'the first instance within living memory of anyone having spoken in Hindustani at such a meeting'.[23] He wore simple Indian dress made of thread he spun himself, *khadi* cloth; he prayed regularly and publicly. The contrast with the old-style politicians, dressed in frock coats, neckties and English boots, even in a Bombay summer, was there for all to see. 'He was like . . . a whirlwind that upset many things,' Nehru wrote, 'but most of all the working of people's minds.'[24]

Gujarat-born like Vallabhbhai Patel, also English-trained in law, Gandhi returned to India in 1915 after twenty-one years (1893–1914) in South Africa where he had fought for the civil rights of Indians against increasingly racist governments. He had relied on techniques of passive resistance – non-violent non-cooperation with, or violation of, repugnant laws, fasts, protest marches and meetings – which he called *satyagraha* ('truth-force' or 'soul-force'). As early as 1909, he advocated the use of *satyagraha* to attain self-government for India.

His first *satyagraha* in India was at Champaran in northern Bihar in 1917. He was persuaded to go to the remote, backward area to champion the cause of tenant-cultivators against their landlords, oppressive British indigo-planters. He met Rajendra Prasad, a lawyer and small landowner, who was to become a devoted disciple and the first president of India in 1950. In 1918, Gandhi led a similar local *satyagraha* of peasants in Kheda District of Gujarat where British officials refused, in spite of a bad season, to reduce the land tax. The cultivators, vowing to pay no tax at all, eventually won the concessions they sought. In Kheda, Gandhi worked closely with 'this stiff-looking person', Vallabhbhai Patel, who 'found himself' during the campaign and began to call Gandhi *'Bapu'* (father).[25] For Gandhi, Kheda 'compelled the educated public workers to establish contact with the actual life of the peasants'. Its achievement was to 'rid the agriculturalists of their fear'.[26] A fearless peasantry was, in Gandhi's view, a prerequisite for self-rule (see illustration p. 66).

Widely known and flushed with success, Gandhi called for a national *satyagraha* in March 1919 against the Rowlatt Acts, which empowered the government to retain wartime measures for detention without trial, and in camera trials for sedition. Gandhi condemned the Acts as 'an *affront* to the nation' and began to form a network of Satyagraha Sabhas, based on the remnants of the Home Rule Leagues and on stalwarts of his work in Bihar and Gujarat, including Rajendra Prasad and Vallabhbhai Patel.[27] The nationwide *hartal* (closure of shops and offices as a form of protest), which Gandhi called on 6 April, was a remarkable success in Bombay, Ahmedabad, Lahore and a number of other places. For the first time, the British were confronted with a militant, all-India challenge to their rule. When on 9 April Gandhi was removed from a train in which he was travelling to Delhi and forcibly returned to Bombay, the news led to rioting in a number of north Indian towns. In Amritsar in Punjab, four Europeans were murdered, and the government lost control of the town.

The government regained control of Amritsar on 13 April with one of the most brutal and shameful blunders in British imperial history. Brigadier-General Reginald Dyer ordered his men to open fire without warning on an illegal public meeting of more than 10,000 people in an enclosed ground called the Jallianwalla Bagh. Fifty men fired rapidly for nearly ten minutes. When they ran out of ammunition, they marched away, leaving 400 people dead and 1200 wounded. The Punjab was cowed into silence.

Although the British government condemned Dyer and forced him to retire, relations between British and Indians would never again be the same. 'My blood is boiling,' Motilal Nehru wrote to his son, Jawaharlal.[28] The 'wrong' of the Rowlatt Acts was now dwarfed by the 'wrong' of Jallianwalla Bagh and the racist arrogance it revealed.

A third 'wrong' began to emerge in 1919: the treatment of Turkey, one of the defeated countries in the First World War. In the early months of 1919, Turkey was being carved up among the victors. Its Sultan, the Khalifa, or spiritual head of Islam, was being humiliated in a way that angered tens of thousands of Muslims in India. In September 1919, an all-India committee to save the Khilafat was formed, and within two months, Gandhi became its only Hindu member. His time in South Africa had made him a passionate advocate of Hindu–Muslim unity, while the support of Muslims gave him the broad base that he still lacked within the Congress. In June 1920, the Central Khilafat Committee announced that it would start a programme of 'non-co-operation' – the choice of word was Ghandi's – from 1 August. It appealed for Hindu support.

THE CONGRESS AND NON-CO-OPERATION

In the next six months, the character of the Congress changed dramatically, and Gandhi acquired the influence he was to retain until his death. His supporters came from groups that had not previously taken prominent parts in Congress sessions. They came, according to one historian, from 'areas which were backward by the canons of Presidency politics' and from 'Muslims, merchants and prosperous cultivators, English-speakers who had little say in Congress because their areas were politically backward, and vernacular literates whose political potential the Congress leaders had only begun to grasp.'[29]

Old-style Congress leaders were uncertain about the response they should make to the Punjab and Khilafat 'wrongs' and whether they should contest the elections under the new constitution scheduled for November 1920. At a special meeting of the Congress in Calcutta in September 1920, many of them opposed Gandhi's resolution for non-co-operation, including boycott of the elections. The resolution passed narrowly. By December when the regular meeting was held in Nagpur, the temptation of the elections had passed. The boycott had been fairly successful: only six of the 637 seats were uncontested, but polling booths were picketed and turnout was low. At Nagpur, the non-co-operation resolution was resoundingly reaffirmed. It decreed that patriots should return British titles and honours, boycott the new constitution and foreign goods, establish 'national' law courts and schools, resign government jobs and, in the last stage, refuse to pay taxes and revenue. The aim was to right the Punjab and Khilafat 'wrongs' and attain *swaraj* within one year.[30]

The British were aware of the change in character of the Congress. A police official wrote: 'The intelligentsia, which dominated earlier Congresses seems to have been swamped in a mass of semi-educated persons swept up from all parts of India . . . many thousands of men who are available for propaganda amongst the masses of the most unscrupulous, reckless and dangerous character.' The Viceroy, Chelmsford, expressed the fear explicitly: 'It is the small people in the villages who do the mischief'.[31] Towns could be cowed, as Dyer had shown in Amritsar. Unrest in the countryside, however, was far more difficult for a government to suppress. The entry of 'the small people in the villages' changed even the physical appearance of nationalist meetings: 'European clothes vanished and soon only khadi was to be seen ... the language used become increasingly Hindustani ... as many of the delegates did not understand English.'[32]

A new Congress constitution, devised by Gandhi and adopted in 1920, embodied these changes. The membership fee was reduced to four annas (one-quarter of a rupee) a year, and provision was made for committees to be established even in villages. Instead of accepting the administrative divisions of the British, the Congress now based its provinces on vernacular languages: a separate province for Tamils, another for Bengalis, etc. At the top, a working committee of fifteen members was set up to give the day-to-day supervision of business and tactics that Congress previously lacked. The All-India Congress Committee (AICC) was increased from 200 to 350 members, elected on the basis of each province's population.

The non-co-operation campaign that followed throughout 1921 was 'probably the worst moment for Britain's imperial rulers in India in the ninety years between the Mutiny and 1942'.[33] According to government statistics, more than 16,700 people were convicted of non-co-operation offences. But convictions told only a small part of the story. Often the government chose not to press criminal charges against demonstrators and contented itself with breaking up meetings with police *lathi*-charges or arresting demonstrators and later releasing them. The picketing of liquor shops and the appeals to give up alcohol cost the provincial governments hundreds of thousands of rupees in revenue. Imports of foreign cloth fell by nearly half, as the *charkha* (spinning wheel) and *khadi* (homespun cloth) spread as popular symbols of independence and self-help. Enrolments in high schools and colleges fell by about 50,000 students; nearly 100 policemen resigned from service and nearly 200 lawyers from the bar.[34] In a country of poverty and economic uncertainty, where a Western education and government job provided sought-after security, it was significant that so many men were prepared to jeopardise their futures. The decline in high school and college enrolment represented about one student in every twenty-five. In effect, every classroom in India had one or two boys leave it for the excitement and idealism of the movement. Their example stirred the emotions of those who remained.

Although for Gandhi the keystone of the movement was the doc-trine of non-violence, violence came increasingly to intrude in the latter half of 1921. During the *hartal* against the arrival of the Prince of Wales on 17 November 1921, the police temporarily lost control of the centre of Calcutta, while in Bombay there were widespread demonstrations and rioting. By December, the British government 'found itself on the run' and came close to convening a conference with the Congress at which responsible government in the provinces might have been conceded. But Gandhi was increasingly distressed at the growing violence. After the riots on 17 November, he postponed the no-tax campaign scheduled to begin a week later in Bardoli taluk in Gujarat. The climax of Gandhi's dismay came on 4 February 1922 when a mob burned to the ground the police station at Chaura near Gorakhpur in the eastern United Provinces; twenty-two police and minor officials were burned to death inside. Gandhi immediately suspended the entire non-co-operation campaign. The British government allowed the movement to peter out in disarray before it arrested Gandhi on 10 March and had him sentenced to six years' imprisonment. By the end of March 1922, the non-co-operation movement was finished. Throughout India, Congress workers were bewildered and appalled at Gandhi's decision at a time when the campaign appeared so strong. 'Our mounting hopes,' Jawaharlal Nehru later wrote, 'tumbled to the ground.'[35]

The movement had used religious symbolism to stir the rural areas as no political campaign had ever done. 'I used to be troubled sometimes at the growth of this religious element in our politics,' Nehru wrote, 'both on the Hindu and the Muslim side.' He consoled himself with the thought that Gandhi used such words and images 'because they were well known and understood by the masses. He had an amazing knack of reaching the heart of the people.'[36] For Muslims, the question of the Khilafat; for Hindus, Gandhi's talk of *Rama Rajya*, the golden age of the god, Rama — such religious themes rallied groups which had been little involved in constitutional politics. But in using religious symbolism for political ends, leaders were unintentionally fostering the process that was to lead to the partition of 1947.

The experience of 1920–2 made the Congress a mass organisation. One estimate calculates that at the height of the movement in 1921, Congress had 1,946,000 members. By March 1923, that number had fallen to about 110,000, and paid-up membership seems to have stabilised at roughly 100,000 until the 1930s. But, most importantly, by 1923 'the centres of Congress activity were shifting rapidly into the countryside', which provided twice as many members as the cities.[37]

ELITE SETBACKS, PEASANT TRIUMPHS

Though the mid-1920s were bleak years for elite, secular nationalists, for sections of the peasantry inspired by Gandhi's ideas, 1928 marked a high point of success, hope and promise.

With the abandonment of non-co-operation, moderate Congressmen formed the Swaraj Party to contest the 1923 elections with the aim of wrecking the legislatures from within, as the Irish nationalists had challenged the British parliament. Although the Swarajists did well in the elections to the Central Legislative Assembly and a few of the provinces, they were unable to destroy the constitution, and 'a demoralising dribble', in Jawaharlal Nehru's phrase, began co-operating with the government.

A new rancour between Hindus and Muslims also revealed itself. The Muslim League, which since 1918 had held its annual meeting in conjunction with the Congress, met separately in 1924. Communal riots increased strikingly, and hundreds died and thousands were injured throughout north India between 1923 and 1927. Common cause over the Khilafat dissolved in 1924 when the Turks themselves abolished the institution. 'The only education the masses are getting', Motilal lamented to Jawaharlal Nehru in March 1927, 'is in communal hatred.'[38]

Away from the towns and the concerns of legislative politicians, however, one could discern another picture, near the centre of which was Vallabhbhai Patel. In 1923, the government of Bombay accused villagers of Borsad taluk in Patel's native Kheda District of protecting robbers. Punitive police were billeted on the area, and a special tax to pay for them was imposed. Patel led the villagers in a calm, steadfast *satyagraha* in which they refused to pay the tax. In January, 1924, the government withdrew its orders rather than risk the spread of such a resolute, troublesome campaign.

A greater triumph, in some ways the high point of peasant *satyagraha*, was to come. In 1928, the regular revision of the land tax in neighbouring Surat District resulted in an increase of 22 per cent. Demanding a new inquiry, the landowners in Bardoli taluk refused to pay the revenue, and minor officials resigned from the government in protest. Though lands were seized for default, the peasants remained firm, and in July 1928, the government sanctioned an inquiry which cut the tax increase to 5 per cent and confiscated land was returned.[39]

As a result of his leadership of the Bardoli *satyagraha*, Patel became a national figure, dignified by the title 'sardar', or leader. He found himself in his element: 'plain speaking in a language that the tiller of the soil could relish. Patel's sarcasm was vindictive, his tongue acid, his jokes barbed and biting like farmers' jokes.' When told that confiscated buffaloes were turning white as a result of poor fodder, he replied that the British didn't like anything black so they were making the buffaloes as white as their women.[40]

To men like Patel, the no-revenue *satyagraha* now appeared 'a weapon of extraordinary potency'.[41] If the landowning peasantry steadfastly refused to pay the land revenue, which accounted for about 15 per cent of the government's income in 1930, British rule would effectively cease in the countryside. But could the limited local successes of Borsad and Bardoli be replicated nationally for a goal as nebulous as *swaraj*? Patel thought so, and advocated a national no-revenue campaign when civil disobedience began in 1930. Gandhi, however, overruled him, and no-revenue movements were attempted only sporadically in 1930–3, as we shall see.[42] British governments, however, were increasingly sensitive to the fact that they could not afford to permit a sense of grievance in the countryside; they were contending for the loyalty of India's prosperous peasants, without whose participation, government, as the British understood it, was not possible.[43]

Outbursts in 1928 revealed ferment in other sections of society. In Bombay, a six-month, communist-led strike in the cotton mills ended in victory for the 100,000 strikers and raised for the British the bogey of 'bolshevism'. And the visit of the Simon Commission, appointed to report on the working of the 1919 constitution, angered both the demoralised legislative politicians and a younger generation eager for a confrontation with the British. The Commission, named for its chairman, Sir John Simon, was drawn from the British parliament and therefore contained not a single Indian. It was greeted with *hartals*, demonstrations and cries of 'Simon go back'. Although Indian attempts — notably a report prepared by Motilal Nehru — to devise a constitution agreeable to the

Congress, Muslim League and rightwing Hindu groups failed, some
sort of national demonstration against British rule was unavoidable.

CIVIL DISOBEDIENCE

The civil disobedience movement of 1930–3 revealed the short-
comings of *satyagraha* and the complexities of the relationship
between peasants and nationalist politics. First, *satyagraha* could not
break a determined, ruthless government, Second, some peasants
were more welcome than others in the Congress camp.

In December 1928, the Congress passed Gandhi's resolution
threatening civil disobedience if the British government did not grant
Dominion status on the Canadian or Australian model within a year.
Tardily, in October 1929, Irwin, the Viceroy, declared that the
'natural issue of India's constitutional progress' was Dominion status
and promised a conference to draw up proposals for a new constitution. Congress ultimately rejected the offer, and at Lahore in
December, it overwhelmingly endorsed a resolution giving Gandhi
the authority to start a national movement of civil disobedience for
purna swara – complete independence, not Dominion status.

Gandhi's genius led him to focus the movement initially against
the salt tax. Although the tax from the sale of salt provided only
4 per cent of the Government of India's revenues, it touched every
man and woman. People were prohibited from manufacturing salt
even for their own use. Announcing that he would walk to the
Arabian Sea and make salt by boiling sea water, Gandhi gathered
eight of his most faithful disciples at his Sabarmati *ashram* at
Ahmedabad, and on 12 March 1930, with the hot weather about to
begin, they set out on a march of 240 miles to Dandi on the coast.
The area was ideally chosen. They were passing through the rich
fields and lush mango groves of Gandhi's and Vallabhbhai Patel's
own Gujarat, where the Patidar peasants had successfully confronted
the British in *satyagrahas* in 1918, 1923–4 and 1928. Moving off in
the early morning, the party covered about ten miles a day. It would
halt in a village in the midday heat when the temperature pressed
towards 100 °F. Then in the early evening, the marchers would
move on to another village where they would spend the night.
Gandhi was sixty, lean, fit and creating a legend. Thousands
attended his meetings along the way. Millions followed his progress

in newspapers throughout India and the world, conscious that a great political event was taking place, not in Calcutta, New Delhi or London, but on a hot, dusty road in the Indian countryside. The party reached Dandi on 5 April and began to make salt. The ensuing encounters with the police, particularly the ruthless attacks when the marchers attempted to disrupt the government saltpans at Dharsana on 21 May, won sympathy, publicity and idealistic recruits.

Refusal to pay land revenue to the government, which Vallabhbhai Patel felt should be the crux of the campaign but which Gandhi regarded only as the last resort, began to occur in some areas with little prompting from the Congress. In the late 1920s, reassessment of the land had resulted – as in Bardoli – in large increases in the tax demand, based on the high prices prevailing after the war. Even in 1930, these increases were resented; but as the effects of the economic depression began to pummel India, the increased land tax often became intolerable. Peasants were bewildered, angry and frightened; like the peasants of Bardoli in 1928, many sought a way of escaping from the grinding extractions of an alien government. In Gujarat, the eastern United Provinces, Bihar and the Andhra delta, no-revenue campaigns began.

Such campaigns were complex. To be sure, the great, aristocratic landlords were aligned closely with the British; but the peasantry beneath them was far from being cohesive and united. It tended to be the richer peasants – men who had more land than they could cultivate alone and who grew cash crops – who quickly associated themselves with the Congress. In Andhra, a district magistrate reported that the 1930 campaign was strongest 'where the people are most prosperous'.[44] In the United Provinces, 'small zamindars and the "upper tenantry" provided the most important organisation men of the Congress.' Using their 'strong links with rural castes', they 'carried the Congress message into the villages at a time when both the small zamindars and tenants were hard pressed by the depression and receptive to the call for reductions in land revenue and rents.'[45] In the village of Ras in Kheda District, 'the largest landowner was prepared to sacrifice his lands'.[46] However, when poorer peasants tried to link with the Congress to pursue their grievances, they found they were often rebuffed. Congress leaders feared rural turmoil. In Bihar, they proved 'utterly indifferent to the woes' of the lower strata of peasantry, while in the United Provinces, there was reluctance 'to extend unambiguous support to the poorer classes in the countryside.'[47] The attraction of Gandhian *satyagraha* lay in its promise to remove the British and their allies without destroying the whole fabric of society.

Even without a concerted no-revenue campaign, civil disobedience shook the British. After the arrest of Gandhi on 4 May, the Governor of Bombay wrote that 'it is now necessary frankly to recognize the fact that we are faced with a more or less overt rebellion . . . and that it is supported by a very large section of the population. We have . . . practically no openly active friends.'[48] By April 1933, about 135,000 people had been to prison (illustration, p. 66); nearly 5000 were women. Boycott had cut the value of foreign cloth imports from Rs 590 million in 1929–30 to Rs 250 million in 1930–1. In spite of the repression of 1932–3, Congress membership held steady at about 500,000, the majority of whom were now outside the major cities.[49]

Yet even while civil disobedience was convulsing India, the British constitution-making process ground slowly on. Willingdon, who succeeded Irwin as Viceroy in 1931, wrote at the height of repression early in 1932: 'our policy must be to push on as rapidly as possible with regard to Reforms . . . We ought to show real sympathy with regard to giving Indians more responsibility in every way we can.'[50] Civil disobedience had been suspended in March 1931 to allow Gandhi to attend the second Round Table Conference in London, at which attempts were made to arrive at an all-party agreement on a future constitution. The conference failed, largely over the question of safeguards for Muslims.

After the breakdown, Willingdon, a flintier man than Irwin, abandoned the wait-and-see policy that the British had followed in 1920–2 and 1930. The government prepared legislation giving it powers later described as 'civil martial law'. On 4 January 1932, six days after Gandhi landed back in India, the government outlawed the Congress and arrested all leading Congressmen. By June, the draconian powers of the government had broken the movement, though it was two years before Congress officially abandoned civil disobedience. The British had shown that they were still capable of governing India, that their Indian employees and dependants were still ready to do their bidding.

'THE MAGIC OF THE CONGRESS NAME'

The futility of further civil disobedience, added to the political possibilities of a new constitution, led growing numbers of Congress supporters to the view that civil disobedience should be abandoned. One leading Congressman argued that the party should contest elections and use 'the magic of the Congress name and memory of its past sacrifices' as electoral assets.[51] This view eventually prevailed, and the Congress, once more a legal organisation, scored a stunning victory in the elections to the Central Legislative Assembly in October 1934; it won forty-four of eighty-eight elected seats.

The passage of the Government of India Act of 1935 took nearly three years from the end of the third Round Table Conference in January 1933. To enact a constitution that would appease the reactionaries like Winston Churchill in the Conservative Party, yet still have a chance of attracting Indians to work it, was a slow, delicate business. The new constitution granted responsible government in the provinces, where the franchise requirements now gave the vote to about 13 per cent of the population (36 million people), five times as many as under the Act of 1919. The provisions for the central government, based on a federation, were frustrated by the rulers of the 580 princely states and never came into force.

With its connections in the countryside, reputation for self-sacrifice and organisational skills resulting from the 1930-3 struggle, the Congress brought important assets to electoral politics. Brennan has written of the United Provinces: 'the work of local Congressmen, especially those with links with the rural castes, brought them into contact with a large proportion of those who in 1937 would vote for the first time in a provincial election: the small landowners paying Rs. 5 and more in land revenue (that is, owning about two acres); and tenants paying Rs. 10 and more in rent (that is, cultivating about two acres).'

The rivals of the Congress – the aristocratic landlords with whom the British had long been in informal alliance – were, as Willingdon himself wrote, 'a flabby lot'.[52] Such men were disdainful of – if not downright hostile to – the electorate whose approval they had to win. In the United Provinces, Bihar, Madras and elsewhere, the old aristocrats were crushingly defeated by the Congress in the elections of February 1937. They came to see, as one landlord wrote in consternation, 'before their very eyes . . . their own tenants voting

TABLE 2.1

Seats won by Congress and the Muslim League, 1937 and 1946 elections

Province	Total seats	Congress 1937	Congress 1946	Muslim 1937	Muslim 1946	Muslim-reserved seats
Madras	215	159	165	10	29	28
Bihar	152	95	98	0	34	39
Orissa	60	36	47	0	4	4
Central Provinces	112	70	92	0	13	14
United Provinces	228	134	153	27	54	64
Bombay	175	86	125	20	30	29
Assam	108	35	58	9	31	34
North-West Frontier Province	50	19	30	0	17	36
Bengal	250	60	86	39	113	117
Punjab	175	18	51	2	73	84
Sind	60	7	18	3	27	33

against their wishes'.[53] On polling day, a police official wrote, 'many villagers observed fast ... and broke it after exercising their franchise in favour of the Congress candidate ... Village voters bowed before the Congress candidate boxes [each candidate had a separate ballot box] as a mark of respect to Mahatma Gandhi.'[54] Such was 'the magic of the Congress name', the handsome legacy of previous suffering.

The Congress won a majority in the legislatures of six of the eleven provinces, and was the largest single party in two others. Only in the Muslim-majority provinces of Bengal, Punjab and Sind was the Congress a small minority. (See table 2.1).

The original intention of Congress had been to contest the elections in order to disrupt the legislatures and destroy the constitution. But as early as June 1935, the Governor of Madras had written that 'down here the leaders are simply panting to take office'.[55] After face-saving negotiations with the provincial governors about the use of the governors' special powers, Congress ministries accepted office in seven provinces (Madras, Bihar, Orissa, CP, UP, NWFP and Bombay) in July 1937. Congressmen later joined coalition governments in Assam and Sind.

Once the party decided to contest elections, membership rose from 473,000 in 1935-6 to 636,000 in 1936-7 and — once in power — to 4,512,000 in 1938-9. Clearly, the large majority of these new members had not stood with the Congress in the dangerous days of 1930-3. 'A substantial portion of this new membership came from the ranks of rich peasants and small and middle landlords. Many of them had stayed out of the Congress until then for fear of losing their property or security,' an historian has written.[56] One Congress leader insisted that its ranks should be opened as wide as possible: 'He appealed to businessmen not to fear the party; rather, they should join it to defend their interests through the Congress.'[57] An alignment between the rural rich and the prosperous business classes was in the making.

The relationship between the Congress and the Indian industrialists of Bombay and Calcutta was often close. Indeed, one historian has estimated that Marwari businessmen alone poured Rs 100 million into nationalist coffers between about 1920 and 1947.[58] Vallabhbhai Patel was central to much of this. In Bombay, many of the capitalists were also Gujaratis, while in Calcutta, the Marwaris who controlled much of business came originally from an area of western India within 200 miles of Kheda District. Patel was recognised as 'definitely the closest' political friend of the leading Marwari capitalist, G. D. Birla, and as if to sanctify this association between Indian capitalists and nationalists, it was in the gardens of Birla's New Delhi house that Gandhi was assassinated in 1948. The big industrialists had to tread warily to avoid British reprisals; but their sympathies and support for nationalist causes were often undisguised.[59]

The Congress governments of 1937-9 attempted little radical reform. Efforts were made to introduce prohibition, cut official salaries and propagate Hindi as the national language. But the Tenancy Act, passed in the United Provinces in 1939, for example, placed only those who paid more than Rs 250 a year in land revenue in danger of expropriation; such men would have held in excess of 100 acres. According to one historian, "the poor man's party" of 1920' in the UP had become 'a rich peasants' party, by 1940'.[60] The Congress emphasised the importance of its rural base by holding its four annual meetings between 1937 and 1940 in small towns or villages deep in the countryside, the first time in its history it had met outside a major town. The most spectacular of these sessions took place in February 1938 with Congress governments in office in the provinces. To honour the *satyagrahas* of 1928, 1930 and 1932, Gandhi chose as the site the sixty-house hamlet of Haripura in Gujarat's legendary Bardoli taluk where Vallabhbhai Patel had won his honorific 'sardar' in 1928. The Congress camp, named Vithalnagar in homage to the late Vithalbhai Patel, was eleven miles from the nearest railway station.[61]

The central leadership of the Congress – Gandhi, Nehru, Vallabhbhai Patel and others – had decided to stay out of the ministries formed in 1937 and to attempt to control and direct them. As disputes about and within ministries multiplied, central leaders were hard pressed to find solutions. When the British declared without consultation with Indian politicians that India was at war with Nazi Germany in September 1939, Congress eagerly took the opportunity in October to have its unruly ministries resign in protest. Resignation, Gandhi himself admitted privately, 'covered the fact that we were crumbling to pieces'.[62]

THE WAR AND QUIT INDIA

The Congress was deeply divided over its attitude to the war. Some leaders, like Subhash Chandra Bose, urged total opposition. Bose later fled India and recruited Indian prisoners of war in Malaya into the Indian National Army (INA) which fought with the Japanese in Burma. Other Congressmen, like Nehru, hated fascism and were reluctant to appear to support Hitler or the Japanese. Gandhi's solution was an insipid campaign requiring individual Congressmen to make anti-war speeches and undergo arrest. 'Individual *satyagraha*' began in October 1940 and dragged on through 1941 with 25,000 convictions but little impact on the British (see illustration, p. 67).

The fall of Singapore to the Japanese on 15 February 1942 led to a last British attempt to win the support of 'political India' for the war. Sir Stafford Cripps, a Labour member of the British coalition government, came to India in March to offer complete independence after the war and, in the meantime, virtual responsible government at the centre – except in the case of the defence ministry. Although the negotiations failed over the question of defence and the veto powers of the Viceroy, the Cripps mission had two crucial consequences. In the long term, it made independence inevitable. The promise, once made, could scarcely be retracted. Second, the British government declared that it was prepared to treat provinces that did not wish to join the projected Indian Union on the same basis as the Union itself. This was a large step towards the acceptance of Pakistan, for it meant that Muslim-majority provinces like Punjab and Bengal would have the opportunity to stand apart as separate countries.

Like its predecessors in 1920–2 and 1930–3, the last great Gandhi-inspired movement against the British failed to drive them out of India. But it profoundly shook them. Areas of the countryside passed out of their control for weeks, and one can see in the movement 'a groundswell coming up from within peasant society ... decisive in loosening the hold of colonial rule.'[63]

The AICC met in Bombay on 7 August 1942 to endorse Gandhi's resolution calling on the British to 'Quit India' and leave Indians to negotiate with the Japanese, who were advancing rapidly through Burma. Attempting to nip the campaign in the bud, the government banned the Congress and arrested every Congressman it could catch; but far from dying, the movement blossomed. From August to October, northern India, particularly the eastern United Provinces and Bihar, produced anti-British violence of a kind not seen since 1857. Easily crushed in the towns, the revolt spread to the countryside. 'The well known and mainly moderate Congressmen were escorted to jail,' wrote the District Magistrate of Benares, 'leaving those whom we found later to be the real plotters of the rebellion still happily plotting away.'[64] Quit India was crushed by early 1943, but it required eighty battalions of British troops, training in India to fight the Japanese, to complete the suppression. Collective fines were levied, punitive troops billeted in hostile villages, houses destroyed, exemplary beatings, tortures and murders carried out. At least 1000 people were killed and probably many more.

The Communist Party of India (CPI) backed the British government and denounced Congressmen as 'fifth columnists'. Illegal and underground from 1934 until July 1942, the CPI had about 5000 members in 1940. They had ridiculed the equivocation of the Congress in 1939–41 and themselves had immediately followed the Soviet Union's directive in 1939 that the war was an 'imperialist war' and must be opposed in every way. However, when Hitler invaded the Soviet Union in June 1941, the 'imperialist war' was suddenly transformed into a 'people's war' which all communists were dutybound to support. Indian communists agonisingly performed this intellectual somersault, though it forced them to fly in the face of national feeling (see illustration, p. 68). They were released from jail in July 1942, and Congressmen filled the vacant cells in August. Communists were stigmatised as betrayers of the national cause and puppets of a foreign government. They thereby alienated the large part of a generation.

'KINDLY SEND MAULVIES'

The war and the Quit India movement had vital consequences for the Muslim League. With the Congress banned from August 1942, the League's major competitor was removed.

The Congress and the League had not always been bitter rivals, though the attempts of Muslim and Hindu politicians to unite against the British invariably broke down. By the late 1920s, and at the Round Table Conferences in 1930–3, Muslims were demanding a federation for independent India in which most powers would reside with the provinces, where Muslims would have separate electorates returning only Muslims. A majority of the seats in Bengal and Punjab, as well as a weighted minority of seats in other provinces and one-third of any central assembly, should be reserved for Muslims.

At this stage, Muhammad Ali Jinnah, the nattily dressed, British-trained barrister, was an apostle of unity. He told the All-Parties Conference in 1928: 'nothing will make me more happy than to see the Hindu-Muslim union'.[65] Denounced by Muslims at the Round Table Conferences for his accommodating line towards Hindus, he stayed in Britain from 1931–4 and practised at the bar of the Privy Council. Many saw him as a minor – and a spent – force.

The 1937 elections revealed that the Muslim League had a weak hold on the affections of the new classes of Muslim voters. It won

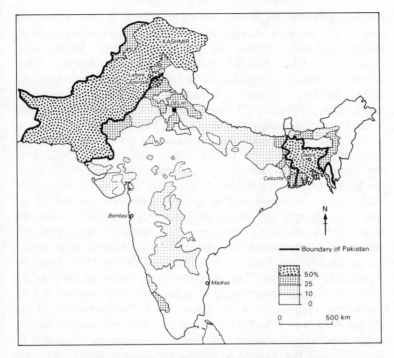

India: Muslim population density and boundary of Pakistan

only 109 out of 482 reserved Muslim seats that it contested (see table 2.1). In the Muslim-majority provinces of Bengal and Punjab, it won only 39 out of 117 and 2 out of 84 seats respectively. It enjoyed significant support only in the UP and Bombay, where Muslims were in a minority and felt themselves under pressure. Jinnah reproached the League for being 'a preserved conclave of titled and conservative people' unable to understand or move the electorate.[66]

Congress, however, had fared even worse in attracting Muslim voters, and a race now began to reach Muslim electors, a competition that intensified communal consciousness and animosity. At the Muslim League's annual meeting in Lucknow in 1937, Jinnah attacked Congress for its 'demand for unconditional surrender and attempts to liquidate the League.' The League made its first efforts to broaden its base by opening its membership to all Muslims over the age of eighteen. It won agreement from non-League Muslim politicians in the Punjab and Bengal to follow its lead in all-India questions.[67] Soon the League was organising campaigns to publicise Muslim grievances against the Congress ministries, which were portrayed as Hindu chauvinist, seeking to downgrade Islamic culture wherever possible. In by-elections in 1938, the League won four out of the five seats it contested. When the Congress ministries resigned, the League celebrated 22 December 1939 as 'Deliverance Day', which enjoyed startling popularity among Muslims.

The idea of a separate Muslim state had been discussed among students in London in the early 1930s. Out of such discussion came the acronym, 'Pakistan' — Punjab, Afghania, Kashmir, Iran, Sind, Tukharistan, Afghanistan and Baluchistan. *Pak*, moreover, meant pure; the new country would be the land of the pure and faithful. At this stage, Bengal, the largest Muslim-majority province, was not mentioned. It was not a great jump from powerful provinces with a weak central government to an independent state owing allegiance to no government but itself. In the aftermath of the 1937 elections, Jinnah and the League became increasingly aware of the need to mobilise far larger numbers of people—whether to vote or take to the streets—than they had ever done before. The insensitivity of the Congress ministries, and the potency of Islam as a way of waking men's interest and winning their hearts, enhanced the attraction of the symbol of Pakistan. At its meeting in Lahore in March 1940, the League agreed not to hinder the British war effort and passed the 'Pakistan resolution' demanding that 'the areas in which the Muslims are numerically in a majority ... should constitute "independent states" ... autonomous and sovereign'. For the rest of the war, Jinnah appeared increasingly as a national figure, the equal of Gandhi or Nehru.

'Kindly send Maulvies [Muslim religious teachers]', an organiser of the Unionist Party in Punjab, desperately trying to turn back the Muslim League wave, telegraphed to party headquarters on the eve of the 1945-6 elections.[68] The Unionists, a party of both Hindu and Muslim landlords, had held power in Punjab since 1923. In 1946, however, the Muslim League reversed its dismal performance in the 1937 elections, defeated the Unionists and became the largest single party in the legislature, kept from power only by an ill-assorted coalition. The League's victory rested in considerable measure on the support of local religious leaders, excited by the prospect of an Islamic state and exercising influence in rural areas once regarded as the strongholds of Unionist landlords. Punjab, 'the cornerstone of Pakistan' in Jinnah's words, had accepted the League and the idea of Pakistan itself.[69]

The results of the elections starkly revealed the intense religious antagonism that pervaded India. The Congress, whose members had been released from prison in 1944–5, won majorities and formed ministries in eight of the eleven provinces. But it could capture only a handful of Muslim-reserved seats (see table 2.1). The Muslim League won all 300 of the seats reserved for Muslims in the Central Legislative Assembly and 427 out of 482 Muslim seats in the provinces. In Bengal and Sind, it formed governments.

The British will to retain India had drained away during the war. Quit India demonstrated that it would require tens of thousands of troops to control the countryside if a fourth civil disobedience movement were begun. For this, the British public and the Labour government elected in July 1945 had neither desire nor stomach. By July 1946, Wavell, the Viceroy, was working on a 'Breakdown Plan' for a British strategic withdrawal from India, based on the assumption that no agreement between Congress and the League was possible and that anarchy threatened.[70]

Wavell had good cause for anxiety. At the level of high politics, an all-parties conference to discuss a new constitution had failed at Simla in June 1945. The Cabinet Mission, composed of three ministers, including Cripps, negotiated in India for three months and left behind it in June 1946 a complicated scheme for a federation with three levels of government (provincial, regional and national). Congress and the League rejected it in July after a brief, half-hearted flirtation. In the same month, provincial assemblies elected members of a national constituent assembly to draft a new constitution; the League boycotted it. In September, with no settlement in prospect, Wavell formed an interim government which ultimately included members of both Congress and the League, two nations, as many saw it, warring within the bosom of a single ministry.

In the streets and the countryside, violence and revolt stalked the government. In February 1946 sections of the Royal Indian Navy mutinied in Bombay, found the support of the communists and held out for five days. Vallabhbhai Patel, seeking power not revolution, was instrumental in persuading them to surrender. Communist-led peasant insurgencies began in Malabar and Travancore on the south-west coast, in north Bengal and in Telengana in the princely state of

Hyderabad. The Muslim League declared 8 August 'Direct Action Day' to protest at the failure of the British and the Congress to concede Pakistan. In Calcutta, it became the 'Great Calcutta Killing', the worst communal violence in India up to that time. More than 4000 were killed in four days; thousands more were injured. A chain reaction of communal killing was triggered and spread throughout India during the next year.

To break the impasse, the Labour government replaced Wavell as Viceroy on 20 February 1947 and announced that power would be transferred to Indians by June 1948, regardless of whether agreement was reached on a constitution for a united country. The new Viceroy was Louis Mountbatten, 46, the wartime chief of South-East Asia Command (SEAC). Noted for his charm and drive, Mountbatten soon discarded in his own mind the three-tier Cabinet Mission scheme. He and his staff devised a plan for partition of the country, which they saw as the only way of extricating the British and possibly avoiding civil war. On 3 June 1947, after much negotiation and many last-minute alarms, the plan to divide the subcontinent into India and Pakistan was announced and formally accepted by both Congress and the League within two weeks.

The mechanics of partition were as complex as the negotiations that led to it. By the first week of July, however, the provincial legislatures in Bengal and Punjab had voted for division of their provinces, and in other areas where the Muslim population was significant, the decision for India or Pakistan had also been made. In Britain, the Indian Independence Act became law on 18 July. Everything from the army (two-thirds to India, one-third to Pakistan) to office stationery had to be divided between the two new dominions. Sir Cyril Radcliffe, the chairman of the two commissions set up to trace boundaries in Punjab and Bengal, arrived in India on 8 July.

This hectic rush among leaders and constitution-makers left little time for consideration of the future of the minorities – Sikhs and Hindus in Pakistan and Muslims in India – who would be left in the new dominions. Yet the transmission to the villages of the communal concerns of the elites had made partition, or a settlement of some kind, so urgent. Religion had mobilised the countryside as no constitutional or economic issue ever could, but by the summer of 1947, the countryside was mobilised not for politics, but for bloody violence. This was particularly true in Punjab, where Sikhs did not form a majority in any single district and could expect to find their community bisected by the boundary between India and Pakistan. As early as March 1947, a Sikh leader suggested that provision should be made to transfer populations in Punjab: Hindus and Sikhs to India, Muslims to Pakistan. Dismissed at this stage as 'almost impossible',[71] a transfer of populations in fact occurred. Murder and arson began in March and spread throughout Punjab in July. With the announcement of the precise boundaries on 17 August, the province exploded. Before the transfer of population subsided in November, more than 3 million people had moved in each direction; probably 200,000 were killed, and thousands wounded, raped and mutilated. In Bengal, the violence and the transfer at this stage were much less, but they were to continue for years, even in a sense until 1971 and the emergence of Bangladesh.

THE NEW GOVERNMENTS: THE RISE OF THE RICH PEASANT

The governments of India and Pakistan evolved very different characters after August 1947.

In Pakistan, Jinnah chose to become governor-general, not prime minister. Within a year, he was dead, and Pakistan lapsed into a political uncertainty that has endured for thirty years. A constitution was not framed until the mid-1950s; in its first ten years, only one set of elections -- to provincial assemblies -- was held, and until the emergence of Bangladesh in 1971, there had been only one general election (1970) for the national government. In West Pakistan, power was shared among a tight group of soldiers, bureaucrats, industrialists and great landlords, mainly from Punjab. 'Political parties . . . have not turned their attention toward the primary voter. This has not been necessary. The national legislature has never been chosen by popular vote.'[72]

In India, general elections on a universal franchise were held in the winter of 1951–2 and repeated in 1957, 1962, 1967, 1971, 1977 and 1980. The first general elections brought the Congress Party an overwhelming victory. Nehru was left its undisputed master, for Gandhi had been assassinated by a Hindu fanatic in January 1948 and Patel died in 1950.

The Congress had its roots in the countryside as few Afro-Asian nationalist parties have done. Gandhi had constantly emphasised that more than 80 per cent of Indians lived in the villages and that the Congress should find its support and do its work there. But in becoming a strong rural party, the Congress did not become the party of all rural interests. The process was neatly illustrated in a letter Patel wrote to an ex-Royal Air Force officer and aristocratic landlord whom the Congress adopted as a candidate in 1946:

We have selected you because our policy is to adopt suitable persons available in the Defence Forces for nomination in the Assemblies wherever possible. . .

Forget that you are a landlord; also try to forget that you are a superior person. Try to be one of the people . . . and learn to talk with them and live with them on their own level. . . Above all, learn to talk to them in their own language.[73]

An economist has written of 'the deal between urban elites and big farmers'.[74] Vallabhbhai Patel was well equipped to execute that deal. It appears true also that there had been a 'a shift in power within the Congress from urban to rural groups', [75] and, not surprisingly, it was the rich peasants, families owning roughly 10 to 100 acres of land, who came 'to dominate the Congress in the rural areas'.[76]

Emphasising that prosperous peasants embraced the Congress, and were embraced by it, in the 1920–50 period is not to say that India's countryside experienced a Gandhian reformation after independence. The new men were substantial landholders, and they were allied, as Vallabhbhai Patel's activities so clearly showed, with the industrial and administrative elites in the cities. In owning or controlling significant amounts of land, the rich peasants were a minority: most of the population of rural India held only very small areas (less than five acres) or no land at all. Those who held between 10 and 100 acres comprised only about 10 per cent of the rural population.[77] But they had scores to settle with the old aristocratic landlords who held hundreds or even thousands of acres and conducted themselves as feudal lords. The land reforms of Congress governments in the 1950s were directed against such men.[78]

But once placed in the driver's seat themselves, the rich peasants had no desire to share control of the bus with other passengers. Radical land legislation, providing for low ceilings on landholding, confiscation, redistribution or co-operative farming, have either not been enacted or remained a dead letter.

Rich peasants have, to be sure, found opportunity for much conflict among themselves. 'Factional' is a favourite adjective to describe the politics of India's states since 1947. Governments have risen and fallen, ministers come and gone, often with great rapidity. But the structure has remained intact; the rules of the game have survived for thirty years. When threatened from below, or from the demands of certain classes of city dwellers, the rich peasants have been able to defend their interests (for example, abolition of land tax, guaranteed prices for grain, cheap irrigation, electricity and fertiliser). Nor is this surprising, for a rich-peasant family may have one or two members in the village and on the land, another in the administration, another perhaps in the police or the army, still another in teaching, law or politics. Such families know how to work the legal and political system to keep their own tenants, labourers and social inferiors in order. Such families, moreover, are based in the villages. They know what goes on, what strangers come and go, the state of the harvest and the state of men's and women's minds. They are not the effete, absentee landlords of the British period who often lost touch with their estates. The rich peasants control resources in the villages, and this in turn has often enabled them to control votes. They are not a majority, but they are a substantial, widely distributed, powerful minority. Their rise to political power through the Gandhian national movement – a movement to overthrow the British and their allies but not to overturn the social order – is well illustrated in the proudly spoken, but perhaps slightly calculated boast of India's first Home Minister and boss of the Congress Party: 'I am the son of a peasant'.

NOTES

1. Kewal L. Panjabi, *The Indomitable Sardar* (Bombay: Bharatiya Bhavan, 1962) pp. 43–4.
2. There is a vast literature on peasants and the differences among them. Hamza Alavi, 'Peasants and Revolution', in *The Socialist Register* (London: Merlin Press, 1965) pp. 241–77, and Eric R. Wolf, *Peasant Wars of the Twentieth Century* (London: Faber and Faber, 1973; 1st pubd, 1971) are starting points. The National Sample Surveys, published by the Cabinet Secretariat, have been compiling and analysing Indian agricultural statistics for nearly thirty years. One such table is in Angus Maddison, *Class Structure and Economic Growth. India and Pakistan since the Moghuls* (London: Allen and Unwin, 1971) p.106.

3. Ravinder Kumar, 'The Rise of the Rich peasants in Western India', in D. A. Low (ed.), *Soundings in Modern South Asian History* (London: Weidenfeld and Nicolson, 1968) pp. 25–58.

4. V. Shankar, *My Reminiscences of Sardar Patel*, vol. II (New Delhi: Macmillan, 1974) p.81.

5. Panjabi, *Indomitable Sardar*, pp. 106, 17 and vii.

6. P. D. Reeves, 'The Politics of Order: "Anti-Non-Cooperation" in the United Provinces, 1921', *Journal of Asian Studies*, XXV, 2 (Feb. 1966) p. 262.

7. T. B. Macaulay, Minute on Education, 2 Feb. 1835, in Christine Dobbin (ed.), *Basic Documents in the Development of Modern India and Pakistan 1835–1947* (London: Van Nostrand Reinhold, 1970) p. 18.

8. B. B. Misra, *The Indian Middle Classes. Their Growth in Modern Times* (London: Oxford University Press for the Royal Institute of International Affairs, 1961) p. 304.

9. John R. McLane, *Indian Nationalism and the Early Congress* (Princeton: Princeton University Press, 1977) p. 54.

10. Dipesh Chakraborty, *Communal Riots and Labour: Bengal's Jute Millhands in the 1890s* (Calcutta: Centre for Studies in Social Sciences, Occasional Paper no. 11, 1976) pp. 40–3.

11. B. R. Nanda, *Gokhale. The Indian Moderates and the British Raj* (Delhi: Oxford University Press, 1977) p. 287.

12. Quoted in Bipin Chandra, *Modern India* (New Delhi: National Council of Educational Research and Training, 1977; 1st pubd, 1971) p. 213.

13. McLane, *Congress*, p. 362.

14. Sumit Sarkar, *The Swadeshi Movement in Bengal, 1903–8* (New Delhi: People's Publishing House, 1973) provides a lengthy account.

15. A. C. Bose, *Indian Revolutionaries Abroad, 1905–22* (Patna: Bharati Bhawan, 1971) pp. 159–73.

16. H. F. Owen, 'Towards Nationwide Agitation and Organisation: The Home Rule Leagues, 1915–18', in D. A. Low (ed.), *Soundings*, p. 181.

17. M. K. Gandhi, *An Autobiography or The Story of My Experiments With Truth* (Ahmedabad: Navajivan Publishing House, 1966; 1st pubd, 1927) p. 337.

18. S. Gopal, *British Policy in India, 1858–1905* (Cambridge: Cambridge University Press, 1965) p. 182, quoting Lansdowne, the Viceroy, to Cross, Secretary of State for India, 1 Jan. 1889.

19. J. H. Broomfield, *Elite Conflict in a Plural Society: Twentieth-Century Bengal* (Berkeley: University of California Press, 1968), p. 54; A. B. Keith, *A Constitutional History of India, 1600–1935* (London: Methuen, 1936) pp. 229–32.

20. H. F. Owen, 'Negotiating the Lucknow Pact', *Journal of Asian Studies*, XXXI, 3 (May 1972) pp. 561–87.

21. Broomfield, *Elite Conflict*, p. 202.

22. Jawaharlal Nehru, *The Discovery of India* (London: Meridian, 1951; 1st pubd, 1946) p. 336.

23. Gandhi, *Autobiography*, p. 336.

24. Nehru, *Discovery*, p. 336.

25. Panjabi, *Indomitable Sardar*, pp. 27, 41.

26. Gandhi, *Autobiography*, pp. 332, 330.

27. Judith M. Brown, *Gandhi's Rise to Power* (Cambridge: Cambridge University Press, 1972) p. 164.

28. *Ibid.*, p. 244.

29. *Ibid.*, p. 302.

30. *Ibid.*, pp. 202, 221, 254-5, 265. See also Richard Gordon, 'Non-Co-operation and Council Entry, 1919 to 1920', in John Gallagher, Gordon Johnson and Anil Seal (eds.), *Locality, Province and Nation* (Cambridge University Press, 1973) pp. 443-73.
31. Brown, *Gandhi's Rise*, pp. 293, 262.
32. Jawaharlal Nehru, *An Autobiography* (London: Bodley Head, 1953; 1st pubd, 1936) pp. 65-6.
33. D. A. Low, 'The Government of India and the First Non-Cooperation Movement, 1920-22', *Journal of Asian Studies*, XXV, 2 (Feb. 1966) p. 257.
34. Brown, *Gandhi's Rise*, pp. 309-18.
35. Nehru. *Autobiography*, p. 82.
36. *Ibid.*, p. 72.
37. Gopal Krishna, 'The Development of the Indian National Congress as a Mass Organisation, 1918-23', in Thomas R. Metcalf (ed.), *Modern India* (London: Collier-Macmillan, 1971) pp. 262-5. The full version of this paper is in the *Journal of Asian Studies*, XXV, 3 (May 1966) pp. 413-30.
38. Judith M. Brown, *Gandhi and Civil Disobedience* (Cambridge: Cambridge University Press, 1977) pp. 9-12.
39. Panjabi, *Indomitable Sardar*, pp. 54-62; David Hardiman, 'The Crisis of the Lesser Patidars: Peasant Agitations in Kheda District, Gujarat, 1917-34', in D. A. Low (ed.), *Congress and the Raj* (London: Heinemann, 1977) p. 62; Ghanshyam Shah, 'Traditional Society and Political Mobilization: the Experience of the Bardoli Satyagraha (1920-1928)', *Contributions to Indian Sociology* (n.s.), 8 (1974) pp. 89-107.
40. Krishnalal Shridharani, *The Big Four of India* (Delhi: Malhotra Brothers, 1951) pp. 81, 83.
41. Hardiman, 'Crisis', p. 63.
42. *Ibid.*, p. 62.
43. D. A. Low, 'Introduction: The Climactic Years, 1917-47', in Low (ed.), *Congress and the Raj*, pp. 26-7.
44. Brian Stoddart, 'The Structure of Congress Politics in Coastal Andhra, 1925-37', in Low (ed.), *Congress and the Raj*, p. 43.
45. Gyanendra Pandey, 'A Rural Base for Congress: The United Provinces, 1920-40', and Lance Brennan, 'From One Raj to Another: Congress Politics in Rohilkhand, 1930-50', both in Low (ed.), *Congress and the Raj*, pp. 214, 477. See also Gyanendra Pandey, *The Ascendancy of the Congress in Uttar Pradesh, 1926-34* (New Delhi: Oxford University Press, 1978).
46. Hardiman, 'Crisis', p. 65.
47. Binay Bhushan Chaudhuri, 'Agrarian Movements in Bihar and Bengal, 1919-39', in B. R. Nanda (ed.), *Socialism in India* (Delhi: Vikas, 1972), p. 220. Pandey, 'Rural Base', p. 214.
48. Brown, *Gandhi and Civil Disobedience*, p. 131. For the prelude to civil disobedience, see', D. A. Low, 'Sir Tej Bahadur Sapru and the First Round Table Conference', in Low (ed.), *Soundings*, pp. 294-329.
49. Brown, *Gandhi and Civil Disobedience*, pp. 124, 129, 282, 286.
50. D. A. Low, ' "Civil Martial Law": The Government of India and the Civil Disobedience Movements, 1930-34', in Low (ed.), *Congress and the Raj*, p. 176.
51. *Ibid.*, pp. 189-90.
52. Brennan, 'From One Raj', p. 478. Low, 'Civil Martial Law', p. 190.
53. Rai Amar Nath Agarwal, Secretary, Agra Provincial Zamindars' Association, quoted in P. D. Reeves, 'Landlords and Party Politics in the United Provinces, 1934-37', in Low (ed.), *Soundings*, p. 282.
54. Low, 'Introduction', p. 30.

55. David Arnold, 'The Politics of Coalescence: the Congress in Tamilnad, 1930–37', in Low (ed.), *Congress and the Raj*, p. 274.

56. Pandey, 'Rural Base', p. 216.

57. Arnold, 'Politics', pp. 274–5.

58. Krishna, 'Development', p. 426.

59. Shankar, *Reminiscences*, vol. II, p. 20. See also Brown, *Civil Disobedience*, pp. 120, 290; and A. D. Gordon, *Businessmen and Politics* (Canberra: ANU South Asian History Section, 1977) pp. 228–9.

60. Pandey, 'Rural Base', p. 218.

61. *Hindu* (Madras), 3 Feb. 1938, p. 9.

62. Nehru, Notes, 'W. C. Wardha. Bapu. 18.6.1940', quoted in Johannes Voight, 'Cooperation or Confrontation? War and Congress Politics, 1939–42', in Low (ed.), *Congress and the Raj*, p. 354.

63. Eric Stokes, 'The Return of the Peasant to South Asian History', *South Asia*, 6 (Dec. 1976) p. 105.

64. Max Harcourt, 'Kisan Populism and Revolution in Rural India: The 1942 Disturbances in Bihar and East United Provinces', in Low (ed.), *Congress and the Raj*, p. 342. Francis G. Hutchins, *India's Revolution, Gandhi and the Quit India Movement* (Cambridge, Mass.: Harvard University Press, 1973) p. 235.

65. *Proceedings of the All Parties National Convention* (Allahabad: 1928), quoted in Uma Kaura, *Muslims and Indian Nationalism. The Emergence of the Demand for India's Partition, 1928–40* (Delhi: Manohar, 1977) p. 45.

66. *Ibid.*, p. 111.

67. *Ibid.*, p. 117.

68. Quoted in David Gilmartin, 'Religious Leadership and the Pakistan Movement in the Punjab', *Modern Asian Studies*, XIII, 3 (July 1979) p. 515.

69. Quoted in R. Coupland, *The Future of India* (London: Oxford University Press, 1943) p. 9.

70. Penderel Moon (ed.), *Wavell, The Viceroy's Journal* (Delhi: Oxford University Press, 1977; 1st pubd, 1973) pp. 330–2.

71. Lt-Gen. Sir Frank Messervy, 24 Mar. 1947, quoted in Robin Jeffrey, 'The Punjab Boundary Force and the Problem of Order: August 1947', *Modern Asian Studies*, VIII, 4 (Oct. 1974) p. 495.

72. Keith Callard, *Pakistan. A Political Study* (London: Allen and Unwin, 1957) p. 67. See also Gilmartin, 'Religious Leadership', p. 517.

73. Patel to Ranjit Singh, 22 Feb. 1946, in Durga Das (ed.), *Sardar Patel's Correspondence*, vol. II (Ahmedabad: Navajivan, 1972) pp. 325–6.

74. M. Lipton, 'Urban Bias and Rural Planning in India', in Henry Bernstein (ed.), *Underdevelopment and Development: The Third World Today* (Harmondsworth: Penguin, 1976; 1st pubd, 1973) p. 246. See also *India Today*, 1–15 Jan. 1978, p. 33.

75. George Rosen, *Democracy and Economic Change in India* (Berkeley: University of California Press, 1966) p. 116. See also pp. 196–7, 214–19, 240–1.

76. Stanley A. Kochanek, *The Congress Party of India. The Dynamics of One-Party Dominance* (Princeton: Princeton University Press, 1968) p. 360. See also Myron Weiner, *Party Building in a New Nation. The Indian National Congress* (Chicago: University of Chicago Press, 1967) pp. 30–54, 459–81.

77. One survey in the 1970s suggested that roughly 15 per cent of India's rural households owned 80 per cent of the land. See *Social Scientist*, no. 75 (Oct. 1978) p. 81.

78. W. S. Neale, *Economic Change in Rural India. Land Tenure and Reform in Uttar Pradesh, 1800–1955* (New Haven: Yale University Press, 1962).

Indonesia:
Illustrations

DJENDERAL VAN HEUTSZ.
KAGET MELIHAT HATSIL PEKERDJA'ANNJA.
Manebarkan benih persatoean Hindia-Belanda. tetapi Persatoean-Indonesia
jang toemboeh .;;

'General van Heutsz is astonished to see the fruit of his labour. He plants the
seeds of Netherlands Indies unity (Persatoean Hindia Belanda), but it is
Indonesian unity (Persatoean Indonesia, represented by the red and white flag)
that springs up'.

Sukarno's journal, *Fikiran Ra'jat*, pleads for unity among nationalist leaders (*pemimpin*) in 1932. While the nationalists fight each other, the masses are threatened by the monster of imperialism, capitalism and the depression. The caption reads: 'The Voice of the Marhaen Masses' "Hey, you hungry people, unite! The enemy is ever more tyrannical!" '

Jakarta, 1945. A roadside poster urges Indonesians to boycott the returning Dutch. The Indonesian figures, from left to right, are saying: 'There's no room for Dutch COLONIALISTS'; 'The Dutch won't get any [postal deliveries]'; 'Even for 10 guilders a bunch, I won't sell'.

Glossary for Chapter 3

batik	Textile patterns formed by Javanese wax-dyeing method.
beamtenstaat	State controlled by officialdom.
bengkok	Allocation of village land as remuneration for village officials.
bupati	Regent; highest Javanese official, partly hereditary, under Dutch rule; since 1948 second-highest bureaucratic rank.
diplomasi	Diplomacy.
Djawa Hokokai	Java Service Organisation.
GERINDO	Gerakan Rakyat Indonesia—Indonesian People's Movement.
Giyugun	Volunteer army (under Japanese).
Kenpeitai	Military Police (Japanese).
KNIL	Koninklijk Nederlands Indisch Leger—Royal Netherlands Indies Army.
KNIP	Komite Nasional Indonesia Pusat—Central Indonesian National Committee.
MASJUMI	Majlis Syuro Muslimin Indonesia—Consultative Council of Indonesian Muslims.
MIAI	Majlisul Islamil a'laa Indonesia—Great Islamic Council of Indonesia.
NIT	Negara Indonesia Timor—State of East Indonesia.
Pangreh Praja	Literally, 'Rulers of the realm', Javanese semi-aristocratic administrative corps, after 1946 called *pamong praja*.
PARINDRA	Partai Indonesia Raya—Greater Indonesia Party.
PARTINDO	Partai Indonesia—Indonesia Party.
pemuda	Youth.

perjuangan	Struggle.
PETA	Pembela Tanah Air—Defenders of the Fatherland.
PKI	Partai Komunis Indonesia—Indonesian Communist Party.
PNI	Partai Nasional Indonesia—Indonesian National Party.
priyayi	Member of Javanese aristocracy.
puputan	Ritualised suicidal attack (in Bali).
PUTERA	Pusat Tenaga Rakyat—Centre of People's Strength.
raja	King.
SI	Sarekat Islam—Islamic Association.
ulama	'The learned'; Islamic teachers.
Volksraad	People's Council.

3 Indonesia: Revolution without Socialism

Anthony Reid

PROCLAIMING INDEPENDENCE

We the people of Indonesia hereby declare Indonesia's independence.
Matters concerning the transfer of power and other matters will be
executed in an orderly manner and in the shortest possible time.

These simple words were read by Sukarno to a few hundred people
gathered outside his house in Jakarta on the morning of 17 August
1945. They have been celebrated every year since by a grateful people.
  Two days earlier the proclamation had been the subject of an
angry exchange between two generations of nationalists. The Japanese had surrendered to the Allies on 14 August, just too soon to
allow the implementation of their last-minute preparations to grant
'independence' to Indonesia. Sukarno and his then colleague Hatta
were anxiously seeking a way to proceed on the agreed path to
independence in a manner which would not provoke the intervention of the still-powerful Japanese occupying army. A delegation of
young revolutionaries, including the future communist leader
D. N. Aidit, came to Sukarno's house to deliver an ultimatum.
Sukarno must, they insisted, 'for the last time, proclaim independence at once and break all ties and connections with the promise
of "a gift of independence" from the Japanese'. They demanded a
revolutionary proclamation by Sukarno in the name of the people.
The older leaders, knowing they could not fight the Japanese, replied
that this was impossible 'until we hear what the attitude of the
Gunseikan and the *Somubucho* [the senior military administration
officials] is to the independence which has been promised'. The
young men taunted Sukarno with cowardice, and threatened that
they would not be answerable for the violence if independence was

not proclaimed that very night. Sukarno leapt out of his chair in a fury, shouting, 'Here is my neck . . . go on, cut my head off . . . Don't wait until tomorrow'. Aidit replied bitterly, 'You have crushed the hopes of our generation', and the youths had to return empty-handed, 'overwhelmed with mixed feelings of anger and dejection'.[1]

The proclamation of 17 August represented a characteristic compromise between the two positions, though not before the angry youth leaders had kidnapped Sukarno and Hatta to try to force them into a bolder stance. The conflict between a romantic vision of revolutionary struggle and the desire to obtain the maximum pragmatic advantage from the objective situation has been at the heart of Indonesian nationalism throughout this century. The difference between the two parties was one of age and of closeness to power. They shared the same revolutionary rhetoric and the same goals. They could and did frequently change sides.

THE PEOPLES OF INDONESIA

Indonesia is a new word for a nation which has taken clear shape only in our own century. Coined by European ethnologists in the late nineteenth century, the word was adopted by nationalism in the 1920s in an extraordinarily rapid discovery of national unity. It was scarcely two decades earlier that Dutch conquest or control had forced into a centralised polity the varied array of peoples and cultures that made up the archipelago.

The enormous linguistic and cultural complexity of Indonesia can be crudely categorised into three broad types of historical experience, each of which had its own relationship with Dutch colonialism and with independent Indonesia. In addition to the immigrant Chinese and European cultures, these were the Javanese, the coastal-Islamic, and the non-Islamic (see map, p. 115).

The Javanese are by far the largest single ethno-linguistic group, comprising over 40 per cent of the Indonesian population. Inhabiting the most densely-cultivated eastern two-thirds of the island of Java, the Javanese had supported for more than a millenium a succession of brilliant kingdoms, whose twentieth-century relics remained in baroque but ineffective splendour at the four courts of Surakarta and Yogyakarta. Despite the poverty and the low literacy level of the Javanese as a whole, non-Javanese were ready to concede that

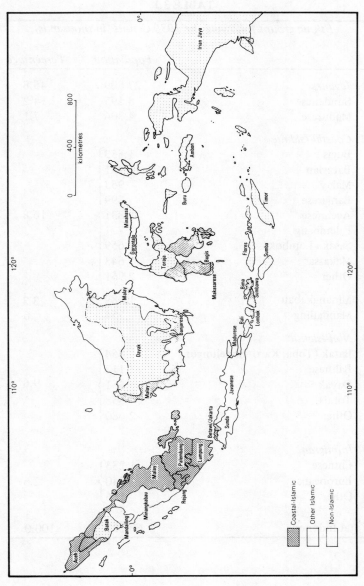

Indonesia: ethno-religious divisions

TABLE 3.1

Ethnic groups following the 1930 Census (in thousands)

	Population	Percentage
1. *Javanese*	27,809	45.8
Sundanese	8,595	14.2
Madurese	4,306	7.1
2. *Coastal-Islamic*		
Bugis	1,533 ⎤	
Batavian	981 ⎟	
Malay	953 ⎟	
Banjarese	899 ⎟	
Acehnese	831 ⎬	16.8
Palembang	771 ⎟	
Sasak (Lombok)	659 ⎟	
Makassar	643 ⎟	
Other	2,961 ⎦	
Minangkabau	1,989	3.3
Mandailing	354	.6
3. *Non-Islamic*		
Batak (Toba, Karo, Simelungun)	854 ⎤	
Balinese	1,112 ⎟	
Dayak	651 ⎬	9.6
Toraja	558 ⎟	
Other	2,680 ⎦	
4. *Immigrant*		
Chinese	1,233 ⎤	
Europeans	240 ⎬	2.6
Other	116 ⎦	
Total Indonesia	60,727	100.0

they possessed an exceptionally high culture, based on the dance, the *gamelan* orchestra, the theatre and especially the *wayang kulit* shadow puppets which carried the ideology of the courts into the lowliest villages. Java had accepted Islam in the sixteenth century, but without surrendering the Hindu epics or the cultivation of inner spiritual strength which had marked its pre-Islamic religious system.

The gradual adaptation of the Javanese ruling class to the realities of Dutch power over three centuries had strengthened the passive, hierarchic elements in the value system of the *priyayi* aristocracy at the expense of an earlier warrior ethos. Twentieth-century formulations emphasised the mystical unity of ruler and ruled in an ordered and mutually dependent harmony. The various levels of *priyayi* rank were reinforced by speech levels, by prescribed patterns of *batik* dress, and by an exquisite degree of deferential politeness which was of course taken advantage of by non-Indonesians. Dr Wahidin, a lower *priyayi* who founded the earliest nationalist organisation, Budi Utomo, in 1908, saw no contradiction between his progressive goals and refusing a proferred seat higher than his lowly origins merited, or prostrating himself before the desk of a Dutch official he wished to win to his cause.[2]

The coastal-Islamic peoples, less numerous than the Javanese, were also diverse and geographically scattered. Their cultures had for the most part been defined in one of the Islamic harbour-principalities of the sixteenth and seventeenth centuries, such as Aceh, Palembang, Riau-Johor, Makassar, Ternate or Banjarmasin. They had in common not only Islam but a commercial orientation, and Malay as the language of literature, trade and religion. Long before Indonesian nationalism, these coastal peoples had been conscious of Islam as a basis of unity against the Dutch infidels.

The third group, still more heterogeneous, comprise those communities which came abruptly into contact with Dutch colonialism without prior incorporation into the Muslim world. The Toba Bataks of North Sumatra underwent a rapid Christianisation from the late nineteenth century, while the Ambonese and Menadonese had already allied with the Portuguese and Christendom in the sixteenth century. The people of Bali, on the other hand, clung to the Hindu-animist culture they had once shared with pre-Islamic Java, even when faced with a brutal Dutch conquest in 1908. Throughout the outer islands of Indonesia there were slash-and-burn, or swidden, cultivators little affected by the outside world even in the twentieth century, though their isolation prevented them from playing any substantial role in the struggle against Dutch imperialism.

This tripartite division is of course too neat, and some important ethnic groups sit firmly astride the dividing lines. The Sundanese and Madurese absorbed a large degree of *priyayi* culture from their Javanese neighbours, although both are more Islamic in orientation than the great majority of Javanese. Similarly the largest single ethnic group outside Java, the Minangkabau of Central Sumatra, have features of both the second and third categories. They are firmly within the Islamic camp, yet they share with many of the more isolated peoples a strong kinship system and a very weak tradition of kingship.

ECONOMIC CHANGES

The genius of Dutch colonialism was always its indirectness, making use of traditional authorities wherever these would serve the economic monopoly the Dutch had at heart. The more commercially oriented peoples and leaders had the worst of a frequently violent competition with the Dutch, whereas the more hierarchic and agrarian were able to flourish in a complementary relationship with European and Chinese business. Although profound changes occurred during the three centuries the Dutch were in the archipelago, they were in the direction of isolating Indonesia's people from the more important effects of capitalism. The 'ethical policy' inaugurated by a consciously Christian Dutch Government in 1900 was meant to change this. Indonesia would be repaid for decades of alternate oppression and neglect by an interventionist colonial policy directed towards native welfare, education and advancement. This policy shift came at a time of great European self-confidence, when the machine gun and the steamship provided a decisive military superiority over any indigenous opponent, and capitalism demanded the right to transform the whole world in its image. The first two decades of this century therefore marked a period of astonishing change for Indonesia, and especially for the islands outside Java.

In these Outer Islands, as we shall see, the building of roads and the more active penetration of the money economy had very mixed effects, bringing wealth to some, resentment to others and social upheaval to most areas. In rural Java, on the other hand, the Ethical

Policy had little chance of fundamentally changing the increasingly sombre economic pattern. Already in 1905 Java supported almost 30 million people in one of the densest agricultural settlement patterns in the world. Buoyant sugar prices and the increased productivity which European capital made possible kept Java's sugar exports growing until 1928, creating a superficial impression of prosperity. The profits of the sugar industry had only been possible, however, because of the extraordinarily low level of wages, and especially rent, in this overcrowded island. Sugar had been grown in alternation with peasant rice, by leasing irrigated rice land on a rotation basis, and the collapse of the industry in the 1930s was a source of relief to the Javanese peasantry. 'The garden of the East', as Java had been known in the nineteenth century, was having increasing difficulty in feeding itself, let alone producing anything for export. In the 1930s the rice production available per head of population in Java was about 82 kg a year[3] or 220 grams a day, less than half the normal requirement. Rice imports had made up the balance in the more affluent years before the First World War, but these declined again after 1913.[4] Javanese could only live by increasing their production of less preferred subsidiary crops like cassava and maize — eaten only by the poor. Looked at in global figures it is difficult to escape the conclusion that despite a possible small improvement in the first decade of the century, the welfare of Javanese continued to decline thereafter.

Java no longer had a functioning middle class independent of government. Centuries of interdependence between Dutch and Chinese commerce on the one hand and the Javanese aristocracy on the other had seen to that. By 1865, near the end of the system of forced cultivation of export crops through the agency of the *bupati* (regents, or highest *priyayi*), a Dutch report had judged that 'the *bupati* are the only group left in Javanese society with a high income, and it is wise of the Dutch to keep it so'.[5] A thorough survey of the Javanese economy in 1904-5 concluded: 'A true Javanese trading class virtually does not exist, not even in the trading cities'.[6] One prominent nationalist remembered of his youth at the beginning of the century that 'the average person thought only about the glory connected with becoming a member of the *priyayi*', so that to aspire to being even a doctor or teacher seemed a revolutionary act.[7] Colonial Java's elite was based not on property but on the extraordinary power and rewards of official position.

At the apex of the pyramid (outside the royal courts of South-Central Java) were the sixty-six *bupati*, with about half-a-million subjects each, salaries of 1000 guilders a month, palaces at the very fulcrum of the district capital and enormous powers of patronage throughout the subordinate Javanese officialdom. Nevertheless, life was not easy for the *bupati*, caught between the traditional loyalty the Dutch wished to see him inspire and demand, and the contempt with which both Dutch and modern-minded Indonesians increasingly regarded him for doing so. At the base of the pyramid, the *lurah* (village head) had fewer real challenges to his authority. Instead of salary, village officials in Java received (and still receive) an allocation of communal village land. For the *lurah* himself, always among the wealthiest village landowners in his own right, this was likely to mean an additional twenty hectares in a village in which the average holding was less than half a hectare. The *lurah* also controlled the allocation of water, the distribution of collective village land, the leasing of land to the sugar estates and the imposition of tax and various 'welfare' measures by the government. A large proportion of villagers were frequently in his debt, so that he gained half the product of their land as well as his own.

At the bottom of the scale was an ever greater proportion of Java's peasants who either had no land or not enough to support themselves. In some areas, more than half the villagers appear to have been already in this position in 1903. Buchler calculates that by 1932, 62.5 per cent of peasants in Cirebon regency had no rice land, while others must have lost control of their land through indebtedness.[8] There is some truth in the picture of 'shared poverty' to describe the Javanese village: private landlordism was not marked, the product of a given piece of land might be divided to feed a variety of people with different claims upon it, and an ethos of mutual obligation was maintained through village ceremonies and feasts. Yet the nature of these relationships was one which reinforced the authority of the *lurah*, and through him the whole bureaucratic structure, over Javanese life. Unlike the position in other parts of Asia, and indeed Indonesia, there appears to have been no tendency for capitalism to erode this authority, perhaps in part because the *lurah* had to remain in and of the village to exercise it.

The position was entirely different in the so-called 'Outer Islands' which had a population density of only 11 per square kilometre in 1930 in contrast to Java's enormous 316. There, the bureaucratic control the Dutch sought to impose in the first decade of the century was something quite new and came at the same time as remarkable changes in the economic sphere. The vigorous Dutch policy in the Outer Islands was attributable to three men who had made their reputations by apparently putting a forceful end to the last and costliest of Holland's colonial wars, in Aceh, at the turn of the century. They were General van Heutsz, who became Governor-General (1904-9), the later arch-conservative prime minister Hendrik Colijn, who became his chief adviser for policy in the Outer Islands, and the great Islamicist C. Snouck Hurgronje. Their energetic policy for the first time subjected the whole archipelago to effective control from Batavia, imposing direct taxes and corvée labour for massive road-building projects on societies which had never known such things.

Dutch power became universally felt, and almost as universally resented. Many societies, such as Aceh, South Bali, Lombok and the Bugis area of South Sulawesi, had to cope with the physical and psychological burden of ruinous military defeat. In others, which included Tapanuli, Jambi, Minangkabau and parts of South Sulawesi and Lombok, there were vigorous 'anti-tax' revolts which reached their peak with a widespread imposition of new direct taxes in 1908. In this first stage, it was typically the traditional chiefs who led resistance. Later these were effectively made dependent on the colonial system — leaving to the *ulama*, or religious teachers, the role of potentially rebellious counter-elite. Resentment against taxation and corvée was manifested anew with each political movement to sweep the country, and it was still a factor in the welcome given the Japanese in 1942.

The Outer Islands were also the scene of most of the colony's economic expansion in the period 1905-30. Oil was discovered in North and South Sumatra and in eastern Borneo, while the jungle was felled to provide the expanding needs of European and American industry for rubber, palm oil, copra and other tropical crops. By the 1930s 'the Netherlands Indies could well claim to represent the apogee of tropical export agriculture'.[9] It then supplied the bulk of the world's needs for pepper, kapok and cinchona, about a third of its rubber and copra, a fifth of its palm oil and tea and about 5 per cent of its sugar and coffee. Rubber and oil, both Outer Island products, had replaced Javanese sugar as the colony's biggest export earners.

Indonesian 'smallholders' outside Java grew a major share of some of these export crops – 43 per cent of the rubber, 30 per cent of the coffee, 90 per cent of the copra and 65 per cent of the pepper in 1940. The rapid expansion in the export of these crops and others brought a large number of small farmers into the modern world economy. There were estimated to be 800,000 such farmers growing rubber in 1930, a figure which would have to be doubled if we add the coffee growers of Central Sumatra, the pepper growers of Lampung, and the copra growers in the coastal districts of every island, but especially Sulawesi.

These cash-croppers typically retained some stake in the more labour-intensive rice economy, as a security against fluctuations in the price of export crops. Indeed, the major reason for the small-holder's better performance than the estate in the 1920s and 1930s was that he could cut costs to virtually nil in times of low rubber prices, leaving the trees untapped while he concentrated on his rice fields. Nevertheless, there was a substantial influx of money into Indonesian hands, which reached its peak during the 1920s. In 1921 the export value of Indonesian-grown crops amounted to 7.26 guilders per head of Indonesian population in the Outer Islands, though only 1.88 guilders in Java (a discrepancy which continued to widen). In the income tax assessments for 1929, there were 239,000 Indonesian households in Java, or 2.9 per cent of the total, earning over 300 guilders a year, whereas in the whole Outer Islands the figure was 698,000 households or 19 per cent. In West Sumatra, an area of relatively high adaptation to the cash economy, the proportion was about 28 per cent.[10]

The permanent effect of this wealth in consolidating a functioning middle class was perhaps less clear than might have been expected. Much of it undoubtedly went to Chinese and European dealers, in exchange for bicycles, sewing machines, radios and other consumer durables. Much certainly went on taking 400,000 Indonesian pilgrims to Mecca in the period 1911–31. During these boom years Indonesians, especially from Sumatra, Borneo and West Java, were disproportionately represented in Mecca, providing half the total number of pilgrims in some years. Although not directly productive, the pilgrimage did in another sense contribute towards the creation of a middle class, for the returning *haji* (pilgrim) tended to be set apart from the community as a whole, not only by his presumed piety but by his social and economic status. A degree of entrepreneurial skill and miserliness was almost expected of him.

The wealth of the smallholder export boom did make it possible for a number of Indonesians, particularly Muslims in Sumatra, to move into bulk trade, transportation, shopkeeping and even finance and manufacturing. In 1941 there were 2800 buses and 8000 taxis owned by Indonesians, frequently on a co-operative basis.[11] A handful of small banks had been formed to promote the business activity of a particular ethnic group or interest. A few rubber traders of Palembang and Padang in Sumatra became large enough during the prosperous 1920s to diversify their activities in the more difficult years that were to follow. Some moved into textile manufacture during the Great Depression when Indonesia's exports dropped to a third of their 1924 value. Only this crisis, at its worst in 1933–4, forced the Netherlands Indies government to create the opportunity for an indigenous textile industry to again arise, and even then chiefly in the hope that excluding Japanese and British cloth would help the ailing industry in Holland. The indigenous industry responded by growing with enormous speed, especially in the Bandung plateau of West Java. Most Indonesian entrepreneurs operated by 'putting-out' the yarn to five or ten home weavers, but there were also seventy-seven factories with more than fifty looms in Indonesia by 1937, where there had been none in 1930.[12]

The economic opportunities of the 1920s contributed to the atmosphere of hope and progress which took hold of much of Outer Indonesia. They also provided the basis for a great deal of social conflict. New wealth put strains on the older status system and on the collective manner in which many communities had allocated land. The position of many Dutch-backed chiefly families was politicised by the way they used official position to enrich themselves, while at the same time the rivals of these officials found new sources of strength in commerce, religious organisation, the press and eventually the nationalist movement itself. In some areas of Aceh, West Sumatra and Karoland, there was by 1940 a polarisation of society between the Dutch-backed aristocractic hierarchy and its opponents that could almost be labelled a class conflict. The opponents were too heterogeneous to be seen as a real middle class, but they were beginning to forge some of the weapons which would make them independent of government. Insofar as there was comparable conflict in Java, it tended to be created by Dutch education and the challenge which the 'new *priyayi*', of educated professionals offered to the established hierarchies of race and official rank.

The collapse in the price of all export commodities in 1929 threw much of this economic advance into reverse. Cash-cropping had to be neglected in favour of a return to subsistence farming, and the need to meet the continued high levels of taxation left little if any margin. The depression of the 1930s can be seen as the beginning of a period lasting until 1950 in which export opportunities were minimal and the return on any capital investment highly uncertain. The return to their home villages of thousands of refugees from the devastated cash economy of city and plantation restored some power to the village heads and the aristocracy. At the same time, the Dutch continued to experiment with further ways of reinvigorating threatened traditional rulers, including the restoration of rajas in Bali and in Goa (South Sulawesi). These changes tended to accentuate the social conflicts described above rather than to ease them. In the long run, however, the economic setbacks of the 1930s and 1940s undoubtedly weakened cash-cropping as the basis for a strong Outer Islands middle class. Entrepreneurial elements remained very significant in many societies, but they had not captured the high points of the economy before their energies had to be diverted into the more complicated game of economic and political survival in an unstable post-colonial Indonesia.

FROM DARKNESS TO LIGHT[13]

For the cultural leaders of every part of Indonesia, the discovery of Dutch domination around the turn of the century had been both painful and bewildering. At one extreme, the ruling elite in Bali could only respond to their crushing military defeats in 1894 (Lombok) and 1908 (Badung and Klungkung) by a ritual suicide or *puputan*. Whole ruling families were wiped out, thereby seeming to release their subjects to find their own way in a new era. Muslim Acehnese or Bugis, in the same dilemma, could only explain the victory of the unbelievers as a product of Muslim sinfulness, perhaps as a sign of the approaching end of the world. Even the Javanese courts, whose humiliation had been gradual and disguised by every aristocratic artifice, sensed a crisis in the late nineteenth century. Before his death in 1873 the last court poet of Surakarta saw that 'there is no example left. . . everything is darkened; the world immersed in misery'.[14] No successor could be found to celebrate the grandeur of the royal dynasty. Only another generation of Indonesians, armed with the new weapon of education, could find a way through this sense of gloom.

Only with the Ethical Policy did the Dutch accept any serious responsibility to educate the people of the Indies. In 1901 a small handful of Indonesians – 1600 at primary level and fewer than fifty at secondary – had struggled among a sea of white faces. Four years later the Indonesian numbers had tripled, and by 1930 there were 60,000 pupils in Dutch-medium government-supported primary schools. The pioneers at the beginning of the century had been marginal men, alienated from both Indonesian and Dutch societies. Parents were inclined to believe that they would never see their children again, that pupils would be Christianised or at least that they would suffer terrible punishments in the next life for sitting at the feet of the infidels. By the second decade of the century, however, there were already enough Indonesians at secondary schools to create a constituency for new ideas, and by the third decade a Dutch education began to seem the new talisman, the magical key to status, to progress and eventually to power. Indonesians demanded much more than the colonial authorities were prepared to give. A private Indonesian school system grew up to meet this thirst for a Dutch-style education, and by 1940 it catered for more than twice as many pupils as the government system.[15] Netherlands India continued to lag behind most of its neighbours in literacy – 6.44 per cent of all Indonesians in 1930, though more for Sumatra (13 per cent) than for Java (5.5 per cent), and for men (10.8 per cent) than for women (2.2 per cent). Those literate in Dutch were less than one in 300. Nevertheless Dutch education was rigorous and a startling departure from traditional Indonesian ways, and there is no denying its impact on the new elite who experienced it (see illustration, p. 107).

This change from reluctance to enthusiasm for a Western type of education was part of a fundamental adjustment from the pessimism of defeat to a new faith in progress and modernisation. This transition was easiest in the colonial cities, whose cosmopolitanism formed the nucleus around which a new urban Indonesian superculture would form. It was based on Malay/Indonesian as a language medium, on economic rather than personal relationships and on an assumption of ethnic conflict between Indonesians, Chinese and the dominant Dutch. By 1930, 1.87 million Indonesians inhabited centres which could be considered fully urban, and they changed in step with the cities themselves. For most Indonesians, however, it was by no means obvious how one could become 'modern' while still remaining Javanese on the one hand, or Islamic on the other.

Among the first Western-education generation in Java were some who insisted that no one could be considered Javanese who abandoned his uncut hair wrapped inside his traditional headcloth. Long hair was nevertheless the first thing to go in a wholesale shift towards Western dress during the second decade. If for some this was betrayal, for most it represented liberation. 'It is always surprising to see a slavish attitude and manners, yes even opinions, change into ways which are unforced, free, but still polite in the Oriental fashion, through the change of clothes', remarked Ki Hadjar Dewantara.[16] Radicals like Tjipto Mangoenkoesoemo demanded the abandonment of Javanese culture altogether, including even its language — 'a language of slaves', with its hierarchic speech-levels — as the price of progress.[17]

The first organisation to mobilise a substantial section of the new Javanese elite, Budi Utomo, was born out of this struggle for a new definition of identity. The student activist who initiated it in 1908, Dr Soetomo, suggests that what inspired him in his older mentor, Dr Wahidin, was a new way of being Javanese: 'His tranquil features, his wise manner and tone. . .his conviction. . .his melodious serene voice. . .brought me new ideals and a new world that could, it seemed, console my wounded heart.'[18]

One of the most radical young nationalists of this first generation, Ki Hadjar Dewantara, later gave birth to a still more influential syncretism in his Taman Siswa school system, founded in Yogyakarta in 1922. 'Government Western education', he argued, 'provides an abundance [of knowledge] but not the capacity to bring it to a synthesis. It enables youth to take note of everything, but gives them no centre, no cultural basis of their own. They thereby neither remain Javanese nor become Western, they break into pieces.'[19] His *Panca Darma* (Five Duties), foreshadowing the nationalist *Panca Sila* of 1945, were freedom, natural harmony, culture, nationality and humaneness. In practice, this meant a relaxed, family atmosphere in the classroom, development of the whole person, and 'socialism without class conflict' in which fees and teachers' salaries would be adjusted to need rather than rank. As the movement spread outside Java in the 1930s, it developed a pattern of integrating other cultures as well as the Javanese into its national-progressive format. Although the number of students in its school system never rose above 25,000, Taman Siswa provided remarkable leadership in developing a new and secure identity which belonged to the modern world. It also reinforced the point that once a *modern* identity had been defined for Javanese, as for Muslims, the step to a *national* identity was a relatively short one.

Muslims had a less complicated path to follow, since religion itself was the guarantee that they had not sold their birthright to the West. Some of the most profoundly individualistic and iconoclastic Indonesians of this century have been strict Muslims. The modernists of Egypt in the late nineteenth century had already provided the argument that Islamic societies were in decline because they had not been truly Muslim, failing to learn from the world around them. Islamic reformism made its earliest Indonesian impact in West Sumatra, but the appearance of a Dutch-educated generation gave it new impetus everywhere. In 1912 Indonesia's most successful religious organisation, Muhammadiah, was founded in Yogyakarta precisely to cater for disoriented Muslims in Dutch schools. Gradually it developed its own modern school system, and by the 1930s it had almost 1000 branches throughout the archipelago, each supporting one or more schools as well as women's, youth and scouting organisations. In Yogyakarta itself, and in West Sumatra from the 1920s, it developed strong populist roots. Elsewhere, it had a predominantly urban and Western-educated membership. Even as an irritant to the more traditional rural *ulama* it was important, however, for these in turn eventually formed their own movements which imitated Muhammadiah's organisation even while opposing its theology. Such traditionally oriented organisations as Nahdatul Ulama in East Java (1926), Perti in West Sumatra, Al Jamiatul Wasliyah in North Sumatra (1930) and PUSA in Aceh (1939) did have an enormous potential rural constituency. Gradually, the distance between these organisations and Muhammadiah narrowed, and their common ground against the alien government became more marked. In 1937 the major Islamic organisations joined in a federative council called MIAI, which in turn joined forces with the secular nationalists in a number of political campaigns in 1939–41. Under the Japanese, the same organisations were again united on a Java-wide basis into MASJUMI, which provided the name and much of the leadership for independent Indonesia's biggest political party in the period 1945–53. By independence, in other words, the Indonesian Islamic community had as its spokesman a modern organisation quite different from, and frequently hostile towards, the rajas, chiefs and *bupatis* who had official control of the Muslim juridical apparatus under the Dutch.

Its basis was not the *kadi*, the religious judge, but the Islamic school — whether of traditional or modern type. It could form a powerful ally of the secular nationalists against the Dutch and Japanese but its fundamental goal could only be an Islamic State based on religious law. It was therefore also a rival of secular nationalism, and the relative strength of the two forces remained uncertain until 1955 when Islamic parties took 45 per cent of the vote in Indonesia's first election.

THE POLITICS OF ANTI-COLONIALISM

As we have seen, ideas of progress, solidarity and party formation had begun to be important in Indonesia at least from the time of the first political organisations — Budi Utomo (1908), the Indische Partij and Sarekat Islam (both 1912). These parties, like all those that followed, were led by Dutch-educated intellectuals sensitive to Dutch power and arrogance on one hand and anachronistic aristocratic pretension on the other. It was a small group of privileged urban people. Even in 1940, when the numbers of Dutch-educated had expanded many times, only about 50,000 Indonesians were associated with nationalist parties. Aided by the Japanese occupation this small group would succeed in 1945 in making itself both spokesman and leader of the Indonesian people. At no point, however, did it mobilise mass support in really effective political organisations at grassroots level.

The very weak position of an indigenous middle class of financiers and traders limited the opportunities for building organisations which could reach the rural mass. The most important linkages between city and country remaining in indigenous hands were the bureaucratic hierarchy and the *ulama*. The first was effectively controlled by the Dutch, who quickly dismissed any official who joined a political party. The second, in conjuction with the embryonic middle-class elements described above, became the basis for Indonesia's first experiment with mass politics in 1912–26.

Sarekat Islam (SI), which pioneered this experiment, was not initially inspired by the Dutch-educated element at all. It sprang from the resentment of Javanese *batik* makers in Surakarta at Chinese economic pressure, and thus it had a populist anti-Chinese base from the start. Its founder saw the need for educated *priyayi* leadership, however, and he turned to H. O. S. Tjokroaminoto to organise an association for mutual self-help among Muslims — which in 1912 was still the most common term by which Indonesians designated themselves in contrast to Europeans and Chinese. Within two years the organisation had received membership fees from 366,000 people, almost all in Java. This astonishing growth owed something to the desire of Western-educated lower *priyayi, ulama* and small traders for a vehicle for their interests in a time of rapid change, but more to the messianic longings of a downtrodden people whose traditional leaders had long since ceased to be a source of hope. Tjokroaminoto was widely identified with the *Heru Tjokro* or *Ratu Adil*, the messianic deliverer of Javanese prophecy, and secret oaths and rituals underlined the supernatural power the organisation was thought to possess.[20]

After 1914 this popular following declined in Java as more cautious leaders discouraged the messianic elements. The loss was for a time made good by the Outer Islands, where there were already 83,000 members by 1916. Here, where the Dutch conquest was still a recent memory, SI was embraced as a new and more promising way to continue the struggle. As a propagandist in Aceh put it: 'Formerly we became *Muslimin* [Muslim fighters] by carrying a gun, but now that is no longer necessary, now unity [through SI] is enough. If we have unity we are already numerous and we will achieve whatever we want.'[21] Violent incidents began to frighten the Dutch and even the urban leadership of SI in the period 1918-20. Numerous rural activists were arrested, and the movement lost its enthusiasm for rapid expansion of membership.

At its height, however, Sarekat Islam had become the voice of the national awakening, and any who wished to participate in that awakening had to join it. Among them were a handful of able Indonesian Marxists in the Semarang stronghold of the Indies Socialist Party. The pioneers of Marxist activism in the Indies had been Dutch, but the exile of the European leaders in 1918 only made it easier for their young Indonesian protegees, Semaun and Darsono, to argue that imperialism and capitalism were the same enemy. The same men led the militant Semarang branch of Sarekat Islam, the radicalism of which was a constant challenge to the original SI leadership. In its anxiety to preserve its role as the united voice for all oppressed Indonesians, Sarekat Islam was forced by Semarang to condemn 'sinful' capitalism in October 1917 — a compromise which retained for a time the indispensable support of the small Muslim entrepreneurial group. The conflict between the left and right wings could not be papered over for long, however, especially when the former became increasingly influenced by the Comintern and the latter by pan-Islam. In 1920 Semaun and Darsono formed the Partai Komunis di Hindia (from 1924, Partai Komunis Indonesia, or PKI), though they remained in the executive of SI. There were stormy scenes at each subsequent SI Congress, until the PKI members walked out for the last time in February 1923.

The SI henceforth became an urban party catering for Islamic nationalists. Many of its wealthier supporters transferred their energies to Muhammadiah, concluding that the quality of religious practice had to be improved before entering the political arena. It was left to the PKI to pursue the dangerous course of mass mobilisation, between the twin perils of government repression and popular expectations of the millenium. It was no use for some Dutch Marxists to argue that Indonesian capitalism had to grow stronger before there was any chance for the proletariat. The demand from politicised rural Indonesians, whether Sumatran coffee and rubber growers, Javanese sugar and railway workers or village schoolteachers, was for an end to taxes, forced labour and domination by foreigners. Marxism was irresistible as long as it not only gave a modern name to the enemy, 'capitalism', but promised rapid success against it. As one leftwing newspaper ended its explanation:

Communism knows that as long as this world is ruled by capitalism, there must be misery and general difficulty. So in short 'communism' is anti 'Capitalism', or better 'Communism' is the science [*ilmu*] of people who are at present squeezed, milked, oppressed, etc.

Now do you understand and agree with the existence of communism? 'Oh sure – really great if that's what it is. When is the hour of this "Communism" coming?' Wait on, in a little while it must rule the world, for its turn has nearly come.[22]

In its attempt to avoid these dangerous pressures the PKI dissolved its peasant branches in 1924, complaining about their 'petty bourgeois' values and tendency 'to give up in despair or go over into terrorism'.[23] The tightrope act nevertheless soon broke down and a suicidal revolt was planned on the grounds that it was 'better to die fighting than let oneself be killed'.[24] Scheduled for 12 November 1926, the revolt was very poorly co-ordinated, largely as a result of pre-emptive Dutch action. The disturbances which took place in West Java in November 1926, and in West Sumatra in early 1927, gained strongest support from the despised rural branches but were suppressed within a few days. They provided the pretext for the Dutch to arrest 13,000 people associated with the PKI, and to intern 1308 of them in the swamps of Boven Digul, New Guinea. From having been the strongest communist party in Asia, the PKI was now entirely removed from the public arena. Even had it sought a Maoist retreat to a rural stronghold, there was nowhere it could have gone and no hope of help from abroad. Marxist ideas remained influential and the PKI's reputation as arch-revolutionary was unchallengeable, but when the party reappeared two decades later it was extremely weak in organisation.

The revolt marked the end of mass mobilisation as a feasible tactic. Government bureaucratic control was sufficient to ensure that no later party could penetrate the rural areas, had any sought to do so. Except in cities and some Christian areas of whose loyalty the Dutch were very sure, there were no popular elections before independence. Indonesian members of the *Volksraad*, established in 1918 but never developed beyond its weak co-legislative functions, were either appointed or elected by minute electoral colleges of elite Indonesians.

Nevertheless, the national ideal continued to develop rapidly among the nearly two million urban or educated Indonesians. Taking from Marxism the opposition to capitalism, from Sarekat Islam the solidarity of 'us' against 'them', and from European scholarship the name Indonesia and the rediscovery of a glorious pre-European past, secular nationalism became the dominant political force after 1926. The first organisation to use the term Indonesia, in 1917, had been a non-political association of students in the Netherlands. Becoming steadily more radical, this adopted in 1925 the name Perhimpunan Indonesia and issued a militant journal called *Indonesia Merdeka* (Free Indonesia). Dominated in the period 1924-31 by a thoughtful Minangkabau economist, Mohammad Hatta, this association developed many of the ideas and symbols which would inspire the struggle of the 1930s. As we have seen, the PKI incorporated 'Indonesia' into its title in 1924, Sarekat Islam followed suit in 1929 and even Budi Utomo, originally restricted to Java, fused into the Indonesian nationalist PARINDRA in 1935. Student activists in Indonesia were especially quick to respond to the new national symbols. At a

national Youth Congress in 1928 a pledge was made by all delegates
– 'We the youth of Indonesia have only one fatherland, Indonesia.
We have only one nation, Indonesia. We have only one language, the
Indonesian language'. The same Congress first heard the composi-
tion 'Indonesia Raya', which quickly gained the status of the anthem
of nationalism (see illustration, p. 107).

The most popular spokesman for the nationalist position soon
became a young architecture graduate in Bandung named Sukarno.
As a student, Sukarno had lived with Tjokroaminoto and taken his
daughter as his first wife. He shared the older man's concern for
unity as well as his faith in charismatic oratory rather than careful
organisation. In July 1927 he founded the PNI (Indonesian Nationalist Party) on a platform of complete non-co-operation in government-
sponsored councils such as the *Volksraad*, drawing into the party a
number of returned members of the Perhimpunan Indonesia in
Holland. Only five months later he had succeeded in forming the
first federation of nationalist political parties, the PPPKI. Sukarno
wrote and spoke tirelessly on the theme that Muslims, Marxists and
nationalists all had the same central aim, to rid Indonesia of imperialism, but could never achieve it unless united (see illustration,
p. 108). At his urging the PPPKI adopted the 'Indonesian way' of
reaching decisions by consultation (*musyawarah*) and consensus
(*mufakat*). The major policies of Sukarno as future president were
already clearly delineated before he was thirty.

The superficial unity he had built up did not outlast his first
imprisonment (December 1929–January 1932). Another young
Minangkabau intellectual, Sutan Sjahrir, established a 'New PNI'
dedicated to the education of party cadres rather than the cultivation of 'sacred unity' at all costs. Hatta joined this new party on
his return in 1932, whereas Sukarno after his release joined
PARTINDO, the successor to the first PNI. Both the rival leaderships
were put out of circulation altogether by the reactionary Governor-
General de Jonge by early 1934. Hatta and Sjahrir were exiled to
Boven Digul, while Sukarno had a more comfortable exile in Flores,
perhaps as a reward for the abject letters he wrote the Dutch after
his second arrest. The tactics of Sukarno and Hatta were in striking
contrast, though neither had been a great success. Hatta's party
structure barely survived on a harried semi-legal basis until 1942,
while Sukarno had to hope that he lived on in the memory of his
people.

Since 1920 Dutch colonial policy had grown steadily more conservative. To understand the intransigence of Holland one must recall the importance in popular consciousness of its oversized colony. This alone gave Holland the status of a major power. By 1930, US$2000 million had been invested in Netherlands India, and 73 per cent of it was Dutch. It was estimated that between one in five and one in ten of the Dutch population depended directly on the Indies for their livelihood.[25] Many took it as axiomatic that 'if the bonds which attach the Netherlands to the Indies are severed there will be a permanent reduction in the national income of the Netherlands which will lead to the country's pauperisation.'[26] The two men who dominated colonial policy in the 1930s, Hendrik Colijn (Prime Minister, 1933-7) and B. C. de Jonge (Governor-General, 1931-6), were both former Directors of Royal Dutch Shell — the largest single economic interest in the Indies. The challenge of Indonesian nationalism led such men to adopt a rigid position excluding even the discussion of movement towards independence. De Jonge inaugurated his term of office by announcing that Holland had been in the Indies for 300 years and would be there for another 300. Under his regime and that of his successor the police silenced nationalist speakers or broke up their meetings if the word 'independence' was uttered, or even if it was implied that the economic difficulties of Indonesians were related to imperialism.

Such repression created a superficial calm, but the alienation of urban Indonesians from the colonial system steadily deepened. The small but vigorous Indonesian press (with a total, overlapping, circulation of about 500,000), the Islamic movement, Taman Siswa and the other private schools, the moderate Indonesian spokesmen in the *Volksraad*, all came to share with the nationalists a sense of identity as Indonesians and a conviction that Dutch intransigence was the principal barrier to progress. Dutch commitment to the *Pangreh Praja* corps (no longer a traditional aristocracy but not yet a professional bureaucracy) as the legitimate leaders of Indonesia placed both in an awkward straitjacket. As Heather Sutherland puts it: 'The theoretically apolitical *Beamtenstaat* became a protective scaffolding supporting indigenous authority. Paradoxically, this imprisoned the *Pangreh Praja*, inhibited its responses and so further weakened a corps already suffering from the contempt of many of its defenders as well as the challenges of new elites. Ultimately, maintenance of the status quo necessitated the development of a police regime'.[27]

Only co-operative, pragmatic political parties were permitted to operate in the late 1930s. PARINDRA, which incorporated Budi Utomo in 1935, attracted many professionals and retired officials with a practical programme of social reforms. GERINDO was born two years later as a vehicle for former members of Sukarno's parties and a number of covert communists, on the basis of the Moscow-approved 'common front against fascism'. The key figure in the latter group was a Surabaya lawyer named Amir Sjarifuddin, an attractive and persuasive Sumatran who had converted to Christianity as a student and was later drawn into the 'underground PKI' through GERINDO.

Unlike their predecessors, these parties did not frighten cautious or pious Indonesians. In a quieter way than Sukarno's, a more effective political front gradually emerged to link the political parties, the Islamic organisations (beginning to lose their fear of politics), and even the union representing much of the more educated *Pangreh Praja*. These elements joined to promote such modest aims as the Soetardjo petition (1936) for a Dutch-Indonesian constitutional conference, the call for an Indonesian parliament in 1939-40, and the wider use of the title Indonesia and the Indonesian language. Dutch rejection of all these requests pushed moderate Indonesians into the arms of the nationalists. Despite the outward calm, alienation from the colonial regime was universal by 1942, and the Japanese were welcomed as liberators. One leftwing nationalist intellectually committed to opposing the Japanese had to concede: 'For the average Indonesian the war. . .was simply a struggle in which the Dutch colonial rulers would finally be punished by providence for the evil, the arrogance, and the oppression they had brought to Indonesia'.[28]

THE JAPANESE OCCUPATION, 1942-5

Even the Japanese were astonished at the ease of their victory in the East Indies. In some areas, the speed of the Dutch capitulation owed as much to fear of the Indonesian population as to the Japanese advance. By 8 March 1942, only three months after Pearl Harbour and three weeks after the fall of Singapore, the Dutch colonial regime was at an end. Despite the intensity of colonial penetration of Indonesia, with its 300,000 European residents, 100,000 students in Dutch-medium schools and the high degree of Westernisation in the clothes, manners and life-style of millions of Indonesians, it had gone for good. The Dutch language was effectively forbidden from the public arena by the Japanese, giving to Indonesian a primacy which could never again be challenged. The Japanese did not succeed in Japanising Indonesian culture in any significant respect, but they made possible the consolidation of a very strong sense of the meaning of being Indonesian.

The Japanese were welcomed in part because they were assumed to represent change. The contradictions kept under the carpet by Dutch police measures now had an opportunity to emerge. In Sumatra, there were demonstrations against the rajas and demands for their abolition. A number of village and district heads were killed or injured by their angry subjects. Local peace-keeping committees which oversaw the transfer of power usually represented the political activists hoping for an end to the rule of the *Pangreh Praja*. In Jakarta, the Japanese were presented with a list of nationalist politicians to form a Cabinet for the new Indonesia. Javanese *priyayi* and Sumatran rajas were denounced as pro-Dutch collaborators, though they in turn were not slow to point out the dangers their opponents would present to the Japanese. The Japanese, in other words, were 'overwhelmed with willing, yet warring, collaborators'.[29] Indonesian society had never seemed so divided. Sukarno was not far from the truth in labelling the enmity between the national movement and the *Pangreh Praja* 'the most rotten wound caused by the Dutch policy of *divide et impera*'.[30]

The Japanese did bring change, but not of the sort expected. Their primary aim in the Pacific War was to obtain access to the raw materials of the archipelago for industries at home. Independence, even in name, had already been ruled out before the war began for all the islands except Java, the status of which remained for a time uncertain. In terms of administration, the policy laid down in Tokyo had been that 'existing government organizations shall be utilized as much as possible, with due respect for past organization structure and native practice'.[31] The *Pangreh Praja* continued to be used as the backbone of administration. The hereditary element the Dutch had continued to value was removed, and the service moved closer to a true bureaucracy subject to frequent transfer and intervention from above. On the other hand the disappearance of local councils and of the ever-watchful Dutch *controleur*, together with Japanese unfamiliarity with conditions, gave Indonesian administrators more real authority than ever.

Unlike the Dutch, the Japanese also had places for Islamic and political 'counter-elites' even if not the ones they had sought. Indeed, few avenues were open to politicians and journalists except on the government payroll in organisations directly answerable to the Japanese. Political parties were banned, independent newspapers were closed and the opportunities for pursuing a private career in law, engineering or business were sharply curtailed. In this sense the Japanese period drastically eroded the fragile autonomy which Indonesian organisations had prided themselves on in relation to the Dutch. On the other hand, a significant role was provided for politicians and journalists in city administration, in the one official newspaper the Japanese permitted in each major city and in the organisations set up for propaganda and popular mobilisation.

Surprisingly few politicians declined these opportunities. The only significant nationalist group to attempt anti-Japanese activity was the 'Illegal PKI' re-established by Musso during a brief clandestine visit to Surabaya in 1935, though more effective under the GERINDO umbrella of 1937–41. The Dutch, apparently unaware of his communist connection, gave Amir Sjarifuddin 25,000 guilders to finance an anti-Japanese underground. This made it easy for the Japanese to trace the PKI leaders, executing many of them although Amir himself was spared through Sukarno's intervention.[32] Sutan Sjahrir also stood aloof from Japanese-orchestrated activity in order to act as a link between anti-Japanese elements and the co-operating politicians, notably Sukarno and Hatta.

The overwhelming majority had no objection to working with the Japanese, some politicians seeing it as 'a magnificent opportunity to educate and ready our people'.[33] Despite greater restraints than ever on freedom to speak and organise, there were some precious, if unintended, advantages. Favoured leaders were not only allowed but required to stump the country addressing huge rallies, their audiences often trucked in from the surrounding villages. In their determination to mobilise greater sacrifices for the war effort the Japanese gave Indonesians their first experience of real political theatre. Secondly, a unitary leadership was forced upon the politicians of each area. The quarrelling factions which had greeted the Japanese in 1942 were obliged to join single propaganda bodies in each area, responsible to clearly identified leaders. Muslim modernists and traditionalists, Christians, Protestants and Catholics, were obliged to merge into a single representative body. The different elites, secular nationalist, religious and *Pangreh Praja*, were in turn fused at the top of the pyramid in local advisory councils and 'loyalty' organisations in which the leading local politician usually enjoyed the position of chairman. Although the tensions of 1942 were by no means eliminated, all these rival elites found themselves in a very similar predicament. All now enjoyed official status, a relatively high income in a time of general hardship and privileged access to travel, information and scarce resources. In return, they shared a vulnerable role as mediators between the unpredictable, demanding Japanese and an increasingly desperate population.

The leaders who rose to the top under the Japanese proved durable both at local and national level. The overtly pro-Japanese figures without popular support were tried and found wanting during 1942, and the Japanese turned to those who seemed likely to be most effective in the task of wartime mobilisation. Those selected for highest office were seldom challenged either before or after the Japanese surrender, because their colleagues in the wartime elite groups were aware of the dangers such prominence brought with it. Moreover, the power of the official media ensured that only the officially designated leaders were known and recognised at grassroots level, making them indispensable in the struggle that would follow.

In the Outer Islands, this process of developing an Indonesian leadership did not go beyond the Residency level (close to today's Province). Sumatra, seen as strategically vital by the Japanese, had been united with Malaya in 1942 under the command of the 25th Army. Even when its links with Malaya were broken the following year, the 25th Army insisted that Sumatra was not ready for independence and defended its territory from the more liberal ideas emanating from Java. The eastern islands had been entrusted to the Japanese Navy as 'sparsely populated primitive areas, which shall be retained in future for the benefit of the [Japanese] Empire'.[34] Java, on the other hand, had no special strategic value to Japan, and was fortunate that General Imamura Hitoshi established what was known to the Japanese as a 'soft' policy there. In particular, Imamura developed a good relationship with Sukarno, the most obvious potential leader since the deaths of the two major PARINDRA figures shortly before the war. At a meeting in July 1942 Imamura promised Sukarno 'greater political participation by the people and greater welfare than in the Dutch period',[35] though he was replaced before he could persuade Tokyo to sanction any significant concession. The Indonesian politicians were allowed only to establish a Java-wide propaganda body named PUTERA (March 1943–February 1944) and a completely powerless Java advisory council in October 1943. Later, even PUTERA was abolished in favour of the broader Djawa Hokokai, in which the influence of the nationalists was effectively diluted by the *Pangreh Praja* and other groups. Until September 1944, when independence for 'the Indies' was at last promised by a Japan which knew it was losing the war, Sukarno had no substantial concessions whatever to show for his bargaining with the Japanese. Mohammad Hatta, who had decided that co-operation was the only realistic option despite his obvious distaste for Japanese methods, was very lucky to escape a Kenpeitai plan to eliminate him in a traffic 'accident' during 1943.[36] Nevertheless, Sukarno and Hatta, who remained loyal to each other despite profound differences during this difficult period, were unchallenged as Indonesian spokesmen throughout Java. Since so little had been achieved beyond the local level in the other islands, there would be no alternative in 1945 than for the Java leadership to become the Indonesian leadership.

Java's more advanced political climate has to be seen against its appalling shortages of food and other vital supplies. The policy of local self-sufficiency and the collapse of export earnings brought shortages of cloth and other imported articles everywhere. Food production became inadequate even in rice-surplus areas because the increasingly arbitrary Japanese policy of forcible requisitions reduced any incentive to produce. Java, already unable to feed its 50 million people before the war, was in a critical situation by 1944–5. Possibilities of import had disappeared, the Japanese were preparing large stockpiles for a last-ditch defence of the island, and 40,000 tons were even ordered to be sent to Singapore. In their determination to keep themselves, the cities and workers in strategic industries well fed, the Japanese imposed requisitions on rural areas which rose as high as 50 per cent of the crop in 1944. Lucas has calculated that the rice remaining for the Indonesian population in Pekalongan Residency may have fallen as low as 63 grams per head per day – less than one-seventh of a healthy ration. The effects of starvation could be seen throughout Java. The promised time of deliverance had become a time of despair.

All over Java and Sumatra there were incidents of rural rebellion, sometimes directed against the Japanese themselves but more often against the local officials through whom Japanese demands for rice and forced labour were imposed on the people. A number of village and district heads were killed in these spontaneous outbursts of anger, and many more would be punished in the 'social revolutions' which followed the departure of the Japanese. Had there been a more effective underground guerrilla movement, it could have capitalised on this popular bitterness, at its peak in 1945. But the political elite seemed now to be a captive of the Japanese, clinging to the hope that the increasingly frenzied preparations for the final military struggle would at last bring real independence to Indonesia.

If the Japanese distanced the pre-war elites in this way from the masses in whose name they professed to speak, they also created a wholly new class without parallel in the Dutch time. They made a complete break with the Dutch educational system, which they considered elitist, academic and impractical. Japanese training would emphasise physical fitness, discipline, toughness and above all a spirit of sacrificial patriotism. Indonesians who were taught by the young, idealistic Japanese teachers testify to their closeness to their students and to the self-confident spirit they produced in young Indonesians. Beyond the relatively small number of Japanese schools, a wide sector of Indonesian youth experienced at least some form of military drilling and patriotic rhetoric. About half-a-million youths in Java were trained in the urban *Seinendan* (Youth Corps) and over a million in the rural *Keibodan* (Vigilance Corps). At the end of the occupation some radical nationalists were encouraged to set up further paramilitary groups of this type, the Sukarnoist *Barison Pelopor* in Java being the biggest, on the grounds that these would have the strongest motivation to fight against the returning Allies. The numerous young people who were radicalised in an inchoate way by this training at a time of general crisis would become the *pemuda* (youth) of the revolution, ready for action, though uncertain what its object would be.

The elect of this Japanese-influenced generation were the young men selected for officer training in the embryo Indonesian army. Known as PETA in Java and as *Giyugun* in Sumatra and Bali, this force amounted to about 60,000 men by the surrender. The officer training was the same as that provided for junior Japanese officers, emphasising group solidarity, discipline, physical toughness and a spirit of heroic patriotism. This intensive training was designed to equip educated youths of 18-25 to become company and platoon commanders. Although there was probably no conscious bias on the part of the Japanese, most of those selected appear to have been from well-placed *priyayi* families and their Sumatran equivalent. In Java alone, older men thought to have some popular influence, typically as religious leaders, were given a shorter training to become battalion commanders. Although this gave a superficial Islamic cast to the PETA army, these men were intended as political advisers rather than professional soldiers and most of them did not remain in the army after independence. The PETA/*Giyugun* represented potentially the most effective legacy of the Japanese period in both organisational and ideological terms, but its leadership in 1945 was still very young and extremely decentralised.

THE REVOLUTIONARY REPUBLIC

Preparation for independence was going on at two levels during the middle of 1945. Politicised youth leaders and the shadowy leftwing underground were banking on a Japanese defeat followed by some kind of revolution for which they were hopelessly unprepared. Meanwhile the political leadership which had emerged under the Japanese umbrella was, when it seemed almost too late, being given the opportunity it had sought since 1942. Although 'independence' had been promised in September 1944, little was done to implement it except at the symbolic level of flag and anthem until May 1945 — and then only in Java. On 28 May, a sixty-two-man assembly met in Jakarta to debate the shape of a future state. Some of the potential for disagreement was removed by the underrepresentation of the Outer Islands, Muslims and liberal constitutionalists. The delegates voted convincingly for a unitary Republic under a strong president. The most divisive issue was the religious one, and instead of polarising the country through a vote, a compromise was arranged whereby a prologue to the draft constitution pronounced 'the obligation for those who profess the Islamic faith to abide by Islamic laws'. Although the '1945 Constitution', as it later became known, was authoritarian and integralist in tone, it was a remarkable achievement to have reached agreement in less than a month on a document which still serves as the constitutional basis for the world's fifth most populous state.

The further collapse of Japanese defences in July caused a rapid acceleration of preparations for a recognition of independence, now scheduled for 7 September. In Java, capable *Pangreh Praja* had already been appointed substantive or deputy Residents in late 1944, while each department of the Military Administration received an Indonesian adviser as a shadow minister. Now in Sumatra and the Navy area, similar moves were belatedly made, usually appointing the leading local politician as deputy Resident and capable aristocrats at the lower levels. For the first time, the Japanese brought together a committee representing all three military administrations, scheduled to begin the final preparations for independence on 16 August. The twenty-two delegates, including three flown in from Sumatra, two from Sulawesi and one from Bali, were therefore on hand to witness the dramatic events surrounding the proclamation of Indonesian independence on 17 August. When they finally did meet the following day, Sukarno and Hatta were able to tell the Japanese that they were simply following the plans laid down under previous Japanese authority, while attempting to explain to suspicious youth leaders that this was at the same time a revolutionary national committee.

Despite some initial misgivings from the Outer Islands delegates, this committee unanimously elected Sukarno to fill the all-powerful role of president under the '1945 Constitution' which it adopted. Hatta would be vice-president. These two men continued to have the major responsibility for delicate diplomacy with the Japanese commanders to prevent their moving against the new republic at least until its authority was firmly established. To this end, they sought to give the appearance of adhering as closely as possible to the Japanese-sponsored preparations. Sukarno's first Cabinet (4 September–11 November 1945) was made up almost entirely of ministers already acting as 'advisers' to their respective departments under the Japanese. *Pangreh Praja* members were appointed to the positions of Resident (in Java) or Assistant Resident (in Sumatra) for which they had been prepared. Similarly, the Preparatory Committee which dispersed on 22 August had made few changes to the agreed Constitution. The concessions to an Islamic state were dropped in the hope of improving the Republic's appeal to potentially pro-Dutch Christians in the East, and a high degree of autonomy in practice, if not in constitutional provision, was given to the Provincial Governments established in Sumatra, Borneo, Sulawesi, the Lesser Sundas and Maluku. Provision was made for a single state party, though this quickly became a dead letter, and for national committees at national, province and residency levels. The delicate question of an armed force was left unresolved by defining a People's Security Body but appointing no one to head it.

These measures were successful in avoiding the kind of provocation which might have obliged the Japanese to intervene. Real change was very gradual for the first month after the proclamation, as Indonesians gradually gained more courage in disregarding their now dispirited Japanese superiors and acting in the name of the Republic. There was an explicit 'gentlemen's agreement' at the national level, replicated locally, that Indonesians could proceed along the promised path to independence provided they did not make the position of the Japanese impossible by violence against Japanese or overt rejection of nominal Allied authority. The *Pangreh Praja* to whom power was meant to devolve at most levels, however, were not the men to take risks on behalf of a revolutionary Republic. They were typically wary of their position with the victorious Allies, some of them going so far as to remove Republican flags and insignia from public places. A positive force for change had to be mobilised before the Republic could acquire real substance. The *diplomasi* of the older elite had to be complemented by the *perjuangan* (struggle) of revolutionary youth.

It would be fair to say that most Indonesians were initially bewildered by news of the Japanese surrender, and found it hard to know whether the noises of independence coming from Jakarta were the last act of the Japanese play or something entirely new. Only two groups had prepared themselves for this moment -- older leftwingers who had been anti-Japanese all along, and angry youth leaders whom the Japanese had mobilised but failed to control. The revolutionary youth movement started most quickly in towns where these two elements were able to find each other. They began by putting up red-and-white insignia and revolutionary posters, and proceeded to call the bluff of Japanese guards by replacing the Japanese flag with the Republican flag on public buildings. During September in Java, and October in Sumatra, they organised mass rallies to show their strength. Where necessary they forced reluctant officials to take a tougher line with the Japanese. By the time the first Allied forces arrived, at the end of September in Jakarta, and the middle of October in Sumatra, they had ensured that the Japanese had withdrawn to their barracks and power was in Indonesian hands – however ill-co-ordinated.

The officers of the PETA/*Giyugun* army were initially at a greater disadvantage than semi-militarised urban youth, since their Japanese commanders had disarmed and dispersed them before the surrender was generally known. In September and October, however, they began to reform as the Republican Army, officially designated as such on 5 October. They took an increasingly large part in the struggle which now turned on the control of Japanese arms. A pattern quickly emerged to be replicated in one centre after another, where crowds of militant youth armed only with sharpened bamboos, knives and a few pistols would descend on a Japanese post and demand weapons. The Japanese always agreed to negotiate, and some or all of their arms would then be transferred, as if under compulsion, to some Republican authority. In Central and East Java alone it appeared that 26,000 rifles and over 1300 machine guns and mortars passed into Indonesian hands.[37] Most went to the official army whose officer corps was overwhelmingly Japanese-trained, but much also fell to politically oriented youth groups bold enough to seize them. The ease of these victories must have appeared to validate the lesson of Japanese training that spirit was the key to military success.

The eventual arrival of British Indian troops, representing the Allied military administration whose task was to preserve law and order until the Dutch administration could resume, interrupted these relatively bloodless exchanges (see illustration, p. 109). In Jakarta, *diplomasi* with the Republican leaders prevented any serious violence, and the city slipped gradually out of Republican control. In Bandung, British pressure induced the Japanese to retake the city from Republican forces on 10 October. In Semarang the following week, a small war developed between Japanese and Indonesians before British troops took over. The climax to this phase came in Surabaya, where uniquely well-armed Indonesian forces had been aggravated by the fact that the first Allied representatives were all Dutch. When the first British brigade arrived on 25 October, the militant youth were in a mood to resist, and wholesale fighting broke out on 28 October. The intervention of Sukarno, Hatta and Amir Sjarifuddin established a tense ceasefire, but the ground was cut from under their feet when an undisciplined sniper killed the British commander, General Mallaby. On 10 November the outraged British launched a massive air, sea and ground operation against the city, whose leaders announced that they would resist to the last.

In the 'Battle of Surabaya' which ensued, the Republic received its baptism of fire. Less startling to the British than the tanks and field artillery which opposed them were the hordes of villagers armed only with bamboo stakes and knives, throwing themselves before British guns in a frenzy of religious fervour. About 15,000 Indonesians probably died in the fighting.[38] Despite the enormous sacrifice of lives and of armament, Indonesians had convinced the British and themselves that their country was not to be reconquered by force alone. Since then 10 November has been celebrated as 'Heroes' Day' – a holiday second only in importance to 17 August.

Even though the leaders of *diplomasi* had had to oppose the *perjuangan* of Surabaya, they knew that without it their bargaining position with the British would have been very weak. The same could not be said when revolutionary zeal was turned against its internal enemies. As we have seen, there was a widespread revulsion among villagers against the power-holders who had enforced Japanese demands for rice and labour. Once it was clear there was no longer any power structure behind these men, there was spontaneous action in village after village to dismiss the village headman, sometimes with violence. In one seemingly typical district of Central Java, we know that eighty village heads were overthrown within a few months, out of a total of 180.[39] In most areas a change of office-holder was all that was achieved – the system through which the headman was able to dominate the village was shaken but not fundamentally altered. Where a more ambitious radical leadership existed, however, the revolutionary impetus could be carried to higher levels of government. In the strongly Islamic northern coast of Java, from the Sunda Strait in the west to Semarang in the east, a series of such actions in the last three months of 1945 eliminated most of the *Pangreh Praja* even though they were now designated Republican officials. In December the ruling class of Aceh was permanently removed from power, in March 1946 the same thing happened to the Malay Sultans of East Sumatra, and in April–June it was the turn of the rulers of Surakarta. Except in Surakarta and East Sumatra these were rural phenomena in which the Japanese-trained *pemuda* whom we have met in the towns played a relatively small role. Three types of leadership were involved, frequently in combination – semi-bandit figures, Islamic teachers and communist veterans of 1926 or the anti-Japanese underground. The first category, very prominent to the west of Jakarta and in Tegal (Central Java), often went in for social banditry claiming to help the small man, but they were better equipped for tearing down than for building up. The more politicised Islamic leaders were involved everywhere, playing their time-honoured role as spokesmen for discontent. Only in Aceh were they united and strong enough not only to oust the secular elite but to replace them effectively in control of the local Republican government. In this sense, Aceh's was the only 'social revolution' to succeed. It did put a new class into power, but one which in the long run proved too difficult for the central Republican government to handle, resulting in the Aceh rebellion of 1953.

The communist element in these revolutionary actions is the least understood, partly because the people concerned were not supported by the Party. It had been so difficult for any party structures to survive the decades of Dutch and Japanese repression that individuals and small cells appeared everywhere in 1945 believing that they acted in the interests of communism. In the western part of Pekalongan Residency (Central Java), such a group had continued the tradition of the 'Illegal PKI' to the best of its ability, carrying out some sabotage against the Japanese and preparing for their defeat. Though only a handful of men, they steered the action committee which co-ordinated the ousting of the *Pangreh Praja* and eventually took over the Residency capital itself for a few days in December. In a similar way, a small group of communist veterans in North Sumatra were able to guide the chaotic youth bands around Medan for a time in a social revolutionary direction, and even to exercise a guiding hand on the Islamic revolutionaries of Aceh. These few individuals had such disproportionate influence because they offered legitimation and further direction to the angry popular mood. However, in none of these revolutionary outbursts did the Left stay in power for more than a few weeks. The reasons were that their enemies – the Republican army apparatus, sometimes assisted by modernist Muslim forces – were too strong, that their presumed friends in the central Government failed to support them and that they lacked any organised popular base.

The urban intellectuals who were the national-level leaders of the Left were at best embarrassed by these 'social revolutions'. Amir Sjarifuddin, who was appointed from a Japanese prison to Sukarno's first Cabinet and became the strong man of the succeeding four cabinets (November 1945–January 1948), washed his hands of the

'Illegal PKI' raducals of Pekalongan who looked to him as their leader. In East Sumatra he campaigned vigorously and with some success against the 'social revolution', arguing that 'as a Marxist. . . I want an egalitarian society with fair distribution. But every theoretician of revolution must accept that that aspiration must be attained in stages'.[40] The reason for this stance was less that he and the other Marxist intellectuals were remote from popular aspirations (although they may have been) than that they were playing the same game as the local social revolutionaries for higher national stakes. That game was not the forming of an organised mass base, for which the communists were badly placed in 1945, but the direct capturing of the revolution from within by making use of their revolutionary credentials at an extraordinarily favourable moment. For Amir this meant *diplomasi* with the Allies to prevent any external attack on the Republic, while doing his utmost to strengthen his position in the government and especially in the Army where control of the revolution would finally be decided.

It is the great virtue of revolution to produce such bewildering change that leadership can be assumed by wholly unrepresentative radical intellectuals who had been outsiders until the day before. Such men were the Marxists who had opposed the Japanese or held aloof from them. Because of this they became in the first months of independence the heroes of the young activists who wanted a complete break with the Japanese. With the arrival of Allied forces, even their rivals who had co-operated with the Japanese could see that men with 'anti-fascist' records were indispensable. Sjahrir and Amir Sjarifuddin were given a free hand in October 1945 to 'democratise' government by making the Central National Committee (KNIP) a provisional legislature, whose functions between sessions would be exercised by a working committee chosen by themselves. On 14 November they formed a cabinet responsible not to the president (as provided in the Constitution) but to the KNIP, with they themselves holding the key portfolios of foreign affairs, interior and defence. The initiative in the capital was so much in the hands of these two men that they might have chosen to dispense with Sukarno as president; but two young Sumatran intellectuals could not afford to do without the massive popularity of Sukarno in Central and East Java. The only serious challenger as president was another Sumatran, Tan Malaka, a veteran 'national communist' whose writings of the 1920s had given him a wide following, and who reappeared in

Jakarta in August 1945 after decades of shadowy underground existence. However, after meeting him Sjahrir came to distrust Tan Malaka as irresponsibly leftist, while Amir opposed him as an alleged 'Trotskyist' who had broken with Moscow. An alliance was therefore struck with Sukarno. Initially he was a passive 'parliamentary' president suffering from his pro-Japanese image, but during each subsequent crisis of the Sjahrir-Amir government, he became more powerful as a bridge to mass support.

In the jockeying for power at the national level in the Republic, the conflict between *perjuangan* (struggle) ideals and *diplomasi* reality was the most powerful weapon. As we have seen, none of the national level leaders, including Tan Malaka, gave any support to *perjuangan* in practice when it meant social dislocation within the Republic. All (with the possible exception of Tan Malaka, who was never put to the test) accepted when in government the need for negotiating with the Allies. But the euphoria marking the early months of total independence, improvised government and spontaneous revolution was such that every subsequent compromise was highly unpopular with the armed youth who provided the muscle of the revolution. Sjahrir and Amir had profited from the desire for *perjuangan* against the Japanese. Now it was Tan Malaka who became the spokesman for *perjuangan* against the compromises Sjahrir and Amir had to make with the Dutch. Tan Malaka was arrested in March 1946 and many of his political allies were arrested on 3 July. The cabinet was steadily enlarged in an attempt to increase its support, seducing some modernising intellectuals of the Muslim and nationalist parties (MASJUMI and PNI) away from the opposition. Sjahrir himself, as the man most closely identified with *diplomasi*, was eventually sacrificed in June 1947. Amir Sjarifuddin now carried on the same policies with an even broader cabinet. However, it was Sukarno, who had successfully identified himself in the public eye with *perjuangan* while backing the *diplomasi* government at each crisis, who was now in the most strategic position. When Amir in turn was forced to resign in January 1948 because of the unpopularity of his diplomatic concessions, Sukarno was able to appoint a presidential cabinet with Hatta as prime minister. Amir's controversial tenure of the defence portfolio, where he had striven since 1945 to make the army more responsive to leftwing control, was ended. In disgust the communist parties went for the first time into opposition. The policy of capturing the revolution from within appeared to have failed.

Whether it could have succeeded will long be debated by revolutionary theorists. As in 1965, the strategy appeared extraordinarily close to fulfilment. Subsequent PKI analysis attacked Amir for his 'very important error. . . that the cabinet resigned voluntarily, without offering any resistance whatever'.[41] What is certain is that the alternative policy of attempting to acquire a mass base with which to attack the 'bourgeois' leadership, was a far more complete and disastrous failure. Once again, as in 1926, the PKI found itself pushed by its own rhetoric and by pressures from below into an armed struggle for which it was not ready. Also as in 1926 Moscow probably opposed the communist rising, although the Soviet contribution to the Cold War – the 'two-camp' doctrine which had replaced the conciliatory 'common front against fascism' by early 1948 – helped to polarise Indonesian politics to the point where a clash was inevitable.

In his time as Defence Minister, Amir Sjarifuddin had built some support among regular Army units, as well as a loyal leftist force in the PESINDO youth movement. This was not enough to balance the hostility the majority of Japanese-trained officers felt towards him for his 'anti-fascist' stand and his attempt to politicise the Army. When PESINDO began the communist revolt in Madiun on 15 September 1948 and the leading communists felt obliged to join it, the government of Sukarno and Hatta threw against them all the forces it could muster. By the end of November, the last communist forces had been hunted down. Most significant PKI leaders including Amir were executed the following month. Their belated attempt to mobilise the peasants of Java had been no more successful. The short period of communist control of some rural areas appeared to be remembered as a time of confusion and bloodshed rather than of developing reliable rural cadres. In any case, the defeat of the communist forces which had been the mainstay of government for the first two years of the revolution made in unlikely that any fundamental restructuring of Indonesian society would take place.

THE VICTORY OF THE REPUBLIC

The Dutch response to the revolutionary Republic was a policy of federalism emphasising minority interests. The Republic had been able to form effective governments only in Java and Sumatra. The 'national' politics described above took place in Java, where the

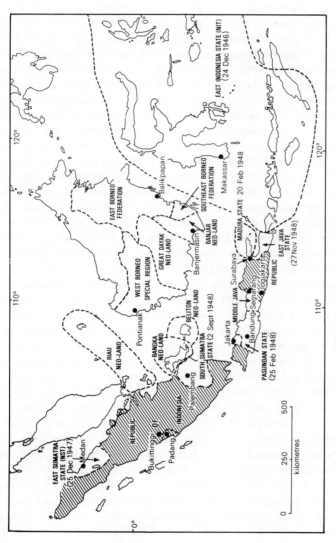

Federal Indonesia, 1948–9

Republic had moved its capital to Yogyakarta in January 1946 as the Allies became too strong in Jakarta. The autonomous revolutions which had taken place in each Residency of Sumatra gradually began to be co-ordinated with Yogyakarta during 1946. In Borneo and the East, the Allies, represented by Australian troops, had arrived before any Republican authority could be established, and they proceeded to pass authority to the Dutch according to plan. Since the British were unwilling and the Dutch militarily unable to move beyond their seven urban enclaves in Java and Sumatra, there was no alternative for the Dutch than to use the Outer Islands as a base to surround the Republican stronghold. Once they had accepted the painful reality that some form of independence would have to be conceded, the Dutch therefore aimed at a federal 'United States of Indonesia', the diversity of which would provide a continuing role for a Dutch 'referee'. A host of semi-autonomous federal bodies were developed in the very fragmented area under Dutch control, but they failed to conceal the strong arm of the Dutch holding the whole structure together. The culmination of this policy was the State of East Indonesia (NIT), established in December 1946 to embrace all the communities of eastern Indonesia except New Guinea.

Meanwhile, under strong British and American pressure, the Dutch had negotiated the Linggajati Agreement (12 November 1946) with the Republic, whereby the two sides would work together to create a United States of Indonesia whose three constituents would be the Republic (Java and Sumatra), Borneo and the East. Neither side was happy with this compromise, and the Dutch were particularly frustrated to be making no progress politically at a time when their military forces grew stronger. On 20 July 1947 the Dutch launched a swift military action to occupy the wealthiest parts of Java and Sumatra, which were also the homes of potentially anti-Javanese ethnic groups – notably the Sundanese, the Madurese and the Malays of East Sumatra. Republican forces retreated, and the Dutch set about extending the federal idea by the erection of further states there. The most important was Pasundan, occupying the Sundanese-speaking area of West Java. Instead of the federal model appealing to Republicans, however, pro-Republican sentiment gradually took over the federal states, which knew that Dutch concessions to them had been won by the struggle of the Republic. As a concept, federalism made a great deal of sense for a country as large and diverse as Indonesia, but the fact that the Dutch had backed it, and backed it unsuccessfully, made it a dirty word for independent Indonesia.

Frustrated by the steady erosion of their position even in Dutch-occupied areas, the Dutch launched a second attack on 19 December 1948. This time the object was to eliminate the Republic by a direct attack on Yogyakarta and all other significant cities, hoping desperately that this *fait accompli* would vitiate United Nations attempts to pursue a negotiated solution. It was a suicidal move, which was to ensure the final frustration of Dutch plans. Despite the military success of taking all the cities of Java within a week, no Republican leaders went over to the Dutch side. Instead, anti-Dutch guerrilla activity commenced on a considerable scale while the governments of NIT and Pasundan resigned in sympathy with the Republic. Holland was eventually forced by the pressure of the United Nations, in particular the United States, to reopen negotiations with the Republican leaders they had captured, and eventually to restore them to power in Yogyakarta on 6 July 1949. With this, the moral victory of the Republic seemed complete. Although a Federal Indonesian Republic (RIS) was duly formed under United Nations auspices in December 1949, its federal components were all dissolved into the unitary Republic within eight months. With appropriate symbolism the date chosen for the final destruction of federalism was 17 August 1950, while the date on which sovereignty was formally transferred from the Dutch to the RIS was almost forgotten.

The period when the Dutch controlled all the Republican cities (December 1948–July 1949) is known in Indonesia as the 'guerrilla period'. The civilian leaders of the Republic had allowed themselves (or so it seemed to the military) to be captured by Dutch paratroops despite Sukarno's constant promises to fight to the bitter end. Leadership of the guerrilla struggle was therefore contested between the three elements which had most effectively organised armed support – the Army, the Muslims and the communists. Since the orthodox communists were still reeling from their defeat at Madiun, Tan Malaka renewed his bid for ideological leadership of the revolution, but he was killed on military orders in February 1949. A separate Islamic army known as Darul Islam also clashed frequently with other units in West Java, and remained as a thorn in the side of the Republic for years after the Dutch had departed. Yet it was the official Republican Army who pre-eminently 'felt themselves to be boss' during the guerrilla period.[42]

Because the Japanese-trained officers were all so young and inexperienced in higher staff functions, the Army had faced leadership difficulties ever since 1945. In attempting to set up a general staff in October 1945, the Republican leaders had turned to a small group of officers trained in the pre-war Dutch colonial army (KNIL). Urip Sumohardjo, who had been a KNIL major, was made General and Chief-of-Staff, while a number of younger and better-educated officers like A. H. Nasution filled the major staff positions. Meanwhile, the Japanese-trained officers, who had not been taught to accept orders from civilian politicians, were sorting out their own leadership. Their choice for commander fell in November on a former PETA battalion commander and Muhammadiah teacher, Sudirman, aged only thirty. It was not until six weeks later that Amir as defence minister and Sudirman as commander accepted the legitimacy of each others' positions, with obvious reluctance on both sides. Sudirman did, however, establish a good working relationship with Urip, twenty-five years his senior, and deferred to him on the technical questions of supply and organisation.

Sudirman and his ex-PETA colleagues were among the more consistent supporters of *perjuangan*, and bitterly distrustful of the compromises Dutch-educated civilians kept making with the Dutch. The 'guerrilla period' confirmed that suspicion, while underlining the army's image of itself as the true saviour of the Republic working in harmony with the rural masses. When the Republic was restored to Yogyakarta, Sudirman made no secret of his great reluctance to leave his guerrilla headquarters and embrace Sukarno again as president.

There seems little doubt that if Sudirman had lived he would have presented an immediate threat to civilian control of the independent Republic. However, he was mortally ill in 1945 and his colleague Urip already dead, the commander attributing both ailments to grief caused by the inconstancy of the civilian leadership. At the level of the Residency, the military continued to wield enormous power which civilians could do nothing to override. At the centre, however, there was a long breathing space for civilian leadership while the young officers gained experience and developed some unity of action among themselves.

THE REVOLUTIONARY PATH TO INDEPENDENCE

The major achievement of the Indonesian revolution was the creation of a united nation with an assured sense of its own identity and significance. The national idea had by 1950 become an irresistible myth, sanctified by the blood sacrificed for it. Subsequent challenges would be made only in the context of a sovereign, united Indonesia, by dissidents with their own distinct sense of the goal for which the revolutionary struggle had been fought. Nationalism acquired a moral urgency which would create problems both for Indonesians who sought a pragmatic process of nation-building, and for some of the country's neighbours.

The revolution had begun as a series of autonomous but parallel uprisings in a dozen parts of the archipelago. These sought to find each other, and succeeded in eliminating most of the barriers that impeded a fuller union — federal state structures, traditional rajas and even separate ethnic nationalisms. What bound the country together positively, however, were ideas and sentiment rather than political institutions. Because the contest between *diplomasi* and *perjuangan* had ended in a draw through United Nations intervention, none of the various elements which made up the revolutionary struggle had succeeded in making it fully their own. On the surface, it appeared as though the Dutch-educated nationalist politicians had emerged victorious. They dominated the politics of the 1950s, occupied Cabinet posts and distributed government positions to their colleagues through the patronage system. Yet the basis for their power was far from strong. The weakness of an indigenous middle class, accentuated by the instability of the 1940s, made the politicians heavily dependent on the state they had themselves created. Their political parties had not been required to mobilise for elections; they possessed few economic resources except the patronage which power alone conveyed; they tended to flourish by identifying with a particular cultural stream rather than by mobilising reliable cadres. Despite its decimation in 1948, the PKI quickly proved itself again the strongest party in organisational terms although—as was demonstrated again in 1965 — its supporters too were less than reliable in a contest against the apparatus and ideology of the state.

Nor was the Indonesian bureaucracy the integrated professional force it was in some former British colonies. Having had such an ambiguous role under the Dutch, it was much attacked in the 1940s

Asia – The Winning of Independence

for the 'feudal' attributes which lingered around it. In principle, its
scope was enormously expanded by the victory of the revolution. A
uniform bureaucratic structure now covered the whole country.
Because government position was now seen as the reward for an
earlier anti-government stance, bureaucratic numbers swelled enormously – about 2.8 million were estimated to be employed by the
Central Government in 1953. The system of patronage brought the
morale of the administrative corps to a low ebb. Towards the people
they governed, the administrators preserved much of the extraordinary power they had held in the past, but they seemed powerless
to protect themselves against constant intervention from political
and military power-holders. It was the Army which was institutionally
strongest by the end of the revolution, though as we have seen it was
not until 1966 that the Army became unified enough to take and
keep power at the national level.

There remains Islam – a permanent source of ideas and leadership
outside the government's power to control. Since independence, as
for centuries before, it has acted as a vital focus of opposition rather
than as a basis for state power. In the 1950s it appeared as if there
was a natural alliance of interests between Islam and the embryonic
middle class whose major sources of strength were the Outer Islands.
In the first great crisis of the post-revolutionary Republic, however,
the alliance of Army, PKI and Sukarno – all predominantly based in
Java – proved too strong for that fragile alliance. The crushing of the
Outer Island rebellions of 1953–8, the banning of the MASJUMI
party, the transition to Guided Democracy in 1959, and the gradual
unification of the Army on a more Javanese base than previously,
were all part of a process which moved Indonesia still further away
from a path which might have led to the strengthening of these
middle-class elements.[43]

The result was neither socialism nor capitalism but a system in
which the state itself dominated the formation of capital and the
crucial relationships with foreign economic enterprise (especially in
oil). The revolutionary experience had weakened or broken most of
the political, administrative or economic institutions of pre-war
Indonesia. The legal system became a less reliable safeguard for
investment than political patronage. In seeking to characterise this
type of pre-revolutionary state, modern commentators have used
such terms as 'bureaucratic polity', 'neo-traditional' and 'neo-
patrimonial' – the last referring to Max Weber's 'patrimonialism'

where the ruling power is exercised personally and intense competition occurs between court factions for access to the spoils of office.[44] While none of these labels is entirely satisfactory, each seeks to explain the enormous economic predominance of the nation's capital and (since 1959) the presidency, and the rivalry of military/political or military/bureaucratic factions for access to the wealth derived from foreign, Chinese or government investment.

The pursuit of the heirs of colonial power in Indonesia does not, in other words, lead us to a single dominant 'class' in the Marxist sense. It does lead to a remarkably cohesive, expanding, urban elite which is firmly Indonesian in identity even while drawn from more than twenty diverse ethnic backgrounds. Some of the values of this elite derive from the colonial and pre-colonial past, but its confidence and its cohesiveness are the fruit of its successful anti-colonial revolution. It believes in Indonesia, distrusts the machinations of outside powers, yet it is essentially cosmopolitan in its love for the verbal play of different languages and cultures. If it has not brought the golden age of prosperity and justice of which Sukarno dreamed, it has undoubtedly wrought a nation with a profound sense of unity and purpose out of the world's largest and most diverse archipelago.

NOTES

1. The primary sources for this episode are the following Indonesian memoirs: Sidik Kertapati, *Sekitar Proklamasi 17 Agustus 1945*, 3rd ed. (Jakarta: Pembaruan, 1964) pp. 94–7; Adam Malik, *Riwajat dan Perdjuangan sekitar Proklamasi Kemerdekaan Indonesia 17 Agustus 1945*, rev. ed. (Jakarta: Widjaya, 1970) pp. 35–7; *Sukarno, An Autobiography as told to Cindy Adams* (Hong Kong: Gunang Agung, 1966) pp. 206–9; Mohammad Hatta, *Sekitar Proklamasi 17 Agustus 1945* (Jakarta: Tintamas, 1970) pp. 33–7. It is described in Anthony Reid, *The Indonesian National Revolution 1945-1950* (Hawthorn: Longman, 1974) p. 26, and Benedict Anderson, *Java in a Time of Revolution, Occupation and Resistance* (Ithaca: Cornell, 1972), pp. 71–3.
2. Nagazumi Akira, *The Dawn of Indonesian Nationalism* (Tokyo: Institute of Developing Economies, 1972) pp. 27, 32.
3. Figures derived from *Statistical Pocketbook of Indonesia, 1941* (Batavia: Central Bureau of Statistics, 1947) p. 142.
4. J. S. Furnivall, *Netherlands India* (Cambridge: 1939) p. 401.
5. Onghokham, 'The Residency of Madiun. Priyayi and Peasant in the Nineteenth Century', (Yale University, PhD thesis, 1976) p. 143.
6. C. J. Hasselman, *Algemeen Overzicht van de Uitkomsten van het Welvaart-Onderzoek Gehouden op Java en Madoera in 1904-1905* ('s-Gravenhage: Nijhoff, 1914) p. 115.
7. Dr Soetomo, cited Nagazumi, *Dawn*, p. 24.
8. F. Buchler, 'Land Hunger and the Growing Power of Regional Elites in

Cirebon Regency, 1903-1930', paper presented to Second Asian Studies Association of Australia Conference, Sydney, 1978.

9.   D. W. Fryer and J. C. Jackson, *Indonesia* (London: Ernest Benn, 1977) p. 153.

10. Derived from Furnivall, *Netherlands India*, p. 348, and Oki Akira 'Social Change in the West Sumatran Village', (Australian National University, PhD Thesis, 1977) p. 64

11. *Statistical Pocketbook of Indonesia, 1941*, p. 96.

12. Richard Robison, 'Capitalism and the Bureaucratic State in Indonesia; 1965-1975', (Sydney University, PhD thesis, 1977) pp. 34–8 and 155. Matsuo Hiroshi, *The Development of the Javanese Cotton Industry* (Tokyo: Institute of Developing Economies, 1970) pp. 19–40.

13. These words, from the title of the collected letters of Raden Adjeng Kartini, are taken as a theme by Benedict Anderson in his perceptive essay on Dr Soetomo in *Perceptions of the Past in Southeast Asia*, eds. Anthony Reid and David Marr (Singapore: Heinemann Asia for the ASAA, 1980) pp. 219-48. On this theme see also Anthony Reid, *'Heaven's Will and Man's Fault': The rise of the West as a Southeast Asian dilemma*, Flinders Asian Studies Lecture 6 (Bedford Park: Flinders University, 1975).

14. R. Ng. Ranggawarsita, *Serat Kala Tida,* quoted in Anerson, *Perceptions,* p. 219.

15. Reid, *Indonesian National Revolution*, pp. 2-3.

16. 'Onze Nationale Kleeding', 2 July 1914, in *Karja K. H. Dewantara,* vol. IIA (Jogjakarta: Persatuan Taman Siswa, 1967) p. 267.

17. Ki Hadjar Dewantara, 'Taal en Volk', 1917, in *ibid.*, p. 106.

18. Dr Soetomo, *Kenang-kenangan,* quoted in Anderson, *Perceptions,* p. 243.

19. In interview with H. J. Kiewiet de Jonge, 20 October 1932, in S. L. van der Wal (ed.), *Het Onderwijsbeleid in Nederlands-Indie 1900-1940. Een Bronnenpublikatie* (Groningen: J. B. Wolters, 1963) p. 537.

20. The best short survey of the rise of SI is in Bernhard Dahm, *History of Indonesia in the Twentieth Century* (London: Pall Mall Press, 1971) pp. 38-55.

21. Speech by Abdul Manap, 1920, quoted in Anthony Reid, *The Blood of the People: Revolution and the End of Traditional Rule in Northern Sumatra* (Kuala Lumpur: Oxford, 1979) p. 16.

22. *Rasa Doenia* (Yogyakarta), 1-8 March 1923.

23. Aliarcham, 1924, quoted in Ruth T. McVey, *The Rise of Indonesian Communism* (Ithaca: Cornell University Press, 1965) p. 263.

24. Darsono, quoted in *ibid.*, p. 298.

25. G. C. Allen and A. G. Donnithorne, *Western Enterprise in Indonesia and Malaya* (London: George Allen & Unwin, 1957) p. 288.

26. P. S. Gerbrandy, *Indonesia* (London: Hutchinson, 1950) p. 27.

27. Heather Sutherland, *The Making of a Bureaucratic Elite: The Colonial Transformation of the Javanese Priyayi*, Asia for the ASAA, (Singapore: Heinemann, 1979) p. 145.

28. Soetan Sjahrir, *Out of Exile*, (trans.) Charles Wolf (New York: John Day, 1949) p. 219.

29. *Continuity and Change in Southeast Asia: Collected Journal Articles of Harry J. Benda* (New Haven: Yale University Southeast Asia Studies, 1972) p. 72. On this theme see also Anthony Reid 'The Japanese Occupation and Rival Indonesian Elites: Northern Sumatra in 1942', *Journal of Asian Studies*, **XXXV**, 1 (Nov. 1975), pp. 49-61.

30. Sukarno, 9 March 1943, quoted in Benda, *Continuity and Change,* p. 71.

31. 'Principles Governing the Administration of Occupied Southern Areas', 20 November 1941, in *Japanese Military Administration in Indonesia: Selected Documents*, eds. H. J. Benda, J. K. Irikura and K. Kishi (New Haven: Yale University Southeast Asia Studies, 1965), p. 1.

32. The importance of this 'Illegal PKI' will become clear for the first time in the forthcoming PhD thesis of Anton Lucas (Australian National University).

33. *Sukarno. An Autobiography*, p. 173.

34. Benda, Irikura and Kishi (eds.), *Japanese Military Administration*, p. 7.

35. *Imamura Hitoshi Taisho Kaisoroku* (Tokyo: Jiyu Ajia-sha, 1960) **IV**, p. 185, translation by Oki Akira (awaiting publication). *Sukarno. An Autobiography*, pp. 175-6, also describes this meeting, though Sukarno's admiration for Imamura is even more apparent at pp. 244-5.

36. Miyoshi Shunkichiro, in *Kokusai Mondai* (Tokyo), vol. 73 (April 1966), pp. 64-6, trans. Oki Akira (forthcoming).

37. These figures, derived from Nasution, are in Dahm. *History*, p. 116.

38. The British counted 4185 Indonesians killed up to 30 January 1946, but estimated that about another 13,000 must have died or been seriously wounded. British casualties throughout Indonesia were only 348 killed and 225 missing by May 1946, by which time the estimate of Indonesian dead had passed 20,000. Most of these losses were in the Surabaya fighting. Cables of 30 January and 28 May 1946, in Public Records Office, London, WO 203/5013 and 203/5015, respectively.

39. Soeyatno Kartodirdjo, 'Social and Political Changes in Surakarta after 1945', *RIMA* 8, no. 1 (1974), p. 39.

40. Amir Sjarifuddin, 9 April 1946, cited in Reid, *Indonesian National Revolution*, p. 75.

41. Musso, 1948, cited in Ruth McVey, *The Soviet View of the Indonesian Revolution* (Ithaca: Cornell Modern Indonesia Project, 1957) p. 62.

42. Reid, *Indonesian National Revolution*, p. 154, quoting Iwa Kusuma Sumantri.

43. This process is best described in Robison, 'Capitalism and the Bureaucratic State in Indonesia: 1965-1975', partly summarised in R. Robison, 'Toward a Class Analysis of the Indonesian Military Bureaucratic State', *Indonesia*, 25 (April 1978) pp. 18-23.

44. Karl Jackson and Lucien Pye (eds.), *Political Power and Communications in Indonesia* (Berkeley: University of California Press, 1978) especially two articles on 'Bureaucratic Polity' by Karl Jackson. Ann Ruth Willner, 'The neo-traditional accommodation to political independence: the case of Indonesia', in L. Pye (ed.), *Cases in Comparative Politics: Asia* (Boston: Little, Brown, 1970). Harold Crouch, 'Patrimonialism and Military Rule in Indonesia', *World Politics*, XXXI. 4 (July 1979) pp. 571-84. For Weber's concept see Max Weber, *Economy and Society. An Outline of Interpretive Sociology* (New York: Bedminster, 1968) pp. 231 ff; and for its modern application S. N. Eisenstadt, *Traditional Patrimonialism and Modern Neo-Patrimonialism* (London: Sage Publications, 1973).

Vietnam:

Illustrations

'Let's follow the example of Nghe-Tinh! Workers, Peasants, Soldiers! Exterminate the gang of imperialists, mandarins, capitalists and big landlords. Communist Party.' An Indochinese Communist Party sticker of late 1931, probably printed in France and designed for smuggling into Indochina. The Nghe-Tinh 'soviets' of 1930, though crushed, had shaken the French.

'The Communist Spider.' French counter-propaganda leaflet distributed in 1931 as a response to the revolts of the previous year.

Năm thứ nhất — Số 4 -- **CƠ-QUAN CỦA THANH-NIÊN**   Ra ngày 15 Novembre 1938

MẶT TRẬN CÁC DÂN TỘC

Một tháng 2 kỳ   **28 trang**   **Giá : 0$10**

The Gioi (The World), a Popular Front publication, promotes a 'Front of Many Nationalities', unity among white, black and yellow peoples. Published in Vietnam, 15 November 1938.

Glossary for Chapter 4

colons	European residents of a French colony
corvée	Unpaid labour demanded by the state
DRV	Democratic Republic of Vietnam, proclaimed in Hanoi, 2 September 1945
ICP	Indochinese Communist Party
indigènes	Local people; in this case, Vietnamese.
VNQDD	Viet Nam Quoc Dan Dang – Vietnam Nationalist Party

4 Vietnam: Harnessing the Whirlwind

David Marr

MAY DAY 1930

Responding to Communist Party exhortations, tens of thousands of Vietnamese peasants took to the roads on 1 May 1930 to demonstrate against corvée, high taxes and exhorbitant land rents. They also demanded redistribution of communal property held by local officials and suspension of debt repayments. And they expressed solidarity with the hundreds of urban workers and intellectuals who had been jailed in previous months.

In Thai Binh province of northern Vietnam (Tonkin), peasants marched in the direction of the government bureau carrying a large red flag and banners listing seven specific grievances. A French officer dispersed them by shooting the flag bearer and ordering his troops to fire into the crowd. Far to the South (Cochinchina), in Long Xuyen province, peasants surrounded the house of a local Vietnamese official and forced him to sign a tax deferral statement. On the same day in Nghe An province of central Vietnam (Annam), peasants marched into Ben Thuy town to support a local strike by sawmill workers. They had just finished singing the Vietnamese version of the 'Internationale' together when a volley from colonial troops killed seven and wounded eighteen. Meanwhile 50 km away, some three thousand villagers were sweeping into the grounds of the Ky Vien plantation, owned by a particularly detested retired Vietnamese official, and were proceeding to sack and burn it.[1]

What made the May Day 1930 demonstrations truly memorable, however, was the manner in which they stimulated hundreds of additional peasant actions over the next twelve months. Instead of collapsing into confusion or sullen acquiescence following the first French attacks, participants continued to press their demands on local representatives of colonial authority. When that failed, they sometimes took control of village affairs themselves, establishing administrative committees, self-defence units, literacy classes and welfare units. This was no traditional *jacquerie*, but an attempt to operate and defend an alternative social system. Realising the gravity of the challenge, French officials responded with a type of brutality not seen since the time of conquest half-a-century earlier. Aircraft bombed and strafed villagers, foreign legionnaires were ordered to kill nine out of ten prisoners taken and search-and-destroy operations became routine. In the end, colonial law and order was restored, but at a price that would haunt everyone thereafter[2] (see illustrations, pp. 158, 159).

May Day 1930 marked the beginning of the end of colonial rule in Vietnam, although the French would not be forced to withdraw for another twenty-four years. Vietnamese Communists were amazed at the size and momentum of peasant actions. While their leaflets and speeches had provided the spark, communist leaders quickly came to realise how poorly prepared they were to predict, plan and co-ordinate anti-colonial operations at even the provincial level, much less to implement a realistic national strategy. For the next decade they grappled with the problem of how to tap the power of an aroused peasantry without being trapped by spontaneous peasant outbursts. They also had to convince poor peasants not to alienate everyone in the village who was more prosperous, but rather to focus discontent on colonial officials and on landlords or village functionaries who refused to co-operate with the revolutionary movement.

Events of 1930-1 also had major repercussions in France. Although it was still possible for a tourist pamphlet blandly to proclaim that the main north-south road in Indochina was 'excellent, but encumbered with beasts and people'[3], the majority of French citizens were now vaguely aware that more serious problems existed in their most important overseas possession. In June 1930 two solutions were mooted in full-scale parliamentary debate. The Socialist Party argued for gradual decolonisation, with practical emphasis on identifying and nurturing those native elements most committed to 'modern civilization' and most likely to participate voluntarily in some post-colonial relationship with France. The rightwing coalition then in government called instead for a revitalisation of colonial institutions, so that the rural Indochinese economy would prosper, peasants would turn a deaf ear to Communist propaganda and all anticolonial malcontents would be either silenced or eliminated. This position was vigorously endorsed by ranking colonial officials in Indochina, who added that the government should be looking to recent Dutch success in crushing the Indonesian Communist Party rather than being led astray by reference to the British dominions. When the issue was brought to a vote the Socialist proposal was defeated. There would not be another such parliamentary debate until 1946.[4]

THE COLONIAL SETTING

The French arrived in force in Vietnam in 1858, much later than most Western colonisers in Asia. They encountered people who possessed a reasonably homogeneous cultural tradition, a well-defined political structure and immense pride at having been able to stave off numerous Chinese encroachments from the north while simultaneously seizing territories from other ethnic groups to the south. Although the Vietnamese court in Hue proved incapable of organising an effective defence, this did not prevent the Confucian-educated elite from mobilising widespread resistance to the French. The conflict, often bitter and protracted, left permanent scars.[5] Armed opposition was quelled in 1897, at which time the French were able finally to fashion the desired colonial system. It featured a surprisingly large French administrative corps and numerous state benefits to private metropolitan investors. Existing tax and corvée systems were greatly expanded; huge land grants were provided to French nationals and faithful Vietnamese officials; and an ever increasing number of peasants were induced to become tenants or wage labourers.

Twenty-five years later French colonialists had reason to be satisfied with their Indochina venture. Capital was pouring into the colony from Paris and Lyon. Output of rubber, rice and assorted minerals was expanding rapidly to meet international demand. And the supply of cheap native labour was proving adequate. Success was symbolised by the Bank of Indochina, which had managed to multiply its profits forty times between 1895 and 1922.[6] Indeed, the Bank had become one of the most precious jewels in the French colonial crown, its influence extending far beyond Indochina to the financing of railroads in China, trade with Japan and investment

Vietnam, 1930–54

in such distant French possessions as Djibouti and Guyana.

With the advent of the Great Depression the bottom fell out of the rubber and rice markets. By early 1931 the Indochina economy was in serious trouble — landowners defaulting on bank loans, companies going into bankruptcy, *colons* banging on government doors demanding assistance, uncounted thousands of Vietnamese tenants, agricultural labourers, plantation hands, miners and factory workers thrown out of employment.[7] A few of the largest corporations found this situation much to their advantage, buying out scores of smaller firms at rock-bottom prices. The Bank of Indochina, for example, purchased cultivated rubber plantations at one-twentieth of former cost. By the end of the turbulent 1930s it controlled 110 enterprises worldwide and had a direct capitalised value 75 per cent greater than at the outset of the Depression.[8]

Although the primary French objective in Indochina was to develop a modern export sector, colonial policies inevitably had an impact throughout the economy. When granting large land concessions to French companies and Vietnamese collaborators, for example, the government relied on Western capitalist concepts of private property and individual legal responsibility. The small minority of Vietnamese who grasped this new ethic quickly were able to amass wealth beyond the wildest dreams of their parents or grandparents. By the same token, those who ignored the new ethic or were slow to adjust often found themselves being evicted or converted into tenants. Still others who *thought* they had protected themselves legally were outmanoeuvred by means of usurious loans, cadastral manipulations, seizure for back taxes or bribery of local officials.

All rural Vietnamese had to learn how to survive in an impersonal cash economy, instead of relying on the more personal and varied system of interaction that had characterised the pre-colonial economy. Often the first shock came when the government ordered taxes to be rendered on an individual rather than corporate village basis. Moreover, payment was now to be made in solid silver *piastres*, rather than in rice or in copper or zinc as before. Many peasants had to acquire the necessary silver coins from landlords or moneylenders at marked-up rates of exchange. Corvée obligations could also be rendered in cash for those who had it. Increasingly exchange relationships within the village also came to be expressed in monetary terms. Local artisan activity declined as workshops multiplied in the towns and peasants focussed on producing a rice surplus for cash income. By the 1920s it was no longer possible in most rural areas to obtain by barter such basic consumer products as cloth, straw mats, cooking utensils or farm implements. Those who lacked the cash to purchase commodities either went into debt or did without.

The nature of the Vietnamese village changed significantly during the colonial period. In many places communal land, the basis of traditional social welfare palliatives and the means of support for local temples and schools, fell into the hands of one or more village families, or even came to be controlled by outsiders. As disparities in wealth increased, the selection of village notables, the observance of village festivals, the organising of weddings, funerals or honours to returning scholars became more the sources of contention and conspicuous consumption, less the symbolic reinforcements of community self-consciousness and solidarity. The ultimate breakdown of corporate ties occurred in those villages where individuals amassed enough property to be able to go and live in some distant city or town. Such absentee landlords, especially prevalent in southern Vietnam, controlled the fates of hundreds or thousands of villagers without ever having to meet them face-to-face, or, worse yet, showing up only at rent or loan collection times.

If the French had come earlier to Indochina, or if the Great Depression and Second World War had not disrupted the colonial process subsequently, the changes described above might well have added up to a complete transformation of Vietnamese society. As it was, nothing could be said to be complete in 1930. The French had not invested sufficiently to possess a solid modern sector. They still relied heavily on force or the threat of force to obtain what they wanted. Some Vietnamese were still alive who could tell nostalgically of a time when life was less troubled, when people knew who they were and where they were going. Other Vietnamese were well enough informed about events beyond Indochina to know that there were viable alternatives to French colonial rule. These two visions — the one backward-looking and romantic, the other forward-looking and programmatic — would combine to fuel the Vietnamese revolution.

The consolidation of these visions into a mass ideology may have spelled the difference between success and failure. Vietnamese peasants had rebelled against rulers (indigenous and foreign) many times before, usually without lasting benefit to themselves. Widespread Vietnamese resentment at French overlordship had not prevented metropolitan capitalists from making fortunes in Indochina. Nor had a long line of anticolonial militants been able seriously to threaten French control. The Indochinese Communist Party (ICP), despite its sophisticated Leninist credentials, was smashed twice before 1941. From a strictly organisational perspective, several other Vietnamese groups had fully as much talent and opportunity as the Communists. What they failed to perceive, however, was that millions of ordinary Vietnamese were primed for ideological transformation, not merely ejection of the French. Several religious groups understood this popular craving, but were unable to project their messages at the national level.

From early 1945, if not before, the ideology of national and social revolution that had captured the imagination of the Vietnamese intelligentsia in the 1930s found a much broader constituency, enabling people to focus their emotional wrath, to turn existing organisational skills to far more ambitious goals. The ICP was only partly responsible for this transformation, just as the Bolsheviks under Lenin had been only partly responsible for the upheavals of 1917 in Russia. In both cases the ability of revolutionaries to comprehend what was happening proved more important than their structural initiatives.

COLONIAL SOCIETY BEFORE THE SECOND WORLD WAR

At the top of Indochina's colonial society before the Second World War stood 42,000 Europeans, all but 3100 residing in Vietnam (Cochinchina, Annam, Tonkin).[9] Approximately one-quarter were military personnel, another one-quarter ran the various government agencies and private firms, and the remaining half were women and children classified as 'without profession'. Most notable were the Europeans who had lived in the colony for at least one or two decades. Known as *colons*, they had economic interests and political perspectives which did not always coincide with either the French government of the day or the big capitalist enterprises with head offices in faraway Paris, Lyon or Marseilles. Badly hit by the Depression, *colons* in Indochina were just recovering when the Japanese marched in and the economy was dealt yet another heavy blow.

The overall population of Vietnam in 1937 was estimated to be 19 million. Of these, about 1.6 million were highland peoples of diverse ethnolinguistic background living along the Chinese, Laotian and Cambodian borders. Another 326,000 were Cambodians living in Vietnam (while 191,000 Vietnamese resided in Cambodia). Overseas Chinese totalled 217,000 people, ranging from the wealthiest rice merchants to small-town moneylenders and shopkeepers, poor dockworkers and sweatshop labourers. Rounding off the minority elements were 5000 Indian moneylenders and brokers, almost all in Cochinchina.

The remaining 16.7 million people, or 87 per cent, were ethnic Vietnamese. Only about 1 million, or 6 per cent, lived in the cities and towns. The other 15.7 million were country folk, living mainly in the tightly packed Red River delta, the somewhat more open Mekong delta and several smaller alluvial plains of central Vietnam. Vietnamese numbers were estimated to be growing by at least 200,000 per year, the result of French success in reducing mortality from malaria, smallpox, cholera and plague. However, the death rate among mothers and small children remained extremely high, since there were no modern health facilities in or near most villages.

At the top of the Vietnamese social pyramid were the absentee landlords, mentioned above, together with a small number of entrepreneurs and ranking government officials. These three groups styled themselves the indigenous bourgeoisie (*tu san ban xu*). They may have totalled 10,500 families in 1937, up to 70 per cent living in or near Saigon, perhaps 15 per cent in Hanoi, the rest scattered in such towns as Da Nang, Hue and Nam Dinh. From the early twentieth century the Saigon bourgeoisie had projected a coherent ideology, combining general acceptance of French colonial rule with special pleas for increased political representation and improved educational and commercial opportunities. From 1917 the Constitutionalist Party began to take shape, led by Bui Quang Chieu, a colonial functionary who had amassed enough land to 'retire' to journalism and politics. In northern and central Vietnam there was no specific party to represent the bourgeoisie, partly because the legal system was more restrictive, but mainly because the constituency was so much smaller and less identified with plantation estates. Nor was there a leader who could be said to represent bourgeois interests in Tonkin and Annam. Perhaps the closest was Pham Quynh, a former interpreter, researcher, editor and essayist who had become a ranking mandarin at the royal court in Hue upon the return of the young King Bao Dai from schooling in France in 1932.

Although the Vietnamese bourgeoisie wanted to achieve solid economic and political status, the prospects were not good. Large metropolitan corporations were disinclined to give *indigènes* any power on their executive boards. French *colons* were prepared to work closely with Vietnamese absentee landlords, but they often drew the line at commercial competition. Industrial opportunities were limited severely by metropolitan tariff preferences. Even the purchase, transport and milling of rice was largely in the hands of Chinese businessmen. The Constitutionalist Party had been founded to change all this, yet ten years later it had lost all momentum. Peasant upheavals in 1930–1, income losses during the Depression and political humiliations during the Popular Fromt period (1936–9) made members of the Vietnamese bourgeoisie extremely defensive about whatever rights they possessed, yet also incapable of mounting any further challenge to the status quo. Henceforth small groups would link their destinies to the French, the Japanese, the religious sects or parties of the radical left.

In a rather different position stood the small landlords, who generally continued to live in home villages and conduct affairs with tenants or wage labourers directly, without resort to agents. Depending on local soil fertility and intensity of cultivation, such landlords might own as many as fifty or as few as four hectares of arable land. Although perhaps totalling 55,000 families in 1937, and thus five times as numerous as the bourgeoisie,[10] they seldom organised themselves effectively beyond the province level. Despite the essentially commercial character of their dealings with subordinates, most small landlords thought of themselves as inheriting the mantle of authority previously worn by the local Confucian scholars and village elders. Hence they staunchly defended local status hierarchy, traditional festivals, patriarchal family institutions and various religious doctrines upholding harmony, human compassion and rewards in the afterlife. Small landlords were often more nationalistic than the bourgeoisie, dwelling proudly on ancient Vietnamese heroes, condemning Western-induced cultural alienation and, on safe occasions, at least, displaying rancour at the way in which the French lorded it over the Vietnamese.

During the 1930s there remained a significant stratum of middle-level farmers, perhaps 750,000 families, or close to 30 per cent of the rural Vietnamese population. Basically they focussed on producing enough from their own property to subsist and pay taxes. Unlike the small landlords, most middle farmers favoured the diffusion of village decision-making, the restoration of viable village schools and, above all, preservation of communal lands from private alienation. To avoid going into debt to landlords or moneylenders they often organised small mutual credit and mutual-aid associations. However, this provided scant protection in the event of major family reversals. Several bad seasons in a row were sufficient to convert scores of subsistence farmers in a particular village into poor peasants or tenants, with little chance of reversing the process. Acutely aware of their precarious position, subsistence farmers were often the first to respond positively to anticolonial overtures from outside the village, thence recruiting a few relatives and friends to form a clandestine cell.

By the late 1930s nearly 70 per cent of rural Vietnamese either owned no land or were hanging on to tiny scraps that could not produce enough to support their families. This was most obvious in Cochinchina, where tenants and rural wage labourers had tilled the plantations of the Vietnamese bourgeoisie and French companies for two generations. However, a more subtle process of land aliena- tion was also underway in the Red River delta and parts of central Vietnam as well. Generally the immediate cause was a family default- ing on taxes or being unable to repay a loan. Some portion of land would be sold, female members of the family would make renewed efforts to supplement income by petty commerce or handicraft production, and one member might be sent into the 'modern' sector of the economy. With luck the family might avoid further land sales. Without it there was a choice between tenantry and sending more able-bodied members to the mines, factories or rubber plantations. Colonial businessman often complained that the pres- sures to migrate were not building up fast enough. For them it was essential that rural Vietnamese come to the 'modern' sector prepared to accept low pay and poor working conditions, in full knowledge that there were plenty of other desperate villagers ready to take their place.[11] Some French officials were not so sanguine, however, fearing social and political repercussions in both village and work- place.

During the 1920s it seems likely that at least 600,000 Vietnamese men and women accumulated several years' experience as non-rural wage labourers. Numbers were substantially lower during the 1930s. Although never more than 2 per cent of the population at any given time, this proletariat possessed disproportionate significance. For one thing, members tended to be detached from traditional mechanisms of social control (father, family elders, village notables) and thus were more likely to act 'erratically'. They were also located physically in positions of most economic and psychological concern to the French. Finally, small groups of workers in league with radical intellectuals demonstrated an uncanny ability to influence other elements of the population to challenge the existing system.

Between French *colons*, wealthy overseas Chinese and Vietnamese proletariat on the one hand, and the Vietnamese proletariat on the other, stood a volatile component of shopkeepers, small traders, artisans, clerks, managers, interpreters, primary-school teachers, journalists and technicians. Perhaps numbering half-a-million people in 1937, this petite bourgeoisie felt the psychological degradations of foreign rule more directly than others and was quick to participate in nationalist organisations, political demonstrations or diverse cultural initiatives. Until 1926 most petit bourgeois Vietnamese had followed the bourgeoisie, assuming that it could extract major concessions from the French. When this proved incorrect a number of clandestine anticolonial groups took shape, the most notable being the Vietnam Nationalist Party (*Viet Nam Quoc Dan Dang*, or *VNQDD*). In February 1930 the Nationalists attempted a *coup de force* in northern Vietnam but were quickly defeated; survivors fled to China. Subsequent petit bourgeois attention tended to focus on either the existing Marxist–Leninist parties (Indochinese Communist Party or Trotskyist Left Opposition) or the example provided by Japan.

While most of the developments outlined above were not uncommon in other colonies in Asia, certain factors helped to make the Vietnamese colonial experience unique. First of all, the French were dealing with people who had seen themselves as part of a national entity long before the Western idea of a nation–state was introduced. There was much less room for the French to manoeuvre than if no majority nationality existed, or if the ethnic Vietnamese had been fragmented into small principalities. The French did indeed divide Vietnam into three parts. However, no one ever was able to parlay that into strong regional loyalties. By the same token, even small gestures of political liberalisation by the French were taken by many Vietnamese to mean that national independence was not far away. Each time those hopes were dashed, communication became more difficult, the opportunities for compromise more remote.

The Vietnamese possessed a national identity in large part because

of a two-millenia history of both conflict and accommodation with
the Chinese. This set them apart from the rest of South and Southeast Asia. It also bothered the French, who worried about any
renewal of Chinese interest in Vietnam, and who felt uneasy when
elite Vietnamese refused to be content with Aristotle, Voltaire
or Henri Bergson, but insisted on retaining expert knowledge of
Chinese philosophy as well. Finally, this unique historical relationship with China insured that the Vietnamese would be acutely
aware of contemporary events in East Asia, especially as war and
revolution spread during the 1930s.

More than any other Western power, France wished not only to
obtain commercial and strategic advantages from its colonies, but
to accomplish a 'civilising mission', to transform the way of thinking
of its subjects. In Vietnam, this urge had been evident from the
seventeenth century, when French Catholic priests (together with
Portuguese and Spanish clergymen) managed to convert several
hundred thousand people. The French government as well as the
French clergy retained a special interest in Vietnam because of that
minority. When Napoleon III sent troops to invade Vietnam in
1858, not the least of his motives was to protect Vietnamese Catholics from persecution. His influential wife, the Empress Eugénie,
fully expected that the Church would be as successful in Vietnam
as it had been in the Philippines. Although Catholics never came to
total more than 10 per cent of the Vietnamese population, they
were still extremely important to the French. In the early years
they provided the bulk of collaborators, a fact that anticolonial
Vietnamese never forgot. As late as the 1920s Catholics held considerably more than 10 per cent of indigenous administrative positions. Conservative Catholic priests were the first to raise a hue
and cry over 'Bolshevism', indeed before most Vietnamese had
the slightest idea what they were talking about. By the 1930s,
however, some Catholic intellectuals were deeply ashamed of
their past and anxious to gain acceptance from the non-Catholic
majority.

Meanwhile, French 'civilising' ideology had been rendered far
more complex by the ascendency in the métropole of anticlerical
political parties. Catholic priests continued to press for mass conversions after the fall of Napoleon III in 1870, but they received
no support from most colonial administrators. Instead, the Third
Republic began to evolve a hybrid message for the colonised peoples,
combining faith in French idealism, admiration for its contributions

to 'world culture' and respect for its military prowess as demonstrated by Napoleon Bonaparte and recent 'pacification' experts. For decades some officials and pedagogues fully expected that all Vietnamese would learn the French language. Even in the 1920s it was assumed that the Vietnamese elite would want always to use French as its first language, despite the fact that Vietnam already possessed a rich oral and literary tradition. Indeed, at that moment the elite was experimenting eagerly with the replacement of both Chinese and French by a romanised script (invented by the missionaries) that greatly simplified the problem of mass education.[12]

Traditional Vietnamese reverence for learning combined with French cultural pride to produce the Vietnamese intelligentsia. Emerging from French and Franco-Vietnamese schools in the 1920s, these young men and women took their own 'civilising mission' very seriously. With French agreement if possible, against the French if necessary, they would create a vibrant, strong and independent Vietnam. Although coming largely from bourgeois, petit bourgeois and small landlord families, the Vietnamese intelligentsia was in a sense outside the social structure, defined more by its propensity to analyse, argue, publish, exhort and demonstrate than to defend specific class interests. Its seminal political experiences included the failure of a Socialist governor-general, Alexandre Varenne, to institute fundamental reforms in 1925, the widespread student strikes of 1926-7, and the sweeping colonial repression of 1929-31 (see illustration, p. 159). Henceforth it took on specifically Marxist coloration, although other doctrines were not excluded. By 1937 the intelligentsia probably numbered 10,000 individuals, with a growing minority coming from subsistence farmer and proletarian backgrounds. Literacy had increased substantially in the previous decade, so that perhaps 1.8 million people, or at least 10 per cent of the population, could read Vietnamese newspapers, pamphlets and leaflets.[13] While this was still very low by contemporary European standards, it was probably high when compared with most colonised societies. It was certainly sufficient to provide a foundation for subsequent mass literacy campaigns in Vietnam.

THE POPULAR FRONT PERIOD

In May 1936 the French Left scored a spectacular election victory. The Socialist Party displaced the Radicals from their traditional position as the strongest party in the Chamber of Deputies; the

Communists became for the first time a major force in French electoral politics. Leon Blum took over as prime minister and a fellow Socialist, Marius Moutet, was designated minister of colonies.

In Indochina, French administrators, bankers and plantation managers shuddered at the thought of the Socialists implementing a policy leading to democratic self-government. The Vietnamese bourgeoisie was nonplussed, being eager to receive self-governing responsibilities, but extremely anxious that the French maintain order and not allow the initiative to be seized by radical elements. The Vietnamese intelligentsia was ecstatic, seeing an unprecedented opportunity to conduct politics openly and to press for sweeping changes. Workers now expected to obtain the right to form unions and bargain collectively. Peasants looked to a sharp reduction in rents and interest rates.

Aware of Socialist promises to canvass colonial grievances and aspirations, a group of southern Vietnamese intelligentsia conceived the idea of an Indochina Congress, which would encourage people to make their feelings known, organise sentiments in written fashion, ascertain priorities and begin the dialogue with representatives of the Blum government. Beyond that clearly was the intention that the Indochina Congress would evolve into a 'national' representative assembly. At the heart of this project was Nguyen An Ninh, supported by a unique coalition of Communists and Trotskyists, and with the cautious endorsement of one faction of the Constitutionalist Party. Nguyen An Ninh was the Vietnamese intelligentsia in its ideal type, son of a prominent scholar-businessman, graduate of a Paris law school, biting essayist and consummate public speaker. Equally at home in a newspaper room debating Marx versus Nietzsche or in a peasant hut discussing taxes, Buddhism and popular medical remedies, he had already been jailed twice, and would be jailed twice again before dying of illness on the prison isle of Con Son in 1943. Although taking a political line increasingly akin to that of the Indochinese Communist Party, he never accepted party discipline and enjoyed the respect of many Trotskyists and Constitutionalists.

Respect was one thing, political solidarity something else. As the Indochina Congress movement gathered momentum in August 1936 it quickly became evident that different participants had different objectives. Trotskyists were most interested in forming local 'action committees' which would serve as the basis for a general strike and possible armed insurrection if the Blum government reneged. Communists were equally involved with the action committees (which soon came to total 600 throughout Saigon and the Mekong delta), but current Comintern policy ruled out any violent challenge to French rule, above all a Popular Front government. Bourgeois participants generally opposed the action committees, preferring that grievances be channelled through 'recognised' leaders such as landlords, village notables and factory managers. In September, Governor-General René Robin prohibited the organisation of local committees in Tonkin or Annam; this was a signal too for some Constitutionalists to break with the Congress movement in Cochinchina.

The Blum cabinet, preoccupied by continuing domestic social and economic problems, not to mention the growing threat from Germany and Italy, was not inclined to make precipitous changes in the colonies. Marius Moutet's first concern was to re-evaluate the function of each overseas possession vis-à-vis the French economy. More precisely, the Socialists, now that they were in power, dropped talk of dominion status in favour of ascertaining how the colonies could help France pull out of the Depression. French policy debate on Indochina thus centred on whether to permit increased local industrialisation.[14] Moutet also declared his intention to establish a parliamentary commission of inquiry, patterned on the 1927-8 British Simon Commission to India. In the meantime, however, he secretly instructed Governor-General Robin to prevent any large Indochina Congress assembly in Saigon.

Robin, a professional colonial administrator infamous among Vietnamese for having directed part of the brutal repression of 1930-1, took the liberty of exceeding his instructions. He banned public meetings in general, instructed Congress organisers to submit grievance lists and ordered local committees to cease activities forthwith. When these orders were ignored, Nguyen An Ninh and a number of other leaders were jailed. District and village officials began to harass committees in the countryside. In imitation of Mohandas Gandhi, Nguyen An Ninh and two fellow internees responded with a hunger strike which generated tremendous public sympathy and sent reverberations as far as Paris. Released after eleven days of fasting, yet observing no other signs of government repentance, the three heroes encouraged their followers to continue a series of strikes begun a few days earlier.[15]

By the end of 1936 the battle lines were drawn. The French Popular Front government was prepared to bestow certain reforms at a pace set by itself, but would not see them extracted by Vietnamese intellectuals, workers and peasants employing modern techniques of political struggle. Unwilling to wait, and increasingly suspicious of Moutet and his colonial advisors, Vietnamese leftists decided that only well-organised strikes, mass meetings and demonstrations could convey their message effectively. The first test of strength came in early 1937 with the arrival of a Popular Front minister, Justin Godart, and the new governor- general, Jules Brévié. Despite police harassment, tens of thousands of citizens were mobilised to 'greet' these officials at each city on their tour. Participants yelled slogans in unison and held banners demanding higher pay, better working conditions, reduced land rents, an amnesty for all political prisoners and promulgation of a general bill of rights. French officials were duly impressed, especially by the careful planning and discipline as compared with the upheavals of 1930-1. Instead of causing a speed-up in the timetable of reforms, however, such signs of political sophistication convinced Brévié to look for conservative Vietnamese who might provide an alternative to the Marxists.

Blum's domestic political coalition came unstuck soon after, forcing his resignation in June 1937. The two ministries which succeeded the Blum government still gave lip service to the Popular Front (see illustration, p. 160), but by April 1938, when Edouard Daladier assumed leadership, it had no practical meaning. The commission of inquiry, on which so many Vietnamese hopes had centred, never came to Indochina and was quietly disbanded in July 1938. Governor-General Brévié remained on until August 1939, implementing some significant economic programmes (hydraulic construction, new industries, improved tariff formulas, limited tax relief for the poor). He also released the majority of political prisoners. None the less, the political climate became ever more tense. From mid-1937 Vietnamese Trotskyists condemned the entire popular-front concept as an imperialist and Stalinist plot to deceive the working class. In the April 1939 elections to the Cochinchina Colonial Council, a limited franchise advisory body, the Trotskyist slate managed to trounce both the Constitutionalists and the Communists.

Vietnamese Communists had to work hard from mid-1937 to

avoid being tagged French government apologists. According to the strategy enunciated at the Seventh Comintern Congress in 1935, struggles for national liberation and land redistribution were to be deferred in the interests of building a broad united front for 'democracy' and against 'fascism'. This was not impossible in Vietnam, providing that 'democracy' included substantial French concessions on civil rights and political representation. Without those concessions, however, ICP identification with the French Popular Front was damaging on both patriotic and social revolutionary grounds. Realising the danger, Vietnamese Communists took the offensive, thrusting the glowing rhetoric of French Popular Front politicians in the faces of colonial administrators, *colons* and native landlords alike. The favourite political medium continued to be local grievance lists, which served simultaneously as platforms and public accusations. Although each list was different, most demanded that metropolitan labour laws should be applied in Indochina, that the head tax and salt and liquor monopolies should be eliminated, that the sale of opium should be banned, that land rents should be reduced and corvée terminated, that tariffs should be readjusted to the advantage of the colony and that privileges granted to the Bank of Indochina should be removed.[16] During this period ICP intellectuals also prepared detailed studies of current social and economic problems, which were used both as a means of public education and as the basis for challenging government policies. Thus, Truong Chinh and Vo Nguyen Giap, two young Communists of many talents, analysed the increasingly desperate position of the majority of Vietnamese peasants.[17]

Together with sixteen other prominent Hanoi intellectuals, Truong Chinh and Vo Nguyen Giap spearheaded a remarkably successful united front campaign in northern and north-central Vietnam. As in Saigon it was pointedly called the Indochina Democratic Front, and the hub was an editorial office, from which poured French and Vietnamese language newspapers, books, pamphlets and leaflets. Beyond that office existed a bewildering number of affiliates. Thus, one organisation developed hundreds of private literacy classes, another tried to provide free professional services for the poor, still another agitated for an end to censorship. As Japanese troops marched across China in late 1937 and 1938, the Democratic Front joined with overseas Chinese organisations to raise funds, to demonstrate and to warn of the growing threat to Indochina. Meanwhile, separate semi-legal ICP networks operated among workers and peasants, assisting them to convene meetings, to express grievances publicly and to form 'mutual-aid associations' (unions remained illegal outside of Cochinchina). By 1938 it was not uncommon to see peasant spokesmen addressing working-class and intelligentsia audiences, not always the reverse as had been the case.

The ICP-led Democratic Front was more effective in the north partly because there were very few Trotskyists to worry about, partly because the bourgeoisie was much smaller and lacked a political party such as the Constitutionalists in the south. Nevertheless, not all was smooth sailing. Front participants continued to be threatened, beaten up, detained, fined heavily or imprisoned. Operations were particularly difficult in the countryside, where peasants remained vulnerable to harassment from village notables or landlords. On the other end of the Front, bourgeois members were lured by local members of the French Socialist Party or by self-styled liberals within the colonial administration. The ICP responded by infiltrating several of its members into the Hanoi branch of the Socialist Party, one of whom, Phan Thanh, proved extraordinarily successful in publicly criticising the French authorities for failing to institute reforms.

On May Day 1938 in Hanoi the Democratic Front proved its capacity to mobilise the masses. An estimated 20,000 people marched in twenty-five functional divisions, from factory workers to rickshaw pullers, from peasants to petty merchants. Even the barbers, leatherworkers, laundrymen and unemployed were grouped together under symbols. The tricolour and the red flag were displayed side by side, and the crowd sang both the 'Marseillaise' and the 'Internationale'. Slogans ranged from demanding universal education to reducing inflation. At the market place where marchers converged to listen to speeches hung a huge banner on which were written the words 'Rice, Peace, Liberty'.[18] One year later the colonial police were under instructions to prevent any repetition. As it happened, however, the sudden death from anthrax of Phan Thanh led thousands of people to ignore warnings and to participate in a combined May Day celebration and funeral procession.

Ironically, the last such public demonstration under French rule commemorated Bastille Day 1939, the 150th anniversary of the French Revolution. On the broad Boulevard Norodom in the heart of Saigon, the colonial authorities had organised a splendid military parade. Simultaneously the Democratic Front organised several thousand people to march behind the military units, yelling for an amnesty for political prisoners (Nguyen An Ninh and associates had been arrested once again), freedom to organise unions (withdrawn again), sweeping tax reforms and an effective defence of Indochina against Japan.[19] Within eight weeks of that Bastille Day, most Democratic Front leaders were in jail or frantically trying to evade capture.

THE JAPANESE INTERVENE

From the Marco Polo Bridge incident in July 1937 that precipitated full-scale Sino-Japanese hostilities, both French and Vietnamese observers were acutely aware that events to the north had a direct bearing on the future of Indochina. Indeed, every few months Tokyo made the point explicit by sending formal protests against shipments of military supplies through Haiphong to Kuomintang armies in southern China. By 1939 the Japanese were in a position to punctuate their protests with air raids on the French-owned Yunnan railway.

Georges Mandel, who replaced Marius Moutet as minister of colonies in 1938, devised a plan for strengthening Indochina's capacity to resist the Japanese. Among other things it involved creation of a specifically Indochinese army, commanded by French officers but otherwise composed of volunteers and conscripts from the local population. As a result, non-commissioned officer schools greatly increased indigenous enrolments. Wealthy Vietnamese families were assured that the officer ranks as well would soon be open to their sons. As had been the case during the First World War, French officials suggested that those natives who demonstrated loyalty in time of greatest need would be duly rewarded once peace was restored. On the assumption that Indochina might become isolated from the métropole, new attention was given to local industry and to expanding regional trade. To pay for expansion of the armed forces, not to mention a local aeroplane factory, arsenal and blast furnace, the government authorised a defence loan of 400 million francs. To cover the interest on the loan, Indochinese taxes on imports, exports and consumer goods were increased.

Mandel's defence plan proved extremely controversial. Conservative elements in Paris favoured accommodation with Tokyo, not confrontation. Their counterparts in Indochina were too busy making money from the trade with Kuomintang China to agree. On the other hand, most *colons* vigorously opposed the Indochinese army concept, fearing that it might be used by the natives to threaten French rule. They preferred massive reinforcements from home. After the September 1939 outbreak of war in Europe reinforcements were out of the question; indeed, people in France clamoured for troops, supplies and money to be sent in the opposite direction. In July 1940 the Indochinese authorities went hat in hand to Washington, hoping for fighter planes and anti-aircraft guns. However, the Roosevelt administration denied the request as the impending battle for Britain was considered far more deserving of military aid than a group of French colonialists who had already recognised the Vichy government.

The defence issue also split the Vietnamese bourgeoisie. Some responded eagerly to the Mandel plan, subscribing to the defence loan, participating in new industrial ventures, even sending their sons to military academies for the first time. Others were more cautious, recalling how many French promises made during the previous world war had failed to materialise in peacetime. One particularly vocal group suggested an immediate return to the letter of the 1884 Treaty which had established the French protectorate over Annam and Tonkin. This would have meant restoring a number of powers to Bao Dai and the royal mandarinate, an idea repugnant to both *colons* and Vietnamese radicals. Still other members of the bourgeoisie, sensing that whatever its intentions France could not protect Indochina from the Japanese, looked increasingly to the latter as potential benefactors. By 1939, if not earlier, they had established covert links with Japanese agents and were exchanging messages with Prince Cuong De, a pretender to the Vietnamese throne long resident in Japan.

The Vietnamese Left divided no less sharply. Trotskyists condemned the entire anti-fascist alliance, believing that it played into the hands of the imperialists and undermined the chances for worldwide proletarian revolution. Citing Lenin's stance in the First World War, they called on Vietnamese youths to avoid conscription and encouraged citizens not to pay any defence levies. Trotskyists ridiculed military preparations, predicting that French and Japanese imperialists would instead find a way to share the spoils in Indochina. Their prediction came true, but not before the French had rounded up most Trotskyist leaders and thrown them in jail.

The ICP was placed in an embarrassing position by the Mandel plan. On the one hand it supported serious French efforts to defend the colony against Japanese attack. On the other hand it could not condone a rise in regressive taxes, nor did it like the idea of a bigger standing army. The possibility of a bourgeois Vietnamese officer corps was chilling. It resolved its dilemma by demanding that the French arm a substantial portion of the native population, cancel plans to manufacture aircraft or other sophisticated weapons and be prepared to emulate the Chinese by waging unconventional warfare. If there had to be a new tax, then the target should be the profits of the monopoly capitalists, not the meagre incomes of ordinary Indochinese. Finally, ICP writers stressed that colonised peoples had very little motivation to fight the Japanese unless the French demonstrated good faith by accepting some of the Democratic Front reform proposals. There is no record that Paris ever considered these ICP demands seriously.

Realising the probable futility of ever convincing the French, ICP leaders went ahead to develop their own plans for armed struggle in the event of Japanese attack. As might be expected, they drew inspiration from the anti- Japanese united front in China, especially operations of the Red Army led by Chu Teh. Rather surprisingly, colonial censors allowed Vietnamese Communists to publish extensive reports on Chinese guerrilla warfare, as well as political statements by Mao Tse-tung. Vo Nguyen Giap and others explained such concepts as 'total mass mobilisation', 'protracted resistance' and 'national salvation associations'.[20] A series of informative letters from China, probably written by Ho Chi Minh, were published in Hanoi in early 1939.[21] Such widespread media discussion of the Chinese precedent proved invaluable to the ICP, paving the way for formation of the Viet Minh in 1941. After September 1939, of course, the French banned all ICP publications. Indeed, until 1944 colonial security was so tight that even clandestine written communication between ICP units was tenuous. This meant that ICP leaders often had to depend on cadres having read the pre-war essays, in which case oral transmission of simple instructions such as 'total mass mobilisation' might serve as the basis for unified action.

The Mandel plan had been only partially implemented when it was put to the test in mid-1940. On 19 June, the day after the French government accepted defeat at the hands of the German Army and asked Hitler for an armistice, the Japanese handed an ultimatum to Indochina's Governor-General Georges Catroux, demanding that he admit a sizeable military mission to 'supervise' suspension of all aid to China. Catroux reluctantly agreed, and ironically was sacked by the new collaborator Pétain government in France as a result. After the Japanese presented new demands, his successor, Jean Decoux, seriously considered armed resistance. What led him to back away, other than the knowledge that chances of victory were slim, was a growing conviction that the Japanese would countenance a *modus vivendi* preserving some degree of French authority in Indochina. Following numerous military feints and intense diplomatic bargaining, an agreement was finally signed on 22 September 1940, whereby the Japanese recognised French (Vichy) sovereignty in exchange for the right to station up to 25,000 troops in Tonkin and complete renegotiation of economic relations.

A few hours after signature of the agreement in Hanoi, Japanese forces in south China launched attacks from land, sea and air. Particularly notable were the ground assaults on important French positions in the vicinity of Lang Son, which caused heavy French casualties and forced capitulation of several units. To this day it remains unclear whether the Japanese negotiating team in Hanoi was a party to this attack, whether there was a temporary breakdown in radio communications or whether rightwing officers in south China tried to force a different solution. Whatever the cause, the effect was to convince almost all French military officers that armed resistance was futile. Shortly thereafter, Thailand also decided to capitalise on French weakness, seeking to occupy several provinces in Cambodia ceded at the turn of the century. Outraged, the French managed to counterattack successfully by sea and air, whereupon the Japanese government stepped in and 'mediated' an agreement in Bangkok's favour. Deeply embittered, the French in Indochina tried to make domestic life as normal as possible, which included not only immaculate linen suits, aperitifs and discussion of the latest latex figures, but also making absolutely certain that the natives knew their place.

Although Germany's quick, crushing defeat of France surprised

Vietnamese of all political tendencies, most were quick to make adjustments. Longtime collaborators became more circumspect, less willing to exhibit unqualified loyalty. Pro-Japanese groups became quite excited, fully expecting the French to be expelled and some form of self-government permitted within the Greater East Asia Co-prosperity Sphere. The ICP, in accordance with the Comintern line promulgated following Stalin's pact with Hitler in August 1939, took a plague-on-both-your-houses position remarkably akin to that of the Trotskyists earlier. However, it did anticipate that the Soviet Union would be attacked by one or more major powers, thus causing further dramatic realignments. It also continued to prepare for an armed uprising against whatever imperialist(s) controlled Indochina.

The sheer complexity of affairs was nowhere more evident than in the rough limestone hills west of Lang Son following the Japanese attack on 22 September. In the panic of defeat hundreds of native colonial soldiers dropped their rifles or were disarmed by local tribespeople, some of whom immediately began to shoot at French Legionnaires and artillerymen stumbling towards the delta. Meanwhile, a unit of several thousand Vietnamese recently armed and trained by Japanese officers in south China eagerly awaited orders to sweep across the frontier. Instead, they were informed of the Japanese agreement with Governor-General Decoux and instructed to withdraw. One Vietnamese unit obeyed, but another crossed into Lang Son province and began to assault colonial personnel and installations. Local ICP cadres, observing how eager everyone was to hit the French, whatever the odds, joined the movement and broadened it to include the establishment of people's courts, village revolutionary committees and armed propaganda teams. Collaborators were executed and the property of 'reactionaries' seized and distributed to victims of French terror.

Once military officials in Hanoi had sorted out the 'misunderstanding', the Japanese permitted the French to reoccupy Lang Son province. They did this with particular brutality, perhaps in compensation for the Japanese-inflicted defeat. Skirmishes continued to the end of 1940, but the outcome was obvious by November. Several leaders were captured and executed, about 1000 resisters fled towards Kuomintang-held territory in China, and the others dispersed to the nearby forests. Within a year some of the latter survivors would regroup under ICP auspices and become the first unit of the Vietnam Army for National Salvation.[22]

In late November 1940 an even larger upheaval occurred in Cochinchina, precipitated by Governor-General Decoux's order to mobilise troops for the counterattack on Thailand. During the previous ten months the ICP's Southern Region Committee had made some preparations for an uprising, relying particularly on discontent arising from wartime economic dislocations and troop conscriptions. A representative was despatched to faraway Bac Ninh province, adjacent to Hanoi, to convince the Central Committee to order a nationwide uprising. The proposal was rejected as premature. Meanwhile, however, Vietnamese colonial soldiers from several garrisons in Cochinchina appear to have successfully pressed the Southern Region Committee to order an uprising before their units were sent to Cambodia. Forewarned by about twelve hours, the French ordered a curfew, confined a number of suspect military units to quarters without weapons, closed all schools and began to pick up alleged ringleaders.

Because word had already been passed, however, the uprising went ahead on 23 November. It involved tens of thousands of peasants, tenants and agricultural labourers as well as a smattering of soldiers and workers. Police posts and district officers were attacked, roads torn up, collaborators punished, revolutionary committees formed and the red flag with yellow star flown for the first time. French military units were desperately indiscriminate in their counterattacks, employing aircraft, armoured units and artillery to destroy whole villages. Thousands of people were killed and up to 8000 detained. More than a hundred ICP cadres were executed. Unlike their comrades in the mountains along the Sino-Vietnamese frontier, who recovered from defeat within a year, ICP survivors in Cochinchina would not be able to pull themselves together and begin to influence events again until early 1945.

Assessing all these developments in early 1941, ICP Central Committee members realised once again that it was not enough to respond to popular pressures or to take advantage of immediate tactical opportunities. The results could still be disastrous. To break out of the vicious circle of colonial oppression, local anti-colonial initiatives and effective colonial counteractions required methodical planning, organising, training, proselytising, testing and revision. On the other hand, given problems of command and communication, it was quite impractical to expect to control the rhythm of diverse local preparations from a central headquarters. The objective, therefore, was to combine broad political discipline with local spontaneity. Holding people back became as crucial as urging them forward. Beyond that, it was essential to predict strategic trends in the World War with sufficient accuracy so as to modulate strategy inside Vietnam, and to be able to select the most opportune moment for a general uprising. Fortunately for the ICP it had in Ho Chi Minh a leader uniquely qualified to assess the direction and pace of international events.

NON-COMMUNIST ALTERNATIVES

The ICP was by no means the only Vietnamese group intent on taking advantage of new historical circumstances. Mention has already been made of those Vietnamese who served as auxiliaries for the Japanese in south China, only to see their hopes dashed in later 1940. That component which straggled into Kuomintang-held territory was permitted to join several hundred adherents of the Vietnam Nationalist Party in preparing for a possible Chinese offensive into Tonkin. Although such an attack was seriously considered several times during the war, it would not be until after the Japanese surrender that Chinese troops actually marched on Hanoi. In the meantime, Nationalist Party and other associates of the Kuomintang failed to build an underground network inside Vietnam, which left the field to rivals.

In 1938 and 1939, as the French government hardened its colonial policy and the Japanese army came closer to Indochina, a number of Vietnamese intellectuals met secretly in Hanoi to formulate a strategy that was militantly anti-colonial but also anti-revolutionary. Most participants were the sons of mandarins, big landowners and professionals. Although Western-educated, they felt that French rule had produced only moral decay, cultural chaos and social disorder. While they did not see themselves as pro-Japanese, they were of the opinion that only Japan among Asian nations had demonstrated the capacity to face up to modern threats, regain order and strengthen 'Eastern' values. Their specific objective was to create a relatively small, tight-knit, clandestine apparatus that could step into power at the right moment. Unlike the Communists, they believed that it was undesirable to excite the peasants to revolutionary action. If large numbers of people were needed at a particular time, then it was best to recruit them through established patron–client networks. In this way one could be certain that the mass who understood only the need for more food or better health care would follow the few who understood high politics. Ironically these several score intellectuals could not agree on a single set of leaders, so that by 1941 three or four such organisations were functioning in and near Hanoi.

In late 1941 the French police uncovered one Hanoi organisation, the Greater Vietnam Legitimate People's Party. Dozens of arrests were made and the Japanese Kenpeitai (Military Security Agency), which had previously given the group quiet encouragement, did not intervene. The party chairman, Nguyen Tuong Tam, a well-known novelist, fled to China to join those Vietnamese who awaited a Kuomintang offensive. In 1943, after the French had made further arrests among other groups, the Kenpeitai put a number of Vietnamese intellectuals under its protection, in some cases sending them as far away as Taiwan, Singapore or Bangkok. Although the Vietnamese involved were not happy to be removed from the scene at such a critical juncture in their nation's history, they were not of a mind to flee to the countryside and seek sanctuary with ordinary peasants.

Meanwhile, two non-communist movements of much more substantial character were underway in southern Vietnam. The Cao Dai Church, founded in 1925 by retired colonial functionaries and wealthy landowners, was continuing to attract many thousands of less fortunate people with its spirit mediums, elaborate hierarchy and colourful ritual. Drawing from Christian as well as Confucian, Buddhist and Taoist precedents, Cao Dai leaders promised to restore morality on earth and harmony in the universe. Although the French were pleased to see a conservative alternative to ICP and Trotskyist groups in Cochinchina, they were not amused to discover that some Cao Dai leaders had established contact with Japanese agents and pledged themselves to Prince Cuong De, the royal pretender. In August 1940 the French raided the largest Cao Dai temple in Tay Ninh province. The next year they arrested the Cao Dai Pope, Pham Cong Tac, and deported him to Madagascar. After that incident, however, the Japanese began to provide protection to Cao Dai leaders who were prepared to provide them with regular intelligence reports and to recruit and supervise labourers for

Japanese military installations. In 1944 the Japanese were persuaded to give basic military training to 3000 Cao Dai shipyard workers in Saigon. Each time the French protested to the Japanese they were assured that no Vietnamese paramilitary units would be armed except in the event of Allied invasion.

In 1939 yet another religious sect blossomed in western Cochinchina, centred on Huynh Phu So, the frail, haunted son of the head of Hoa Hao village in Chau Doc province. In one sense Huynh Phu So was simply another Buddhist mystic in a region long known for its prophets, magicians and faith healers. Because of fortuitous timing, however, he quickly became leader of the Hoa Hao movement, encompassing several hundred thousand people. Previously the colonial authorities would have been able to halt such a mass movement in its tracks. Indeed, the colonial police did detain Huynh Phu So in a psychiatric ward in August 1940, after he predicted the imminent humbling of the French by the Japanese. When his disciples continued to convert whole villages in the lower Mekong delta, the French made plans to banish Huynh Phu So to Laos. At this point the Japanese 'liberated' Huynh Phu So and placed him in a Kenpeitai building in Saigon, from where he disseminated prophesies of damnation for non-believers and independence for Vietnam.

Despite risk of offending the French, some Vietnamese landlords soon converted to the Hoa Hao faith. Undoubtedly there was a sincere religious component to these conversions, as it was quite common for wealthy, Western-trained Vietnamese, feeling that something deep and meaningful was missing from their lives, to patronise traditional adepts. None the less, it is hardly coincidental that western Cochinchina represented the most extreme case of colonial latifundia in Indochina, and that part of Huynh Phu So's message to his followers was Buddhist compassion, brotherhood and non-violence. During the Popular Front period landowners had been outraged by the increasing tendency among tenants to break contracts. Outrage turned to fear on the occasion of the November 1940 uprising, when poor rural participants declared their intent to abolish all debts, redistribute land and place all 'agents' of the French on trial. Realising that the fortunes of war and international politics might make it impossible for the French to crush the next such uprising so successfully, some southern Vietnamese landlords saw the Hoa Hao movement as the answer to their prayers, hopefully inducing tenant followers to eschew class confrontation. Several landlord converts soon became close advisers to Huynh Phu So and were seen to represent him in meetings with other religious and political organisations.

By 1943 military reverses in the Pacific led the Japanese to revise policy in relation to local independence movements. As encouragement to collaborate more energetically, political promises were stated more explicitly and selected indigenous organisations were given increased administrative responsibility. In Indochina, however, Japan was constrained by its agreement with the French. For example, it seems that the French successfully prevented the Japanese from recruiting Indochinese to work or fight in other parts of Southeast Asia. Also, local government personnel within Indochina remained under firm French control. Any Japanese promises of political rewards for their Indochinese followers had to be made privately, and were subject to formal disavowal by Japanese Foreign Ministry representatives in Saigon and Hanoi.

The delicacy of this relationship became evident following Japanese-sponsored revival and expansion in May 1943 of Prince Cuong De's organisation, the Vietnam Restoration League. Although Cuong De himself was kept safely in Japan, some of his associates who had obeyed orders in September 1940 and retreated to Kwangsi were now slipped past the French and given Kenpeitai protection. Restoration League leadership was broadened to include Greater Vietnam Party representatives from Tonkin and Cao Dai and Hoa Hao religious dignitaries from Cochinchina. Some longstanding members of the Constitutionalist Party, now bravely styling themselves the Vietnam Independence Party, also affiliated with the Restoration League. As rumours spread of Japan's intention to permit formation of a Vietnamese 'provisional government', the League's prestige soared accordingly. However, the French decided to call the Japanese bluff, swooping down on League hideouts and arresting anyone within reach. The Kenpeitai provided safe haven to individuals who evaded French arrest, but nothing more. When on 5 November 1943 Prime Minister Tojo Hideki convened a Greater East Asia Assembly in Tokyo, to include a number of eminent Southeast Asian personalities, there was no mention of Indochina in general or Vietnam in particular. The Restoration League, perhaps the closest thing to a national non-communist organisation that would ever exist in Vietnam, had lost its historical opportunity.

In late 1944, with the Vichy regime in France dismantled, American troops invading the Philippines, and Franco-Japanese relations increasingly tense in Indochina, another flurry of rumours spread of imminent self-rule for Vietnam. Ngo Dinh Diem, former court mandarin and a member of the country's leading Catholic family, was brought from Hue to Saigon by the Japanese for consultations. The immediate crisis passed, however, when Governor-General Decoux was able to restrain French subordinates working for the Gaullist cause, and Ambassador Matsumoto Shunichi was able to convince Tokyo that drastic action was unnecessary. Several months later Tokyo would listen instead to its military commander in Indochina, with very different results.

THE EFFECTS OF THE WAR IN INDOCHINA

Governor-General Decoux's single objective was to maintain the French colonial presence in Indochina pending the outcome of the global war. He was prepared to concede the Japanese anything if French administrative control was not jeopardised in the process. Realising that such concessions did have something of a corrosive effect on French power, however, Decoux tried to compensate in other directions. Essentially he gambled for time – and lost.

Nowhere was Decoux more vulnerable than in economic affairs. German occupation of France in June 1940 had led the British navy to terminate commerce between Indochina and the métropole. From May 1941 Indochina's trade was reoriented entirely towards Japan. Further, Decoux had already been forced to allocate a portion of local revenue to support Japanese forces in Indochina. Following Hitler's attack on the Soviet Union in June 1941, the Japanese government demanded and received permission to move its air, sea and ground units southward to Cochinchina. This helped to precipitate the Western economic embargo of Japan, which in turn led Tokyo to decide on a full-scale Pacific war. The French were spared this holocaust, merely being ordered on 9 December 1941 to make available to the Japanese facilities 'necessary to pursuit of the war'.[23] As time went by, this clause was applied ever more extensively by the Japanese.

Japan's demand for Indochina's rice, corn, jute and vegetable oils was limited only by the availability of transport. Japan sent very few products in exchange, however, so that a large Indochina credit soon accrued in Tokyo banks, and the Indochinese economy began to suffer from lack of machinery, spare parts, chemicals and consumer goods normally imported from France. Perhaps the single most disruptive wartime practice was to force Vietnamese peasants to shift some of their arable land to the cultivation of industrial crops. This was especially risky in northern and north-central Vietnam, where a permanent grain deficit already existed, and where the margin of error for most peasant families was paper thin.

Inevitable wartime inflation was made far worse by the French practice of cranking out ever larger quantities of paper money, so that they could be sure of paying the salaries of French residents, native soldiers and functionaries, and so that they could meet the monthly bill for maintaining Japanese troops in Indochina. Eventually farmers were ordered to sell half of their rice crop to the government at artificially low prices, a policy which led some landlords to push tenants off the land so that it could be left fallow, while some middle and poor peasants tried merely to grow enough for their own families and then concentrate on hiding it from the authorities.

Beginning in 1943 American submarines torpedoed Indochina coastal shipping and mined the approaches to harbours. Bombers stationed in Yunnan destroyed a number of industries in Tonkin. From mid-1944 longer range aircraft wrecked roads and railroads along the central coast. In early 1945 American carrier-based aircraft increase the threat, making it almost impossible to transport rice northward by ship or rail. Neither the French nor the Japanese were willing to risk military trucks for civilian purposes. The French did try to recruit private truckers, but the pay was far too low for the dangers involved.[24] As rice piled up in Cochinchina the French ordered the construction of new silos. When these proved inadequate thousands of tons of rice began to spoil and eventually were burned.

Meanwhile, in Tonkin and northern Annam in late 1944, rainstorms had helped to cut the autumn rice harvest to well below the margin of survival. Subsidiary supplies of corn, sweet potatoes and beans were already extremely low because of compulsory crop shifting. To make matters worse, the Japanese now refused to purchase the resulting industrial crops because nothing could be shipped to the home islands. During the first months of 1945 hundreds of thousands of Vietnamese villagers wandered the northern countryside or drifted into the cities, hoping to scavenge or beg some food. Others sat at home quietly awaiting their fate. Although it will never be known how many died, subsequent estimates suggested between one and two million people.[25] What especially angered those who survived was knowledge that the Japanese continued to fuel their vehicles from alcohol made from grain, and continued to seize and store rice in anticipation of future military needs. A minority of Vietnamese families were also known to be eating well from accumulated stocks. In addition, there were persistent reports of speculators hiding grain in expectation of further price rises. The Communist-led Viet Minh not only helped to publicise such information but also encouraged citizens to storm government and landlord granaries. From March 1945 the Viet Minh was in a position to assist some villagers in making these attacks.

Prior to the fall of the Vichy regime in France in mid-1944, Governor-General Decoux had attempted to offset the reality of collaboration with the Japanese by promulgating a curious brand of Indochinese nationalism. Marshal Pétain became something of a Confucian father-figure, his picture being hung everywhere, his epigrams on patriotism, family loyalty and hard work cited constantly. Under the friendly guidance of the French, each ethnic group of Indochina was expected to develop its unique characteristics to the utmost. The symbol of Vietnamese identity clearly was meant to be 'Emperor' Bao Dai, to whom Decoux showed appropriate deference. More Vietnamese were allowed to enter the middle and upper echelons of colonial administration. Pay and allowance differentials between French and non-French government employees were reduced substantially. The first batch of Vietnamese military officers was selected and trained. University and vocational school enrolments increased sharply. Vietnamese primary-school enrolments jumped 57 per cent between 1939 and 1944. The fact that Decoux was paying for these improvements with new paper money only began to dawn on Vietnamese as inflation got out of hand in 1944.

Decoux's most novel experiment was to permit at least 100,000 young Vietnamese men and women to join with several thousand French youths in mass calisthenics, track and field meets, swimming competitions, soccer matches, scout jamborees and long hikes through the countryside. Designed in the first instance to offset the example of Japanese warriors swaggering around Indochina and to divert young people from direct political action, Decoux did not object when participants gave the movement an increasingly Vietnamese patriotic slant, complete with visits to important historical monuments, composition of heroic marching songs and promotion of the idea that only determined minds and healthy bodies could produce a strong and independent Vietnam. As long as French military officers, police inspectors and civil administrators were intimately involved, Decoux felt it possible to control what was in any event a largely urban movement.

THE FRENCH DEPOSED

At 7.00 p.m. on 9 March 1945, Ambassador Matsumoto delivered an ultimatum to Governor-General Decoux, ordering that all French armed forces, transport facilities and war materials were to be placed immediately under Japanese control. Anticipating a negative or non-committal response, the Japanese Army was already poised to attack. Decoux, still hopeful that French authority could be sustained, even if in the most adumbrated form, summoned his staff to discuss delaying tactics, whereupon the Japanese detained them all and proceeded to mount a classic *coup de force*. Within twenty-four hours the Japanese had broken French resistance and were busy organising internments. A few isolated French garrisons decided to fight longer and were given no quarter. One unit of several thousand soldiers made a desperate retreat to Yunnan, where it was promptly disarmed by the Chinese.

While the Japanese high command in Tokyo had been considering such a move ever since the collapse of the Vichy government in August 1944, it was the threat of American amphibious forces moving beyond the Philippines to land in Indochina that finally tipped its hand. Well informed of Gaullist organising efforts among Decoux's subordinates, the Japanese had no desire to be attacked from front and rear simultaneously. Ironically, only three weeks later the Japanese coup was rendered unnecessary, American forces invading Okinawa far to the northeast, thus by-passing Indochina and all other Japanese positions to the southwest.

What had been done in Vietnam could not be undone, however. The Japanese had already authorised Bao Dai to abrogate the protectorate treaty of 1884 and to proclaim the independence of his kingdom. Bao Dai's French-approved cabinet, led by Pham Quynh, duly resigned on 19 March. The Japanese coup was a signal too for diverse Vietnamese organisations to try to gain the political initiative. Large 'independence' meetings were held in Saigon, Hanoi and Hue under the watchful eyes of the Kenpeitai. Anti-French feelings ran high, to the point where the Japanese found it impossible to guarantee the safety of French technicians who had been permitted to continue working after the coup. Inflation, famine, psychological strain and political anticipation combined to make the atmosphere electric.

In April Bao Dai was provided with a new cabinet, headed by Tran Trong Kim, a retired primary school inspector and historian flown back from Bangkok by the Japanese. Most of Tran Trong Kim's ministers were teachers, lawyers and physicians. Notable by his absence was Ngo Dinh Diem, who may have disapproved of the Japanese decision not to replace Bao Dai with Prince Cuong De, or perhaps anticipated the slim prospect of overcoming critical problems of the day. As it was, the Japanese retained direct control over matters of defence, internal security, foreign affairs and communications. Only in July did they relinquish control of the cities of Hanoi, Haiphong and Da Nang. And it was not until 14 August the day before the Japanese lost all authority by virtue of unconditional surrender, that the government's jurisdiction over Cochinchina was recognised. In the meantime, the Tran Trong Kim cabinet had managed to issue a number of edicts condemning corruption, reducing taxes, loosening censorship, introducing the Vietnamese language to the civil bureaucracy and substituting its own political symbols for those of the French colonial period. It also persuaded the Japanese to moderate rice confiscations and to allow selected Vietnamese youth organisations to assume informal police roles. However, it could not prevent the Japanese from printing millions of new paper *piastres*, nor could it convince them to divert military transport or fuel to help feed starving civilians.

Meanwhile, a great deal was happening beyond either Japanese or royal Vietnamese direction. In March, ordinary people were awed that the French colonialists, after eighty years of superiority, could be reduced to prisoners in a mere twenty-four hours. Initially the Japanese and their Vietnamese associates benefited from this feeling. By June, however, as it became apparent that neither authority was resolving Vietnam's dire economic and social problems, the mood shifted to one of spontaneous self-assertion, to over-coming obstacles through direct action. In the cities youth organisa-tions previously under French supervision stepped forth to help allocate scarce resources, prevent pillaging, organise public works projects and exhort everyone to patriotic sacrifice. Sensing that the Japanese were rapidly losing the war, meetings were held to debate the character of a truly independent Vietnam.

In the countryside, which lacked either a French-controlled security apparatus or a Japanese substitute, landlords and peasants alike began to realise that social relationships could be dramatically altered. Some villages became the scene of intense debates over con-tracts, social welfare and local security. Others saw poor peasants simply seizing rice from wealthier neighbours. Although there still existed local police and civil guard units, few intervened vigor-ously. Stripped of their French commanders, only tenuously con-nected to new Japanese or royal government superiors, unsure of the future, most Vietnamese security forces preferred to avoid commitment.

THE VIET MINH

On 6 June 1941, Ho Chi Minh sent an emotional 'Letter from Abroad' to his countrymen, urging them to recognise the importance of recent international events and prepare to seize Vietnamese independence. Metropolitan France, defeated by Germany the previous year, was incapable of assisting the colonialists in Indochina. Japan, bogged down in China and 'hampered' by the British and Americans, was in Ho Chi Minh's opinion unable to crush a resolute national liberation movement in Vietnam. Ho asked everyone to hark back to their bronze-age forebears, to emulate the thirteenth-century defeat of the Mongols and to recall those many Vietnamese who had already sacrificed their lives fighting the French. Borrow-ing rhetoric from the current anti-Japanese struggle in China, he requested each person to contribute whatever he had most of, whether it be money, physical strength or talent.[26] There was in his 'Letter' not a hint of class struggle, and no mention of pro-letarian internationalism.

To implement this appeal, Ho Chi Minh and the ICP Central Committee had the previous month designed a strategy of united front 'from below', in which each social class and interest group would be represented by a national salvation association, and each association guided from within by clandestine Communist Party members. Within a particular village the various salvation associations (peasants, youth, women, elders, etc.) would elect representatives to a joint committee. Those committees would send representatives to a district committee, and so on, gradually forming a parallel administration that would challenge and eventually replace the colonial system. Meanwhile, ICP leaders would also try to work out a united front 'from above' with other organisations which had either declared themselves against the Vichy French and Japanese already, or which might be convinced to take that position. The name for this entire structure was to be the Vietnam Independence League, or Viet Minh in abbreviated Vietnamese.

In June 1941 all of this organising was merely a gleam in the eye of a few Vietnamese Communists. For the next three years, the few thousand souls who did join the Viet Minh were subject to constant colonial harassment, unable to defend securely the two areas in Cao Bang and Lang Son selected as liberation zones, experiencing extreme difficulty communicating with small units in more distant provinces. By the summer of 1944, however, they could compare themselves favourably with their predecessors of 1930–1 and 1940, having not only built but somehow sustained under fire a rudimentary revolutionary apparatus. Elated, the ICP Central Committee prepared to order a three-province armed uprising. It was dissuaded at the last moment by Ho Chi Minh, who had just recrossed the Sino–Vietnamese frontier after being a prisoner of the Kuomintang for twenty-two months. Convinced from conversations with his captors that both Germany and Japan were going to be defeated in the not-too-distant future, Ho Chi Minh wanted more time to prepare for a much more favourable opportunity.

Five months later the Japanese *coup de force* on 9 March 1945 appeared to some Vietnamese Communists the proper historical context for an uprising. Ho Chi Minh was once again in China, this time successfully convincing the Americans to work with the Viet Minh. The ICP Central Committee pointedly rejected the idea of an immediate uprising, instead keying all subsequent action to either an Allied invasion of Indochina or a general Japanese surrender. In either case, the Central Committee emphasised, it was essential that the Viet Minh was the prime force co-operating with the Allies, and that Viet Minh representatives should be able to greet Allied units as they entered each town and village. The Central Committee looked beyond the coup, beyond whatever indigenous administrative apparatus the Japanese would permit, to the creation of more armed propaganda teams, the introduction of basic Viet Minh symbols (flag, songs, slogans) throughout the country and confrontation with the enemy at his moment of greatest weakness.

Between March and early July, Liberation Army units made life increasingly difficult for Japanese patrols in the six hill provinces north of Hanoi. Eventually the Japanese consolidated to several defensive positions, which left local Vietnamese government officials and militia units feeling very exposed. After a few officials were killed by the Viet Minh, the remainder either agreed to co-operate or fled the region. Militiamen occasionally joined the Viet Minh or turned over their weapons in exchange for safe passage home. By the end of July the Viet Minh could boast a six-province liberation zone, a provisional capital at Tan Trao (Tuyen Quang province), five fledgling government ministries, and a central training academy for military and political cadres. ICP members released or recently escaped from jail re-established contact. Viet Minh committees began to blossom throughout the Red River delta and in several provinces of central Vietnam. Word of rural Viet Minh successes spread to the cities, leading young people in particular to seek out representatives of the various clandestine national salvation organisations. In only a few weeks the public image of the Viet Minh changed dramatically, from that of a distant band of poorly equipped anti-colonials tilting at windmills to a nationwide movement capable of seizing and defending true independence for Vietnam. While the latter feat had yet to be proven, the popular wish helped to father the deed.

On 15 August 1945 Communist cadres in the outskirts of Hanoi listened to Allied radios report the unconditional surrender of Japan and Allied plans to send Chinese Kuomintang and British troops into Indochina to disarm the enemy. Following the strategic guidelines disseminated in March, the ICP's Northern Region Committee decided to seize power in Hanoi without waiting for instructions from Tan Trao. Since the closest Liberation Army units were still at least 100 km from the city, and since very few local Viet Minh participants possessed firearms, it was decided to organise mass demonstrations which could then be transformed into revolutionary assault forces. Before encouraging people to take to the streets, however, the Northern Region Committee needed to ascertain Japanese intentions. Two days later it had reason to believe that the Japanese would not respond violently, providing their personnel and installations were not threatened. Further, the Viceroy of Tonkin, Phan Ke Toai, indicated his willingness to co-operate with the Viet Minh. Instructions thus went out to convene a mass rally on 19 August that would be converted into a general uprising.

The morning of 19 August saw tens of thousands of peasants surging into Hanoi, many armed with machetes, knives or bamboo spears. After the rally, Viet Minh squads led crowds to occupy a number of key buildings. Although there were several tense confrontations with Japanese troops and Vietnamese militia, bloodshed was averted by referring problems to higher echelons for negotiated settlement. In the process Viet Minh leaders apparently convinced the Japanese general staff of their capacity to maintain public order. This informal channel of communication was also employed to help terminate or avoid combat between Japanese and Viet Minh units in more distant locations. Having occupied the Viceroy's office, Northern Region Committee members used his telephone network to order provinical administrators to surrender to local Viet Minh representatives. In scores of district and provincial seats during the next ten days crowds marched on government offices, detained mandarins, ransacked files, hung Viet Minh flags, talked incessantly, collected whatever firearms were available and organised revolutionary committees. Although there was almost no resistance and very little bloodshed overall, some particularly well-known mandarins or landlords were summarily executed, including Pham Quynh and the elder brother of Ngo Dinh Diem.

On 23 August an estimated 100,000 peasants marched into the royal capital of Hue, seized government buildings without opposition and cheered urban Viet Minh intellectuals as they announced yet another liberation committee. At that point Bao Dai declared his readiness to abdicate, whereupon three ranking Viet Minh leaders drove hastily from Hanoi to receive the royal regalia in a public ceremony on 30 August.[27] A thousand years of Vietnamese monarchism was at an end.

News of Bao Dai's intention to abdicate had reached Saigon quickly by telegraph, causing consternation and confusion among leaders of the Restoration League, who had Japanese approval to take power in the name of the Vietnamese monarch. Already Communist Party leaders had convinced the largest Saigon paramilitary organisation, the Vanguard Youth, to join them in forming a Southern Region Provisional Administrative Committee to meet the Allies. The fear of being labelled enemy collaborators now caused the Restoration League to defer to the Communists and Vanguard Youth, who proceeded on 25 August to occupy key buildings and to organise a large rally in the name of the Viet Minh.

The first two Allied representatives to appear in Vietnam were Major Archimedes Patti of the US Office of Strategic Services (OSS) and Jean Sainteny of the Free French government. Although both flew to Hanoi airport on the same plane on 22 August, each was treated very differently. As the man charged with preparing for the arrival of the Allied surrender commission, Patti received every possible assistance from the Japanese and Viet Minh alike. Patti attended Viet Minh ceremonies and allowed himself to be photographed in what appeared to be official conversations with Viet Minh leaders, a precedent that was continued by his commanding officer, General Philip Gallagher, upon arrival in Hanoi several weeks later. On the other hand, Sainteny, having no status with the surrender commission, was politely detained by the Japanese and made the object of public protests by the Viet Minh.

THE DEMOCRATIC REPUBLIC OF VIETNAM

Ho Chi Minh reached Hanoi from Tan Trao on 26 August; the first Liberation Army units marched in five days later. Amidst huge celebrations the Democratic Republic of Vietnam (DRV) was proclaimed on 2 September, seven days before Chinese troops arrived in Hanoi and ten days before British troops made it to Saigon. In his Declaration on behalf of the fifteen-member provisional government, Ho Chi Minh began with quotes from the American Declaration of Independence and French Declaration on the Rights of Man. He ended by arguing that Vietnam was already independent by virtue of the French having fled and Japan having surrendered. If anyone tried to reverse that reality, Ho Chi Minh warned that 'the entire Vietnamese people are determined to mobilize all their physical and mental strength, to sacrifice their lives and property in order to safeguard their independence and freedom'.[28] That this was no idle boast became evident in following weeks, as even Vietnamese Catholic bishops, former mandarins, big landlords and entrepreneurs identified themselves with Ho Chi Minh's government. Although such a honeymoon could not last, it endured long enough to help spell the difference between victory and defeat.

Perhaps better than any other communist leader, Ho Chi Minh understood that the August 1945 Revolution was above all a giant outpouring of emotion and only secondarily a well-engineered seizure of power. Millions of Vietnamese wanted to consider the colonial period as a bad dream and to seek a glorious future. The problem, therefore, was to sustain emotion, retain faith and aim popular enthusiasm in directions of most value to the party and government. Henceforth Ho Chi Minh's most important role was that of national figure, the embodiment of people's will. Much of his time was spent meeting local delegations informally, visiting work sites, preparing radio talks and drafting pithy messages to different interest groups. During this period he came to rely increasingly on three lieutenants selected in 1941: Truong Chinh for Communist Party affairs; Pham Van Dong for government co-ordination; and Vo Nguyen Giap for military operations. Although there was never any doubt that Ho Chi Minh could override the wishes of subordinates, he generally held that power in reserve. This functional relationship was to continue unchanged for another decade at least.

Within days of the founding of the DRV, Ho Chi Minh initiated mass campaigns to vanquish three 'bandits' — foreign invaders, famine and ignorance. With countless volunteers for the armed forces, the main problem became one of gaining enough time to train and equip a wide range of units, from elite shock battalions to village self-defence platoons, from specialised services (communications, supply, transport, intelligence, security, medical, engineering) to independent guerrilla teams who depended more on guile, surprise and ingenuity than on technology. Beyond that, there was the realisation that Vietnam could not expect to win a classic military confrontation, so that all fighters would need to grasp some of the more subtle economic, political and diplomatic components of struggle. By December 1946, when full-scale war broke out, a great deal had been accomplished.

In late 1945 famine still stalked northern Vietnam. Early fighting in the south meant that no food relief could come from that direction. No foreign powers stepped forward to assist. Sparked by Ho Chi Minh's slogan that 'an inch of earth is worth an ounce of gold', people planted seeds everywhere, without reference to land ownership. Top priority was given to dry crops such as sweet potatoes, corn, manioc and soya beans. Urban citizens were called out to repair the dikes alongside their rural cousins. By March 1946 it was clear that no one was going to die of starvation that year, although undernourishment was still common.

Between September 1945 and December 1946 the DRV's Department of Mass Education reported 95,665 voluntary instructors as having taught 2,520,678 people to read and write. Although it is impossible to verify such figures, there can be no doubting that one characteristic of newly independent Vietnam was the barefooted peasant walking to evening classes, tiny oil lamp in one hand, battered literacy primer in the other. Classes were held in village communal houses, pagodas, private homes, shops and offices. For those who could not or would not attend evening sessions, special classes were organised at the marketplace, in the rice fields, aboard fishing boats. 'We must be literate to emerge victorious in the Resistance' became a national slogan.[29] Eventually this movement had important social consequences, as it meant that poor peasants could carry out many of the tasks previously monopolised by wealthier individuals trained in colonial schools.

Second only to such mass mobilisation programmes were issues of foreign policy. It was here that people's trust in Ho Chi Minh and the new government was put to the ultimate test, as there was no way they could comprehend the complex diplomatic manoeuvres that occurred during the period from September 1945 to September 1946. The most serious problem until February 1946 was the presence of up to 100,000 Chinese troops in northern and north-central Vietnam. Not only did ordinary Chinese soldiers live entirely off the fruits of Vietnamese labour, but Kuomintang generals concocted the most brazen schemes to manipulate currency exchanges, black-market operations and private-property transactions to their own advantage. For the ICP, one positive effect of this Chinese pillaging was to weaken greatly the political potential of the Vietnam Nationalist Party, whose leaders had arrived along with the Kuomintang generals. On the other hand, it was important that the DRV authorities did not allow popular anger to result in attacks on Chinese personnel, which might have been sufficient grounds for a Chinese *coup de force*. Ho Chi Minh also tried to ensure that the Chinese did not reverse policy and for suitable rewards invite the French to return to the north.

The British needed no rewards to help the French back to southern and south-central Vietnam. On 12 September 1945 a company of French paratroopers accompanied the first battalion of British troops flown into Saigon. Ten days later, General Douglas Gracey, commander of Allied forces taking the Japanese surrender south of the sixteenth parallel, authorised the re-arming of French military units interned in March. From that point on a bloody confrontation was inevitable. DRV capacity to deal with this crisis was significantly reduced by the relative weakness of the Communist Party in the south and its need to rely almost entirely on a united front 'from above' with the Cao Dai and Hoa Hao religious organisations. As a combination of Gurkha, French and Japanese troops forced the Vietnamese anti-colonials out of Saigon in early October, the united front crumbled quickly, and it was not long before some leaders of the Cao Dai and Hoa Hao were responding to French overtures to collaborate in fighting the DRV.

Diplomatic activity reached a climax in February 1946. The Chinese Nationalist government in Chungking, although a public advocate of Vietnamese independence, was quite prepared to make a deal with the French if the price was right. On 28 February it agreed to withdraw Chinese troops in exchange for France relinquishing all territorial and concession rights extracted from China in the nineteenth century, providing a free port and customs-free transit for Chinese goods moving through Tonkin, and granting special status for Chinese nationals residing in Indochina. While some Kuomintang generals in Hanoi wanted more, and managed to delay withdrawals until mid-June, French troops began landing at Haiphong on 8 March.

Aware from early January 1946 that Sino–French negotiations were in process, Ho Chi Minh realised that if he did not reach some diplomatic understanding with Paris before French troops moved to replace Chinese troops, then full-scale war was inevitable. Although the Vietnamese populace was psychologically primed for war, Ho Chi Minh also knew that the Communist Party, the army and the government needed more time to organise an effective resistance. By means of extended discussions with Jean Sainteny it became clear that the DRV's main, perhaps sole diplomatic card was the French desire to return to Tonkin minus the bitter confrontation and continuing guerrilla combat that characterised their return to Cochinchina. In mid-February Ho Chi Minh made a concrete proposal which became the basis for the 6 March Franco-Vietnamese Preliminary Convention. In exchange for receiving 'amicably' 15,000 French troops, the DRV gained formal recognition as a 'free state having its own government, parliament, army and finances, and forming part of the Indochinese Federation and the French Union'. The unification of Cochinchina with the rest of the country was to be the object of a popular referendum, the results of which the French government agreed to accept.[30]

For a brief moment it appeared that both governments had overcome history, surmounted opposition within their own ranks and made the key concessions that could produce a long-term, peaceful relationship. The Preliminary Convention seemed to represent French acceptance of Vietnam's independence and Vietnamese acceptance of a close post-colonial association with France. Eight days later, however, everything began to come unstuck. Marius Moutet, back again as minister for colonies (now renamed 'overseas territories'), declared in Paris that Cochinchina was to be treated as a *separate* 'free state' within the Indochinese Federation, an interpretation totally unacceptable to the DRV. As for the status of the DRV itself, it soon became evident that whereas the Vietnamese considered 'free state' to mean the development of a special relationship by mutual consent, the French saw it as ruling Vietnam with native support. Subsequent diplomatic encounters at Dalat and Fontainebleau failed to resolve these fundamental differences.

As the months went by, both sides conducted affairs increasingly on the assumption that war was likely. By late 1946 the DRV probably had 100,000 men and women under arms, compared to a mere 2000–3000 fourteen months earlier. The point of no return came on 23 November, when a dispute over customs controls in Haiphong harbour escalated to include a French naval bombardment of the city that killed at least 6000 people. Four weeks later the DRV ordered a nationwide counterattack. Within months French forces had seized almost all of Vietnam's cities and towns, but were experiencing difficulty pacifying the villages or penetrating the forests. This remained the basic military situation until early 1954, when the French made the mistake of committing 16,000 troops to a distant valley bearing the name of Dien Bien Phu. In an unprecedented logistical manoeuvre, Vo Nguyen Giap shifted sufficient soldiers, artillery, anti-aircraft guns, food and ammunition 220 km across the mountains of northern Vietnam to isolate and eventually force the surrender of the entire French garrison on 7 May.

Dien Bien Phu finally brought home to the French public the fact that something important had changed in Indochina since 1940. In June 1954, Pierre Mendes–France started his term as prime minister with the promise to resign if a general ceasefire was not obtained by 20 July. On that date in Geneva an Agreement on the Cessation of Hostilities was indeed signed, by which terms the French withdrew their military forces south of the seventeenth parallel and the Vietnamese withdrew north of that line. This was followed the next day by a Final Declaration, in which the United Kingdom, the Soviet Union and China joined the two antagonists in affirming the ceasefire and promising nationwide elections two years hence. Ominously, the United States declared itself dissatisfied with both documents and issued a unilateral declaration, which became the basis for its political and military support of the State of Vietnam, headquartered in Saigon.

The State of Vietnam was a composite of those former colonial officials, landlords, entrepreneurs and intellectuals who had either opposed the DRV from the start in Cochinchina, or who had backed away from participation in Tonkin and Annam between 1946 and 1949. It had been established in June 1949 after prolonged discussions between the French and Bao Dai, who had parted company with the DRV in March 1946. Although on paper Bao Dai received all that Ho Chi Minh had asked for in 1946, in reality his government was still under French protection. Only in 1953–4, as the United States began to assist Bao Dai's armed forces directly, rather than via the French, did he gain some leverage. As it turned out, however, the United States preferred an alternative Vietnamese leader, Ngo Dinh Diem, who moved audaciously to quell first the Bao Dai loyalists, then the Cao Dai and Hoa Hao religious sects and finally the Communist Party south of the seventeenth parallel. With American blessing Ngo Dinh Diem had himself declared President of the Republic of Vietnam in October 1955 and proceeded to ignore the provision for nationwide elections in 1956. The stage was thus set for the Second Indochina War.

As DRV soldiers returned unobtrusively to Hanoi in late 1954, the job of constructing a new society and economy was begun. Eight years of war had decimated an entire generation. During that time too the entire world had become polarised into communist and anti-communist camps. From 1950 the United States had bankrolled the French war effort, while the newly victorious People's Republic of China had provided considerable assistance to DRV forces. Although the DRV in 1954 made serious overtures to France for post-colonial economic relations, it was inevitable in the context of the Cold War that such initiatives would fail, and that Vietnam north of the seventeenth parallel would come to depend heavily on the Soviet Union amd China for development. Meanwhile, beginning in 1953 in the liberated zones, and covering all low-land provinces by 1956, the DRV implemented a policy of land confiscation and redistribution that eliminated landlords as a social class. This in turn cleared the way for formation of agricultural co-operatives in 1958-9. By 1960 the Party Central Committee was of the opinion that affairs were in sufficient order in the DRV to resume efforts to liberate south and south-central Vietnam, thus reunifying the country. Few could have imagined that this would take another fifteen years, and leave a legacy of death and destruction far greater than the previous struggle against the French.

NOTES

1. Ngo Vinh Long, 'Peasant Revolutionary Struggles in Vietnam in the 1930s', PhD thesis (Harvard University, 1978) pp. 13-19, 75-7, 81-3.

2. *Ibid.*, pp. 19-72, 77-9, 83-93. Milton Osborne, 'Continuity and Motivation in the Vietnamese Revolution: New Light from the 1930s,' *Pacific Affairs* (Spring 1974) pp. 37-55.

3. Quoted in W. Robert Moore, 'Along the Old Mandarin Road of Indo-China', *The National Geographic Magazine* (Aug. 1931) p. 177.

4. Daniel Hémery, 'Aux origines des guerres d'indèpendance vietnamiennes: pouvoir colonial et phénomène communiste en Indochine avant la Second Guerre mondiale', *Mouvement social*, 101 (October–December 1977), pp. 4-20.

5. David G. Marr, *Vietnamese Anticolonialism, 1885-1925* (Berkeley: University of California Press, 1971) pp. 7-76.

6. Henri Simoni, *Le Role du Capital dans la Mise en Valeur de l'Indochine* (Paris: Helms Librairie, 1929) pp. 43-5.

7. Pierre Brocheux, 'Crise économique et société en Indochine française', *Revue française d'histoire d'outre-mer*, nos. 232-3 (1976), pp. 655-67.

8. Thomas Schweitzer, 'The French Colonialist Lobby in the 1930s: The Economic Foundations of Imperialism', PhD thesis (University of Wisconsin, 1971) p. 458. André Laurent, *La Banque de l'Indochine et la Piastre* (Paris: Deux Rives, 1954) pp. 35-9.

9. These and subsequent figures are derived from the 1937 census, the first time that reasonably accurate data was obtained and compiled. Charles Robequain, *The Economic Development of French Indo-China* (London: Oxford University Press, 1944) pp. 21–49.

10. Pierre Gourou, *L'Utilisation du sol en Indochine* (Paris: Centre d'Etudes de Politique Etrangère, 1940) pp. 229, 255, 272–3, 282.

11. Ngo Vinh Long, 'Peasant Revolutionary Struggles,' pp. 99–350.

12. John de Francis, *Colonialism and Language Policy in Vietnam* (The Hague: Mouton, 1977).

13. This figure is based on a study of both publishing statistics and school enrolments. For a revealing discussion of the latter, see Gail P. Kelly, 'Franco-Vietnamese Schools, 1918–1938', PhD thesis (University of Wisconsin, 1974).

14. Hémery, 'Aux origines', pp. 22–7.

15. Daniel Hémery, *Revolutionnaires vietnamiens et pouvoir colonial en Indochine* (Paris: Maspero, 1975) pp. 281–332.

16. Tran Huy Lieu *et al, Cach Mang Can Dai Viet Nam* [Vietnam's Modern Revolution], vol. 7 (Hanoi: Van Su Dia, 1956) pp. 62–103.

17. Truong Chinh and Vo Nguyen Giap, *The Peasant Question*, trans. Christine P. White (Ithaca: Cornell SE Asia Program, 1974).

18. Tran Huy Lieu *et al.*, pp. 125–7.

19. Tran Huy Lieu *et al.*, pp. 134–6

20. *Dan Chung* (Saigon), 10–21 Sept. 1938. *Tin Tuc* (Hanoi), 13 July 1938, 14 Aug. 1938, 27 Aug. 1938. Van Dinh (Vo Nguyen Giap), *Muon Hieu Ro Tinh Hinh Quan Su o Tau* [Understanding Clearly the Military Situation in China] (Hanoi: Dan Chung, 1939).

21. See letters signed 'P.C. Lin' in various issues of *Notre Voix* (Hanoi) Jan–Feb. 1939.

22. Chu Van Tan, *Reminiscences on the Army for National Salvation*, trans. Mai Elliott (Ithaca: Cornell SE Asia Program, 1974).

23. André Gaudel, *L' Indochine francaise en face du Japon* (Paris: Susse, 1947) pp. 199–208.

24. *Thanh Nghi* (Hanoi), 5 May 1945.

25. Jean Decoux, *A la barre de l' Indochine* (Paris: Librairie Plon, 1952) p. 267. Tran Huy Lieu *et al.,* vol. 9, pp. 82–6.

26. Ho Chi Minh, *Selected Writings* (Hanoi: Foreign Languages Publishing House, 1977) pp. 44–6.

27. Allan W. Cameron (ed.), *Viet-Nam Crisis: A Documentary History*, vol. 1 (Ithaca: Cornell University Press, 1971) pp. 49–50, contains a translation of Bao Dai's abdication rescript.

28. *Ibid.*, pp. 52–4.

29. Vu Huy Phuc, in *Nghien Cuu Lich Su* (Hanoi) no. 30 (Sept. 1961), pp. 33–42.

30. Cameron (ed.), *Viet-Nam Crisis*, pp. 77–9.

Malaya:
Illustrations

'All the other people have made preparations. Only the Malays wait for their destiny.' As a storm in world affairs gathers, other peoples on the way to shelter have put up their national umbrellas. Only the Malays are unprotected.

Hiboran, 15 September 1947.

'Malay huts and foreign-owned buildings. It is very clear what the position of the Malay people in their own land is.' Malays express increasing resentment at the economic control of non-Malays.

Kenchana, 1 November 1947.

COMING IN TO PORT ?

The Alliance Party, the product of co-operation between Malays and Chinese, used a boat as its symbol. Tunku Abdul Rahman, the Malay, and Sir Cheng Lock Tan, the Chinese leader, steer the boat towards independence.

Straits Times, 21 January 1956.

Glossary for Chapter 5

AMCJA	All-Malaya Council of Joint Action.
API	*Angkatan Pemuda Insaf*, youth wing of MNP.
CIAM	Central Indian Association in Malaya.
hartal	Closure of shops and businesses as a protest, a technique derived from India.
IMP	Independence of Malaya Party.
INA	Indian National Army.
KMM	Kesatuan Malayu Muda, radical nationalist group founded 1938.
kangany	A recruiter of estate labour.
Kaum Muda	Islamic reformist group founded in 1920s.
KRIS	Kesatuan Rakyat Indonesian Semenanjung, radical nationalist organisation set up in 1945.
MCA	Malayan Chinese Association.
MCP	Malayan Communist Party.
MDU	Malayan Democratic Union.
MIC	Malayan Indian Congress.
MNP	Malay Nationalist Party.
MPAJA	Malayan Peoples' Anti-Japanese Army.
Merdeka	Independence.
Mentri Besar	Chief minister.
PAP	People's Action Party of Singapore.
PETA	*Pembela Tanah Air*, auxiliary defence force set up by Japanese.
Putera	Pusat Tenaga Rakyat, 'centre of people's strength'.
UMNO	United Malay National Organisation

5 Malaya: New State and Old Elites

Lee Kam Hing

MEETING AT BALING

On the morning of 28 December 1955, a delegation, escorted by forty armed men and led by Chin Peng, the secretary-general of the Malayan Communist Party (MCP), emerged from the jungle into a clearing near the town of Baling in northern Malaya for a dramatic meeting with the country's newly elected chief minister, Tunku Abdul Rahman. Since the start of the MCP's guerrilla war against British rule in June 1948, this was the first time government officials and communists had met. But more important, the meeting at Baling symbolised two different strategies in the quest for political change in Malaya. On one side were the communists: advocates of armed expulsion of the British and of revolution; on the other, the Tunku and his Alliance party: men aiming for constitutional progress towards independence and gradual change thereafter.

The talks, for which secret negotiations had been going on since October, were an attempt to end the Emergency, as the war against the MCP was euphemistically called. The war had affected the lives of everyone in the country in one way or another and had led the British to deploy thousands of Commonwealth troops and local police and home guards. Regular communist attacks on rubber estates, tin mines and railroads damaged the country's economy. Civilians suspected of working for the government against the MCP were murdered. The government responded with the tough Emergency Regulations which gave powers ranging from arrest and detention without trial to the relocation of thousands of people in new, fenced-up villages. During the Emergency, 34,000 people were detained, 15,000 deported and nearly 500,000 moved to the new villages. Areas of communist strength were declared 'black' and long curfews imposed. Checkpoints on all major roads kept watch on the movement of people, food and medicine. Troops rode as guards on passenger trains, while armoured cars patrolled the roads and surrounding jungles. However, communist attacks on civilians, police and military could not be completely prevented.

Senior British officials had strong reservations about the meeting at Baling. They feared that the inexperienced Tunku might not be firm enough with the hardened revolutionaries whom the authorities labelled bandits and terrorists. At a high-level meeting in Singapore on 19 October, the British argued that the communists were beaten and that the insurgency would end within a year, regardless of whether the MCP agreed to stop fighting and that any meeting should do no more than clarify the amnesty terms offered by the government.

The Tunku, however, viewed his role differently and emphasised that he and his party were the true custodians of the nation's honour: 'One thing I can assure those present is that I am not going to see Chin Peng merely to clarify to him the terms of the amnesty. My strength springs from my straightforward dealing and my sincerity, and I am not going to depart from this principle. Further I would never stand and be charged with being a running dog of the British'.[1] Partly to allay the anxiety of the British, the Tunku suggested the inclusion of David Marshall, chief minister of Singapore, and a successful lawyer, and Tan Cheng Lock, leader of the Malayan Chinese Association (MCA).

For the communists, the Baling talks offered the chance to nego- tiate a return to a legitimate political role. The party had suffered military reverses in the jungle and had not been able to win over a sufficiently large section of the population. It remained largely Chinese. With constitutional changes imminent, Chin Peng, Chen Tian, the party's propaganda chief, and Rashid Mydin, its highest- ranking Malay, hoped to reach some understanding with the Tunku. Harassed in the jungle by government troops, the party in 1955 found itself no closer to its objectives than in 1948.

For his part, the Tunku saw the talks as a chance to end the eight- year war that was costing the country nearly 200 million dollars and hundreds of lives a year. Perhaps more important, however, the Tunku hoped that he could emerge from the talks as the undisputed representative of the people's aspirations. He had already asserted that he would be no 'running dog' of the British. He now sought to show that he was not afraid to talk to the communists but that he could also stand up to them. If he persuaded them to end the fighting, well and good; if not, the MCP would then be shown to have no genuine desire for a peaceful solution. Finally, on the personal side, the Tunku was curious to meet the men who had taken to the jungle.

The Baling talks were cordial and lasted two days. Chin Peng saw little purpose in discussing ideological differences and accepted the Tunku's position as leader of a party that had just won the first national elections ever held. The Tunku sought to reinforce his standing as a nationalist leader with a national mandate: 'I did not come here as the spokesman for the British Government, neither am I the stooge or running dog of colonialism. I am the servant of the people and I represent the people who have elected me to power, and I do genuinely seek peace for this country'.[2]

Chin Peng appeared to accept this claim: 'First and foremost, I wish to say that it is precisely because we realize that you are not the spokesman of the British Government and are not the running dog of the British Government, the stooge of the British that we have come out to meet you at the risk of our lives'.[3]

The Tunku appealed to Chin Peng to accept the amnesty offer and join the fight for independence by constitutional means. Members of the MCP would be permitted to participate in politics or return to China. There were conditions, however. First, the communists would have to lay down their arms and be held in detention while they were investigated. Second, the MCP would not be recognised as a party. Chin Peng replied that such terms were tantamount to surrender: 'Such an investigation, no matter how it is explained, implies that we come out to surrender. ... If you demand our surrender we would prefer to fight to the last man'.[4] David Marshall reiterated the Tunku's argument that the elected leaders were the real custodians of national aspirations. Of the MCP, Marshall said: 'We understand that there are some genuine nationalists in the movement. I distinguish between nationalists and those who seek to make us a colony of a foreign ideology.' He continued: 'The welfare of the 7,000,000 [people in Malaya] must come first. Now that we have elected governments and we are on the verge of independence it cannot be said that your struggle is for independence'.[5]

When the Tunku and Marshall rejected Chin Peng's demand that the MCP be recognised and that there be 'no detention, no investigation and no restriction on movement',[6] the talks broke down. The MCP leaders returned to the jungle to continue their guerilla war, while the Tunku led an Alliance delegation to London and successfully negotiated independence from the British. The MCP's 'war of liberation' now challenged a popularly elected, independent government that proclaimed its dedication to building a modern state. By 1960, the communist threat had so petered out that the Tunku's government withdrew the Emergency. Two years later, Malaya together with Singapore and two Borneo territories (Sabah and Sarawak) formed the state of Malaysia, thus constitutionally phasing out a British presence in the area of more than 150 years.

BEGINNINGS OF POLITICAL ACTIVITY

Earlier in the twentieth century, British political control in Malaya had remained unthreatened, even as nationalist movements gathered strength elsewhere in Asia. This was not because of an absence of political consciousness, but rather because political activity had developed narrowly along communal lines and had identified with events and aspirations outside Malaya. Political activity was neither coherently nor specifically anti-British in character. Such a feature was a natural outcome of the compartmentalised development of the various races. Malaya consisted of an indigenous Malay population and two large immigrant minority groups who made up almost half of the population. The British encouraged the migration of the Chinese and Indians in the nineteenth century as cheap labour for the expanding tin and rubber industries. Differentiation in the economic roles of the various races was accentuated by varying educational experiences. British policy had been to permit the different races to be educated in their own vernacular languages while a minority gained access to English-language schools. Differences in educational background promoted separate political outlooks.[7]

The beginnings of political consciousness among the various communities were most evident from the 1920s. The immigrant community had by this time lost its transient character. This was particularly so with the Chinese and to an extent the Indians. With a settled immigrant population, new organisations arose which served as the forums for their grievances and aspirations. Firstly,

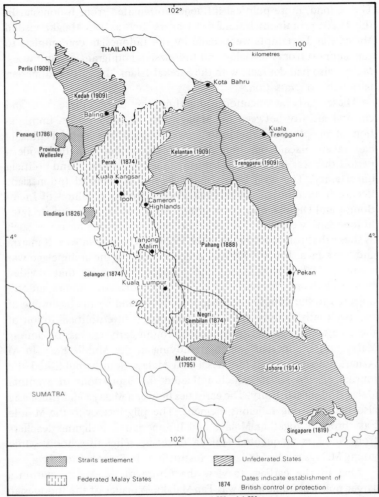

Malaya before the Second World War

fast-moving events elsewhere in Asia had an important bearing upon political thinking in Malaysia. For the Malays, the influence came from two directions. From the Middle East, came the inspiration for an Islamic reform movement. Known as the Kaum Muda group, it aimed at purifying the practice of Islam in Malaya. The new teachings were brought by students who had gone to the Middle East to study, as well as by religious teachers arriving from abroad.

The second, more political influence, originated from Indonesia. In the 1920s prominent Indonesian leaders such as Tan Malaka visited Malaya, and attempts were made by the Indonesian communists to gain support from the Malay and Indonesian immigrant communities. Malays also had contacts with the Sarekat Islam, the early Indonesian nationalist organisation.

These early connections underline the close ethnic ties and cultural affinity between the Malays and the Indonesians. Immigration of people from the Indonesian islands to the Malay Peninsula had taken place from time immemorial, although in the modern period this was most marked during times of economic and political uncertainty. The west coast of the Peninsula received Indonesians fleeing frum unrest such as took place after the rebellion of Imam Bonjol and Diponegoro. These groups served as refuge points to later Indonesians seeking to escape from Dutch repressive measures such as those that followed the abortive 1926–7 rebellion in west Sumatra and west Java. For the Malays and Indonesians, the archipelago was a single Malay world, and the political boundary that divided Indonesia from Malaya was of little importance. Some, indeed, objected to the imposed political separation, and by the beginning of the twentieth century there was talk of a future political union of the two territories. Such aspirations found early expression among Malay and Indonesian students studying in the Middle East. In Al Azhar, students from Indonesia and Malaya jointly published the journal *Seruan Azhar* which reflected the aspirations of eventual Malay–Indonesian unity. The early ties between Malaya and Indonesia also had a strong religious element. The pilgrimages to the Middle East brought together Malays and Indonesians.[8] Religious teachers from Sumatra frequented Malaya to set up religious schools, while young Malays studied in Islamic institutions in Sumatra and Java.

One of the earliest to view the future of the Malays within a larger political framework was Tan Malaka. A leader of the Indonesian Communist Party and a Comintern agent, Tan Malaka travelled to Malaya during the 1920s and made attempts to arouse a revolutionary consciousness among the Malays. He wrote that 'the weak Malay race has for long been divided by various robbers in this world'[9] and called for unity of all the Malay people living in the territories of Malaya, Indonesia, the Philippines and southern Thailand. But his efforts to gain support in Malaya failed. He wrote: 'In the Straits and the FMS [Federated Malay States] there is not a single daily newspaper which is read by the Malays. In short, if one expects a movement in the FMS, it will not be seen from the side of the Malays. It will certainly come from the Chinese and Klings [Indians], whatever the nature of the movement may be'.[10]

The Malay society which Tan Malaka encountered was essentially rural; its economy was largely subsistence and dependent on fishing and rice cultivation. Policies adopted by the British were designed to encourage the Malays to remain attached to the the land to ensure the production of food and insulate them from the vagaries of a modern economy. In these circumstances, the Malay in the village remained loyal to his chief and ruler. The Sultans' standing within Malay society had in fact been enhanced even as their actual power had been reduced by the British. Backed by the British, the rulers feared no political threat to their positions, and in matters of religion and Malay custom they were paramount. The British neutralised the class of powerful territorial chiefs by a policy of incorporation where possible and suppression when necessary. In 1902 the British further absorbed the Malay ruling class into the colonial administration by setting up the Malay College. Modelled on English public schools like Eton, the Malay College provided English education to young Malays from aristocratic families; it aimed at moulding them into English gentlemen. Through the Malay College, children of the Malay upper class were recruited into the colonial service. Thus in the midst of change, the fabric of Malay society remained intact in the twentieth century.[11] Tan Malaka's politics of revolution attracted little support in such an environment.

It was among the Chinese that Tan Malaka seemed most hopeful about support for the communist movement. By the 1920s the Chinese community had lost much of its transient character. The economic depression of the 1930s led to the introduction of ordinances restricting the free immigration of Chinese; many now stayed permanently. The sex ratio, which previously had been predominantly male, became more balanced. During this time, many Chinese in Malaya closely followed the political upheavals that took place in China. In China activists had long realised the financial contribution the overseas Chinese could make to political causes. Furthermore, Southeast Asia, and particularly Malaya, was convenient to Chinese activists seeking temporary refuge. In the revolution against the Manchus, men such as Sun Yat-sen and Kang Yu-wei spent brief periods in Malaya.[12]

The politics of the 1920s and 1930s in China, where the Kuomintang (KMT) and the communists fought each other, were soon reflected in Malaya. Both the pro-KMT and the communists competed for support in the local Chinese community, particularly in the trade unions and the Chinese schools. Students from the schools were the most susceptible to the influence of the China-oriented organisations whose appeal was basically Chinese nationalism. The marked anti-Western character of Chinese nationalism found a sympathetic response among the Chinese-educated in Malaya who themselves felt alienated from the colonial administration. Graduates from Chinese schools had few employment and higher educational opportunities. This dissatisfaction produced ready support for the China-oriented organisations. Later, much of this resentment was directed against the Japanese when the Sino–Japanese conflict began in 1937. Organisations aimed at arousing Chinese patriotism were set up to mobilise support for China, and in this effort, the pro-KMT and the communists were equally active.

Like the Chinese, the Indians had also been a transient population. Most of the Indians were Tamils who came as indentured labour and worked in depressed conditions with low wages on rubber estates. Other groups of Indians such as the Telugus, Malayalis, Tamils from Ceylon, Sikhs and other northern Indians subsequently followed. The later arrivals tended to be better educated and were employed by the British as clerks or lower level administrators. Others occupied professional positions or went into business. Within the Indian community there were therefore class and group cleavages, and political activities in the 1930s reflected these divisions. The professionals and the business group developed the Indian press and elitist associations. Most of these were concerned primarily with developments in India. In 1936 the Central Indian Association in Malaya (CIAM) was set up to bring together all the Indian groups in the country. The community had grown apprehensive at what it regarded as the pro-Malay policies of the British. There was also concern to improve the depressed conditions of the large Tamil labour class. The CIAM successfully petitioned the Indian National Congress and the Indian government against renewed recruitment of unskilled workers in India. With the labour supply thereby limited, the position of Indian workers in Malaya was greatly enhanced, especially their bargaining power for higher wages. But despite such activities, the CIAM was essentially elitist and had few links with the Tamil-speaking groups who made up the estate population.[13]

It was the kanganys (estate-labour recruiters) and Tamil school teachers who, because of the respected positions they held on estates, managed to reach the Tamils and establish themselves as their leaders. Frustrated by their low salaries, the kanganys and the teachers soon identified themselves with the dissatisfaction of the labour class. Encouraged by visits to Malaya of prominent Indian leaders, several associations, led and supported by Tamils, began to demand recognition of Indians' contribution to the country and call for equal treatment such as parity in wages. They backed their demands for improved conditions with strikes: in February 1941 on eight estates in Klang, and two months later by Indian miners in Batu Arang.

The political and economic activities of the non-Malays caused concern to the Malays, who observed with growing apprehension the increasing assertiveness of non-Malays in most major economic activities (see illustration, p. 209). The Malay community, on the other hand, remained largely a poor peasantry. The Chinese formed the majority of urban dwellers in 1921 in the FMS; Malays living in towns with more than 1000 inhabitants had declined to 5.8 per cent in that year.[14] Labour in the tin and rubber industries, as well as the railways, public works and telecommunications, was overwhelmingly non-Malay, and in commerce the presence of the Chinese was prominent. In education non-Malays benefited from the growth of government and Christian English-language schools in the towns. English-language education was a prerequisite to an administrative or professional career. In 1921 Malays represented only 6 per cent of the enrolment in all the English-language schools in the FMS. The non-Malays also possessed a system of vernacular education to teach their own languages. Furthermore, Malays benefited little from basic social and health services which were chiefly available in the urban areas. Indeed, infant mortality was highest among Malays. Thus resentment arose among the Malays and tended to be directed at non-Malays.

Malays of both radical and conservative persuasions were deeply disturbed by these developments. British policy was supposedly to protect the interest of the Malays, yet increasingly the actual situation suggested that it was the immigrant communities that benefited most. Immigration of non-Malays continued despite Malay protest and by the 1930s the Malays were already in a minority.

Only with the depression did the British end the unchecked flow of immigrants. Troubled by these trends and worried by non-Malay political activities, prominent Malays spoke up in the Federal Council. The first Malay organisations were formed at this time too. These were the Persatuan-persatuan Negeri, or Malay State Associations, set up largely by the English-educated Malays who were closely identified with the traditional ruling class. These early associations were parochially organised and state loyalties were paramount. The first was founded in 1926 in Singapore where the Malays had been exposed to more ideas and changes. It was followed by Malay associations in Malacca and Penang, but only in the 1930s were associations founded in other states. Basically loyal to the rulers and the British, they wanted no radical change, but were anxious that the position of English-educated Malays should be protected and the general interest of Malays promoted.[15]

A number of Malays, however, were critical of the conservative nature of the Malay associations. Led by Ibrahim Yaacob, they left the Malay associations in 1938 and set up instead the Kesatuan Malayu Muda. The KMM represented the more radical wing of Malay nationalism as well as the aspirations of the Malay-educated and lower socioeconomic groups. To Ibrahim Yaacob the KMM was to stand for young and new ideas, opposed to the old and anachronistic position of the traditional ruling class.[16] He placed much of the blame for the prevailing weaknesses of the Malays upon the traditional elite and suggested that the Malay associations, by their encouragement of state loyalties, had worsened divisions within Malay society. Ibrahim Yaacob advocated a broader Malay consciousness and urged Malays to transcend state loyalties. This consciousness should extend beyond the Malay Peninsula to encompass both Malaya and Indonesia. To him Melayu Raya (also known as Indonesia Raya) was based on common blood ties and was a concept supported by history. The realisation of Melayu Raya would prevent the Malays in Malaya from becoming a threatened minority.

Among those who played important roles in the KMM were students of the Sultan Idris Training College (SITC). In contrast to the Malay College, those who studied in the SITC were drawn from the poorer Malays of the rural areas. Coming from the villages, they experienced more of the poverty of their community. The SITC was set up in 1922 to train Malay-language school teachers. One early problem of the SITC was the shortage of reading materials in Malay and because of this Indonesian journals and pamphlets were imported. These were largely political in nature such as those of Sukarno's Partai Nasional Indonesia (PNI). Many in the SITC thus came to be influenced by the writings of Indonesian nationalists, and men like Ibrahim Yaacob were inspired by Sukarno and accepted the vocabulary and ideas of the PNI. They themselves began to write about the economic backwardness of the Malays, and while critical of the Malay ruling class, they attacked British colonialism for many of the problems of the community. These writings marked also an important phase in the development of Malay literature. As with Sukarno's PNI, Ibrahim Yaacob advocated non-co-operation with the authorities, and as a journalist expressed his anti-British sentiments in his writings. In November 1939 he took over the editorship of the *Majlis*, a Malay daily in Kuala Lumpur, but resigned at the end of 1940 when he was warned by the British for his polemical attacks. He then moved to Singapore.[17]

Thus what was marked in the pre-war period was that the political consciousness of the various races was governed largely by a concern for their own separate identities. Each communal group saw little in common with the others and each sought to protect its own economic and cultural interests.

Even the non-racial Malayan Communist Party (MCP) could not escape the communal factor. Largely because its beginnings were associated with politics in China, it had since become largely Chinese in Malaya. Formed in 1930 from the remnants of the Nanyang Communist Party, the MCP failed to get much support early on. It was further hampered by the frequent arrests of its leaders. The turning point came in 1937 when the outbreak of the Sino–Japanese war led to a resurgence of nationalism among overseas Chinese. This proved to be advantageous, and the MCP, because of the Communist–KMT united front in China, gained access to many non-communist Chinese organisations in Malaya. It managed in this way to direct some of the pro-China sentiments towards support for its objectives and organisations.[18] Old-boys' associations, cultural organisations and educational bodies were infiltrated, and the party won over significant sections of the community. Many of these were teachers and students in Chinese schools, workers, and rural squatters who had always been alienated from the colonial authorities.

THE JAPANESE OCCUPATION

Thus prior to the outbreak of the Second World War, the British had to face few serious challenges. The elites of the various communities supported the status quo from which they benefited, while anti-British organisations failed to mobilise broad support. The communal divisions hindered the evolution of an acceptable and coherent platform for effective political action. Nationalism as an idea remained inchoate. Yet it is also generally accepted that British rule had not been, by comparison with elsewhere, unduly harsh; Malaya suffered to a lesser degree the negative effects of colonialism. Furthermore, the British possessed an efficient intelligence service, and through close co-operation with French and Dutch, watched dissident groups and their activities. Opposition groups were infiltrated and successfully neutralised through detention and banishment. The secure position of the British changed only with the invasion of the Japanese in December 1941.

Malay nationalist groups had by then made tentative contact with the Japanese. In April 1941 Ibrahim Yaacob obtained a sum of money from the Japanese and bought the *Warta Malaya*, a Malay newspaper in Singapore which was expected to take a pro-Japanese line. Just prior to the Japanese landing, an espionage network known as KAME was established to assist the invasion. This came to the notice of the British. The KMM was linked to the organisation, and in December 1941 Ibrahim Yaacob and about a hundred members of the KMM were arrested. Ibrahim Yaacob later admitted that he reached an understanding with the Japanese that the invading force would not be opposed by the Malays; in exchange, the Japanese promised that Malay sovereignty, religion and custom would be upheld and that Malay women and property respected. More important to Ibrahim Yaacob, the Japanese were to support the independence of Malaya through a union with Indonesia.[19]

The Japanese advanced rapidly in peninsular Malaya, and by 15 February 1942 they had reached Singapore and forced the British to surrender. Upon the arrival of the Japanese, the Chinese were singled out for some of the harshest treatment. This was in retribution for earlier anti-Japanese activities. In turn, many Chinese supported the Malayan Peoples' Anti-Japanese Army (MPAJA), the armed wing of the MCP which began to symbolise resistance. Japanese policy towards the Malays, on the other hand, was calculated to win their support. Ibrahim Yaacob and KMM leaders, released by the British just prior to the surrender, were immediately appointed to administrative positions by the Japanese. The KMM, banned by the British, was allowed to be re-activated, and in the early months of the occupation Ibrahim Yaacob and other KMM leaders travelled around the country to seek support.

The arrival of the Japanese gave the communists the opportunity to build up an armed wing. The early training of the MPAJA was provided by the British who also supplied arms, medical equipment and money during the war. The MCP–British alliance came about when the communists switched in December 1941 from an anti-colonial stand to one of co-operation in the face of the Japanese military threat. A few weeks before the landing of the Japanese the British Army hurriedly trained about 200 members of the MCP.[20] These went into the jungle to provide the core of the MPAJA resistance. During the war, the Allied forces dropped military supplies and landed members of a commando group known as Force 136 to join the MPAJA. The resistance role of the MPAJA enhanced its standing within the Chinese community and enabled it to broaden its support. Of those who joined the MPAJA during the period were many who were motivated less by ideological than chauvinistic considerations. The MPAJA was able to draw information and supplies from the rural Chinese squatters whose number had greatly increased when many fled the towns to escape the harshness of the Japanese.

The Japanese soon realised that Ibrahim Yaacob did not command the same support or influence as nationalist leaders in Indonesia. Neither Ibrahim Yaacob nor the KMM was to assume a similar role to those held by Sukarno and Hatta in Indonesia in the same period. Even so, the Japanese moved quickly to domesticate Malay political aspirations. The KMM was soon banned, and Ibrahim Yaacob was asked instead to head an advisory committee on Malay affairs. In the middle of 1943 the Japanese set up the *Giyugun* or *Pembela Tanah Air* (PETA) of which Ibrahim Yaacob was given command. An auxiliary force to help in the defence of Malaya against expected Allied attack, the PETA provided some military training to young Malays. A number were later to use this experience when they joined the Indonesian revolution. However, the Japanese came increasingly to rely on former Malay bureaucrats who had more experience and were better educated. More of these Malays were entrusted with taking over the administrative responsibilities previously held by the British. Like the British, the Japanese recognised that the English-educated Malay elite commanded support among the ordinary Malays. KMM members were retained in positions at lower levels of the administration. Many KMM leaders gradually realised that the Japanese had no plans to give independence to the Malays.

The Japanese occupation contributed to a large degree of politicisation in the Indian community as well. This was largely because of the role played by the Indian Independence League set up with Japanese support. Under Subhash Chandra Bose, a militantly anti-British nationalist who made the liberation of India his goal, the League chose Malaya as the centre of its campaign to mobilise the resources of Indians in Southeast Asia against the British. Bose visited various Indian communities in the country and won consider-able support. Several prominent Indians including a few from the CIAM joined the League and were given positions in the Provisional Government of Free India. From the estates came volunteers to join the League's Indian National Army (INA) which was headed by a local Indian and was based on Indian prisoners of war captured in Malaya. Funds were collected, voluntarily or otherwise, from the wealthier sections of the community to help finance the INA. But as with Chinese and Malays, Indians too suffered harsh treatment; thousands, for instance, were taken to work on the notorious Siam railway.[21]

In early 1945 Ibrahim Yaacob and former KMM members learned that the Japanese had permitted the Indonesians to make plans for independence. By October 1944 defeat for the Japanese appeared imminent, and the new Koiso government in Tokyo instructed the adoption of a pro-nationalist policy in Southeast Asia. In Malaya, news of the Indonesian independence preparations encouraged Ibrahim Yaacob to renew efforts, approved of by several Japanese officers, for a political union with Indonesia. In May 1945 the former KMM group under Ibrahim Yaacob set up the *Kekuatan Rakyat Istimewa*, later called *Kesatuan Rakyat Indonesian Semenanjung* (KRIS). Branches of KRIS were formed in various parts of the country. Contact with the Indonesian nationalist movement was established by KRIS, and it was learnt that the Indonesian leaders supported the idea of a political union. When Sukarno and Hatta stopped in Singapore en route to Saigon on 8 August for independence talks with the Japanese, they were met by KMM supporters.

Further discussions were held when Ibrahim Yaacob saw Sukarno and Hatta on their way back. Thus by the time the Indonesian leaders departed, KRIS members were confident that independence would come to both Indonesia and Malaya at the same time.[22]

However, events moved too fast for the KMM leaders. Japan surrendered on 15 August 1945, and two days later Indonesian nationalists declared their independence. Malaya was not included, and there was confusion among KMM supporters. Nevertheless, the leadership continued to urge independence through union with Indonesia. Some KMM supporters talked of seizing Japanese military installations and resisting the return of the British. Others proposed allying the KMM with the MPAJA to fight the returning Allied troops. But such plans collapsed quickly; no support came from the Japanese who ordered Ibrahim Yaacob to disband the PETA. The MPAJA, with whom Ibrahim Yaacob made efforts to arrive at an understanding, chose to co-operate with the returning British. On 19 August Ibrahim Yaacob left for Java. Two weeks later other KMM leaders followed him to join the Indonesian revolution. The KMM was left in disarray.

EMERGENCE OF THE UMNO

Upon the surrender of the Japanese, the MPAJA came out of the jungle and took over a number of towns. British troops did not arrive for another two weeks, and the MPAJA strove to fill the resulting power vacuum before the British could arrive. The MPAJA took reprisals against those they termed collaborators. Many of those attacked were Malays, and Malay reaction to the MPAJA was therefore hostile. Racial fighting occurred in several parts of the country as Malays exacted revenge upon the Chinese for MPAJA killings. Order and security were thus the main tasks confronting the British as they returned. A British military administration was set up and lasted until it was replaced in April 1946 by the Malayan Union. In the face of British military presence, the MCP decided against armed means to achieve their political objectives. The order by the British to surrender all arms was partially obeyed, and the MPAJA was disbanded amidst official recognition of the role it played. Still the MCP remained the best organised party of the time.

Despite the departure of Ibrahim Yaacob, the Malay radical

movement took shape again immediately after the war. In October 1945, the Malay Nationalist Party (MNP) was set up,[23] impelled from three sources. The first of these was the MCP who through its Malay members helped to organise the party. The second came from former KMM members who, tainted with the stigma of war-time collaboration, projected themselves actively in an overtly anti-colonial party. The third element was the inspiration of the Indonesian revolution. The MNP supported the struggle of the Indonesians and thus attracted those Malays who held strongly to the idea of political affinity between Malaya and Indonesia. A youth wing, *Angkatan Pemuda Insaf* (API), was organised which was even more militant in its rhetoric.

The MNP as a party was short-lived. Its leaders came largely from the vernacular-educated, and its members from the lower economic groups. Its language of revolution failed to win much support either from the ordinary Malays or the traditional ruling class. Instead, it drew the attention of the British: they banned API in July 1949. What was later to galvanise the majority of Malays into political action was not the appeal of revolution but the threat to the special position of Malays posed by the Malayan Union. In this opposition to the British plan, it was the conservative Malays who provided effective leadership as they set out to mobilise the masses. The MNP by its own vacillation lost out to the conservatives. Harassed by the British because it linked itself to leftwing, non-Malay politics, the MNP never regained the leadership of the Malays.

Many Malays had trusted that the British would protect their interests and that the rulers with whom the British had entered into treaties would ensure that the objectives were honoured. The Malayan Union plans jolted this faith (see illustration, p. 208). Pre-pared during the war, the plans were largely concerned with providing greater administrative centralisation to replace the four Federated Malay States, five Unfederated Malay States and two Straits Settlements. There was also the realisation that reforms leading towards eventual self-government were necessary. The pre-war position of the Malay rulers, for instance, was thought to inhibit democratic developments, while the continued alienation of the large number of Chinese was deemed inimical to a peaceful political transition in the future.[24] Under the proposals, a Malayan Union was to be established to bring together the pre-war Federated Malay States, the Unfederated Malay States and the Straits Settlements into one political unit. For strategic reasons, Singapore remained outside this new framework. There were two provisions in the proposal that angered the Malays. The first affected the position of the rulers to whom the Malays looked for ultimate protection: in the Malayan Union the rulers lost their pre-eminent positions. Secondly, the Malayan Union liberalised citizenship requirements, thus giving non-Malays equal access to political rights. Thus a prospect which had long been viewed with apprehension was now to be translated into reality.

Alarmed by the proposals and angered by the manner in which Sir Harold MacMichael, the British envoy, negotiated the treaties with the rulers, the Malays held demonstrations throughout the country. The most important of these was led by Dato Onn bin Jaafar who called for the formation of a larger Malay organisation to fight the British proposals.[25] In March 1946 a Pan-Malayan Malay Congress was held in Kuala Lumpur at which forty Malay organisations were represented. The conference agreed to the setting-up of a body to be known as the United Malay National Organisation (UMNO). At the second meeting of the Congress in May, UMNO came into being formally with Dato Onn as its president.[26] Led by UMNO, opposition continued and its leaders called on the Sultans to boycott the installation of the first Governor of the Malay Union. On the day of the installation, Malays throughout the country wore signs of mourning.

In this movement against the Malayan Union, the role of English-educated Malays was vital. An important section of the leadership of the UMNO was drawn from the civil service. Dato Onn, related to the Johore royal family, was himself formerly from the Johore Civil Service, and so were seven of the eleven executive members of UMNO. Their status guaranteed them the support of the Malay rulers and masses, while their training made them confident negotiators with the British. For them, it was not only a response to the crisis faced by their community; it was also a reaction against what they saw as a British attempt to undermine their own special position.

The opposition mounted by UMNO was peaceful and non-militant. Dato Onn called for the repudiation of the MacMichael treaties and a renegotiation of the terms between the British Government on one side and the Malay rulers and UMNO on the other. Throughout the campaign the demands of UMNO were confined largely to matters concerning the position of the rulers and the Malays. The Malay leadership was prepared for change within the existing political framework and showed willingness to co-operate with the British. In London, UMNO found support among former British civil servants who expressed concern for the cause of the Malays[27] (see illustration, p. 208).

The Malayan Union was inaugurated in April 1946. But in the face of continued Malay opposition, the British were eventually forced to back down. In its place a new set of proposals was negotiated which came into effect as the Federation of Malaya Agreement in 1948. The Agreement recognised the Malay rulers as sovereigns with all the prestige and power they formerly enjoyed. More important, while the principle of a common citizenship was accepted, the Agreement made it more restrictive. And although a unified administrative system was established, state rights, which the Malays and Sultans held important, were retained. The replacement of the Malayan Union by the Federation of Malaya thus represented a decisive victory for UMNO, which had taken part in the negotiations. The British had acceded to its demand for re-negotiation, and the Agreement contained much of what UMNO had insisted on. The party thus established itself strongly within the Malay community. Its position was further enhanced when the radical Malay Nationalist Party joined non-Malay organisations in attacking the Federation of Malaya Agreement. The Agreement was also important for UMNO because future constitutional discussions proceeded from the basis of the Federation of Malaya, and the Federation acknowledged the sovereignty of the Malay rulers.[28]

THE COMMUNIST ARMED STRUGGLE

British willingness to concede to UMNO demands was in part influenced by the growing militancy of the political left and the weak support non-Malays had given to the Malayan Union. Even though the Malayan Union contained provisions favourable to them, non-Malays had not, except for cautious approval from the Malayan Democratic Union, demonstrated noticeable enthusiasm. The Malayan Democratic Union, a party led by Western-educated men and espousing moderate socialism, was at the same time critical of the Malayan Union proposals because they did not provide for a fully elected legislature.[29] Other non-Malay organisations objected to the Malayan Union because it excluded Singapore.

The colonial government at this stage was more concerned with the militant Malayan Communist Party. Of all the political organisations the MCP was the best organised. It had also a clear political objective: ending British colonialism. Immediately after the war the MCP leadership decided on a moderate course in its challenge to the British and consequently disbanded its armed wing, the MPAJA. The party chose to work through a National United Front which was to include most major political organisations. Leadership of all the nationalist forces in the country was to be assumed by the Front, and having done so it was to force British withdrawal by constitutional means.[30]

This strategy was also to allow the MCP time to restructure and strengthen itself. Meanwhile, the communists successfully infiltrated the trade unions. This was one area in which they intended to mount a challenge to the colonial authorities. The communists also achieved considerable success in the Chinese schools, which, as in the pre-war period, remained dissatisfied with the authorities over the state of Chinese education. From the unions and the Chinese schools, the MCP gained recruits and support.

In 1946 the MCP inspired a series of industrial strikes. Economic conditions after the war remained depressed. Food was in short supply and wages were low. Although none of the industrial disputes reached serious proportions, the colonial government was none the less alarmed. In a bid to weaken communist influence in the unions, the British introduced a law in July 1946 requiring all trade unions to be registered. Unions were also to furnish information about their officers, membership, finances and rules to the Registrar of Trade Unions. This legislation enabled the British to watch the activities of the trade unions, particularly those that were communist influenced.[31]

Despite the inroads made into the trade-union movement and the Chinese schools, the MCP failed to broaden further its base of support. It won few adherents from the Indians or Malays, the majority of whom were peasants who tended to perceive the MCP as a Chinese organisation. Largely because of this, the MCP found itself concentrating largely on the urban centres. But even here it was not able to reach those who were Western-educated. Both they and the business group regarded the MCP with distrust and fear.[32]

For a brief period the MCP gained the co-operation of non-communist organisations opposed to the Federation of Malaya Agreement. A Pan-Malaya Council of Joint Action (later renamed the All-Malaya Council of Joint Action or AMCJA) was formed with Tan Cheng Lock, a prominent Chinese from Malacca, as chairman, and John Eber from the Malayan Democratic Union as secretary-general. The communists had by this time infiltrated the leadership of the MDU. The AMCJA allied itself with the radical Malay Nationalist Party to oppose the Federation of Malaya Agreement. The MNP viewed the 1948 agreement as collusion between the British and UMNO to maintain the interests of the colonialists and the feudalists. But the AMCJA–Putera alliance was largely Chinese and backed by communist front organisations such as the Singapore Federation of Trade Unions and the Pan-Malaya Federation of Trade Unions. Tan Cheng Lock, who had close links with the Chinese chambers of commerce, was expected to win over the Chinese business and professional communities.[33]

In protest against the draft Federation of Malaya Agreement, the AMCJA–Putera coalition launched a nation-wide *hartal* on 20 October 1947. This was a political weapon which the Indian nationalists had used to some effect. On the day of the *hartal*, shops were closed throughout the country. Despite the successful show of strength, the British made no concession. A second *hartal* was suggested, but by this time the Associated Chinese Chambers of Commerce had decided to end its co-operation with the AMCJA–Putera alliance. It recognised the intransigence of the British on the issue, and its members were unhappy at the financial losses involved in a *hartal*. Furthermore, events in China, where Kuomintang forces were fighting the communists, influenced many in the Chinese chambers of commerce, some of whom had pro-Kuomintang sympathies. Others too were willing to accept British assurance that non-Malay concern would be taken into account when the Federation of Malaya Agreement was implemented. With that, the AMCJA–Putera coalition was dismantled and opposition to the British–UMNO agreement ended.[34]

With the failure of its move to establish a National United Front through the AMCJA–Putera alliance, and having to face increased British harassment in the labour movements, the MCP decided to abandon constitutional means in its offensive against the British. Its declining influence in the unions was evident. This was partly caused by its concentration on the political arena. Further, from March 1947 European employers in the mining and rubber industries felt more confident in dealing toughly with the militant unions and refused to grant concessions. Against the MCP-backed unions, the employers felt more certain of government support. With declining commodity prices and the rise in labour costs, employers were far less inclined to accept union demands. The position of the employers was strengthened by improved production methods which led to a steady reduction of employment, and with more Malays entering the rubber industries, employers needed to rely less on the Chinese and Indians who made up the bulk of union membership. In the face of what they regarded as communist-inspired industrial disorder, employers demanded that the government introduce tough legislation.[35]

By 1948 the MCP, under its new secretary-general, Chin Peng, felt it had no option but to take up an armed struggle. Following the murder of several British planters, the authorities in June 1948 proclaimed a state of emergency, and the armed conflict against the MCP began. Several thousand members of the communist party withdrew to the jungle where they had hidden their wartime arms.[36]

At the height of the Emergency nearly 6000 armed communists were in the jungle, and until 1957 the government was spending about $200 million a year fighting the insurgency. The conflict was most serious in 1951, up to which time nearly 2000 civilians had been killed, most of whom were Chinese. British planters were also selected as targets. In an attempt to disrupt the economy and thus force out the British, the MCP attacked rubber estates and tin mines. Nearly 7000 communists were killed or captured by 1953, while casualties among government troops were 1500 killed and 2000 wounded. In the course of the Emergency, one of the most serious problems faced by the British were the squatters in the outlying areas. These squatters were largely Chinese, driven by the economic depression of the 1930s into the rural areas where they opened up jungle land for cultivation or livestock rearing. The number had increased during the Japanese occupation. They had no title to the land they worked, and in general their economic condition was depressed. As with the rural Malays, they were generally neglected by the government. Through persuasion or coercion, the squatters became an important source of food, medicine and information to the communists. In a drastic move to disrupt this supply, General

Briggs, who directed the military operations against the insurgency
in 1950 and 1951, ordered the shifting of nearly half-a-million
squatters into fenced-up and more easily defended new villages. This
was a massive population movement involving one out of every four
Chinese in the country, and was to have social and political implications later. Its strategic effect upon the war was almost immediate,
for it isolated the armed communists who now began to experience
difficulties in obtaining supplies and recruits.[37]

A COMMUNAL COALITION FOR ELECTIONS

By the end of 1951 the turning point in the war had been reached.
Despite the assassination in October 1951 of Sir Henry Gurney, the
High Commissioner, the military initiative had been wrested by
government forces. Under Templer, the new High Commissioner,
some of the toughest measures in the war – for example, the resettlement of the Chinese squatters – were vigorously pursued. But even
so, the security situation remained difficult. To obtain support from
the civilian population, the British decided that some measure of
local participation in government ought to be granted. In 1951,
therefore, the first Malayans were appointed to the Federal Executive
Council.

By this process, the British encouraged and supported local
leaders whom they considered moderate and pro-British. The
dominance of the moderates, to whom power could be handed if
the situation warranted, was seen as advantageous to the vast British
economic interests. In the tin and rubber industries, for instance,
European participation was formidable. In 1953, 60 per cent of
Malaya's tin was produced by European-owned mining companies.
In rubber, Europeans owned 83 per cent of total acreage under
cultivation. Estates of more than 1000 acres made up the majority
of this land. European control of oil palm and coconut industries
was similar. Furthermore, it was estimated that in 1953, European-
owned firms held between 65 and 75 per cent of the import trade.
British involvement in the economy was reflected in the dominance
of several large agency houses which controlled extensive trading,
plantation and other economic activities. In manufacturing, banking
and insurance, British companies also played a preponderant role.[38]

In seeking out and supporting moderate leaders, the British paid close attention to the communal problem. Events in the post-occupation period had heightened racial feelings, and the Emergency had set the various communal groups further apart. Both the British and the local leaders recognised racial discord as a major inhibiting factor in any future political development. The examples of Palestine and India were recent reminders of the danger, and in Malaya the communal question was made all the more difficult by the communist challenge.

The British saw two early leaders as possessing the vision and capability to fashion a political format that was moderate, multi-racial and presumably pro-British. They were Dato Onn bin Jaafar and Tan Cheng Lock. Both had been active in politics and in endeavours to foster interracial harmony. In January 1949 the two men had set up the Communities Liaison Committee, largely to promote closer interracial links. The successful campaign against the Malayan Union had made Dato Onn the undisputed leader of the Malays, while Tan Cheng Lock was widely respected in Chinese business and professional circles. Long an advocate of unity among the Chinese, Tan Cheng Lock envisioned a political role for the Chinese that would help create a Malayan identity.

The Emergency left the Chinese community in political disarray. There was a tendency to identify the entire community with the communists of whom the majority were Chinese. In turn, the Emergency alienated large numbers of Chinese. The new, protected villages and group punishment affected mainly the lower socio-economic class of the Chinese, most of whom were vernacular-speaking. Concerned at this, the British authorities were anxious that there should be a non-communist organisation that could not only assist in relief work to the thousands of Chinese uprooted by the resettlement programme but also offer alternative leadership. The emergence of a non-communist leadership would prevent a complete political alienation of the community that would make the insurgency still more difficult and protracted. It would also force the British to rely more on the Malays to help prosecute the jungle war and thus strengthen the political position of UMNO. Some British were concerned that constitutional development could not ignore the Chinese, and a non-communist leadership had therefore to be promoted to represent the Chinese effectively.

The British turned to a group of Chinese businessmen and Western-educated professionals. These were men who wielded

236 Asia − The Winning of Independence

236 Asia − The Winning of Independence

considerable influence in Chinese society. Through Tan Cheng Lock and the Chinese Chambers of Commerce, Sir Henry Gurney encouraged the start of a Chinese organisation in January 1949. The Malayan Chinese Association was formally launched in February 1949 with Tan Cheng Lock as president. Consisting of Chinese Chambers of Commerce personalities and pro-Western English-educated professionals, the MCA was strongly anti-communist. Its leaders decided that the best option was to work closely with the British and the Malays to ensure the political future of the Chinese. All sixteen of the Chinese in the Federal Legislative Council were co-opted into the first Central Committee of the MCA.[39]

Meanwhile, Dato Onn proposed that UMNO, the party founded to defend Malay rights, should offer membership to non-Malays. Dato Onn believed that unless there was a party that comprised all the major races, the British would not agree to self-government for Malaya. UMNO would consequently have to accept non-Malays if it was to be the party to win political reforms and lead the country to independence. Dato Onn felt confident that his stature within UMNO was high enough to persuade its members to support his proposals. However, for a party founded to oppose the Malayan Union and moves to liberalise citizenship for non-Malays, Dato Onn's proposal was almost heretical. Even his standing within UMNO was not strong enough to win the party over completely. Disappointed, Dato Onn left UMNO in mid-1951. He could visualise no other format than a party structured on multiracial lines.

In September 1951 Dato Onn formed the Independence of Malaya Party (IMP) to reassert his leadership.[40] To gain support, he made independence the party's objective, within a framework of non-communalism. The initial support encouraged Dato Onn. Several leaders of UMNO including Dato Panglima Bukit Gantang, the Mentri Besar (chief minister) of Perak, joined him. Among the non-Malays, Tan Cheng Lock, several members of the Legislative Council, prominent Indians and the MCA indicated approval of the IMP. They shared Dato Onn's hope of a single multiracial party to weld the communities together to obtain constitutional reforms. Briefly, then, the IMP seemed to be on the point of becoming the party that might be supported by Malays and non-Malays, as well as being acceptable to the British. The UMNO that Dato Onn left maintained its communal character.

But the influence of the IMP, and the idea of non-communalism in Malayan politics, were short-lived. In 1951 elections were introduced to the local councils. One of the first was for the Kuala Lumpur municipality, and this became an important test of strength for all the parties. The IMP contesting on non-communalism fielded candidates in all twelve seats and many expected it to win, for none of the other parties appeared organised enough to do well. But to defeat the IMP, local representatives of the UMNO and MCA engineered an electoral alliance that was to prove an important turning point in the country's political history. They reached the agreement without prior approval from the central leadership of their parties.[41]

Many in the MCA who were sympathetic to the IMP were furious on learning of the electoral alliance. They saw the IMP as a truly multiracial party that the MCA ought to support. They had strong reservations about UMNO. The issue of the electoral alliance with UMNO thus threatened to split the MCA leadership. Tan Cheng Lock was in a dilemma — personally he was closer to the IMP, but he was not prepared publicly to instruct the Selangor branch of the MCA on the course it should take. The crisis clearly indicated significant divisions within the MCA leadership arising largely from differences in social and educational backgrounds. At this point, the more Chinese-conscious of the MCA leaders found themselves able to co-operate with a very aggressively Malay party, while the English-educated felt greater affinity with the more cosmopolitan IMP. To the English-educated Chinese, Tunku Abdul Rahman was clearly taking UMNO towards a narrow chauvinistic course.

A brother of the Kedah Sultan, the Tunku involved himself closely in politics only after he returned from his studies in London at a relatively late age. He did not get along well with his brother early on, and thus when he took over as president of UMNO and began to talk of self-government and eventual independence there was some unease, it was said, within aristocratic circles about his possible intentions regarding the future of the rulers. The Tunku spent a considerable length of time in Britain where he acquired a fondness for most things British. But despite this he had unpleasant personal experiences of aspects of British colonialism in Malaya. He remembered that in his early years as a Malay Deputy Public Prosecutor he was always assigned the more difficult cases, the easier ones going to his expatriate colleagues. Inevitably he made few successful prosecutions and earned an unfavourable reputation.

Later, as leader of UMNO, the Tunku encountered what he regarded as the obstructionist behaviour of many local British civil servants. To such slights and attitudes, the Tunku was sensitive.[42]

The IMP was badly defeated in the Kuala Lumpur municipal elections; it won only two seats with the rest going to the UMNO–MCA alliance. The successful UMNO–MCA arrangement was repeated in local elections elsewhere. What had essentially been in contest were two formats of multiracial politics. On one hand, the IMP not only espoused multiracialism but incorporated it structurally in the party organisation. The UMNO–MCA alliance, on the other hand, took the form of co-operation between two parties whose basic appeal as individual parties was communal. The results showed that the IMP's approach commanded little support among the masses. Undoubtedly the result was a testimony to the better organisation and wider financial resources of the UMNO–MCA alliance. But the victory underlined the fact that interracial co-operation was easier to comprehend when individual communal interests were maintained. Those in the MCA who had reservations about working with the UMNO therefore found it necessary to do considerable re-thinking. Out of this successful experiment emerged the Alliance, which assumed a more formal character when leaders of the UMNO and MCA and later the Malayan Indian Congress (MIC) agreed to work closely. As a start, the leaders of the parties consulted regularly at what were simply referred to as the Round Table Talks[43] (see illustration, p. 210).

The electoral defeats left Dato Onn politically isolated. He felt let down by both his Malay and non-Malay supporters. Noting the rejection of his multiracial approach and sensing the continuing appeal of communal symbols. Dato Onn adopted once again a strong Malay emphasis in his political rhetoric. Dato Onn's altered posture disillusioned many of his non-Malay supporters such as Tan Cheng Lock. The Malayan Indian Congress now threw in its lot with the UMNO and MCA. To non-Malays, Dato Onn came across as increasingly pro-Malay, just as the Tunku began to assume the image of a moderate.

ALLIANCE FOR INDEPENDENCE

With the convincing success over the IMP and the declining political support of Dato Onn, the Tunku felt confident enough to talk more of interracial co-operation. As with Dato Onn earlier, he came to realise that the British would not agree to a transfer of political power to UMNO only and that UMNO–MCA co-operation had to be the minimal basis for any future constitutional talks. At this time, too, a number of Chinese leaders from the MCA began to move closer to the Tunku.

The British reaction to the success of the Alliance was mixed. There was satisfaction that the response from the political parties to limited constitutional change and elections had been encouraging. The British were further assured by the fact that the winning party was led by men largely committed to moderate constitutional reforms and prepared to work with the colonial authorities. None the less, there was some disquiet that the UMNO–MCA alliance had won so decisively and in the process virtually emasculated the IMP. The potential of the UMNO to mobilise Malay mass support, combined with MCA's links with Chinese commercial interests and the guilds and associations, was clearly evident; such potential could encourage the demand for speedier political reforms.

In fact, the Alliance was already caught by the momentum of events. Flushed with electoral success and the evidence of workable communal co-operation between UMNO and MCA, rank-and-file members of the coalition, especially UMNO members, called for self-government and independence. On 5 April 1953, the Malacca branch of UMNO urged federal elections by the next year. Failing this, representatives of the UMNO and MCA in the Legislative Council should resign. The cry of *Merdeka* (Independence) was made at the end of the meeting.[44] Tan Cheng Lock in his address to the annual general committee meeting of the MCA in December 1953 asked for a speedier approach to self-government and criticised the '"autocratic Colonial Government" which talked of fighting for the hearts and minds of the people yet refusing them equal standing on which to cooperate with the Government'.[45] On 15 October 1954 the youth wing of UMNO at its annual conference passed a resolution calling for independence as soon as possible.[46] In this, the Tunku had a hand, for he quietly encouraged the leader of UMNO Youth to take a more militant posture while the Alliance leaders presented themselves to the British as the moderates.[47] This was political leverage which the Tunku was to use skilfully both with the British and with MCA. UMNO's call for speedy political reforms leading to independence was supported by the MCA, but except for

Tan Cheng Lock, some had misgivings about the pace of change proposed.

The developments were observed with concern by conservative groups, particularly the rulers. Yet there was acceptance that some changes had to come. In the early part of 1953, Templer himself had indicated that political reforms would soon be introduced. It was evident that the first step towards self-government would be to hold elections to the Legislative Council. Mentri Besars (chief ministers) of seven states, in a bid to gain influence over the independence movement, sponsored a meeting called the Malayan National Conference in August 1953, to which were invited all parties, communal organisations and trade unions. Neither the UMNO nor MCA attended. The recommendations of the conference were modest: federal elections by 1956, an enlarged Legislative Council and a national forum to co-ordinate efforts towards unity and self government. A report in the London *Times* commented: 'It is possible that an attempt is being made with official encouragement, to establish an all-party understanding on a wider basis, free from personal jealousies and ambitions, than that envisaged by Tunku Abdul Rahman'.[48]

In January 1954, the Federal Elections Committee published its report. The Committee took the view that ultimately the Legislature should be fully elected. However, while a minority in the Committee favoured an elected majority at once, most of the others argued that at least half the members in the Federal Legislative Council should be nominated.[49] The Alliance leaders were unhappy with the recommendations of the report. They argued that three-fifths of the Legislature should be elected to ensure that the winning party would have a reasonable working majority. The authorities in Kuala Lumpur made no response to the Alliance demand.

On 21 April 1954, the Tunku left for London to take up the matter with Oliver Lyttleton, the Secretary for the Colonies.[50] Just prior to the meeting Lyttleton announced that there would be an elected majority in the new Legislature but it would not be three-fifths. The new Legislative Council would have forty-six nominated members, of whom seven would be chosen by the High Commissioner, and fifty-two elected members.[51] On 15 May, Lyttleton received the Alliance delegation, and the Tunku reiterated the three-fifths demand. A few labour members of Parliament suggested as a compromise that the seven seats to be nominated by the High Commissioner should be filled on the advice of the winning party.[52]

The Tunku's demand for three-fifths of the members of the Legislature to be elected was rejected. However, the Secretary for the Colonies conceded several other points: that civil servants, who formed a significant part of UMNO's membership, should be allowed to contest the elections; that there should be a simple majority vote in all constituencies; that nominated members of the Legislative Council should be eligible for portfolio positions in the Executive Council; and that elections should be held in 1955.[53] There was angry reaction from UMNO and MCA following the publication of Lyttleton's offer. To the Tunku, only the minor points were conceded while the crucial issue regarding the proportion of elected seats had been turned down. On 24 May, the executive committee of the Alliance in Kuala Lumpur called for a royal commission to review the forthcoming elections. Failing this, Alliance members would boycott the elections and serving members in all representative bodies would resign.[54]

The demand for a royal commission was rejected. On 13 June 1954 the Alliance acted. Its members were directed to resign by 28 June from the Legislative Council as well as from all local representative bodies. Thus when the second reading of the bill on federal elections was passed, none of the Alliance members was in the Legislative Council.[55] Sir Donald MacGillivray, the new High Commissioner, worried by the Alliance boycott, wrote to the leaders that appointment to the reserved seats in the Legislature would be made only after consultation with the leader of the majority party.[56] The Tunku finally accepted the proposal and called off the boycott. The demand for a royal commission was renewed.[57]

It was with this understanding that federal elections were held on 27 July 1955. Of the fifty-two seats contested, the Alliance won fifty-one, with one going to the Pan-Malayan Islamic Party, formed from a breakaway religious faction of UMNO.[58] The Tunku became the chief minister. The results once again demonstrated the Alliance's political strength. It also led to the demise of Party Negara and Dato Onn as political factors in the country. Though Dato Onn remained active for a number of years, he never recovered the influence he once wielded. The 1955 elections reflected also the cohesion and understanding that had grown up among the Alliance leaders. With only about 15 per cent of the Chinese eligible to vote, UMNO agreed that the MCA should contest fifteen of the fifty-two seats. In return, the MCA contributed substantially to the campaign funds. Possibly the most significant outcome of the election was the determination of the Alliance to press for early independence.[59]

The refusal of the British to accede to the Alliance demands regarding the composition of the new Legislature, as well as the authorities' quiet backing of the conservative groups, benefited the Alliance politically. These issues became the basis for a relatively militant rhetoric and provided a unifying rallying point for Alliance members. The rejection of the Alliance demands by the British provided an opportunity to launch a peaceful boycott of the representative councils, a rare act of defiance by men who were basically moderate and pro-British. None the less, for some Alliance leaders such actions were essential in any nationalist struggle and had been lacking in the Alliance performance hitherto. The role of Dato Onn in the Legislative Council where he was member in charge of home affairs, the formation of Party Negara and the meeting of the Malayan National Conference, which had called for gradual transition to self-government, were all interpreted by the Alliance as examples of British machinations to balance the Alliance and thereby divide the nationalist movement. Alliance leaders also came to view many actions of expatriate officers as hostile. Yet most of the disputes between the Alliance and the British were conducted in a civil and cordial manner. Much as the Tunku might have expressed fears of his own possible detention, the British were hard put to find a reason to make him a martyr.

The Malay rulers observed political developments with considerable interest. Mindful of the political upheavals elsewhere, the Sultans had come to accept that constitutional changes were inevitable. Events in neighbouring countries such as India and Indonesia, where the ruling princes had been overthrown, worried them. The happenings in Indonesia were probably most alarming since several of those affected were related to Malayan royal families. Yet there was a quiet confidence. Though the signing of the MacMichael treaties in 1946 had for a short while shaken their position, the reaction of the Malay masses, and the British retreats, ultimately strengthened their position. For the Malay masses, the fight against the Malayan Union was at no point directed against the Sultans' representatives consisting of four Mentri Besas before foster Malay unity, and the British in agreeing to renegotiate referred not only to the UMNO but also to the Malay rulers. The Sultans were also reassured by the continued support expressed by UMNO. Indeed, the Tunku even arranged for the UMNO delegates to visit the rulers to pledge their loyalty. Thus the Council of Rulers met in September 1955 and agreed to the holding of independence talks. In a meeting in early January 1956, the rulers also indicated that they were prepared to work with the Tunku and the Alliance.[60]

Towards the end of 1955 the Tunku had obtained agreements from all sides for the next stage of constitutional development. He had presented a credible semblance of racial unity through the Alliance and obtained approval from the Sultans. In arriving at such a broad consensus, the Tunku had acted with considerable skill. He was generous with political allies; he was not vindictive towards opponents. There remained, however, one group with which the Tunku had not established contact: the Malayan Communist Party. In November 1955 the press reported that communication had been made with the MCP and that the Tunku would hold talks with Chin Peng.[61]

The British were unhappy that the Tunku agreed to the meeting. Their military reports suggested that the MCP was already defeated and there was no urgency for a political settlement. When the Tunku insisted on seeing Chin Peng, he was invited to a meeting at which senior colonial administrators were present. The Tunku was briefed on the latest security situation and urged not to agree to recognise the MCP. He was informed that even if the amnesty offer were accepted communist members would certainly be barred from participation in politics and leaders like Chin Peng would be banished. To the British, the MCP was merely changing from a military to a political offensive.[62]

As we have seen, the talks at Baling in December 1955 arrived at no agreement. For the Tunku, this marked the end of any settlement effort with the MCP, and when Chin Peng asked for another meeting in October 1957 his letter was ignored. Alliance policy from then on was decidedly anti-communist, and its leaders accepted no other outcome than a total defeat of the MCP.

TALKS IN LONDON

In early January 1956 the Tunku led a delegation to London for talks on independence. The British had insisted that the rulers should send a separate delegation so that they could be consulted. The Tunku proposed that the Alliance should hold discussions with the Sultans' representatives consisting of four Mentri Besars before arriving in London. The discussions did not turn out to be as difficult as had been feared earlier. The rulers' representatives wanted safeguards for the position of the Sultans and for state rights in matters such as land. The Alliance leaders assured the rulers' representatives that the position of the Sultans would be upheld. More than that, the institution of a paramount ruler was proposed. Elected from among the rulers for a term, the paramount ruler would symbolise the unity of the independent state. For the Tunku, the Sultans were so much a part of the Malay tradition that they could not be done away with. Indeed, they were essential to preserve the Malay character of the proposed state. On the other points, the Alliance leaders insisted that the rulers should do away with British advisers and that future Mentri Besars be chosen from the state assembly, whose members were to be elected.[63]

The Tunku's delegation arrived amidst general optimism that the talks would be successful. Reports from the British press suggested that the British Government had accepted in principle that limited self-government would certainly be granted and that there would be an interim period before full independence. The talks began on 18 January and lasted for three weeks. The discussion concentrated on four areas: defence and internal security, finance, Malayanisation and the setting-up of a constitutional commission to prepare for independence.[64] On 8 February, the Tunku's fifty-third birthday, final agreements were reached. The British Government announced that responsibility in internal government was to be transferred to the Alliance leaders within three months and full independence by 31 August 1957 if possible. During the interim period between April 1956 and the date of independence the High Commissioner in Malaya would act on the advice of the Executive Council. The Tunku now became the chief minister in the full sense. Matters of internal defence became the responsibility of a Malayan minister who was to preside over an Emergency Operation Council to direct the war against the insurgency. From the political point of view, the appointment of a Malayan to head the Emergency Operation Council was crucial, for it meant that the prosecution of the war was to be conducted by the elected representatives of the country. The second area of responsibility to be handed over to

Malayans was finance. The difficult question of Malayanisation was also amicably resolved. While anxious that British expatriate officers should be replaced as early as possible, Malayan leaders were at the same time concerned that the process of Malayanisation should be implemented over a long enough period to allow local people to be trained. The final point in the agreement was on the setting-up of a commission to prepare a constitution. It was accepted that the terms and references had to be approved by the Queen and the Council of Rulers. The agreement also referred to other matters. For instance, the stationing of Commonwealth troops in Malaya was to continue, but the terms were to be worked out in a new defence and mutual-assistance treaty. In turn, the Alliance assured the British that Malaya would remain in the sterling area. British investments in the country would be safeguarded and repatriation of profits allowed.[65]

In its negotiations with London, the Malayan delegation was assisted by several Labour parliamentarians and members of the Malayan League of Friendship. Legal advice was provided by a British law firm which was associated with the League.[66] The role of the Labour group was useful. Not only did they guide the relatively inexperienced Malayan leaders through the various technicalities in the negotiations but they understood enough of the thinking in the Colonial Office to recognise the limits to what the Alliance could obtain. This narrowed considerably the gap between the position of the Tunku's delegation and that of the Colonial Office even before discussions took place.

SEARCH FOR COMMUNAL CONSENSUS

Having successfully negotiated with the British, the Tunku now had to win the support of the people in the preparation of a constitution. Even as the Tunku was returning to Malaya, different reactions to the talks were evident in the country. For the Malays, news of impending independence was received with almost euphoric enthusiasm. Only Dato Onn questioned the basis for the Alliance's confidence that independence would indeed be achieved in 1957. But others, such as Ungku Abdullah who had in fact opposed the *Merdeka* mission, closed ranks with the UMNO and were primarily concerned now that independence was about to be achieved with safeguarding Malay rights.[67] The results of the London talks suddenly made non-Malays realise that a new political order was in the making. They would soon have to deal directly with the Malays; their own political weakness became glaringly evident.

Two groups of Chinese were most apprehensive: first, the pro-British associations of Straits Chinese immediately sent a delegation to London seeking assurances that its members would be allowed to retain their British nationality; second, the Chinese guilds and associations in July 1956 organised a conference which discussed several issues of concern to the community. These were that the principle of *jus soli*, or nationality by birth, should be applied in matters of citizenship, that the Chinese language was to be used together with English and Malay and that racially discriminating laws should be rejected.[68] It also sought to set up a pan-Malayan Federation of Chinese associations as an alternative to the MCA which was regarded as too feeble. This attempt, however, failed.

At this point, the Tunku's role was critical. With the Malays strongly opposed to *jus soli* and the Chinese on the other hand insisting on certain safeguards, the Tunku had to make decisions that would not alienate too many on either side. Confident of the broad support he enjoyed from the Malays following his successful mission, he was prepared to make what he regarded as concessions to the Chinese. He agreed that citizenship should be granted automatically to those born in the country after independence. In return, the non-Malays were asked to recognise the special position of the Malays. Quotas would be reserved for Malays for land, public service posts, business and scholarships. About quotas, the Tunku was firm. In August 1956 he appealed to non-Malays not to question the special position of the Malays.[69] Equally important, the non-Malays were required to accept a new education policy as outlined in the Razak Report through which it was hoped that future generations of Malayan citizens would be inculcated with a sense of a common identity. More important, Malay was to be the official language and Islam the state religion. It was decided that there should be only one memorandum from the Alliance to the Reid Constitutional Commission which arrived in Malaya in July 1956 to obtain views from the various groups.[70]

By taking a posture of compromise and consensus, the Tunku won over many in the MCA, and strengthened the position of those who later urged the Chinese to accept provisions in the Reid Constitution proposal which were regarded as controversial and who argued for close co-operation with UMNO. The MCA could persuade the others that the party was dealing with a man who was moderate and reasonable. Unwillingness to compromise would damage the Tunku's standing within the UMNO, and that could lead to his replacement by more extreme elements.

In April 1956 the transfer of power began. The Tunku took over the portfolio of defence and internal security. Finance as well as commerce and industry were also given to Malayan ministers. An Economic Committee of the Federal Executive Council was established and besides co-ordinating economic policies was entrusted with the tasks of identifying future development needs.[71]

Earlier, in March 1956, a commission to prepare the constitution was appointed with Lord Reid as chairman. There was to be a federal form of constitution for a single, independent, self-governing unit within the Commonwealth. The new nation would have a bicameral legislature and a strong central government, but the states would enjoy a degree of autonomy. The position of the rulers would be safeguarded. At the same time, a constitutional head of state was to be elected from among the Sultans. The constitution was to provide for a common nationality. And finally the special position of the Malays and the legitimate interests of the other races were to be upheld.[72] The constitution represented compromise and reflected the outlook of the political elite who accepted Western political institutions as instruments of change.

MALAYSIA: NEO-COLONIALISM OR DECOLONISATION?

On 31 August 1957 independence was declared in Malaya. The Sultan of Negri Sembilan was installed as paramount ruler and the Tunku became the first prime minister. The process of transfer was relatively smooth. By 1957 there were already a significant number of Malayans in the civil service and they moved up to assume new responsibilities in the following months. As agreed in the London talks, the Malayanisation programme was carried out gradually so that enough Malayans could be prepared to take over. The Alliance government also set about promoting economic development. It committed itself to a free-enterprise system and encouraged foreign

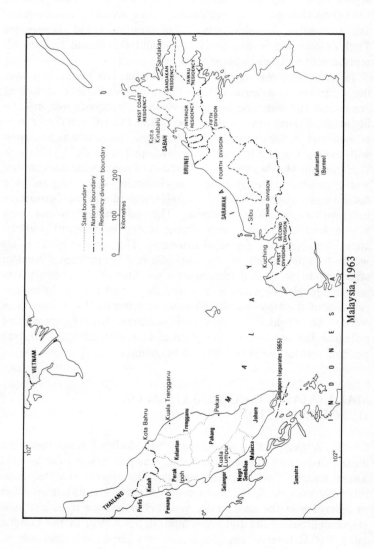

Malaysia, 1963

capital in the development of the economy. At the same time, government leaders emphasised economic and social planning.[73]

The Alliance government retained its strength. It was the party that won independence, and in parliament it enjoyed a huge majority. As leaders of a newly independent country, members of the government commanded important appointments and resources, which represented a great political advantage. Their policies encouraged economic development, and programmes were launched for rural development to benefit the people who constituted so much of UMNO's strength. More encouraging to the newly independent government was the reduction in fighting between Malayan security forces and the MCP; the extent of the 'white area' free from insurgent activities was greatly enlarged. Further, new measures seriously weakened MCP influence in schools and trade unions. Thus by 1960 the Government felt confident enough to declare an end to the Emergency and thereby signify its success over the MCP.[74]

The Tunku also succeeded in easing some serious stresses within the Alliance. These had grown out of rising expectations among all groups. Moreover, discussion of some problems that had been avoided previously in order to maintain a united front had now to be dealt with. The most severe test came in 1959. A year after independence, leadership of the MCA was taken over by men with closer links to the Chinese guilds and associations. The issues of Chinese education and seat allocation were now raised and led to a crisis in relations with UMNO. Confronted with what he viewed as a challenge, the Tunku declared that in the event of a break with the MCA he would continue to work with those Chinese leaders he regarded as reasonable. The MCA leaders backed down and later resigned. Their successors were Western-educated and generally less close to the guilds and associations.

For the British, however, the process of decolonisation remained incomplete. There were still Singapore and the three Borneo territories of Brunei, Sabah and Sarawak. The pace of political development in those states had proceeded at uneven rates, with Singapore more advanced than the rest. It was thought that none could survive independently and that some sort of federation was needed. Otherwise, British withdrawal could create a power vacuum leading to political instability in the region.[75]

On 27 May 1961 the Tunku casually mentioned in a press luncheon in Kuala Lumpur the possibility of a merger involving

Malaya, Singapore and the Borneo territories. The news caught the
journalists by surprise. Yet to many the Tunku's announcement
seemed a very neat way to help phase out British presence in the
region and to tie up various seemingly awkward political ends. By
this time, the Tunku had sounded out local leaders in Sabah and
Sarawak as well as keeping in touch with the Brunei Sultan.

It was evident too that the British approved of the merger
proposal. Some alleged that it was indeed the British who weré
behind the scheme. For the British government, this was the least
complicated manner in which to relinquish its colonial responsibilities
in Southeast Asia and yet retain a significant economic presence.
British investments in all the territories were still considerable.
British leaders were confident of the Tunku's leadership, for his
government so far was a model of stability.

Many political leaders, especially those from the Malay parties,
had always considered it historically logical that Singapore should
be part of Malaya. Furthermore, politician developments in Singapore
had caused considerable concern to leaders across the causeway. In
1959 the People's Action Party (PAP) defeated the conservative
Labour Front-Alliance government under Lim Yew Hock, a man
close to the Tunku. Led by Lee Kuan Yew, the PAP, by its own
acknowledgement, had co-operated with the communists in their
challenge to the British. The PAP promoted a radical ideology with
which the Malayan leaders found themselves uncomfortable. What
was even more alarming to the Tunku was the breakaway of a more
radical faction in 1961 to form the Barisan Sosialis, strongly
supported by the Chinese-educated and leaving the PAP precariously
in power backed by the small English-educated middle class. A
Barisan Sosialis government in Singapore could not be ruled out.[76]
Lee Kuan Yew saw the Tunku several times to discuss a possible
merger. Although the Tunku basically distrusted him, in the context
of recent developments the PAP leaders appeared the more acceptable
group in Singapore. As with the Alliance, the PAP leaders were
largely Western-educated. Lee Kuan Yew was also seen to be strongly
anti-communist. With Singapore in Malaya, Kuala Lumpur leaders
could take steps to neutralise the communist threat which Lee Kuan
Yew, as it appeared then, was unable to do.

Singapore leaders increasingly viewed merger with Malaya as the
only viable strategy to gain independence. Talks held in 1956 on
Singapore independence proved abortive as the Colonial Office

rejected the demands of David Marshall, then the chief minister. London expressed doubts as to Singapore's ability to handle its own internal security and defence.[77] On the other hand, Singapore leaders turned down merger proposals which made Singapore a mere unit within Malaya. This was the form of politicial union which the Tunku had considered in 1956.

But the old distrust in Malaya of a predominantly Chinese Singapore with a highly politicised population remained. The inclusion of Singapore would upset the existing racial balance in Malaya. At this point, therefore, the future of the British territories in Borneo became significant. With the British phasing out their interests in the region, the Tunku envisaged a merger that would include not only Singapore but also British North Borneo (later renamed Sabah), Sarawak and the oil-rich principality of Brunei. This was attractive for several reasons. Firstly, in such a union the Chinese in Singapore would be balanced by the indigenous population of the Borneo territories. Secondly, Malaya would, with the addition of an industrialising Singapore and the resource-rich states in Borneo, emerge as a powerful economic factor in the region. Thirdly, merger ensured a swift and smooth transition towards independence for Singapore and the Borneo territories. For the Tunku and the British, this would complete the phasing out of colonial presence in the area. Finally, the Tunku believed that if the initiative were not taken soon, Singapore leaders might choose to work out a union between Singapore and the Borneo territories as a way by which the city-state could gain independence.

The Malaysia proposals soon encountered difficulties. Unlike the 1955–6 period when the Tunku had only to deal with the British, and when the demand for independence received broad support, the move to form a political union this time was a more complicated issue which involved larger and more powerful forces, some of which were hostile.

Left-wing radicals in Malaya and Singapore immediately saw sinister designs: alleged collusion between the Tunku and the British. Describing the proposed Malaysia formation as a neo-colonial plan to protect Western economic and political interests, the Barisan Sosialis in Singapore and the Socialist Front in Malaya attacked the scheme. In Sarawak, the left-wing Chinese-based Sarawak United People's Party joined in the opposition. The fear of the Barisan Sosialis was that merger would not only strengthen the PAP in

Singapore politics but that Lee Kuan Yew could use Kuala Lumpur to suppress the Barisan Sosialis. Underlying this opposition too was the apprehension among the Chinese-educated, especially in Singapore, that merger meant an extension of Malay-dominated, Kuala Lumpur control, and this could have unfavourable consequences for the economic and cultural position of the Chinese.[78]

It was in Brunei that opposition to the Malaysia proposals quite unexpectedly expressed itself in a violent form. On 8 December 1962, Azahari, the leader of the Brunei Party Rakyat, led a revolt against the British. Azahari's aim was to establish a union of Brunei and the other two British territories. The socialist parties of Malaya and Singapore expressed sympathy with the rebellion. British military action, however, was swift and the uprising was quickly crushed.[79]

In the end, Brunei did not join Malaysia, but the decision had little to do with the rebellion. Rather, it was the Sultan's unwillingness to accept the merger terms offered by Kuala Lumpur. Malaya insisted the Brunei should bear part of the defence expenditure as well as development costs. The two disagreed over the amount of the contributions. To the Sultan of Brunei, the terms fell short of what he believed ought to be the special status of Brunei in the proposed federation, which in his view meant retention of some control of revenue and finance. At this point, the Brunei Sultan indicated that he wished to be the next paramount ruler after Brunei joined. Leaders in Kuala Lumpur interpreted this demand as a gesture by the Sultan of Brunei indicating he wished to end the talks, since everyone recognised that the election of the paramount ruler involved only the Sultans. With that, discussions between Kuala Lumpur and Brunei ended. To the Tunku the non-inclusion of Brunei in Malaysia represented the one major blemish on his statesmanship, and his regret was that the difficulty with Brunei could have been quite easily sorted out if Kuala Lumpur had not insisted on its financial terms.[80]

The Brunei rebellion injected an additional troublesome and dangerous element into the Malaysia question: the hostile reaction of Indonesia and to a lesser extent the Philippines. To the Indonesians, the formation of Malaysia was far from being a withdrawal of the British. Rather, it was the perpetuation of colonialism in a different garb. The Indonesian leadership, which expressed a revolution, had always had reservations about the manner in which Malaya obtained her independence. Where Indonesians had fought the colonial power, Malayans had co-operated with the British. Sukarno, like other leftwing critics, viewed the Tunku as representing the consolidation and strengthening of the feudal class in Malayan politics in collaboration with Western and Chinese economic interests. At this point, the Indonesians put forward into the limelight Ibrahim Yaacob, the pre-war KMM leader, as a contrast to the alleged 'running dog' Tunku. It was also suggested that the proposed federation posed a threat to Indonesia: Malaysia was portrayed as a British–Malayan attempt at encirclement. Indonesia's opposition escalated into a confrontation against Kuala Lumpur and became increasingly serious since the issue was intricately linked to the dynamics of her own internal politics. The Philippines' opposition to Malaysia was lower key. Unlike Indonesia, which made preparations for a military confrontation, the Philippines limited the challenge to the diplomatic level, where it revolved around the Philippines' claim to Sabah.[81]

Efforts were made to resolve the conflict. The Tunku met President Sukarno of Indonesia and President Macapagal of the Philippines in Manila in August 1963. It was agreed to hold a referendum under United Nations supervision to ascertain the wishes of the people in Sabah and Sarawak with regard to Malaysia. In the middle of 1962 a commission led by Lord Cobbold had visited the two territories for the same purpose. The results then indicated a favourable response to Malaysia. But even before the results of the United Nations referendum were made known, the Tunku proceeded to bring Malaysia into effect. On 12 September 1963 Malaysia was formed after having been postponed from its original date of 31 August.[82]

The leaders of the new state were drawn from its old elites. The continued importance of the Sultans was reflected not only in the fact that they remained as constitutional rulers in their own states – the contrast with the Indonesian and Indian princes could not be more striking – but that a new position of paramount ruler of all Malaysia was created, to be chosen regularly by the Sultans from among themselves. The sympathy of the Malay peasantry for its traditional rulers still appeared remarkably strong.

At the political level, men like Tunku Abdul Rahman were products of the ruling houses, and though they had acquired Western educational credentials, they had been able to do so largely because of their privileged extraction. Such men were unlikely to abandon the values of the old elites, particularly so long as those values commanded the support of the newly enfranchised electorate.

It was something of a paradox that most successful political leaders, both Malay and Chinese, were English-educated and cosmopolitan, yet based their power on organisations that were exclusive and communal. Voters and supporters more easily comprehended interracial co-operation when individual communal interests were maintained. Thus any organisation—whether the Malayan Communist Party and its strategy of revolution or Dato Onn's Independence of Malaya Party and its goal of peaceful, multiracial transition—that claimed to embrace all communities, yet could be depicted as dominated by one community alone, was suspect in the eyes of much of Malaya's population. A formal alliance among communal groups committed to constitutionalism and gradual change provided a more practical means of achieving independence than a single nationalist party.

NOTES

1. Unpublished report by Tunku Abdul Rahman of meeting at Government House, Singapore, 20 October 1955.
2. *Report by the Chief Minister of the Federation of Malaya on the Baling Talks* (Kuala Lumpur, 1956) p. 2.
3. *Ibid.*, pp. 2–3.
4. *Ibid.*, p. 12.
5. *Ibid.*, pp. 2, 12.
6. *Ibid.*, p. 12, Tunku Abdul Rahman, *Looking Back* (Kuala Lumpur: Pustaka Antara, 1977) pp. 5–10.
7. Phillip Loh Fook Seng, *Seeds of Separatism: Educational Policy in Malaya, 1874–1940* (Kuala Lumpur: Oxford University Press [hereafter OUP], 1975); V. Purcell, *The Chinese in Malaya*, 1st edn. (1948) [Reprinted in Kuala Lumpur: OUP, 1967.]
8. W. R. Roff, *The Origins of Malay Nationalism* (Kuala Lumpur: University of Malaya Press, 1967), pp. 29–43.
9. Letter from Tan Malaka dated 24 September 1925 from Chiangmei, Thailand and intercepted by Dutch Intelligence.
10. Letter from Tan Malaka written some time in 1925 and intercepted by Dutch Intelligence.
11. Roff, *Malay Nationalism*, p. 120; M. Puthucheary, *The Politics of Administration: The Malaysian Experience* (Kuala Lumpur: University of Malaya Press, 1978) pp. 4–38.
12. Wang Gungwu, 'Sun Yat-sen and Singapore'. *Journal of the South Seas Society*, XV, Pt. 2 (December 1949), pp. 55–68.
13. M. R. Stenson, *Industrial Conflict in Malaya* (Kuala Lumpur: OUP, 1970), pp. 25–33.
14. Roff, *Malay Nationalism*, p. 112.
15. *Ibid.*, pp. 235–47.

16. Cheah Boon Kheng, 'The Japanese Occupation of Malaya, 1941–45: Ibrahim Yaacob and the Struggle for Indonesia Raya', *Indonesia*, no. 28 (October 1979) pp. 85–120.

17. *Ibid.*, pp. 89–92. Also, Abdul Latiff Abu Bakar, 'Ibrahim Haji Yaakub: Kegelisahan dan Impian Seorang Pejuang Melayu', unpublished paper in Malay (April 1980).

18. Stephen Leong, 'The Malayan Overseas Chinese and the Sino-Japanese War, 1937–1941', *Journal of Southeast Asian Studies*, X, 2 (September 1979) pp. 293–320.

19. Cheah Boon Kheng, 'The Japanese Occupation of Malaya, 1941–45'.

20. Edgar O'Ballance, *Malaya: The Communist Insurgent War, 1948–1960* (London: Faber and Faber, 1966), pp. 34–59.

21. S. Arasaratnam, *Indians in Malaysia and Singapore* (Kuala Lumpur: OUP, revised edn., 1979) pp. 102–11; Y. Akashi, 'Japanese Military Administration in Malaya', paper presented to International Conference on Asian History (Kuala Lumpur, August 1968).

22. Radin Soenarno, 'Malay Nationalism, 1900–1945', *Journal of Southeast Asian History*, I, 1 (March 1960) pp. 9–15.

23. Ahmad Boestamam, *Carving the Path to the Summit* (Athens: Ohio University Press, 1979); G. Means, *Malaysian Politics* (London: Hodder and Stoughton, 1970) pp. 89–93.

24. James de V. Allen, *The Malayan Union* (New Haven: Yale Monograph, 1967); also, A. J. Stockwell, 'The Development of Malay Politics during the course of the Malayan Union experiment', PhD thesis (London University, 1973).

25. Radin Soenarno, 'Malay Nationalism, 1900–1945'.

26. Ishak bin Tadin, 'Dato Onn and Malay Nationalism, 1946–1951', *Journal of Southeast Asian History*, I, 1 (March 1960) pp. 56–88.

27. Mohd. Noordin Sopiee, *From Malayan Union to Singapore Separation* (Kuala Lumpur: University of Malaya Press, 1974) pp. 13–20.

28. Yeo Kim Wah, 'The Anti-Federation Movement in Malaya, 1945–48'. *Journal of Southeast Asian Studies*, IV, 1 (March 1973) pp. 31–51.

29. Yeo Kim Wah, *Political Development in Singapore 1945–1955* (Singapore: University of Singapore Press, 1973) pp. 88–98.

30. Cheah Boon Kheng, *The Masked Comrades: A Study of the Communist United Front in Malaya, 1945–48* (Singapore: Times Books International, 1979) pp. 16–42.

31. Stenson, *Industrial Conflict in Malaya*, pp. 181–213.

32. M. Stenson, 'The Ethnic and Urban Bases of Communist Revolt in Malaya', in J. W. Lewis (ed), *Peasant Rebellion and Communist Revolution in Asia* (Palo Alto: Stanford University Press, 1978) pp. 125–50.

33. Yeo Kim Wah, 'The Anti-Federation Movement in Malaya, 1946–48', pp. 21–51.

34. Yeo Kim Wah, *Political Development in Singapore*, pp. 40–4.

35. Stenson, *Industrial Conflict in Malaya*, pp. 153–80.

36. C. Hanrahan, *The Communist Struggle in Malaya* (New York: Institute of Pacific Relations, 1954).

37. See A. Short, *The Communist Insurrection in Malaya, 1948–60* (London: Federick Muller Ltd., 1975); R. Clutterbuck, *The Long Long War* (London: Faber and Faber, 1966).

38. James Puthucheary, *Ownership and Control in the Malayan Economy* (Singapore: Eastern Universities Press, 1960) pp. 23–59.

39. Interview with Tun H. S. Lee, 5 September 1979, Kuala Lumpur.

40. Means, *Malaysian Politics*, p. 26.

41. Interview with Tun Tan Siew Sin (former Finance Minister and President of MCA, 1960–74), 15 October 1979, Kuala Lumpur.

42. Interview with Tunku Abdul Rahman Putra (Prime Minister of Malaysia, 1957–1971), 10 September 1979, Kuala Lumpur.

43. Interview with Tan Sri T. H. Tan, 29 September 1979, Kuala Lumpur.

44. *Straits Times*, 6 April 1953.

45. *Straits Times*, 28 December 1953.

46. *Straits Times*, 15 October 1954.

47. Interview with Tunku Abdul Rahman, 15 October 1979, Kuala Lumpur.

48. *The Times*, (London), 20 August 1953.

49. *Straits Times*, 1 February 1954.

50. *The Times*, 22 April 1954.

51. *The Times*, 28 April 1954.

52. *The Times*, 24 May 1954.

53. *The Times*, 26 May 1954.

54. T. H. Tan, *The Prince and I* (Singapore: Sam Boyd Enterprise and Mini Media, 1979), pp. 84–112.

55. *Straits Times*, 28 June 1954.

56. H. Miller, *Prince and Premier* (London: Harrap, 1959), pp. 156–60.

57. *Ibid.*, pp. 160–1.

58. R. S. Milne and Diane Mauzy, *Politics and Government in Malaysia* (Singapore: Federal Publications, 1978) pp. 23–44.

59. Means, *Malaysian Politics*, pp. 170–1.

60. *Straits Times*, 2 January 1956.

61. Means, *Malaysian Politics*, pp. 265–71.

62. Unpublished report by Tunku Abdul Rahman of meeting at Government House, Singapore, 20 October 1955.

63. Interview with Tan Sri T. H. Tan, 29 September 1979.

64. *The Times*, 19 January 1956.

65. *Straits Times*, 9 February 1956.

66. *Straits Times*, 17 January 1956.

67. *Straits Times*, 11 July 1956.

68. *Straits Times*, 13 August 1956.

69. *Straits Times*, 25 August 1956.

70. Records of Meetings of the Alliance Working Party on Constitutional Problems (unpublished, April–September 1956).

71. *Straits Times*, 31 March 1956. Also, M. Rudner, *Nationalism, Planning and Economic Modernization in Malaysia* (Beverly Hills/London: Sage Publications, 1975) pp. 18–23.

72. *The Times*, 8 March 1956.

73. Rudner, *Nationalism, Planning and Economic Modernization in Malaysia*, pp. 11–12.

74. Means, *Malaysian Politics*, pp. 265–86.

75. W. Hanna, *The Formation of Malaysia* (New York: American Universities Field Service, 1964) pp. 7–30.

76. S. Bedlington, *Malaysia and Singapore: The Building of New States* (Ithaca: Cornell University Press, 1978) pp. 200–6. Also, Pang Chang-lian, *Singapore's People's Action Party* (Singapore: OUP, 1971).

77. *The Times*, 16 May 1956.

78. Mohd. Noordin Sopiee, *From Malayan Union to Singapore Separation* pp. 125–72.

79. *Ibid.*, pp. 172–82; D. S. Ranjit Singh, 'The Internal Politics of Brunei in the 1950s and 60s', unpublished paper presented to the 8th Conference of International Association of Historians (Kuala Lumpur, August 1980).
80. Interview with Tunku Abdul Rahman, 15 October 1979.
81. J. A. C. Mackie, *Konfrontasi: The Indonesia-Malaysia Dispute, 1963–1966* (Kuala Lumpur: OUP, 1974) pp. 111–235.
82. Means, *Malaysian Politics*, pp. 317–18.

Conclusion: Sequence, Crux and Means: Some Asian Nationalisms Compared

D. A. Low

For most of the first half of the twentieth century Western imperial rule had stretched over most parts of South and Southeast Asia—British rule in South Asia, Malaya, Singapore and North Borneo; Dutch in Indonesia; French in Indochina; American in the Philippines.

Between 1942 and 1945 the Japanese conquest of Southeast Asia supervened. Upon the Japanese defeat in 1945 the Western imperial powers returned to Southeast Asia. But there then ensued over the next dramatic eleven years, from 1946 to 1957, the removal of Western imperial domination from country after country in South and Southeast Asia alike, and thereupon the winning by a whole series of major Asian countries of international recognition as independent nations. The Philippines led the way in 1946; India and Pakistan followed in 1947; Burma and Ceylon (now Sri Lanka) in 1948; Indonesia in 1949; Vietnam in 1954; and finally Malaya in 1957.

The individual experiences of five of these countries have been set out earlier in this book. Here in the last chapter an opportunity will be taken to compare some of these experiences in such a way as to underscore the distinctive features of each.[1]

Several sets of comparisons could be readily suggested, many of which would touch on the nature of imperialism and on the colonial reaction to it. Many of these would relate to large economic questions—of dependence, exploitation and development—and to so much that was involved when one people lorded it over another.

There might be some very particular comparisons, such as, for example, on the extent of indigenous participation in higher governmental activity — bureaucratic or 'parliamentary' — prior to independence, and the implications of the different forms which this took for varying occurrences in the post-independence period. There can be fruitful comparisons, as well, of the degree to which indigenous rural leadership was undermined or upheld during the colonial years, and of the implications of this for later developments. There could be interesting comparisons too relating to the composition of armed forces, the extent of Western education and a plethora of other matters besides.

From amongst the issues that might be raised, three have been chosen for discussion. The first relates to the often unappreciated parallels in the experiences of nationalist and other forces in the different countries in the decades preceding independence; the second to the dissimilarities in the critical final years, from the independence of the Philippines in 1946 to the independence of Malaya in 1957; the third to the widely differing sociopolitical processes that determined the means by which independence was secured.

A moment's thought will soon emphasise the similarities in the context of all the countries discussed in this book that stemmed from a series of events of major global significance during the first half of the twentieth century. If the Russo-Japanese War of 1904-5 was in some respects not of quite that order, its importance for the general history of South and Southeast Asia in the first decade of the twentieth century is not to be gainsaid. There was then the First World War of 1914-18, and in 1917 the momentous Bolshevik Revolution in Russia, both of which clearly had major global implications. Although in the 1920s the immediacy of these events gradually receded, and a sense of somewhat quieter times seemed to spread, this was soon rudely shattered for all manner of people across the world from 1929 onwards with the onset of the Great Depression; it was only in the later 1930s that the worst consequences of this came to be weathered. With the outbreak of the Second World War in 1939, and (more especially for the countries under discussion here) its swift and dramatic spread to the eastern hemisphere following the Japanese attack on Pearl Harbour in December 1941, global events of immense magnitude came to dominate the scene once again. In relation to the concerns of this book, the defeat of the Axis Powers in 1945 was no less portentous, while the beginnings of the Cold War shortly afterwards cast its shadow over this region as much as any other.

While these major events at the global level were not the only influences that created commonalities in the histories which were earlier surveyed in this book, a reminder of them indicates something of the importance of moving beyond the particularities of each case to a consideration of the comparisons which appear when one places them alongside each other.

It is, of course, true that in so many respects developments in the first half of the twentieth century in the different countries of South and Southeast Asia which we are considering often took place seemingly quite independently of each other and often, as it were, by fits and starts. For all that, with very obvious qualifications as to different particularities, significant parallels are to be found and in rounding out this book it seems worth exploring some of them.

SEQUENCE: NATIONALIST PARALLELS

Let us consider, in the first place, the sequences in the main political occurrences in South and Southeast Asia which have been discussed here over the first half of the twentieth century, and note the neglected fact that they often had much more striking similarities than have been generally appreciated. Consider the following.

As the twentieth century opened (with, for example, the American annexation of the Philippines at the expense of both Spain and the Filipino revolution), nationalism and independence were both already well developed conceptions amongst the Asian elites in all the countries we have considered, and several others besides—in the Philippines of Aguinaldo; in the India of Tilak, Gokhale, Banerji, Aurobindo and Naoroji; in the Vietnam of Phan Boi Chau and his contemporaries; in the Java of Kartini and Wahidin Sudironusodo; in the Burma of U Ba Pe; even to some extent in Malaya.

A great fillip to their development was then given by the dramatic Japanese defeat of the European power, Russia, in the Russo-Japanese war of 1904-5; and in the ensuing ten years there took place a considerable number of violent nationalist upheavals that had many characteristics in common. They were generally organised by elitist groups; usually on a small scale; and in almost every case were essentially designed to scare the imperialists. They occurred most strikingly in India and in Vietnam. For their participants they were all uniformly disastrous. As a consequence, it became of critical importance for far-sighted nationalists to consider some quite different possibilities.

These as it happened seemed to be adumbrated by the Chinese revolution of 1911 which entailed much more wide-ranging developments. The whole situation was then transformed by the First World War and by the still greater Russian Revolution of 1917.

In these circumstances the similarities between the major movements for change in the major countries of Asia surfaced quite plainly—and for the time being, as we shall see, China should be included in the consideration here. For out of the First World War there came a quite new temper in almost all the larger countries of Asia. One can see this in the May Fourth movement in China; in the mid-war development of the Home Rule Leagues and then Gandhi's first national *satyagrahas* in India; in the agitations of U Ottama and the General Council of Buddhist Associations in Burma; in the important new developments within Sarekat Islam in Indonesia; and so on.

Sarekat Islam was particularly significant. For, while most other movements still tended to have an elitist flavour, Sarekat Islam successfully spread itself during the first quarter of the twentieth century well beyond the small Westernized elite. It represented in fact the Indonesian version of the much broader religiopolitical upheavals which were widely characteristic of the Islamic world in the first twenty-five years of the twentieth century. These reached their climax upon the defeat and final destruction of the centuries-old Ottoman Empire at the end of the First World War. That event not only had an influence in Malaya and in Indonesia, it very directly powered the Khilafat movement in India. Recent scholarship suggests indeed that it was these Muslim movements rather than embryonic nationalist movements as such which in a crucial way first generated extensive support in Asia for anti-colonialism. Although both the Indian nationalist movement and the Indonesian nationalist movement soon loosed themselves from this Muslim tide (which in any case itself soon ebbed), the significant fact is that from this time onwards these movements were clearly inspired by the belief that they could be *mass* movements. They lived in the confidence, that is, that it was quite within the bounds of possibility for them to draw upon country-wide support for their campaigns. Such confidence only came to their contemporaries in some of the other Asian countries later on. Because indeed the Muslim movements in India and Indonesia had no counterpart in the Philippines, or in China or in Vietnam, the course which was followed there differed quite substantially. It is striking, for example, that while by the 1920s, the days of almost unalloyed elitist nationalism in India and Indonesia were all but over, in Vietnam where there was no Muslim movement because there were no Muslims, elitist nationalism persisted, and soon reached its climax with the unsuccessful, violent uprising in 1930 by the recently formed elitist VNQDD (the Vietnamese Nationalist Party).

The change which did then come in Vietnam stemmed largely from the Russian Revolution, which through the Third International elicited significant support for the communist movement from amongst the more ardent opponents of existing regimes—indeed, in several cases, for the Communist International itself, particularly perhaps among the French-speaking Indochinese elite. Some of the most important individuals who were then caught up in this particular development in due course became key figures in their countries. One thinks of Mao Tse-tung, Ho Chi Minh, Tan Malaka, Musso and M. N. Roy. They were not of course confined to Vietnam.

One striking fact however about the 1920s in Asia was that the various communist initiatives which ensued soon suffered very severe setbacks. The Dutch regime in Indonesia very easily crushed the communist revolts in Java and Sumatra in 1926-7. In 1927 Chiang Kai-shek wheeled upon the Chinese Communists and destroyed four-fifths of them. In 1929 the British, by means of the long-winded Meerut Conspiracy Case, swept the Indian Communist leadership into jail; while over the following two years the French in Vietnam ruthlessly crushed a rash of peasant revolts with which the Communists were associated in the provinces of Thai Binh and Nghe An (see illustrations, pp. 158, 159).

Once again a different, though by no means less vigorous, approach was pursued by others. In the late 1920s the Indonesian Dutch-educated elite joined with the young engineer Sukarno to form the Partai Nasional Indonesia to mount a radical nationalist campaign; while in India, Gandhi and the new Congress peasant-oriented leadership, of such as Rajendra Prasad, Vallabhbhai Patel and Abdul Ghaffar Khan, along with several younger leaders like Jawaharlal

Nehru and Subhash Bose, were soon mounting a major new campaign against British dominion in India—knowing that they had done this once already in the Khilafat — non-co-operation movement — of 1920-2.

It soon became clear, however, that almost all the regimes still paramount in Asia were, in the early 1930s, no less determined to crush these other challenges to their dominion than they were to expunge the communists. Thus the French White Terror of 1930-1 was as much directed against the VNQDD as against the Indochinese Communists. The Meerut Conspiracy Case against the Communists in India was soon overshadowed by Britain's ultimately unremitting repression of Gandhi's two Civil Disobedience Movements (1930-1, 1932-4) (see illustration, p. 66). During 1930 the Saya San rebellion was vigorously suppressed in Burma, while first in 1929, and then more particularly in 1933, Sukarno was arraigned by the Dutch, who the second time around all but destroyed the Indonesian nationalist movement. When indeed one looks about in the mid-1930s for the major figures of a decade or so later, one not only sees Mao cooped up in Yenan and Ho in exile in Moscow, but Nehru in Dehra Dun prison and Sukarno in exile in Flores.

Nevertheless in a quite remarkable way the mid-1930s did then see some very significant recoveries. During the preceding decades the American regime in the Philippines had tended to be much more liberal towards its local nationalists than the other imperialist powers. However under the Republicans, Coolidge, Harding and Hoover, and their successive nominees, Wood, Stimson and Welles, the prospects throughout the 1920s for Philippines independence had never been dimmer. But following Roosevelt's presidential victory in 1932, the outlook improved. And out of the toing and froing of the Hoare-Haws-Cutting Act of 1933, its rejection by the Filipino oligarchy and legislature, that was nevertheless followed by Quezon's support for the Tydings-McDuffie Act, there then came the establishment of the Commonwealth of the Philippines under Quezon's presidency in 1935, along with the promise of complete independence a decade later (see illustration, p. 20). In the following year, 1936, the advent of the Popular Front Government in France led to a momentary revival of a few political freedoms in Vietnam, which the lately formed Indochinese Communist Party used in a highly skilful way to build up its popular support (see illustration, p. 160). In December 1936 the Sian Incident gave Mao and the Chinese Communist Party a quite new standing in China as allies against the Japanese of the Kuomintang, of which over the following decade they were to make quite spectacular use. In the early part of 1937 the Indian National Congress successfully capped its recent series of electoral victories by securing control of seven of the eleven provincial governments of India; while that year 'Responsible Government', as the British termed it, came to Burma as well, with Ba Maw as the country's first Premier. In Indonesia alone was there still no movement, with only the collaborating parties possessing the freedom to operate.

Taken together these various developments in the second half of the 1930s were to be of singular importance for the future. While they entrenched the Filipino oligarchy (the only nationalist leadership which had so far secured a clear promise that they would shortly take over from their imperial rulers), they everywhere else undermined the existing regime's local supporters. They gravely weakened the anti-Congress Liberals, etc., in India; Gerindo and Parindra in Indonesia; the Constitutionalist Party in Vietnam; even the supporters of the Kuomintang in China. At the same time they were of great importance on the other side. They saw Mao establishing himself as the prime Chinese Communist leader. The Indochinese Communist Party successfully replaced the VNQDD as the leading Vietnamese nationalist party. Despite patent British opposition, the Indian National Congress convincingly displayed its ability to win a massive electoral victory. In Indonesia Sukarno's pre-eminence as a nationalist leader was becoming firmly entrenched, while Aung San and U Nu were already on the way to becoming well-known nationalist leaders in Burma. The casts were already largely chosen for the greater dramas of the 1940s.

It was then that the Second World War supervened, and late in 1941 extended to all of Southeast Asia. This very directly cut across the older confrontations, and raised some quite new possibilities for their resolution. The Vichyite French stayed on in Vietnam—but only at the mercy of the Japanese. The British were driven from Malaya and Burma; the Dutch from Indonesia; the Americans from the Philippines; and at one stage it even looked as if the Japanese might soon be marching into India. The previous apparent inviolability of the Western imperial regimes was broken, where indeed it was not altogether destroyed.

In these circumstances the future for the nationalist and radical movements was nevertheless very often quite unclear. Given the stark intensity of the moral–political issues which the Japanese onslaughts posed, it was of considerable moment that Mao did not break at this time with Chiang; that Osmena stuck with Quezon and went into exile with him from the Philippines to America; and that Nehru in India, Sjahrir in Indonesia and many others besides, stood out unrelentingly against the Japanese. There were of course others who took a different course – perhaps out of expediency; perhaps in an effort to hold their existing gains intact; perhaps because they saw no end to the Japanese occupation. Thus, in 1940, the former revolutionary and Kuomintang leftist leader, Wang Ching-wei, became the premier of a Japanese puppet government in Nanking. A few months later Subhash Bose, Nehru's rival for the plaudits of the younger Indian nationalists, fled to join the Axis Powers, and in due course formed the Indian National Army to support the Japanese. In the Philippines, Quezon's secretary, Vargas, stayed behind in Manila and then headed up the Philippines Executive Commission which cooperated with the Japanese. Aung San and his 'Thirty Comrades' went to Japan and created the Burma Independence Army; before very long Ba Maw, moreover, who had been premier of Burma under the British, agreed to serve as his country's head of state under the Japanese; while, following his release by the Japanese from detention in July 1942, Sukarno, and his later vice-president, Hatta, both agreed to take prominent positions under the Japanese occupying forces (in March 1943, for example, Sukarno formed PUTERA, an association organized to mobilise the urban elite of Java in support of the Japanese war effort).

As the war then turned against them, the Japanese sought to push these processes further. In October 1943 they established the Republic of the Philippines under the presidency of a typical Filipino oligarch, Jose Laurel. With their concurrence, Aung San became prime minister of an allegedly more independent Burma. In March 1945 (having eventually turned against the Vichyite French) the Japanese elevated the King, Bao Dai, to become the head of an independent Vietnamese state; while in August 1945 some of Japan's by this time defeated military leaders very evidently gave active encouragement to the Indonesian nationalists as they moved towards proclaiming the independent Indonesian republic.

The ambiguities which suffused these situations could be traced out in some detail. It is fascinating to note, for example, the skill with which some of those who walked the knife-edge managed to survive the Japanese defeat—Sukarno for a start, chairman of PUTERA under the Japanese, but president of the Indonesian Republic after their defeat. Likewise, the first president of the post-war American-supported independent Republic of the Philippines was none other than Manuel Roxas, a collaborator with the Japanese, but General MacArthur's protégé following their defeat. Similarly Aung San, who originally actively collaborated with the Japanese, nevertheless linked up in good time with the British commander-in-chief, Lord Mountbatten, and placed himself securely in a position to lead Burma into independence.

As the Asian world teetered on several brinks at once in late 1945 there continued to be parallels in their affairs. It was notable, for example, that the leaders of the radical forces opposing the older and in a number of cases now once again dominant regimes, not only moved very cautiously, but actually entered into negotiations with them. They all began by feeling that more was to be gained by *diplomasi*, as the Indonesians called it, than by *perjuangan* (the Indonesian term for 'struggle'). Thus Chou En-lai and Mao parleyed with Chiang. The Indian leaders met Wavell in Simla in 1945, and negotiated with the British Cabinet Mission in the following year. Ho Chi Minh signed the 6 March Agreement with Sainteny, and attended the Fontainebleau Conference in Paris in 1946. The Indonesian leaders signed the Linggajati Agreement with the Dutch in March 1947, and the Renville Agreement in January 1948.

Nevertheless the most important parallel was also the most striking. It was in the aftermath of the Second World War, particularly between 1946 and 1950, that the final triumph occurred of the main new forces which had been let loose in the twentieth century in all these countries – except in Malaya where independence did not come until 1957, and in Indochina where it was only partly secured in 1954, and not finally until 1975.

This particular recital confirms the impression that the direct interaction between the imperialist and nationalist struggles in the different countries of Asia was in many tangible respects very limited. But it also shows that over forty years and more they seem even so to have oscillated almost in parallel with each other between periods of confrontation and periods of accommodation, and that therefore they have had histories which are more in common with each other than is generally realised.

If one puts it briefly, the story is as follows. In the combination of euphoria and anxiety that came out of the First World War the nationalist and radical forces in Asia first extensively flexed their muscles. As, during the 1920s, the war years receded and western Europe once more regained a degree of self-assurance, very strict curbs came to be placed upon their nationalist (let alone Communist) endeavours. During the depression years of the early 1930s they were indeed often harshly repressed. But as the Western world then moved back to a further time of troubles, there seemed to be some let up, and it was during these years that so many of the new generation of nationalist leaders firmly pegged out their claims on the future. That future was then thrown into considerable confusion by the victories of Japanese armies in the middle years of the Second World War. But with the Japanese defeat in 1945 providing a unique opportunity, the now entrenched Asian nationalists finally moved out to claim their inheritances. To begin with this involved all of them in negotiations with their corresponding colonial power; and the upshot then turned, as we shall see, not on the ability of the nationalists to expel their Western rulers — which was soon no longer in doubt — nor even on whether their particular colonial power had decided to forego its Asian empire or not, but rather on the much narrower issue of the terms on which residual connections acceptable to the imperial power could be established.

CRUX: DISSIMILAR DÉNOUEMENTS

For all the similarities in these stories up to the 1940s, there were nevertheless differences, and it was during the last years of imperial rule in Asia that these became particularly apparent. This raises another set of issues to consider. Striking contrasts began to emerge at the very moment of the Japanese defeat, especially regarding the position which the imperial powers held, or did not hold, in their ex-colonial territories; and they steadily became larger.

Quite remarkably in 1945 the British once again secured imperial control of Malaya. They were still just in control of their empire in India. But they did not so readily regain control of Burma. In the months before the war ended, the Americans for their part effectively re-established their control over the Philippines. But even several months after the Second World War had finished, the Dutch, to their fury, were still not back in control of Indonesia; nor the French of Vietnam. Thus while the British in India and Malaya, and the Americans in the Philippines, could still very largely (in the short run at least) determine the course of events in the territories they claimed as theirs (as the nationalists in each of these cases generally understood), the Dutch found themselves confronted in August 1945 by Sukarno's proclamation of the independent Republic of Indonesia, and the French by Ho Chi Minh's declaration in September 1945 of the independent Democratic Republic of Vietnam. What was scarcely less portentous, both Ho and Sukarno already controlled some of their countries' major cities.

Such contrasts were soon compounded. As in 1946 the Philippines moved peacefully to independence, a full-scale war broke out between the Communists and the Kuomintang in China. Two years later this culminated in Lin Piao's great victory in the Huai-hai campaign, which was soon followed by Mao's declaration in Peking in October 1949 of the People's Republic of China. These massive events provided the ever-present backdrop to contemporary developments elsewhere, particularly in Southeast Asia. They were not, however, readily repeated elsewhere. For none of the colonial territories had suffered the extensive collapse of an ordered society to the extent that China had; none of them saw the decisive military overthrow of the previous dominant regime that China did; and thus, not only was the Chinese revolution unique in its time; its concerns became separated for a decade and more from those which predominated in most of the other Asian countries.

This was not for lack of activity on the part of communist, or at all events markedly leftist, movements elsewhere. In the middle and late 1940s there were considerable leftist revolts in India (in Telengana, Kerala and Bengal); in the Philippines (the Hukbalahap); in Indonesia (under the Moscow returnees, Tan Malaka and Musso); while by the end of the Second World War the Malayan Communist Party was probably the most powerful in the country, and in 1948 took to armed revolt. Nehru's India, however, repressed all of the Indian outbreaks. American support for the Filipino oligarchs just held the Huks at bay in the Philippines. The incautious precipitancy of the Madiun affair in September–October 1948 thwarted the hopes of the Partai Komunis Indonesia, for the time being at least; while in 1948 the British declared the Malayan Emergency and by 1954 had successfully reduced the largely Chinese Malayan Communists to a marginal minority ekeing out a living in the forests. Only Ho Chi Minh, with his Yenan in Cao Bang, managed to survive the post-war onslaughts against the Communists and their like in the ex-colonial territories, and even there Giap's great victory at Dien Bien Phu in 1954 did not come until five years after Lin Piao's in northern China, and even then secured control only of North Vietnam.

In each of these cases we can see the imperial powers seeking to establish regimes with which they could hope to live subsequently. In China General Marshall and other American representatives sought to bolster up the Kuomintang, or at all events ensure that it should be the dominant partner in any coalition with the Communists. They failed of course; the situation was not so amenable to their control. But in the Philippines where the Americans did re-establish their control, Roxas, MacArthur's choice, became in 1946 the first president of the post-war independent Republic of the Philippines. In India Mountbatten in 1947 made his settlements with Nehru and Gandhi and Patel and Jinnah. In Burma, Rance cut Britain's losses and transferred power to Aung San; while in Malaya the British managed to reaffirm their existing alliance with the Malayan elite.

D'Argenlieu in Vietnam tried a variant of these procedures, but with a significantly different objective. Inherently hostile to the Viet Minh, and to its Communist core in particular, he energetically strove to reinstall the former King, Bao Dai, in Vietnam in the hope that France might live with a regime which he headed, and certainly elbow Ho Chi Minh aside. For some years so it turned out, but only at the cost of mounting conflict with the Viet Minh. In Indonesia Van Mook tried a similar line. Despite Musso and Tan Malaka the Indonesian nationalists were never led by their Communists. But they were led by a man whom the Dutch (understandably seared by their experience of the German occupation) considered a quisling. For this, as well as the economic reasons canvassed in the introduction to this book, the Dutch wanted to thrust the radical Indonesian nationalists aside as well. Accordingly Van Mook tried to mobilise the non-Javanese in Indonesia into a Federation under the Dutch Crown so as to confine the Indonesian Republic to its Javanese heartland (see map, p. 149).

It was in these various connections that one of the most striking contrasts in Asia at this time could soon be discerned. For while the Americans in the Philippines and the British in South Asia had by the end of the Second World War clearly decided to depart (and were ready to go from Malaya and Singapore as well, once the Communists there had been defeated), the French and the Dutch still bent every effort to cling on. As a consequence there were strict limits, for the Indonesian and Vietnamese nationalist leaders, to the efficacy of *diplomasi*, and it was not long before armed conflict with their controlling powers broke out in each of their countries.

There was a striking contrast here. On the one hand, those movements which did not need to take military action against the formerly dominant regimes were those which had not had an opportunity during the war to develop their own military forces. On the other, those that did need to take military action against the older regimes did happen, in one way or another, to have had such an opportunity to build up an effective nucleus of their own military forces during the war. Thus Mao had built up the Red Army to an impregnable position in the northern parts of China. In Indonesia, the Japanese had encouraged the creation of PETA, which became the starting point for the Indonesian republican army against the Dutch; while in Vietnam, Ho and Giap had been able to develop a key military base for their revolutionary army in northern Tonkin. Paradoxically, but for this contrast, the divergencies in the stories of the transfers of power in Asia could have been even greater.

Of the five main stories outlined in this book the most straightforward occurred in the Philippines. Here, from the days of their takeover from the Spaniards, the Americans had maintained the Filipino oligarchy in power. This elite managed to hold on to its position throughout the Japanese occupation; and after the war authority was transferred to it remarkably smoothly by the Americans. For this the Americans reaped their reward in the special commercial and military privileges which they enjoyed in the Philippines in the decades that followed. As a consequence the Philippines continued to have one of the most unreconstructed social orders in Asia; while there was a modicum of land reform, power was still held by those who owned its very substantial estates.

A transfer of power was similarly effected in India and Pakistan in the immediate post-war years without armed conflict between the British and the Indian nationalist movement. But by contrast with the Philippines, the transfer particularly in India saw not the entrenchment of a landholding oligarchy, but the coming to power at national level of those who had long held power at village level.

India's attainment of independence was in every respect the outcome of a much more strenuous struggle than it was for the Philippines. It depended greatly on the extraordinarily magnetic leadership of Gandhi. His prime achievement had been to bring into the nationalist movement tens of thousands of activists from the towns and villages of India, who eventually secured hundreds of thousands of supporters. During the period from 1917 to 1937 the tactic the British primarily employed against the Indian nationalist movement had been to extend the franchise for the provincial legislatures in British India beyond the bounds of those groups from which the Indian National Congress had so far recruited support. By enfranchising something like 4-5 per cent of the population, the British were relatively successful in maintaining their position in the years beween 1920 and 1935; the elected provincial legislatures of British India, and the executives partially linked to them in the 'Dyarchy' period, generally withstood the Congress onslaught. At the same time the British deflected the thrust of Congress-led peasant agitations, first by making concessions, and then by displaying a determination to confiscate land when concessions proved ineffectual. But their extensive use of police repression against Congress' two major Civil Disobedience campaigns of 1930-4 nevertheless alienated many people of influence. As a result, when in the mid-1930s they sought once again to undercut the nationalist movement by extending the franchise to nearly 12 per cent of the population, they found that the Congress had now undercut them. The consequence here was that at the provincial elections of 1937 Congress not only achieved a dramatic electoral victory. Because of the provisions of the new Government of India Act of 1935 Congress went on to secure control of seven of the eleven provincial governments in India.

It is true that during the Second World War there was a marked conservative reaction in British Indian policy. But as Churchill's appointee in 1943 to the Viceroyalty, Field Marshal Lord Wavell, immediately appreciated, Britain's interest in maintaining its empire in India had now distinctly declined. British preferences and British trade with India had dropped. India indeed was now becoming costly for Britain. The Indian Army, for example, was not the inexpensive asset it had once been in the past. Accordingly, Mountbatten, Wavell's successor, took energetic steps in 1947 to transfer power to those who at the elections of 1946 had amply demonstrated the very considerable political support they possessed in various parts of India. Since the preceding decade had seen in the movement for Pakistan the most striking case of the classic end-of-empire dispute about how power should be disposed upon the attainment of independence, the eventual transfer ultimately entailed the appalling trauma of the Partition between the two successor states of India and Pakistan. But as between Britain itself and the leaders of these states, the transfer was scarcely less smooth than in the Philippines.

By contrast, the transfer of power in Indonesia involved considerable armed confrontation. Though the Dutch had created a small *Volksraad* (assembly), tney had not made any significant constitutional concessions to the Indonesian nationalists. Ultimately this precipitated Sukarno's unilateral declaration of Indonesia's independenence in August 1945 (see illustration, p. 109). In Java the defence thereafter of the embryonic Indonesian Republic regularly involved violent conflict, often of heroic dimensions as, for example, against the British-led forces assisting the Dutch at the Battle of Surabaya in November 1945. That and various other events which followed, brought about the Linggajati Agreement of 1946 by which the Dutch agreed not, it is true, to Sukarno's independent Indonesia, but to the establishment in due course of a federal Indonesia of which Sukarno's Java would be one part. But since there were soon differing interpretations as to what all this meant, the Dutch in July 1947 eventually sought to settle the issue by mounting their First Military Action against the Indonesian forces. This only precipitated intervention, however, by the United Nations through a Good Offices Committee, which in January 1948 patched up the precarious Renville Agreement. Later that year, in the course of the ill-fated Madiun affair, Sukarno's nationalists outwitted the Indonesian Communists. But, still dissatisfied, the Dutch then mounted their fatal Second Military Action. Since this aroused such strong United Nations, and particularly American, support for the Indonesian nationalist – who had just emerged on top of their Communist associates – international pressure soon forced the Dutch to transfer sovereignty before the end of 1949 to the United States of Indonesia.

Vietnam in some significant respects followed a similar course. Back in 1941 Ho Chi Minh, building upon the Communist experience in Vietnam in the late 1930s, formed a united front nationalist organisation, the Viet Minh. Under Vo Nguyen Giap's remarkable military leadership this formed a military base in northern Tonkin during the Japanese military occupation. Following the Japanese defeat in 1945, Ho dramatically proclaimed the independence of Vietnam. But the French nevertheless re-established themselves in south and central Vietnam, and in March 1946 forced Ho to accept Vietnam's participation in the newly formed French Union, in exchange for French recognition of his Viet Minh government. But such compromises (as in Indonesia) soon collapsed, and before 1946 was out, full-scale war – the first Indochina War (1946-54) – had broken out between France and the Viet Minh.

In the years that followed the Viet Minh forces steadily increased their hold on the northern countryside. But, unlike the Indonesian nationalists, they won little support in the West, particularly when following the victory of the Chinese Communists in 1946 they more openly proclaimed their Communist attachments. French arms, moreover, were more substantial than Dutch. The French were able to play on Communist control of the Viet Minh to hold at least some Vietnamese nationalists to their side; and as we have noted, they once more made the former King Bao Dai head of a Viet-namese puppet state. In the end, however, the Viet Minh forces wore down the French, and at Dien Bien Phu in 1954 delivered their brilliant *coup de grace*. By then the Geneva Conference had been called, and this gave full control over northern Vietnam to Ho Chi Minh and his Viet Minh.

The contrasts were thus plain. In the Philippines the Americans transferred power to the Filipino oligarchy which readily provided them with a continuing commercial and military presence. In South Asia the British accepted the legitimacy of the Indian, Pakistani and Ceylonese nationalist leaderships, and thankfully clutched at their readiness to remain members of the British Commonwealth of Nations. In both these major cases, transfers of power were accord-ingly effected without armed conflict; but it was different elsewhere. The Dutch did not accept the right of what they saw as the Javanese quisling, Sukarno, to rule Indonesia, and they had no confidence that he and his regime would uphold the Dutch notion of an Indonesian federal state within the 'Realm' of the Queen of the Netherlands. Armed warfare accordingly followed. Likewise, many Frenchmen abhorred the Viet Minh leadership in Vietnam for its Communist commitments, and still more questioned its readiness to accept Vietnam's place in the French Union. War followed here too.

The intricacies of these contrasts are all strikingly exemplified in the Malayan case. Here in a situation where the native state structure

was maintained by the imperial power, a strong nationalist movement was as slow to develop as it had been in the Indian states – or in
many of the outer islands of Indonesia. Because of the openings for
able Malays in the state bureaucracies, many ambitious young
Malays found their energies and abilities adequately provided for.
During the Second World War the Malays were by no means
enamoured of their Japanese conquerors. Upon the Japanese defeat
their leaders became particularly anxious, however, that the most
active of the anti-Japanese elements, the Malayan Communists,
should not inherit the future. By trying to impose an impolitic
Malayan Union upon the country, the British nearly bungled the
outcome. But they soon reacted positively to the vehement opposition which this generated, and thereupon fashioned the much more
acceptable Federation of Malaya in its place. The alliance between
the British and the Malayan elite which this entailed thrust the largely
Chinese Malayan Communists, who had developed a strong forest
base during the years of the Japanese occupation, into violent opposition. War (euphemistically termed the Emergency) between the
British and the Malayan Communists then ensued in 1948. But by
contrast with the position of the Dutch in Indonesia, and of the
French in large parts of Vietnam, the British in this Malayan conflict
had the majority of the local population on their side. By combining
successful military operations against the Malayan Communists with
steady constitutional concessions to the Malayan nationalists, and
their Malayan Chinese and Indian allies, the British were eventually
able, to a degree the French and the Dutch never managed, to defeat
the major Communist threat. They then transferred power to a right-
of-centre independent Malayan regime which upon achieving independence in 1957 was happy to remain within the British Commonwealth (see illustration, p. 210).

It needs no emphasising that in every case where an active nationalist movement emerged, independence came by one route or another
eventually. We may still compare, however, the varying sociopolitical
means by which this was secured, and in bringing this book to a
conclusion let us turn finally to consider these.

MEANS: SOCIO-POLITICAL CONTRASTS

Following the example of the Russian Revolution of 1917, it had
long been expected by many of those involved that independence in

the colonial world would most probably come by way of a leftist urban revolt. Here the case of the Communist Party of India is particularly suggestive as to what in the event happened. In the two decades up to the Second World War, the CPI was probably the most substantial urban Communist Party in Asia. In the 1920s it secured a remarkably strong base in Bombay; by the early 1940s it was strong also in other cities such as Calcutta. In 1929, as we have seen, its leaders were imprisoned by the British as a consequence of the long-drawn-out Meerut Conspiracy Case. But by contrast with what occurred elsewhere, in China, Indochina and Indonesia, the leaders of the Communist Party of India were not largely destroyed by their ruling power. During their imprisonment they relied on the Comintern to maintain their position, and on their release in 1933 they mainly returned to their old party bailiwicks in the cities.

Paradoxically this constituted their first serious setback. Unlike their counterparts in Indonesia, Indochina and China, they had had no involvement with a leftist rural revolt: indeed the collapse of these elsewhere may well have reinforced their proneness to concentrate on the cities. But to confine themselves, as they very largely tended to do, to the cities was to limit themselves to less than 15 per cent of India's population. Even in the cities, moreover, they at no time held a monopoly of the available radical impulses. They always had to share these with the very different Indian National Congress.

From the mid-1930s onwards the CPI was caught up in two further difficulties which climaxed in a major disaster. The doctrine of its mentors in the Comintern called at this time for 'united fronts'. In India that meant muting its ideological conflict with the Congress governments who in the late 1930s held power in most of the provinces of British India. There then followed in 1941 the enormously damaging period of the 'People's War', when, just as the Indian National Congress was mounting its final 'Quit India' movement of August 1942 against the British, the CPI in effect aligned itself with the British (see illustration, p. 68). It never fully recovered from this, and by the time the Zhdanov line was being propounded in the late 1940s, the revolutionary moment had passed. With the coming of independence all the levers of power in India passed into the hands of the anti-Communist Congress.

The key failure of the CPI seems in retrospect, and by comparison, to have been its failure to 'go rural'. It should be emphasised that this occurred, not simply because it had had some remarkably strong urban bases for nearly two decades, but more particularly because the position in the rural areas made it difficult for it to do so. For, speaking generally, patterns of political authority at the village level in so many parts of India were at this time still remarkably intact, and leftist movements accordingly encountered great difficulties, as they continue to do, in securing an entry there. The importance of this consideration is most illuminatingly exemplified by the case where, in the 1930s, the Communist Party in India did in fact 'go rural'. In north Malabar in southwestern India, during the transition of the previously dominant Nayar caste from matrilineal to patrilineal succession, a breakdown of the structure of authority in the rural areas occurred. As a consequence, significant numbers of younger, Western-educated Nayars became seriously alienated from their society, and moved into the leadership of a rural Communist movement. Such developments were most unusual elsewhere in India.

Against this particular background the characteristics of the Communist movements in Indonesia, Indochina and China – and the later developing Malayan movement—become the more readily apparent. By the early 1930s the first three had all had their experience of a largely rural Communist revolt, which stuck in their memories. All three moreover had suffered the virtual elimination of their urban parties. All that was open to the remnants that survived was, so it seemed, long-term exile. For the Indonesian Communists there was never to be much relief to this, until Sukarno magically established the Republic of Indonesia in 1945, and made it possible for them to return. Although the Partai Komunis Indonesia had some succcesses in the rural areas in the two decades that followed, their ability to 'go rural' was nevertheless, because of their tardy reappearance on the scene, made very difficult.

In the early 1930s the ability to 'go rural' of the Communist Party of China and of the Indochinese Communist Party was severely restricted as well. Since, however, unlike the CPI, they had been destroyed in the cities, their only hope if they were to operate at all was in fact to 'go rural', and as it happened the opportunities to do so were marginally more favourable for them than for their counter-parts in Indonesia. As is well known, the inability of the Kuomintang government to control effectively the whole of China allowed the CCP to establish a rural base in Yenan. The corresponding opportunity in Indochina came first with the advent of the Popular Front Government in France in 1936 and then with the Japanese invasion in 1941, which allowed the ICP to develop its rural cadres and its rural base sooner than might otherwise have occurred, and also to recover a certain position in the cities. In both these cases, moreover—by contrast with the Indian and the Indonesian ones — the Communist movement came to enjoy a substantial hold on the radical tendencies in their countries: in China as the Kuomintang moved politically to the right; in Vietnam following the French extermination in the early 1930s of the VNQDD.

But more to the present point, in both China and Vietnam (in contrast to so much of India, and for that matter Indonesia and Malaya), the ability of the CCP and ICP to 'go rural' seems to have been substantially assisted because both countries experienced serious breakdowns in the structure of authority at rural level during the crucial period. The circumstances were different from those in Malabar. But in China there were the ravages of warlordism on the one side, and social banditry on the other, while in Vietnam there was the serious dislocation of patterns of authority in the rural areas caused by the sustained French assaults upon the rural scholar-gentry. In both instances the way was opened for Communist intrusion into positions of rural leadership.

In both instances, moreover, there was no question of their being caught at a critical moment on 'the wrong side' of the pre-eminent local issue, as the CPI had been in India in August 1942, or the Malayan Communists were to be in the late 1940s. Mao joined Chiang in fighting the Japanese; Ho Chi Minh and Vo Nguyen Giap fought likewise. Both parties were at the same time able to hold on to their redoubts (in Yenan and in northern Tonkin), while the CCP in particular seems to have benefited greatly from the succour it provided to those devastated by the rural rampages of the Japanese armies. In the event, an armed Communist-led revolution was eventually effected in both these countries, even though to achieve this required major war in China and a grotesquely protracted one in Vietnam.

There were, therefore, successful Communist revolutions in Asia. But they were largely rural Communist revolutions, not (despite the ICP's partial recovery in the cities) the essentially urban ones so many had expected.

The Indonesian story represented a very different case. It is important to note that there were many indications that the structures of power at rural level in Indonesia were kept largely intact during the Dutch period. Indeed, the 'agricultural involution' of which Geertz wrote, may well have served to reinforce the position of the *pamong desa* (village officials) at the head of the grievously hard-pressed, but much interlocked village society, particularly in Java. Certainly the ability of the PKI to 'go rural' was always much restricted. It would also seem that in the 1920s and 1930s the Indo-nesian nationalists of Sukarno's ilk did not 'go rural' either–not even to the extent that Sarekat Islam had done before them. Herein no doubt lay one of the major weaknesses of Indonesian nationalism, which would seem to explain why it was so much more easily crushed by the Dutch in the 1930s than Indian nationalism was by the British.

Accordingly, it would seem highly significant in the present context that when in 1945 the opportunity for Sukarno and his associates did eventually come, it was powered by a ferment *in the cities*, particularly among younger men. In the course of the Indo-nesian Revolution Sukarno and his associates had to be careful not to be outmarched on the left. But they were not unsuccessful in this, as the events of the late 1940s were to show. In their armed conflicts with the Dutch, rural support was of some importance to them; that of many small towns even more so. But the evidence is that the eventually successful Indonesian nationalist movement owed its critically important initial thrust to a series of well co-ordinated non-leftist urban revolts in which young activists were to the fore in the Javanese cities of Jakarta, Bandung, Yogyakarta, Surabaya, etc., along with some corresponding upheavals in Sumatra and Makassar.

The Indian case was different again. In terms of the argument outlined above, the central facts are these: while the CPI, as we have seen, for the most part did *not* 'go rural', the Indian National Con-gress in the 1920s and 1930s under Gandhi's leadership *did* 'go rural'. But it did not do so in a situation where the structure of power at rural and village level had broken down; but rather, and very precisely, through association with those whose power at village level remained intact. In the years between 1919 and 1945, the British successfully repressed both rural and urban revolt in India. The Indian National Congress nevertheless edged its way to power, first by securing the support of leading rural as well as urban ele-ments, and then (as these were enfranchised) by winning the elections the British instituted at local, provincial and eventually national levels. In marked contrast to the Indonesian case, the Indian nation-alists themselves took steps in the 1940s to damp down urban revolt.

Despite events in Kerala, Telengana and elsewhere, they had little to fear from the forces of the left. It was therefore essentially a Congress increasingly linked to established village powerholders that won political independence for India.

Once again the Malayan case underlines the points to be made. The Malayan Communists did in a sense 'go rural'. They based themselves in the forests, and it required a much larger effort on the part of the British in Malaya to destroy their influence there than it did, say, the Indian government to destroy the leftist movements in Bengal or Telengana. But the Malayan Communists, who were largely ethnic Chinese, were unable to move out of their forest redoubts and effectively secure control of the countryside, because traditional rural Malay society remained very much intact, and highly resistant to Communist leadership. Malaya's elitist nationalists meanwhile very successfully established their connections not only in the towns but in the various rural areas of Malaya, and thus secured as effective a power base as the Congress in India had before them.

The heritage of all these changes underlay a great deal of post-independence development in South and Southeast Asia. Even several decades later – in the 1970s – the configurations of politics in all these countries clearly reflected the traditions of the years up to the Second World War and in particular the events of the dramatic decade or so which followed. In Vietnam there had been a successful Communist rural revolution. But except in China this did not occur elsewhere. At the critical moment there was an important non-Communist urban upheaval in Indonesia; but there was no major urban Communist revolution there or elsewhere. Whilst there were significant rural Communist revolts in India, Malaya and the Philippines, in none of these countries did these succeed; and in none of them was there a non-Communist urban revolt such as the Indonesian one. In India and Malaya, the urban elites linked up with existing rural powerholders to form an extraordinarily powerful alliance which neither the imperialists nor the Communists could ultimately withstand. This was still more strikingly the case in the Philippines where the Filipino oligarchy remained at once firmly intact and firmly in control of their countrymen.

Increasing distance casts different reflections upon these events. But recent scholarship has been giving them sharper outlines. It is in the belief that we now have some greater understanding of them that this book has been written.

280

SOURCES

1. In addition to the foregoing chapters and a number of the works cited in the Guide to Further Reading at the end of this book, I have also had occasion to refer to the following.

For the Philippines: Usha Mahajani, *Philippines Nationalism* (St Lucia: University of Queensland Press, 1971). For India: Robin Jeffrey, 'Matriliny, Marxism and the Birth of the Communist Party in Kerala, 1930–40,' *Journal of Asian Studies*, XXXVIII, 1 (Nov. 1978) pp. 77–98; Roger Stuart, 'The Formation of the Communist Party of India, 1927–37: the Dilemma of the Indian Left', PhD thesis, Australian National University, 1979. For Vietnam: John T. McAlister, *Vietnam: the Origins of Revolution* (New York: Knopf, 1969). For Burma: U Maung Maung, *From Sangha to Laity: Nationalist Movements of Burma, 1920–40*, (Canberra/New Delhi: ANU Monographs on South Asia, No. 4, 1980). For China: Lucien Bianco, *Origins of the Chinese Revolution, 1915–59* (Palo Alto: Stanford University Press, 1971); Jerome Ch'en, *Mao and the Chinese Revolution* (London: Oxford University Press, 1965); Jean Chesnaux, *Peasant Revolts in China, 1840–1949* (London: Thames and Hudson, 1973); C. P. Fitzgerald, *The Birth of Communist China* Harmondsworth: Penguin, 1964), Chalmers A. Johnson, *Peasant Nationalism and Communist Power: the Emergence of Revolutionary China, 1937–45* (Palo Alto: Stanford University Press, 1962); S. R. Schram, *Mao Tse-tung* (Harmondsworth: Penguin, 1966), B. I. Schwartz, *Chinese Communism and the Rise of Mao* (Cambridge, Mass.: Harvard University Press, 1951).

I am indebted to my colleagues, Professor Wang Gungwu and Dr Lo Hui-min, for introducing me to the voluminous literature on China.

Biographical Notes

THE PHILIPPINES

AGUINALDO, Emilio (1869-1964). Born Kawit, Cavite Province just south of Manila. Mother was a Chinese *mestiza* and father a prosperous Tagalog farmer who served several times as mayor of his municipality. Forced to withdraw from San Juan de Letran College in his second year when his father died. Returned to Cavite to manage the family farm and was elected town mayor, 1895. Joined the nationalist secret society *Katipunan* and emerged as the revolution's most capable general when fighting began in 1896. Exiled himself to Hong Kong in 1897, but returned to the Philippines the following year to become president of the Republic and command revolutionary forces until his capture in March 1901. Took the oath of loyalty to the United States and retired to his home in Cavite. Unsuccessful campaign for Commonwealth president, 1934. Strong supporter of the Japanese occupation and sought presidency of the wartime Republic, an overture the Japanese rejected.

BONIFACIO, Andres (1863-97). Born in Tondo district of Manila. Little formal education. Worked most of his life as a labourer and self-employed craftsman. Imbibed his anti-colonial nationalism from Jose Rizal's novels, various Propaganda Movement publications and European novels like Victor Hugo's *Les Miserables*. Leader of the revolutionary secret society *Katipunan*, 1892, and spent the next four years planning an armed revolution which began in August 1896. Leadership struggle with General Emilio Aguinaldo, and executed as a traitor on Aguinaldo's orders, May 1897.

BURGOS, Jose (1837-72). Born in the city of Vigan, Ilocos Sur. Father was a Spanish lieutenant in the colonial militia and mother a Spanish *mestiza*. Educated as a charity student in Manila. Graduated from San Juan de Letran College and ordained, 1866, after completing degree in canon law at Santo Tomas University. Leader of tne native clergy's campaign to recover parishes transferred to Spanish missionaries, 1863. During the short-lived 'liberal period' (1869-72), became one of the leading advocates of reforms. Convicted of sedition in 1872, he and two other native priests were executed in Manila's Luneta park.

FELEO, Juan (1896-1946). Born in the central Luzon province of Nueva Ecija where his father was a relatively prosperous tenant farmer. Trained as a school teacher. Defended local tenants threatened with eviction by landlords, 1920s. A passionate and moving speaker, he was one of the founders of the National Society of Peasants (KPMP) in the mid-1920s, and a foundation *Politbureau* member of the Philippine Communist Party, 1930. Active in the wartime *Huk* guerrilla movement. Luzon's most influential peasant leader after the war. Abducted and murdered, 1946, while passing through estates belonging to the wife of President Manuel Roxas.

OSMEÑA, Sergio (1878-1961). Born in Cebu City. Illegitimate child of influential Chinese *mestizo* family. Educated at Santo Tomas University in Manila. Began political career in 1900 as editor of a Spanish newspaper in Cebu. Passed the bar, 1903. Held various public offices, before election to the National Assembly, 1907. Chosen Speaker of the Assembly, 1907 and dominated Philippine politics until he lost the struggle for Nacionalista Party leadership to Manuel Quezon in 1922. Commonwealth vice-president until Quezon's death in 1944 when he succeeded to the presidency. Defeated by Manuel Roxas in 1946 presidential elections.

DE TAVERA, Trinidad Pardo (1857-1925). Born in Manila to wealthy Spanish *mestizo* parents. Graduate in medicine from the Sorbonne University. Studied oriental languages in Paris and published a number of academic studies of Philippine languages, customs, history and botany. Loyal to Spain during the revolution and served briefly as foreign secretary in General Aguinaldo's revolutionary government after Spain's defeat. Declared his loyalty to the United States and was one of main organisers of Federalista Party which favoured union with US. Member of Philippine Commission, 1901-9. Thereafter, devoted himself to writing.

QUEZON, Manuel (1878-1944). Born in the small town of Baler on Luzon's Pacific coast. Parents were Spanish *mestizo* school teachers. Educated in Manila's San Juan de Letran College and Santo Tomas

University. Two years in Philippine revolutionary army. Passed the bar in 1903 and began a career in government service. Elected to new National Assembly, 1907; majority floor leader. Leader of the Nacionalista Party in 1922. Commonwealth president from 1935 until his death in exile.

RECTO, Claro (1890-1960). Born in Batangas Province. Son of local elite family. Educated in Manila at San Juan de Letran College and Santo Tomas University. Passed the bar and entered politics, winning seat in National Assembly, 1919. Known for his nationalist Spanish poetry, but also a skilled political bargainer. Soon emerged as leader of opposition Democrata Party. Elected senator in 1931 on an opposition ticket. Allied himself with Nacionalista Party leader Manuel Quezon and later rewarded with appointments as President of the Constitutional Convention, 1934, and justice of the Supreme Court. Served as foreign secretary under the Japanese. Granted amnesty on the charges of collaboration after the war. Elected to Senate, 1949, and served there until his death.

RICARTE, Artemio (1866-1945). Born in Ilocos Norte Province to local elite family. Educated at Manila's San Juan de Letran College and Escuela Normal. Primary school teacher, 1888, and accepted a position in Cavite Province. Joined *Katipunan*, 1893, and served with Aguinaldo throughout the revolutionary period. Alone among revolutionary generals, Ricarte refused to accept defeat and spent the remainder of his life trying to organise a revolt against American rule. Exiled to Hong Kong until 1915. Organised a number of abortive conspiracies culminating in the failed uprising in Manila on Christmas eve 1914. Lived in Yokohama, Japan, 1915-41. Returned to the Philippines with Japan's invasion forces in 1942. Served as a propagandist for the occupation government and died during the Japanese retreat from Manila.

RIZAL, Jose (1861-96). Born in Laguna Province southeast of Manila where his family were prosperous farmers who leased substantial sugar lands on Dominican estates. Brilliant student. Quit Santo Tomas University in his second year and travelled to Spain where he enrolled in the medical faculty at Madrid University. During his decade in Europe, Rizal became the most influential leader of the reformist Propaganda Movement and published a number of anti-colonial writings, most importantly his anti-friar novel *Noli Me Tangere* (1887). Shortly after his return to the Philippines in 1892, he was banished to a small town in northern Mindanao. After the revolution began in August 1896, Rizal was tried for sedition and died a martyr's death by firing squad in Manila's Luneta park.

ROXAS, Manuel (1892–1948). Born in the Western Visayas province of Capiz of local elite family. Graduated as valedictorian in his law class at the University of the Philippines and married into the wealthy De Leon family of central Luzon. After a term as municipal councillor and governor of Capiz, elected to National Assembly, 1922, and won the Speakership as a protege of Nacionalista Party's Manuel Quezon. Career suffered brief setback when he joined Sergio Osmeña in an unsuccessful challenge to Quezon's leadership, early 1930s. Held several key posts in Japanese-sponsored governments. First president of the Philippine Republic, 1946. Conservative national leader known for his strongly pro-American foreign policy and uncompromising opposition to the *Huk* peasant movement in central Luzon.

TARUC, Luis (b. 1913). Born in the central Luzon province of Pampanga where his family were tenant farmers. Forced to abandon his law studies for lack of funds. Returned to central Luzon where he became a tailor and joined the Socialist Party. Became known as a strike organiser in the late 1930s and influential peasant leader after the merger of the Communist and Socialist parties in 1938. During the Second World War, military commander of the anti-Japanese *Huk* guerrillas. After the war, leader of the left–liberal coalition, Democratic Alliance. Elected to Congress, 1946. Denied his seat by the government's majority. Withdrew into the countryside and assumed command of the communist-led revolt. Surrendered to the government in 1954. After several years in prison, granted amnesty and active supporter of President Marcos' land reform programme after declaration of Martial Law, 1972.

INDIA

AZAD, Maulana Abul Kalam (1888–1958). Born in Arabia of Indian Muslim father. Family resettled in Calcutta when Azad was very young. Traditional education from father, but learned English secretly. Travelled in Middle East, 1908. Began *Al Hilal* (The Crescent), Urdu weekly, 1912; banned 1914 for pro-Turkish line. Interned, 1916-19. President All-India Khilafat Committee, 1920; president INC, 1923, 1940-6. Member Congress Parliamentary Board, 1937. Education minister, Govt of India, 1947-58. Imprisoned, 1921-2, 1930, 1932-3, 1940-1, 1942-5. Author, *India Wins Freedom*, 1959 (posthumous).

BOSE, Subhash Chandra (1897-1945). Kayastha. Born Cuttack, Orissa. Father a lawyer. Educated Calcutta. Passed ICS examination 1920, but resigned in probationary year to take part in non-co-operation movement. Imprisoned 1924-7 for alleged terrorist connections; also during civil disobedience 1930-3. To Europe mid-1930s. President INC 1938, 1939, but Gandhi forced him to resign, 1939. Arrested July 1940 for opposing war. Escaped from India early 1941 and reached Germany. Linked up with Japanese 1943 and founded Indian National Army from Indian prisoners of war; proclaimed provisional government of India in Malaya. Killed in plane crash, Taiwan, Aug. 1945. Author, *The Indian Struggle, 1920-42*, 1934.

GANDHI, Mohandas Karamchand (1869-1948). Mod Baniya. Born in Gujarat. Father prime minister of tiny princely state. Married at 13. Educated locally; in UK to study law, 1888-91; called to bar. Law and civil rights in South Africa, 1893-1914. To India and established *ashram* at Ahmedabad, 1915. Led Champaran, Bihar, peasant movement against indigo planters, 1917. Converted INC to non-co-operation and his doctrine of *satyagraha* for *swaraj* and Khilafat, 1920. Guiding spirit of INC until death, though officially out of INC from 1934. President INC, 1924. Imprisoned, 1922-4, 1930-1, 1932-4, 1942-4. Author, *Hind Swaraj*, 1909, *Satyagraha in South Africa*, 1928, *My Experiments with Truth*, 1927, Assassinated by Hindu fanatic, New Delhi, 30 Jan. 1948.

GOKHALE, G. K. (1866-1915). Chitpavan Brahmin. Educated Kolhapur, Poona, Bombay. BA, 1884. Taught in Poona, 1885-1902. Joint secretary INC, 1895. Member Bombay Legislative Council, 1899; Imperial Legislative Council, 1902. Accepted British honour (CIE), 1904. President Poona municipality, 1905. Refused knighthood, 1914. Founded Servants of India Society, 1905. First went to UK, 1897, and frequently thereafter. President INC, 1905.

JINNAH, Muhammad Ali (1876-1948). Khoja sect of Muslims (followers of Aga Khan). Born Karachi. Father a small merchant. Twice married, second time to a Parsee; this marriage broke up, 1928. Educated Karachi, Bombay. UK, 1892-6; called to the bar. Protested *against* separate electorates for Muslims, 1909. Member Imperial Legislative Council, 1910, from Muslim constituency; in central legislatures, 1913, 1915, 1923, 1926, 1934; resigned, 1919, over Rowlatt Acts. Presided over Muslim League session, 1916, when Lucknow Pact effected. President Bombay Home Rule League, 1917. Resigned from Congress and Home Rule League, 1920; disapproved of non-co-operation. Got Muslim League to boycott Simon Commission, 1928. UK, 1931-4. Into Muslim League on return to India and established it as rival to Congress by 1945; did not oppose British war effort. Governor-General of Pakistan 1947-8.

NEHRU, Jawaharlal (1889-1964). Kashmiri Brahmin. Born Allahabad. Son of Motilal Nehru; father of Mrs Indira Gandhi. Educated Harrow; Trinity College, Cambridge; called to bar; in UK, 1905-12. Married Kamala, 1916; Indira born, 1917; Kamala died, 1936. Imprisoned 1921-2, 1930, 1931-5 (except for 6 mos.), 1940-1, 1942-5. President, INC, 1929, 1936, 1951-4. Prime Minister of India, 1947-64. Author, *An Autobiography*, 1936, *The Discovery of India*, 1946.

NEHRU, Motilal (1861-1931). Kashmiri Brahmin. Born Agra; grew up in princely state in Rajputana. Family moved to Allahabad when High Court established there; elder brother a lawyer. Educated Allahabad; lawyer, 1883. To Europe, 1899 and 1900; increasingly Western style of life. Sent Jawaharlal to Harrow, 1905. Member United Provinces Legislative Council, 1909. President UP Congress Committee, 1912. President Allahabad Home Rule League, 1917. Started *Independent* newspaper, 1919. President INC, 1919. Supported Gandhi at Calcutta, Sept. 1920; resigned from UP Legislative Council Imprisoned, Dec. 1921. Founded Swaraj Party, 1923 and elected to Central Legislative Assembly. Nehru Report attempted to solve Hindu-Muslim problem, 1928. Arrested in civil disobedience movement, 1930, but released on health grounds.

PATEL, Vallabhbhai (1875-1950). Patidar. Born Gujarat. Peasant family. Education locally; lawyer. To UK, 1910; called to bar,

1913. Intimate of Gandhi from 1918. Imprisoned, 1930, 1932-3, 1940-1, 1942-5. Member Congress Parliamentary Board, 1937. Organiser Bardoli *satyagraha* against land revenue increases, 1928. President INC, 1931, Deputy Prime Minister and Home and States Minister, Govt of India, 1947-50; responsible for assimilation of princely states.

PRASAD, Rajendra (1884-1963). Kayastha. Born north Bihar in small *zamindari* family; married at 13. Educated locally and in Patna; BA, MA, ML in Calcutta during anti-partition time (*c.* 1905). Practised law in Calcutta from 1912; to Patna, 1916, when High Court of Bihar and Orissa established. Intimate of Gandhi from Champaran *satyagraha*, 1917. President INC, 1934 and succeeded Bose, 1939. Congress Parliamentary Board, 1937. President Constituent Assembly, 1946. Food and Agriculture Minister, 1946-7. President of Republic of India, 1950-62. Author, *Autobiography*, 1957.

TILAK, Bal Gangadhar (1856-1920). Chitpavan Brahmin. Father a school inspector. Educated Poona; BA, BL. Founder Deccan Education Society; also Fergusson College, Poona, 1885, where Gokhale, his later rival, taught. Publisher *Kesari* and *Mahratta*. Imprisoned for sedition, 1897. Advocate of boycott and national (that is, non-government) education to force British to concede self-government. Imprisoned, 1908-14, for sedition. Started Home Rule League, 1916, and rejoined Congress; had been kept out of Congress after stormy Surat meeting, 1907. Unlike Gandhi, he was prepared to work 1919 constitution.

INDONESIA

AIDIT, Dipa Nusantara (1923-65). Sumatran. Intermediate school only. Joined GERINDO in Jakarta, 1940, and 'Illegal PKI', 1943. Active in Japanese-sponsored youth movements. Member of PKI Central Committee, January 1947, and Politbureau, August 1948. Fled after Madiun rebellion to join Viet Minh in Vietnam, 1949 and attend a conference in Peking. Returned, July 1950, and quickly assumed control of PKI as first secretary, 1951-65. Killed after 1965 coup.

DEWANTARA, Ki Hadjar (1889-1959). Javanese. Born as Suwardi Surjaningrat into the Pakualam princely house of Yogyakarta. Studied at Yogyakarta Teachers' College, 1904, and, without graduating, at STOVIA Medical College in Batavia, 1905-10. Associated with Budi Utomo as a student, but in 1912 joined Tjipto Mangoenkoesoemo and the Eurasian, Douwes Dekker, in the radical nationalist Indische Partij. Exiled to Holland, 1913-19, for anticolonial activity, where he studied modern educational methods and practised journalism. Lived in Yogyakarta from 1921, where his Taman Siswa was founded, 1924. One of four main leaders of Putera under the Japanese, adviser to (Japanese) Education Bureau, December 1944, and first Republican minister of education, August–November, 1945.

HATTA, Drs Mohammad (1902-80). Minangkabau. As his father died young, was brought up by his trader stepfather. Educated in Padang and at a commercially oriented Dutch High School in Batavia, 1919-21. Obtained scholarship to study at the Handels Hoge School in Rotterdam, where he stayed exceptionally long through changes of course and involvement in politics. Chairman of Perhimpunan Indonesia, 1926-30, during its most influential phase, and represented it in the Moscow-backed League Against Imperialism. Expelled from the League at the same time as Nehru as a 'bourgeois' nationalist, and later expelled from PI when it too came under communist influence, 1931. Returned Indonesia, 1932, to head Pendidekan Nasional Indonesia until interned in Digul, 1934-6, and Banda, 1936-41. 'Dwitunggal' (two-in-one) leadership with Sukarno established under Japanese and continued as vice-president, 1945-56. Concurrently prime minister, 1948-50. Resigned vice presidency, 1956, in protest at arbitrary trend in political and economic management.

MANGOENKOESOEMO, Dr Tjipto (1886-1943). Javanese. Son of a school headmaster, he graduated from STOVIA, 1905, and completed the full doctor's degree only available in Europe when he was in exile, 1913-14, for anti-colonial activity. Led radical faction in Budi Utomo before joining the Indische Partij, 1912. Married a Protestant Eurasian woman, 1916. Member *Volksraad*, 1918-21. Interned in Banda Island, 1927-40.

SJAHRIR, Sutan (1909–66). Minangkabau. Childhood in Medan, North Sumatra, as son of a chief government prosecutor. Excellent Dutch education in Medan and Bandung, before going to Leiden, 1929, to study law. Very active in Dutch student socialist club and in Perhimpunan Indonesia, though expelled from latter by dominant communists, 1931. Returned to Indonesia without degree, 1931, to establish Pendidekan Nasional Indonesia. Interned in Boven Digul from 1934 and Banda from 1936. While interned, legally married a Dutch friend, 1936, in vain hope of her being allowed to join him in Indonesia. Refrained from co-operation with Japanese. Prime minister and minister for foreign affairs. November 1945 to July 1947. Headed Indonesian Socialist Party (PSI) from 1948 until it was banned, 1960. Imprisoned by Sukarno, 1962-6.

SJARIFFUDDIN, Mr Amir (1907–48). Angkola Batak. Born in Medan of a Muslim family, but became a Christian as a student. Secondary education in Holland, and law degree (with title Mr) from Batavia, 1933. Private practice until 1940, when joined Government economic affairs department. Deputy chairman PARTINDO, 1933, chairman GERINDO, 1939-40, secretary GAPI, 1938-40. Contact with 'Illegal PKI' at least since 1939. Arrested by Japanese, January 1943, and sentenced to death for leading anti-Japanese underground. Minister of information, August–November 1945, and of defence, November 1945–January 1948. Prime minister, July 1947–January 1948. Leader of the Socialist Party, 1945-8, until its merger into the PKI in August 1948. Executed December 1948.

SOETOMO, Dr (1888–1938). Javanese. The son of a successful *priyayi* administrator, he graduated from STOVIA, 1911, and while a student there organised the foundation of Budi Utomo, 1908. Married a Dutch woman, 1917, and completed study in Holland for his full medical degree, 1919-23. Founded the Indonesia Study Club in Surabaya, which was prominent in nationalist activity and eventually merged into PARINDRA, 1935.

SUDIRMAN, General (1912-1950). Javanese. The son of a sugar plantation overseer, he had a reasonable education in a Dutch-language primary school and Taman Siswa intermediate school through the patronage of an adoptive father. After one year, 1934, of Muhammadiah teacher training in Yogyakarta he taught from 1935 at the Muhammadiah primary school in Cilacap (Central Java). Entered PETA, 1943, and became senior officer (*diadancho*) in Banyumas region. Elected Army Commander by fellow officers, November 1945.

SUKARNO (1901-70). Javanese. Born Surabaya of a lesser *priyayi* schoolteacher father and a Balinese mother. Good Dutch education in Purwokerto and Surabaya, boarding with Tjokroaminoto, 1916-21, whose daughter became his first wife. Graduated as engineer (with title Ir.) from Technische Hogeschool in Bandung, 1926. Joint founder of Algemene Studieclub, 1926, and Persatuan (later Partai) Nasional Indonesia (PNI), 1927. Imprisoned, December 1929 to December 1931. Became principal figure in PARTINDO, which had formed during his imprisonment. Interned in Flores, 1934-8, and Bengkahulu, 1938-42. Remarried a Javanese eleven years his senior, 1923-43, a Sumatran, Fatmawati, 1943 and as secondary wives a Javanese, 1954, a Japanese, 1959, another Javanese and a Menadonese. Leading politician in Java throughout Japanese occupation. Elected President, 1945. Personal rule under 'Guided Democracy', 1959-65, including campaigns against West Irian and Malaysia and growing identification with China. Gradually eased out of power by General Suharto after ambivalent response to Untung coup attempt of 31 September 1965.

TAN MALAKA, Sutan Ibrahim gelar Datuk (1897-1949). Minangkabau. Studied at Bukittinggi (West Sumatra) Teachers' College, and then in Holland, 1913-19, supported by local community. Growing interest in Marxism as student and while on a teaching contract in an East Sumatran plantation, 1919-21. Joined PKI in Semarang, 1921, and became its chairman until exiled, 1922. Comintern representative for Southeast Asia, based in Canton, 1923-5, and Manila, 1925-6. His strong opposition to 1926-7 PKI uprising, together with his belief in a united front with Islamic organisations, led to split with communists. Founded Partai Republik Indonesia (PARI), 1927, in Bangkok. Thereafter moved increasingly among Chinese in Canton, Hong Kong and Singapore, 1937-42, returning to Indonesia clandestinely under Japanese. Spent occupation at coalmine in South Banten, perhaps in some form of detention by

Japanese, emerging in Jakarta only in August 1945. During revolution worked towards unity fronts rather than a disciplined party, though his followers founded Murba Party after his death.

TJOKROAMINOTO, Haji Oemar Said (1882-1934). Javanese. From upper *priyayi* stock in Madiun region, he graduated from the School for Native Officials, 1902, but left government service to settle in Surabaya. Headed Sarekat Islam from 1912 to his death. Member of *Volksraad*, 1918-21. Delegate to Ibn Saud's Al-Islam Congress, 1926.

VIETNAM

BAO DAI (b. 1913). Only son of King Khai Dinh (r. 1916-25). Sent 1922 to France for schooling, returned briefly for 1926 crowning ceremony, then back to France until 1932. Married to wealthy Catholic commoner, 1934. Symbol for royalist reformers in 1930s. With Japanese approval, abrogated French protectorate treaty and proclaimed independent kingdom, Mar. 1945. Abdicated throne Aug. 1945 and accepted membership in first DRVN National Assembly, Jan. 1946. Fled to China Mar. 1946, entered into discussions with French government 1947, and signed agreement for Vietnamese autonomy within French Union, Mar. 1949. Chief of State of Vietnam, 1949-55. Following 1954 Geneva Accords, discarded by US in favour of Ngo Dinh Diem. Author of autobiographical *Le Dragon d'Annam* (1979).

BUI QUANG CHIEU (1873-1945). Born Ben Tre province, Cochinchina. Educated in Saigon, Algiers and Paris. Entered Indochina colonial service as agronomist, 1897. Amassed sizeable Mekong delta properties. Founded Constitutionalist Party, 1917, representing southern Vietnamese landed, high official and commercial interests. Published *La Tribune Indigène* (1917-25) and *La Tribune Indochinoise* (1926-42). President of Société d'enseignement mutuel de Cochinchine, 1918. Visited France in fruitless attempt to extract political and economic concessions, 1926. Member of Cochinchina Colonial Council, 1926-39. Visited India, 1929. Member of Paris-based Conseil supérieur des colonies, 1932-40. Executed by Viet Minh, Sept. 1945.

CUONG DE (1883-1951). Member of the royal family selected as pretender to throne by Vietnamese anti-colonialists, 1903. Except for brief interludes in China and Germany, resided in Japan from 1906 to death. Established contact with Cao Dai religious leaders, 1936(?). Titular head of Vietnam Restoration League, 1939-45. Touted as anti-French replacement for Bao Dai, Mar. 1945, but ignored by Japanese. Attempted return to Vietnam blocked by French, 1950.

HO CHI MINH (1890-1969). Original name Nguyen Sinh Cung. Born Nghe An province, Annam. Father a mandarin. Educated at prestigious Lycée Quoc Hoc in Hue, 1904(?)-10. Signed on French ship as cook's helper to get to Europe, 1911. Circulated widely in radical intellectual and working-class circles. Used name Nguyen Ai Quoc, 1919-40. With four other prominent Vietnamese patriots, unsuccessfully petitioned 1919 Versailles conference. Founding member French Communist Party and energetic journalist in Paris, 1920-3. Studied Marxism-Leninism and participated in Comintern activities in Moscow, 1923-4. Sent to south China to recruit Southeast Asian revolutionaries, 1924. Established Vietnam Revolutionary Youth League in Canton 1925. Published *Duong Kach Menh* (The Revolutionary Path), a training manual for young radical intellectuals. Chaired Feb. 1930 meeting that produced a unified Indochinese Communist Party (ICP). Jailed by British in Hong Kong, 1931-2. Returned to Soviet Union, 1933-7. Minor cadre in Chinese Communist liberated areas, 1938-9. Slipped back to Vietnam Jan. 1941 to assume chairmanship of ICP and to promulgate Viet Minh united front strategy. Jailed by Chinese Kuomintang 1942-4 when trying to contact Allies. Declared independence of Vietnam 2 Sept. 1945. President of DRVN, 1945-69.

HUYNH PHU SO (1919-47). Born Hoa Hao village, Chau Doc province, Cochinchina. Father a rich peasant and head of village council. After prolonged illness, saw visions and preached a form of fundamentalist Buddhism, 1939. His 'Hoa Hao' religion quickly attracted both landlord coterie and mass following in Western Mekong delta. Detained by French, 1940. Liberated by Japanese, Oct. 1942, and allowed to disseminate prophecies of Vietnamese independence. Flirted briefly with Viet Minh, Aug.-Sept., 1945, then again in mid-1946. Helped form Vietnam Social Democratic Party to oppose communist 'class struggle', Sept. 1946. Arrested and executed by Viet Minh for negotiating secretly with the French, Apr. 1947.

NGO DINH DIEM (1901-63). Born Quang Binh province, Annam, to leading Catholic family. Father a ranking Hue court official under King Thanh Thai (r. 1889-1907). Educated at Lycée Quoc Hoc (Hue) and Hanoi Faculty of Law, 1913-21. Entered colonial administration, 1922. Governor of Phan Thiet province, 1929-32. Appointed Bao Dai's minister of interior 1933, but soon resigned. Consulted by Japanese on formation of government, 1944, but they eventually picked Tran Trong Kim. Avoided involvement in either DRVN or pro-French political organisations, 1945-53. Withdrew to Maryknoll seminary in US, 1951-3. Accepted premiership of State of Vietnam in midst of Geneva conference, June 1954. Supported by US Secretary of State Dulles in forcing resignation of pro-French Vietnamese military officers. Outmanoeuvred and suppressed Cao Dai, Hoa Hao and Binh Xuyen organisations. As final rebuff to Bao Dai, declared Republic of Vietnam, Oct. 1955, with himself as president. Mounted anti-communist extermination campaign, 1956-9. Progressively lost support even among Vietnamese bourgeoisie and military officers, 1960-3. Overthrown and killed Nov. 1963.

NGUYEN AN NINH (1900-43). Born Gia Dinh province, Cochinchina. Father Nguyen An Khuong, a prominent literatus and entrepreneur in contact with overseas anti-colonialists. Educated at Chasseloup-Laubat and other private colonial schools. Studied law at University of Hanoi, 1918-20. Obtained licence en droit at Sorbonne (Paris), 1921. Travelled extensively in Europe before returning to Saigon, 1923. Public speech Oct. 1923 criticised current French colonial policy and helped inspire an entire generation of young intellectuals to political action. Edited *La Cloche fêlée*, 1923-6, Jailed by French in 1926, 1928-30, 1936, 1937 and 1939-43. In between, supported family by selling medicinal ointment. Although a committed Marxist from 1931, avoided joining any party. Founded Indochina Congress movement, 1936. Author of *Hai Ba Trung* (The Trung Sisters), *Phe Binh Phat Giao* (A Critique of Buddhism) and *Ton Giao* (Religion). Died of dysentery on Con Son prison island.

NGUYEN TUONG TAM (1906-63). Born Hai Duong province, Tonkin. Father a colonial official in Vietnam and Laos. Studied science in

France, 1927–9. Brief careers as clerk and middle-school teacher. Formed Tu Luc Van Doan (Self-Reliance Literature Group) and began *Phong Hoa* (Customs) journal in Hanoi, 1932. Under the name of Nhat Linh authored a series of popular novels, most notably *Doan Tuyet* (Breaking Off) and *Doi Ban* (Two Friends). Founded elite Dang Dai Viet Dan Chinh (Greater Vietnam Legitimate People's Party) to oppose both the French and the ICP, 1939. Fled to China and joined Viet Nam Quoc Dan Dang (Vietnam Nationalist Party), 1941. Returned with Chinese Nationalist troops, 1945. Accepted foreign affairs portfolio in Ho Chi Minh government, Feb. 1946, and participated in Apr.–May 1946 Dalat negotiations with French. Fled to China and attempted unsuccessfully to build a 'third-force' National Union Front, 1946–7. Returned to French-controlled zone, 1951. Harassed by Ngo Dinh Diem regime from 1960 and committed suicide, July 1963.

PHAM CONG TAC (1893–1958). Born Tan An province, Cochinchina. Attended middle school in Tay Ninh province. Clerk in colonial customs and monopolies bureau, 1910–28. Invested as Ho Phap (Protector of the Law) of new Cao Dai religion, 1926. Famous as spirit medium, traditional medicine practitioner and orator. Split with pro-French Cao Dai colleagues and contacted Prince Cuong De in exile, 1936(?). Head of main Tay Ninh branch of Cao Dai, 1934–56. Deported to Madagascar by French, 1941–6. Returned as part of deal to break with Viet Minh and co-operate with French expeditionary corps. Formed Rassemblement National Cochinchinois, 1947. Visited Europe during Geneva Conference, May 1954. Deposed as Cao Dai leader by Ngo Dinh Diem, 1956. Fled to Cambodia.

PHAM QUYNH (1892–1945). Born Hai Duong province, Tonkin. Literati family. Graduated from French school for interpreters, 1908. Assisted Sûreté in preparing anti-German propaganda, 1914–17. Edited influential pro-colonial Hanoi journal *Nam Phong* (Southern Ethos), 1917–32. Founded conservative Association pour la formation intellectuel et morale des annamites, 1919. Visited France, 1922. Wrote hundreds of essays in Vietnamese and French, the most notable dealing with language, literature and culture. Vice president of Grand Conseil des Interets Financiers et Economiques, 1929–31. Minister at Hue royal court, 1932–45. Resigned following Japanese coup, Mar. 1945. Executed by Viet Minh, Sept. 1945.

PHAN KE TOAI (b. 1892). Born Son Tay province, Tonkin. Entered colonial administration, 1914. Prefect of Tien Hung in Thai Binh province at time of peasant demonstrations, May Day 1930. Governor of Bac Ninh province, 1942. Appointed Viceroy of Tonkin by Bao Dai and Tran Trong Kim government, May 1945. Swung to Viet Minh in Aug. 1945 Revolution. Minister of Interior of DRVN, 1947-? Vice Premier and member of Fatherland Front leadership, 1960.

PHAN THANH (1908–39). Born Quang Nam province, Annam. Contributed to Nguyen An Ninh's *La Cloche fêleé*, 1925–6. Taught school in Thanh Hoa province and Hanoi. Helped found Thang Long private school. Secretary of Association for the Diffusion of *Quoc Ngu* Study, 1936–9. Contributed often to left-wing French-language newspapers in Hanoi and Saigon. As clandestine ICP member, helped found the Vietnam Socialist Party to mount legal criticism of colonial policy, 1938. Elected Quang Nam delegate to Annam Representative Assembly, 1938. Elected to Grand Conseil des Interets Financiers et Economiques, early 1939. Sudden death from anthrax provoked a large May Day 1939 demonstration and funeral ceremony in Hanoi.

TRAN TRONG KIM (1883-1953). Born Ha Tinh province, Annam. Educated at colonial school for interpreters and Ecole Normale d'Instituteurs, Melun, France. Colonial schools administrator, 1911-42, rising to be Tonkin inspector of primary education. Co-authored numerous primary school textbooks. Authored influential *Viet Nam Su Luoc* (Outline History of Vietnam) and *Nho Giao* (Confucianism) in late 1920s. Covert association with conservative anti-colonialists provoked French ire and led him to seek sanctuary with Japanese, who sent him to Singapore and Bangkok, 1944. Invited by Japanese to form government, Apr. 1945. Resigned just prior to Japanese surrender and August 1945 Revolution. Chaired anti-communist conference that demanded more political concessions from French, Oct. 1953. Author of autobiographic *Mot Con Gio Bui* (A Puff of Dust), published in Saigon in 1969.

TRUONG CHINH (b. 1910). Real name Dang Xuan Khu. Born Nam Dinh province, Tonkin. Father a local schoolteacher. Expelled from Nam Dinh school for organising student strikes, 1927. Joined Vietnam Revolutionary Youth League, 1928. Received baccalauréat from Lycée Albert Sarraut in Hanoi, 1929(?). Joined ICP and imprisoned, 1930. Released 1936. Leading member of *Le Travail* and *Tin Tuc* (News) publishing groups in Hanoi, 1937-9. With Vo Nguyen Giap, published *Van De Dan Cay* (The Peasant Question), 1937-8, a pathfinding Marxist analysis of Vietnamese rural conditions. Secretary-General of Communist Party, 1941-56. Authored scores of essays, the most notable dealing with ideology, culture and political struggle. Accepted responsibility for land reform 'excesses' and demoted, 1956. Chairman of Standing Committee of DRVN National Assembly, 1960-present. Ranked second only to Secretary-General Le Duan in Communist Party's Central Executive Council, 1969-present.

VO NGUYEN GIAP (b. 1911). Born Quang Binh province, Annam. Father a village literatus with anti-colonial links. Educated at Lycée Quoc Hoc in Hue, 1923-7. Assisted in publication of *Tieng Dan* (Voice of the People) newspaper in Hue, 1926-9. Joined New Vietnam Revolutionary Party, 1927. Arrested 1930. Joined ICP. After 1931(?) release from prison, studied law at University of Hanoi and taught at private Lycée Thang Long. Leader of Popular Front campaign for greater freedom of the press. With Truong Chinh, published *Van De Dan Cay* (The Peasant Question). Authored several detailed descriptions of Sino-Japanese War, together with an incisive 1939 essay on local political alternatives titled *Con Duong Chinh: Van De Dan Toc Giai Phong o Dong Duong* (The Main and Proper Road: The Question of National Liberation in Indochina). Member of ICP Central Committee, 1941-present. Founder of People's Liberation Armed Forces, 1944. First DRVN minister of interior. Armed forces commander-in-chief, 1945-80. Minister of defence, 1946; 1948-80. Architect of victorious Dien Bien Phu campaign, 1954. Sixth-ranking member of Communist Party's Central Executive Council, 1969-present. Chairman, State Science Committee.

MALAYA

ABDUL RAHMAN, Tunku, Putra Al-Haj (b. 1902). From the Kedah royal family, he studied at the Penang Free School and St. Catharine's College, Cambridge. Returned to Malaya in 1931 and joined the Kedah civil service. Served at Padang Terap and the Langkawi Islands,

Juala Muda and finally Kulim. During the Japanese Occupation he worked in the Audit Department. Earlier, he 'kidnapped' his father, the Sultan of Kedah, to prevent him from being taken to Penang by British and Malay officials. Completed law studies in London after the war. Joined the Kedah legal department. Became involved in politics when he was offered the chairmanship of Kedah UMNO. In 1950 he went to Kuala Lumpur as deputy public prosecutor, and in 1951 took over as president of UMNO when Dato Onn bin Jaafar resigned. Left government service soon after. Appointed to the Federal Legislative Council, and in 1952, the Executive Council. Led the Alliance Party to a sweeping electoral victory in the first federal elections and became chief minister in 1955. Led a successful mission to London for independence talks in 1956. With independence in 1957 he became prime minister of Malaya and in 1963 of newly-formed Malaysia. Resigned September 1970, and has since involved himself in Islamic organisations as well as writing regularly for newspapers.

CHIN PENG (b. 1921). Born in Sitiawan, Perak. A Hockchiu, his real name is Ong Boon Hwa. Second child in a family of 10. Studied up to the senior middle two level at the Nam Hwa Chinese School in Sitiawan where his father owned a bicycle-repair shop. During the Japanese occupation he was senior officer in the 5th Regiment, MPAJA in Perak. Established links with British officers of Force 136. Awarded the Order of the British Empire after the war for his distinguished resistance record and was in the Malayan contingent in the victory parade in London. Reported to have visited communist-held parts of China, 1945-6. Editor of the MCP organ, *The Democrat*. Elected secretary–general of the MCP in 1947 when only 26 years old. Under his leadership the MCP abandoned its constitutional struggle and went into the jungle. In 1955 Chin Peng led a delegation to the talks in Baling. Since 1957 he is believed to have withdrawn to the Thai side of the Thai-Malaysia border.

IBRAHIM YAACOB (1911-79). Born at Temerloh, Pahang, of Bugis descent. Graduated from Sultan Idris Teachers' Training College in 1931 and became language teacher at the Kuala Lumpur Police Depot. Contributed articles critical of the British to Malay news-papers. Resigned as language teacher when warned by British. Joined Malay newspaper *Majlis* which he later edited. Moved subsequently to *Utusan Melayu* in Singapore. Joined the Malay State Association but left to form the Kesatuan Melayu Muda in 1938. Detained in December 1941 for alleged pro-Japanese activities but released a few days before the Japanese invasion. Appointed adviser on Malay affairs to the Japanese administration. Set up the volunteer army *Giyu Gun* for Japanese in 1943. Founded the *Kekuatan Rakyat Istimewa* (KRIS) in May 1945 amidst reports of impending Japanese defeat. Met Sukarno and Hatta to discuss the possibility of a political union between Malaya and Indonesia. Left for Java on 19 August 1945, and placed on the wanted list by the British. Later became a member of the left-wing Partindo Party and during Indonesia's confrontation with Malaysia attacked the new state as a neo-colonial plot. In Indonesia he assumed the name of Iskander Kamel and was a member of parliament. Following the fall of Sukarno with whom he was close, he joined the Murba Party. Retired from politics after the 1971 elections and became President of Bank Pertiwi. Wrote *Sedjarah dan Perdjuangan di Malaya* (History and Struggle in Malaya), 1951, *Sekitar Malaya Merdeka* (On Free Malaya), 1957, and *Melihat Tanah Air* (Observations on the Motherland), 1941.

LEE KUAN YEW (b. 1923). Born in Singapore. Double first in law at Cambridge in 1949. Qualified as barrister-at-law from Middle Temple, 1950. Began law practice in Singapore in 1952. First joined the conservative Straits Chinese British Association, but in 1954 helped set up the socialist-inclined People's Action Party, and became its first secretary–general. Won a seat in Tanjong Pagar, a predominantly working class dock area, in first Singapore elections in 1955. Articulate and forceful opposition leader during the administration of David Marshall and Lim Yew Hock. In 1959 the PAP won elections and Lee became chief minister. In 1962 a militant group split from the PAP and threatened to win the next election. At this juncture, Lee and Tunku Abdul Rahman worked out the Malaysia arrangement. In 1965 Lee took Singapore out of Malaysia and has since led Singapore as prime minister.

MARSHALL, David Saul (b. 1908). Born in Singapore of Iraqi-Jewish descent. Educated at St. Joseph's Institution and St. Andrew's and later at Raffles' Institution. Studied law at the Middle Temple in London. Established a reputation as a brilliant criminal lawyer in Singapore. Enlisted in the Singapore Volunteer Corps in 1938.

Detained by the Japanese. Founded the Workers' Party after the war. In 1955 his Labour Front Party won 10 seats in the new legislature, formed a coalition government with the Singapore Alliance, and Marshall became Singapore's first chief minister. Attended the Baling talks with the MCP, 1955. Four months later he led an all-party delegation to constitutional talks in London which failed and resulted in his resignation. Remained a member of the Legislative Assembly until 1963. Thereafter, concentrated on law practice and social welfare organisations. Appointed by Lee Kuan Yew, a long-time political foe, as Singapore's ambassador to France in 1979.

ONN BIN JAAFAR, Dato (1895-1962). From distinguished family which provided several chief ministers to the Johore state. Completed schooling at the Malay College, Kuala Kangsar. Briefly in civil service until 1919. Left the country for a period and returned to join the *Warta Malaya* which he edited, 1930-3. Moved to the *Lembaga Malaya* in 1934 and the *Lembaga* in 1935. Appointed unofficial member of Johore council of state, 1931-4, and was in the Johore executive council. During the Japanese occupation he was food controller and later district officer in Batu Pahat. Attended the KRIS congress, August 1945. Chief Minister of Johore 1948-51. In 1946 helped to form UMNO and became its first president. In the Communities Liaison Committee with Tan Cheng Lock in 1949. Resigned from UMNO in 1951 and founded the non-communal IMP. In the nominated Federal Legislative Council he was responsible for home affairs, 1951-5. The IMP and Parti Negara, which he later founded, failed in their challenge to UMNO. In 1959 Dato Onn won a seat in Trengganu and was the only Parti Negara MP. His son, Dato Husain Onn, became prime minister of Malaysia in 1976.

TAN CHENG LOCK (1883-1962). From a Baba Chinese family, settled for several generations in Malacca. English-educated, Tan Cheng Lock started his career as a school teacher but turned to rubber planting in which he became wealthy. Served in the Straits Chinese Consultative Committee of the Straits Settlements before 1941. Escaped to India with his family when the Japanese invaded Malaya. Formed the Overseas Chinese Association in India. Returned to Malaya after the war and involved himself in politics while building up his business, including the directorship of the *Malayan Tribune*. Led the AMCJA in 1946 and was in the Communities Liaison Committee in 1949. Elected President of the MCA on its formation in 1949 and held the post until 1958. Close to Dato Onn bin Jaafar and supported the latter's IMP.

Guide to Further Reading

ABBREVIATIONS

Cor MIP	Cornell Modern Indonesia Project
Cor UP	Cornell University Press
CUP	Cambridge University Press
FLPH	Foreign Languages Publishing House
JAS	*Journal of Asian Studies*
JSEAS	*Journal of Southeast Asian Studies*
MAS	*Modern Asian Studies*
OUP	Oxford University Press
PA	*Pacific Affairs*
PUP	Princeton University Press
SEAP	Southeast Asia Programme
UCP	University of California Press
UP	University Press

1. GENERAL STUDIES

Brecher, Michael, *The New States of Asia: A Political Analysis* (London: OUP, 1964; 1st pubd 1963).

Donnison, F. S. V., *British Military Administration in the Far East, 1943-6* (London: HMSO, 1956). Part of the British official history of the war.

Grimal, Henri, *Decolonization: The British, French, Dutch and Belgian Empires* (London: Routledge and Kegan Paul, 1978). An ambitious attempt that pulls together a great deal of material.

Holland, William L. (ed.), *Asian Nationalism and the West* (New York: Macmillan, 1953). Now itself something of an historical document, this collection still has much merit.

Kahin, George McT. (ed.), *Major Governments of Asia* (Ithaca: Cor UP, 1958; 2nd ed., 1963). A useful, though dated, textbook treatment.

——, *The Asian-African Conference. Bandung, Indonesia, 1955* (Port Washington, NY: Kennikat Press, 1972; 1st pubd 1956). A brief sketch of the conference that marked perhaps the highpoint of 'Asian solidarity'. Includes some of the speeches as appendices.

Lebra, Joyce C., *Japanese-Trained Armies in Southeast Asia: Independence and Volunteer Forces in World War II* (New York: Columbia UP, 1977).

Louis, William Roger, *Imperialism at Bay: The U.S. and the Decolonization of the British Empire, 1941-5* (London: OUP, 1978).

McCoy, A. W. (ed.), *Southeast Asia under Japanese Occupation: Transition and Transformation* (New Haven: Yale University Southeast Asia Series, 1980) reassesses this controversial period.

Mansour, Fatma, *Process of Independence* (London: Routledge and Kegan Paul, 1962) attempts a comparative analysis of some Asian and African states.

Pluvier, Jan M., *South-East Asia from Colonialism to Independence* (Kuala Lumpur: OUP, 1974).
Silverstein, Joseph (ed.), *Southeast Asia in World War II: Four Essays* (New Haven: Yale University Southeast Asia Series, 1966).
Smith, Roger M. (ed.), *Southeast Asia: Documents of Political Development and Change* (Ithaca: Cor UP, 1974) has declarations of independence and good post-independence coverage.
Smith, Tony (ed.), *The End of European Empire: Decolonization after World War II* (Lexington, Mass.: D. C. Heath, 1975).
——, 'A Comparative Study of French and British Decolonization', *Comparative Studies in Society and History*, **XX**, 1 (Jan. 1978) pp. 70–102.
Steinberg, David Joel (ed.), *In Search of Southeast Asia* (New York: Praeger, 1971). An invaluable reference work.
von Albertini, Rudolph, *Decolonization* (New York: Doubleday, 1971).
Ward, Robert E. and Macridis, Roy C. (eds.), *Modern Political Systems: Asia* (Englewood Cliffs, NJ: Prentice-Hall, 1963). Dated but handy textbook.

2. THE PHILIPPINES

1. GENERAL HISTORIES

Constantino, Renato, *A History of the Philippines: From the Spanish Colonization to the Second World War* (New York: Monthly Review Press, 1975). Readable social history that attempts a radical re-interpretation of events.
Corpuz, Onofre D., *The Philippines* (Englewood Cliffs, NJ: Prentice-Hall, 1965). A good overview of political history and contemporary government.

2. THE SPANISH PERIOD

Cushner, Nicholas P., *Spain in the Philippines: From Conquest to Revolution* (Manila: Institute of Philippine Culture, Ateneo de Manila University, 1971). The best account of Spanish rule; of interest both to scholars and general readers.
De la Costa, Horacio, *Asia and the Philippines* (Manila: Solidaridad Publishing House, 1967). Insightful interpretations of some key problems in the history of the Philippines during the early Spanish period.
——, *The Jesuits in the Philippines, 1581–1768* (Cambridge, Mass.: Harvard UP, 1967). A classic, enormously detailed study of the role of the Jesuit order in the colonisation of the Philippines.
Robles, Eliodoro G., *The Philippines in the Nineteenth Century* (Quezon City: Malaya Books, 1969). A careful but unexciting study of the structure of Spanish colonial administration in the nineteenth-century Philippines.
Roth, Dennis Morrow, *The Friar Estates of the Philippines* (Albuquerque: University of New Mexico Press, 1977). The development of the religious agricultural estates in central Luzon during the eighteenth and nineteenth centuries.
Schurz, William L., *The Manila Galleon* (New York: E. P. Dutton, 1939). A classic study of the trans-Pacific galleon trade and operation of Spanish commerce in Manila from the sixteenth to early nineteenth centuries.
Phelan, John L., *The Hispanization of the Philippines: Spanish Aims and Filipino Responses, 1565–1700* (Madison: University of Wisconsin Press,

1967). The impact of Spanish colonial rule on Philippine society.

Wickberg, Edgar, *The Chinese in Philippine Life, 1850-1898* (New Haven: Yale UP, 1965). A pioneering study of the origins of the Chinese *mestizos* and their emergence as a key component of the Philippine elite.

3. THE REVOLUTION OF 1896 AND ITS CONSEQUENCES

Agoncillo, Teodoro A., *Malolos: The Crisis of the Republic* (Quezon City: University of the Philippines, 1960). A detailed account of the short-lived Philippine Republic, 1899-1901.

——, *The Revolt of the Masses: the Story of Bonifacio and the Katipunan* (Quezon City: University of the Philippines, 1956). Considered controversial when first published, this work of intellectual passion is now the standard account.

Gates, John M., *Schoolbooks and Krags: The United States Army and the Philippines, 1898-1902* (Westport, Conn.: Greenwood Press, 1973). A useful summary of American military operations in the Philippines during the revolutionary period, marred by its American-centric bias.

Kalaw, Teodoro M., *The Philippine Revolution* (Mandaluyong: Filipiniana Foundation, 1969). A classic narrative of the revolution by a leading Filipino literary figure of the American colonial period.

Schumacher, John N., *The Propaganda Movement, 1880-1895: The Creators of a Filipino Consciousness, The Makers of a Revolution* (Manila: Solidaridad Publishing House, 1973). Detailed, scholarly account of the Propaganda Movement and its impact.

Wolff, Leon, *Little Brown Brother: How the United States Purchased and Pacified the Philippine Islands at the Century's Turn* (New York: Doubleday, 1961). The Philippine–American war from the American perspective.

4. THE AMERICAN PERIOD

Friend, Theodore, *Between Two Empires: The Ordeal of the Philippines, 1929-1946* (New Haven: Yale UP, 1965). An overview of global developments combined with a detailed account of the interaction between American and Philippine leaders.

——, 'The Philippine Sugar Industry and the Politics of Independence', *JAS*, **XXII**, 2 (February 1963) pp. 179–92.

Hayden, Joseph R., *The Philippines: A Study in National Development* (New York: Macmillan, 1972). The most important study of colonial administration by an American participant.

Larkin, John A., *The Pampangans: Colonial Society in a Philippine Province* (Berkeley: UCP, 1972). This lucid study of a single province illumines larger social and economic changes.

Liang, Dapen, *Philippine Parties and Politics: A Historical Study of National Experience in Democracy* (San Francisco: Gladstone Company, 1970). A comprehensive narrative of Philippine party politics from the 1890s to the 1960s.

Owen, Norman G. (ed.), *Compadre Colonialism: Studies on the Philippines Under American Rule* (Ann Arbor: Centre for South and Southeast Asian Studies, 1971). Several of these essays present new interpretations of significant aspects of Philippine colonial history.

Stanley, Peter W., *A Nation in the Making: The Philippines and the United*

States, 1899–1921 (Cambridge, Mass.: Harvard UP, 1974). A carefully documented study of the relationship between Filipino politicians and American officials.

5. THE JAPANESE INTERLUDE

Agoncillo, Teodoro A., *The Fateful Years: Japan's Adventure in the Philippines, 1941–45* (Quezon City: R. P. Garcia, 1965).

Goodman, Grant K., *Four Aspects of Philippine-Japanese Relations, 1930–1940* (New Haven: Southeast Asia Studies, Yale University, 1967). Insightful treatment of Japanese-Philippine relations in the pre-war decade.

McCoy, Alfred W. (ed.), *Southeast Asia under Japanese Occupation: Transition and Transformation* (New Haven: Yale University Southeast Asia Studies, 1980). Essays challenging David J. Steinberg's interpretation of the Filipino elite's response to the Japanese occupation.

Steinberg, David J., 'An Ambiguous Legacy: Years at War in the Philippines', *PA*, **XLV**, 2 (Summer 1972) pp. 165–90.

——, *Philippine Collaboration in World War II* (Ann Arbor: University of Michigan Press, 1967). Stimulating analysis of the response of the Filipino elite to the Japanese occupation.

6. POST-INDEPENDENCE

Jenkins, Shirley, *American Economic Policy Toward the Philippines* (Stanford: Stanford UP, 1954). Strongly critical of the terms of de-colonisation that the United States imposed on the Philippines during the post-war decade.

Kerkvliet, Benedict J. *The Huk Rebellion: A Study of Peasant Revolt in the Philippines* (Berkeley: UCP, 1977).

Lachica, Eduardo, *The Huks: Philippine Agrarian Society in Revolt* (New York: Praeger, 1971). Good journalistic account of the 1946–54 revolt and the armed peasant movement during the late 1950s and 1960s.

Lande, Carl H., *Leaders, Factions, and Parties: The Structure of Philippine Politics* (New Haven: Southeast Asia Studies, Yale University, 1965). An important study of factionalism during the colonial and post-independence periods.

Pomeroy, William J., *American Neo-Colonialism: Its Emergence in the Philippines and Asia* (New York: International Publishers, 1970). An orthodox Marxist interpretation of the economic causes of American diplomacy in the Philippines and Asia at the turn of the century.

7. BIOGRAPHY

Abueva, Jose V., *Ramon Magsaysay: A Political Biography* (Manila: Solidaridad Publishing House, 1971). A readable but partisan account of the political career of one of the Philippines' most important post-war leaders.

Coates, Austin, *Rizal: Philippine Nationalist and Martyr* (Hong Kong: OUP, 1968).

Constantino, Renato, *The Making of a Filipino: A Story of Philippine Colonial Politics* (Manila: Malaya Books, 1969). An hagiographic account of the life of Senator Claro Recto, the most articulate and influential elite nationalist in the post-war period.

Majul, Cesar A., *Apolinario Mabini Revolutionary* (Manila: National Heroes Commission, 1970). The career of a radical revolutionary nationalist and the political ideas of his time.

Pacis, Vicente A., *Sergio Osmena: A Fully-Documented Biography* (Quezon City, Philippine Constitution Association, 1971). A very long account of Osmena's political career which ultimately tells us more about colonial politics than Osmena's own life.

Schumacher, John N., *Father Jose Burgos, Priest and Nationalist* (Quezon City: Ateneo de Manila University Press, 1972). Contains a brief political biography of Father Burgos and a number of key documents about the mid-nineteenth-century nationalist movement.

3. INDIA

1. DOCUMENTS

Banerjee, Anil Chandra (ed.), *Indian Constitutional Documents, 1757-1947*, 4 vols. (Calcutta: A. Mukherjee & Co., 1961; 1st pubd, 1945).

Gwyer, Sir Maurice and Appadorai, A. (eds.), *Speeches and Documents on the Indian Constitution, 1921-47*, 2 vols. (London: OUP, 1957).

Indian Annual Register. A digest of speeches, reports and political events, published from Calcutta, 1919 to 1947. Indispensable for research.

Philips, C. H. (ed.), *The Evolution of India and Pakistan, 1858 to 1947. Select Documents* (London: OUP, 1962).

2. COLLECTED WORKS

Gandhi, M. K., *The Collected Works of Mahatma Gandhi* (New Delhi: Publications Division, from 1958) has reached 70 vols. and the early 1940s.

Nehru, Jawaharlal, *Selected Works of Jawaharlal Nehru* (New Delhi: Orient Longman, from 1972) stands at 10 vols.

Patel, Vallabhbhai, *Sardar Patel's Correspondence, 1945-50*, 5 vols. (Ahmedabad: Navajivan, 1971) has been edited with an eye to Patel's reputation.

3. GENERAL HISTORIES

Chandra, Bipin, *Modern India* (New Delhi: National Council of Educational Research and Training, 1977; 1st pubd, 1971).

Desai, A. R., *Social Background of Indian Nationalism* (Bombay: Popular Book Depot, 1954; 1st pubd, 1948).

Majumdar, R. C., *History of the Freedom Movement in India*, 3 vols. (Calcutta: Firma K. L. Mukhopadhyay, 1962-3). Weigh this against Chandra's *Modern India*.

Masselos, Jim, *Nationalism on the Indian Subcontinent: An Introductory History* (Melbourne: Nelson, 1972).

Pattabhi Sitaramayya, B., *The History of the Indian National Congress,*

2 vols. (Bombay: Padma Publications, 1946 and 1947).

Spear, Percival, *A History of India* (Harmondsworth: Penguin, 1966). Readily available and concise; covers the Mughal and British periods.

——, *The Oxford History of Modern India, 1740-1947* (New Delhi: OUP, 1974; 1st pubd, 1965) is more comprehensive than the former.

Thompson, Edward and Garratt, G. T., *Rise and Fulfilment of British Rule in India* (Allahabad: Central Book Depot, 1962; 1st pubd, *c.* 1935). Though dated, this book still manages to put real flesh on the bones of history.

Wolpert, Stanley, *A New History of India* (New York: OUP, 1977). Well written and comes down to the 1977 elections.

4.   NEW ELITES AND THE EARLY CONGRESS

Broomfield, J. H., *Elite Conflict in a Plural Society. Twentieth-Century Bengal* (Berkeley: UCP, 1968). Splendidly written, still controversial; a good starting point.

Leach, Edmund and Mukherjee, S. N. (eds), *Elites in South Asia* (CUP, 1970). Especially Mukherjee's essay on nineteenth-century Calcutta.

McLane, John R., *Indian Nationalism and the Early Congress* (PUP, 1977). The latest contribution to the literature; good bibliography.

Mehrotra, S. R., *The Emergence of the Indian National Congress* (New Delhi: Vikas, 1971).

Seal, Anil, *The Emergence of Indian Nationalism. Competition and Collaboration in the Later Nineteenth Century* (CUP, 1968). Now partly superseded, it remains a stimulating interpretation.

5.   BRITISH POLICY AND CONSTITUTIONAL DEVELOPMENT

Coupland, R., *The Indian Problem, 1833-1935, The Future of India* and *Indian Politics, 1936-42* (London: OUP, 1942-4) still provide invaluable summaries.

Gopal, S., *British Policy in India, 1858-1905* (CUP, 1965).

Koss, Stephen E., *John Morley at the India Office, 1905-10* (New Haven: Yale UP, 1969) is the most recent of a number of studies of this period.

Moore, R. J., *The Crisis of Indian Unity, 1917-40* (Oxford: Clarendon, 1974).

Robb, P. G. *The Government of India and Reform. Policies towards Politics and the Constitution, 1916-21* (London: OUP, 1976).

Wasti, S. R., *Lord Minto and the Indian Nationalist Movement* (London: OUP, 1964).

6.   THE GANDHIAN CONGRESS

Arnold, David. *The Congress in Tamilnad. Nationalist Politics in South India, 1919-37* (New Delhi: Manohar, 1977). A thorough picture of the development of Congress in a region.

Brown, Judith M., *Gandhi's Rise to Power* and *Gandhi and Civil Disobedience* (CUP, 1972 and 1977) are immensely detailed though rather indigestible.

Gallagher, John, Johnson, Gordon and Seal, Anil (eds.), *Locality, Province and Nation. Essays on Indian Politics, 1870 to 1940* (CUP, 1973; originally pubd as *MAS*, **VII**, 3 July 1973). One of the most important, provocative collections on the subject.

Hutchins, Francis G., *India's Revolution. Gandhi and the Quit India Movement* (Cambridge, Mass.: Harvard UP, 1973).

Krishna, Gopal, 'The Development of the Indian National Congress as a Mass Organization, 1918–23', *JAS*, **XXV**, 3 (May 1965) pp. 413–30 (an abridged version in Metcalf, T. R. (ed.), *Modern India* (London: Collier-Macmillan, 1971), pp. 257–72).

Kumar, Ravinder (ed.), *Essays on Gandhian Politics. The Rowlatt Satyagraha of 1919* (Oxford: Clarendon, 1971) is a collection that provides a good introduction.

Low, D. A. (ed.), *Congress and the Raj. Facets of the Indian Struggle, 1917–47* (London: Heinemann, 1977) contains a number of regional and thematic studies. The articles by Low and Johannes Voigt are particularly helpful for getting a wider view.

Niemeijer, A. C., *The Khilafat Movement in India, 1919–24* (The Hague: Martinus Nijhoff, 1972).

Ray, S. N. (ed.), *Gandhi, India and the World* (Melbourne: Hawthorn Press, 1970). H. F. Owen's brief account of non-co-operation is a handy introduction.

Tomlinson, B. R., *The Indian National Congress and the Raj, 1929–42* (London: Macmillan, 1976).

7. THE PARTITION

Edwardes, Michael, *The Last Years of British India* (London: Cassell, 1963) is a racy introduction to a subject that has generated a large literature.

Jeffrey, Robin, 'The Punjab Boundary Force and the Problem of Order: August 1947', *MAS*, **VIII**, 4 (Oct. 1974) pp. 491–526, notes much of the literature.

Hodson, H. V., *The Great Divide. Britain–India–Pakistan* (London: Hutchinson, 1969).

Lumby, E. W. R., *The Transfer of Power in India* (London: Allen and Unwin, 1953).

Menon, V. P., *The Transfer of Power in India* (Bombay: Orient Longman, 1968; 1st pubd, 1957) is by a leading participant.

Philips, C. H. and Wainwright, M. D. (eds.), *The Partition of India. Policies and Perspectives, 1935–47* (London: Allen and Unwin, 1970) contains both scholarly essays and reminiscences.

Tinker, Hugh, *Experiment with Freedom. India and Pakistan, 1947* (OUP, 1967).

8. MUSLIM POLITICS

Hardy, P., *The Muslims of British India* (CUP, 1972) has an excellent bibliography and makes a good beginning.

Khaliquzzaman, Chaudhury, *Pathway to Pakistan* (Lahore: Longmans, 1961) is perhaps the best version by an insider.

Robinson, Francis, *Separatism among Indian Muslims: The Politics of the United Provinces' Muslims, 1860–1923* (CUP, 1974).

Sayeed, K. B., *Pakistan: The Formative Phase* (OUP, 1968).

9. OUTSIDE THE NATIONALIST MAINSTREAM

Graham, B. D., 'Syama Prasad Mukherjee and the Communalist Alternative', in Low, D. A. (ed.), *Soundings in Modern South Asian History* (London: Weidenfeld and Nicolson, 1968) pp. 330–74, is a starting point for the orthodox Hindu right.

Haithcox, J. P., *Nationalism and Communism in India* (PUP, 1971) is concerned with M. N. Roy, but includes an extensive bibliography.

Jeffrey, Robin (ed.). *People, Princes and Paramount Power: Society and Politics in the Indian Princely States* (New Delhi: OUP, 1978) introduces the princes.

Menon, V. P., *The Story of the Integration of the Indian States* (New York: Macmillan, 1956) is by a crucial participant.

Misra, B. B., *The Indian Political Parties. An Historical Analysis of Political Behaviour up to 1947* (New Delhi: OUP, 1976) is long and meandering, but provides a digest of the activities of communists, liberals, terrorists and the Hindu right.

Overstreet, G. D., and Windmiller, M., *Communism in India* (Berkeley: UCP, 1959) is dated but compendious.

10. BIOGRAPHY AND AUTOBIOGRAPHY

Azad, Maulana Abul Kalam, *India Wins Freedom* (Calcutta: Orient Longman, 1959).

Bolitho, Hector, *Jinnah. Creator of Pakistan* (London: John Murray, 1954). Jinnah still lacks the biography he deserves.

Brecher, Michael, *Nehru. A Political Biography* (London: OUP, 1959) is able and admiring.

Chaudhuri, Nirad C., *The Autobiography of an Unknown Indian* (Berkeley: UCP, 1968) is a splendid, idiosyncratic memoir.

Dalton, Dennis, 'Gandhi during Partition: A Case Study in the Nature of Satyagraha', in Philips and Wainwright, cited in Section 7, pp. 222–44. Dalton's writings on Gandhi are invariably helpful.

Gandhi, M. K., *An Autobiography or the Story of My Experiments with Truth* (Ahmedabad: Navajivan, 1972; 1st pubd, 1927) is immensely readable.

Gopal, S., *Jawaharlal Nehru. A Biography*, 2 vols. (Cambridge, Mass.: Harvard UP, 1976 and 1978). The latest and most reliant on official sources; a third volume is still to be published.

Nehru, Jawaharlal, *An Autobiography* (London: Bodley Head, 1953; 1st pubd, 1936).

Panjabi, Kewal L., *The Indomitable Sardar* (Bombay: Bharatiya Vidya Bhavan, 1962). Patel still awaits a first-rate biography.

Pyarelal, *Mahatma Gandhi: The Last Phase*, 2 vols. (Ahmedabad: Navajivan, 1956 and 1958).

Rudolf, L. I. and S. H., *The Modernity of Tradition* (Chicago: University of Chicago Press, 1967) has a stimulating chapter on Gandhi.

Tendulkar, D. G., *Mahatma: Life of Mohandas Karamchand Gandhi*, 8 vols. (New Delhi: Publications Division, 1960–3).

Tandon, Prakash, *Punjabi Century, Beyond Punjab, Return to Punjab* (Berkeley: UCP, 1968, 1971, 1980). Memoirs of a Punjabi family from the mid-nineteenth century.

11. FICTION

Anand, Mulk Raj, *Coolie* (New York: Interculture, 1974) attempts to capture the life of the Bombay poor in the 1920s.

Joshi, Arun, *The Apprentice* (New Delhi: Orient Paperbacks, 1974) focusses on the scramble for a government job.

Malgonkar, Manohar, *A Bend in the Ganges* (London: Hamish Hamilton, 1964). A racy tale of partition and independence.

Narayan, R. K., *Waiting for the Mahatma* (London: Methuen, 1955) looks lightly at Gandhi's effect on a man and a woman.

Rao, Raja, *Kanthapura* (New York: New Directions, 1967; 1st pubd, 1963). Gandhi's movement comes to a south Indian village.

Sivasankara Pillai, Thakazhi, *Scavenger's Son* (New York: Interculture, 1975) is set among night-soil carriers in Kerala in the 1930s.

4. INDONESIA

1. DOCUMENTS

Benda, Harry *et al.*, *Japanese Military Administration in Indonesia: Selected Documents* (New Haven: Yale University Southeast Asia Studies, 1965).

Benda, Harry and McVey, Ruth, *The Communist Uprisings of 1926-7 in Indonesia: Key Documents* (Ithaca: Cor MIP, 1960) presents three official Dutch reports.

Feith, Herbert and Castles, Lance, *Indonesian Political Thinking: Selected Readings, 1945-65* (Ithaca: Cor UP, 1966) gives a good sample across the spectrum of Indonesian ideas.

Penders, C. L. M., *Indonesia: Selected Documents on Colonialism and Nationalism, 1830-1942* (St Lucia: University of Queensland Press, 1977) selects interesting reports, mainly from Dutch archives.

2. INDONESIAN MEMOIRS AND MANIFESTOS

Aidit, D. N., *Problems of the Indonesian Revolution* ([Peking]: Demos, 1963). A leading communist's analysis.

Hanifah, Abu, *Tales of a Revolution* (Sydney: Angus and Robertson, 1972). A reaction to Sukarno.

Hatta, Mohammad, *Portrait of a Patriot. Selected Writings* (The Hague: Mouton, 1972).

Kartini, Raden, *Letters of a Javanese Princess* (New York: Norton, 1964) portrays well the early impact of Western education.

Mangkupradja, Gatot, 'The Peta and My Relations with the Japanese: a Correction of Sukarno's Autobiography', *Indonesia*, 5 (April 1968) pp. 105-38.

Nasution, A. H., *Fundamentals of Guerrilla Warfare* (Singapore: Donald Moore, 1965).

Sastroamidjojo, Ali, *Milestones on My Journey: The Memoirs of Ali Sastroamidjojo* (St Lucia: University of Queensland Press, 1979).

Simatupang, T. B., *Report from Banaran: Experiences during the People's War* (Ithaca: Cor. MIP, 1972).

Sjahrir, Soetan, *Out of Exile* (New York: John Day, 1949). Primarily pre-war letters.
——, *Our Struggles* (Ithaca: Cor MIP, 1968). A 1945 pamphlet.
Sukarno: An Autobiography, as Told to Cindy Adams (Hong Kong: Gunung Agung, 1966).

3. GENERAL MODERN HISTORIES

Alisjahbana, S. Takdir, *Indonesia: Social and Cultural Revolution* (Kuala Lumpur: OUP, 1966). Introductory.
Dahm, Bernard, *History of Indonesia in the Twentieth Century* (London: Pall Mall, 1971) is the most detailed and reliable survey.
Feith, Herbert, 'Indonesia', in Kahin, G. McT. (ed.), *Governments and Politics in Southeast Asia* 2nd ed. (Ithaca: Cor UP, 1964).
Fryer, Donald and Jackson, James, *Indonesia*. (London: Ernest Benn, 1977). Introductory.
Kahin, G. McT., *Nationalism and Revolution in Indonesia* (Ithaca: Cor UP, 1952) is a classic of political reporting, still valuable for developments to 1949.
Legge, John D., *Indonesia* 2nd ed. (Englewood Cliffs, NJ: Prentice-Hall, 1977). Introductory.
——, *Sukarno: A Political Biography* (Harmondsworth: Penguin, 1973) covers twentieth-century political history from an important perspective.
McVey, Ruth (ed.), *Indonesia* (New Haven: Human Relations Area Files, 1963).
Reid, Anthony and Marr, David (eds.), *Perceptions of the Past in Southeast Asia* (Singapore: Heinemann for Asian Studies Association of Australia, 1980) illustrates the way Indonesians have rewritten their own history in modern times.
Soedjatmoko *et al*, *An Introduction to Indonesian Historiography* (Ithaca: Cor UP, 1965).
Zainu'ddin, Ailsa, *A Short History of Indonesia* (New York: Praeger, 1970).

4. NETHERLANDS INDIES ECONOMY AND SOCIETY

Boeke, J. H., *The Evolution of the Netherlands Indies Economy* (New York: Institute of Pacific Relations, 1946) is still very valuable.
Furnivall, J. S., *Netherlands India: A Study of Plural Economy* (CUP, 1944). Still valuable.
Geertz, Clifford, *Agricultural Involution: The Process of Ecological Change in Indonesia* (Berkeley: UCP, 1963) takes a long, depressingly convincing view of economic change.
Kartodirdjo, Sartono, *Protest Movements in Rural Java: A Study of Agrarian Unrest in the Nineteenth and Early Twentieth Centuries* (Kuala Lumpur: OUP, 1973).
Sutherland, Heather, *The Birth of a Bureaucratic Elite: The Javanese Priyayi and the Dutch* (Singapore: Heinemann for Asian Studies Association of Australia, 1979).
Vlekke, B. H. M., *Nusantara. A History of Indonesia* 2nd ed. (The Hague: Van Hoeve, 1959). A standard colonial history.
Wertheim, W. F., *Indonesian Society in Transition* 2nd ed. (The Hague: Van Hoeve, 1964). A very perceptive view of social change.

5. THE NATIONAL MOVEMENT TO 1942.

Abeyasekere, Susan, *One Hand Clapping: Indonesian Nationalists and the Dutch, 1939-41* (Melbourne: Monash Centre of Southeast Asian Studies, 1976).
Brackman, *Indonesian Communism: A History* (New York: Praeger, 1963). Perhaps the handiest of the numerous lighter works on Indonesian communism.
Dahm, Bernard, *Sukarno and the Struggle for Indonesian Independence* (Ithaca: Cor UP, 1969).
Ingleson, John, *Road to Exile: The Indonesian Nationalist Movement, 1927-34* (Singapore: Heinemann for Asian Studies Association of Australia, 1979).
McVey, Ruth, *The Rise of Indonesian Communism* (Ithaca: Cor UP, 1965) is a painstaking study of the PKI to 1926.
——, 'Taman Siswa and the Indonesian National Awakening', *Indonesia*, 4 (Oct. 1967) pp. 128-49.
Nagazumi, Akira, *The Dawn of Indonesian Nationalism: The Early Years of Budi Utomo, 1908-18* (Tokyo: Institute of Developing Economies, 1972).
Noer, Deliar, *The Modernist Muslim Movement in Indonesia, 1900-42* (Kuala Lumpur: OUP, 1973).

6. THE JAPANESE OCCUPATION

Anderson, Benedict, 'Japan: "The Light of Asia" ', in Silverstein, Josef (ed.), *Southeast Asia in World War Two: Four Essays* (New Haven: Yale University Southeast Asia Studies, 1966) is the most interesting short treatment.
Benda, Harry, *The Crescent and the Rising Sun. Indonesian Islam under the Japanese Occupation, 1942-5* (The Hague: Van Hoeve, 1958).
Kanahele, George, *The Japanese Occupation of Indonesia: Prelude to Independence* (Ann Arbor: University Microfilms, 1967).

7. THE INDONESIAN REVOLUTION AND ITS AFTERMATH

Anderson, Benedict, *Java in a Time of Revolution, Occupation and Resistance, 1944-6* (Ithaca: Cor UP, 1972) is a masterly coverage.
Boland, B. J., *The Struggle of Islam in Modern Indonesia* (The Hague: Nijhoff, 1971). A bookish survey of ideological debates over religion.
Crouch, Harold, *The Army and Politics in Indonesia* (Ithaca: Cor UP, 1978).
Feith, Herbert, *The Decline of Constitutional Democracy in Indonesia* (Ithaca: Cor UP, 1962). A brilliant chronicle of 1950-7.
Harvey, Barbara S., *Permesta: Half a Rebellion* (Ithaca: Cor MIP, 1977) carefully covers one of the major post-independence revolts against Jakarta.
Higgins, Benjamin and Jean, *Indonesia: The Crisis of the Millstones* (Princeton: Van Nostrand, 1963) shows the economic costs of the revolution.
Lev, D. S., *The Transition to Guided Democracy: Indonesian Politics, 1957-9* (Ithaca: Cor MIP, 1965).
McVey, Ruth, *The Soviet View of the Indonesian Revolution* (Ithaca: Cor MIP, 1957).
——, 'The Post-Revolutionary Transformation of the Indonesian Army', *Indonesia*, 11 (April 1971) pp. 131-76.
Reid, Anthony, *The Indonesian National Revolution, 1945-50* (Melbourne: Longman, 1974) is concise.

——, *The Blood of the People: Revolution and the End of Traditional Rule in Northern Sumatra* (Kuala Lumpur: OUP, 1979).

Smail, John, *Bandung in the Early Revolution, 1945-6. A Study in the Social History of the Indonesian Revolution* (Ithaca: Cor SEAP, 1964).

Sutter, John O., *Indonesianisasi: Politics in a Changing Economy, 1940-55*, 4 vols. (Ithaca: Cornell Southeast Asia Studies, 1959) is painstaking and thorough.

8. SOCIETY IN HISTORICAL PERSPECTIVE

Fox, James, *Harvest of the Palm: Ecological Change in Eastern Indonesia* (Cambridge, Mass.: Harvard UP, 1977).

Geertz, Clifford, *The Religion of Java* (Glencoe, NY: Free Press, 1960). One of the many products of the Massachusetts Institute of Technology team that worked in Pare, East Java, in the 1950s.

——, *The Social History of an Indonesian Town* (Cambridge, Mass.: MIT Press, 1965).

Jay, Robert, *Religion and Politics in Rural Central Java* (New Haven: Yale University Southeast Asia Studies, 1963). Another product of the MIT group.

——, *Javanese Villagers: Social Relations in Rural Modjokuto* (Cambridge, Mass.: MIT Press, 1969).

Liddle, R. William, *Ethnicity, Party and National Integration: an Indonesian Case Study* (New Haven: Yale UP, 1970) deals with northern Sumatra.

Selosoemardjan, *Social Change in Jogjakarta* (Ithaca: Cor UP, 1962) is a brilliant description of one province by an 'insider'.

Siegel, James, *The Rope of God* (Berkeley: UCP, 1969) focusses on Aceh in Sumatra.

Skinner, G. William (ed.), *Local, Ethnic and National Loyalties in Village Indonesia* (New Haven: Yale University Southeast Asia Studies, 1959).

9. FICTION

Idrus, 'Surabaja', trans. by S. U. Nababan and B. Anderson, *Indonesia*, 5 (April 1968) is a bitter short story about the Surabaya fighting in 1945.

Lubis, Mochtar, *A Road with No End*, trans. by A. H. Johns (London: Hutchinson, 1968). Deals with middle-class Indonesians in the revolution.

——. *Twilight in Djakarta*, trans. by Claire Holt (London: Hutchinson, 1963). Set in the early 1950s.

Mihardja, Achdiat K., *Atheist*, trans, by R. J. Maguire (St Lucia: Queensland University Press, 1972). Sets the crisis of an individual against the revolutionary conflict of ideas.

Toer, Pramoedya Ananta, *A Heap of Ashes*, trans. by H. Aveling (St Lucia: University of Queensland Press, 1975) is a collection of vivid short stories of the 1940s and 1950s by Indonesia's most successful novelist, recently released from fourteen years' imprisonment.

5. VIETNAM

1. GENERAL STUDIES

Buttinger, Joseph, *The Smaller Dragon: A Political History of Viet-Nam* (New York: Praeger, 1958) provides a useful entry to French sources prior to 1900.

——, *Viet-Nam: A Dragon Embattled*, 2 vols. (New York: Praeger, 1967) is a massive attempt to grapple with twentieth-century developments. The discussion of 1940–54 remains cogent, but the account of earlier events is dated, and the analysis of post-Geneva affairs is coloured by the author's involvement with the Ngo Dinh Diem regime. Vietnam still lacks a good history textbook.

Duiker, William J., *The Rise of Nationalism in Vietnam, 1900–1941* (Ithaca: Cor UP, 1976) fails to analyse nationalism, but manages to replace Buttinger as a political chronology for the period.

Marr, David G., *Vietnamese Anticolonialism, 1885–1925* (Berkeley: UCP, 1971) focusses on the political and intellectual responses of the last two generations of Vietnamese Confucian literati.

Osborne, Milton E., *The French Presence in Cochinchina and Cambodia: Rule and Response, 1859–1905* (Ithaca: Cor UP, 1969) treats early Franco-Vietnamese 'culture contact'.

Smith, Ralph B., *Vietnam and the West* (London: Heinemann, 1968).

Steinberg, David J. *et al.*, *In Search of Southeast Asia* (New York: Praeger, 1971) has a thoughtful Vietnam section.

Vien, Nguyen Khac *et al.*, *Viet Nam: A Historical Sketch* (Hanoi: FLPH, 1974) avoids a number of key issues, for example what happened during the thousand years of Chinese rule.

——, trans. 'Confucianism and Marxism', in *Tradition and Revolution in Vietnam* (Berkeley: Indochina Resource Centre, 1974) pp. 15–52.

Woodside, Alexander P., *Vietnam and the Chinese Model* (Cambridge, Mass.: Harvard UP, 1971) introduces Vietnamese institutions just prior to the French invasion.

——, *Community and Revolution in Modern Vietnam* (Boston: Houghton Mifflin, 1976) is a complex, issue-oriented study, particularly useful for fathoming sociocultural trends.

2. COLONIAL SOCIETY

Brocheux, Pierre, 'Grands propriétaires et fermiers dans l'ouest de la Cochinchine pendant la période coloniale', *Revue Historique*, **CCXLVI** (July–Dec. 1971) pp. 59–76, provides an introduction to the author's important Sorbonne thesis.

——, 'Crise économique et société en Indochine française', *Revue française d'histoire d'outre-mer*, 232–3 (1976) pp. 655–67, discusses the impact of the depression.

Chesneaux, Jean *et al.*, *Tradition et revolution au Vietnam* (Paris: Anthropos, 1971) has a number of important essays.

Chinh, Truong and Giap, Vo Nguyen, *The Peasant Question, 1937–8*, trans. Christine P. White (Ithaca: Cor UP, 1974). An early Vietnamese communist assessment.

Cook, Megan, *The Constitutionalist Party in Cochinchina: The Years of Decline, 1930-42* (Melbourne: Monash University Papers on Southeast Asia, 1977) examines the Vietnamese bourgeoisie and its politics.

Hémery, Daniel, *Révolutionnaires Vietnamiens et Pouvoir Colonial en Indochine* (Paris: Maspero, 1975) provides a stunning portrait of colonial society as seen by ICP and Trotskyist intellectuals in Saigon in the 1930s.

Kelly, Gail P., *Franco-Vietnamese Schools, 1918-38* (Ann Arbor: University Microfilms, 1975) discusses the educational institutions which helped to produce the intelligentsia.

Long, Ngo Vinh, *Before the Revolution* (Cambridge, Mass.: MIT Press, 1973) translates a number of intelligentsia depictions of the dismal rural conditions of the 1930s.

——, *Peasant Revolutionary Struggles in Vietnam in the 1930s* (Ann Arbor: University Microfilms, 1978) is filled with fascinating detail but lacks analytical precision.

Marr, David G., *Vietnamese Tradition on Trial, 1920-45* (Berkeley: UCP, 1981) focusses on the intelligentsia.

Popkin, Samuel L., *The Rational Peasant* (Berkeley: UCP, 1979) carries the scholarly debate about Vietnamese peasants to battlefield proportions.

Porter, Daniel Gareth, *Imperialism and Social Structure in Twentieth Century Vietnam* (Ann Arbor: University Microfilms, 1976) follows the constitutionalists beyond 1945 and also tells us something about the bourgeoisie in Tonkin and Annam.

Robequain, Charles, *Economic Development of French Indochina* (New York: OUP, 1944) is still a necessary work for students of economic history.

Scott, James C., *The Moral Economy of the Peasant* (New Haven: Yale UP, 1976) enlivens the debate about the Vietnamese peasant.

Smith, Ralph B., 'Bui Quang Chieu and the Constitutionalist Party in French Cochinchina, 1917-30', *MAS*, **III**, 2 (1969) pp. 131-50, introduces the bourgeoisie.

——, 'An Introduction to Caodaism', *Bulletin of the School of Oriental and African Studies*, **XXXIII** (1970) pp. 335-49, 573-89, opens up the world of Vietnamese religious movements.

——, 'The Vietnamese Elite of French Cochinchina, 1943', *MAS*, **VI**, 4 (1972) pp. 459-82.

Werner, Jayne S., *The Cao Dai: The Politics of a Vietnamese Syncretic Religious Movement* (Ann Arbor: University Microfilms, 1976) benefits from access to Vietnamese source materials and interviews with surviving dignitaries.

Woodside, Alexander P., 'The Development of Social Organizations in Vietnamese Cities in the Late Colonial Period', *PA*, **XLIV**, 1 (Spring 1971), pp. 39-64.

3. POLITICAL HISTORY

Chi, Hoang Van, *From Colonialism to Communism* (New York: Praeger, 1964). Bitterly anti-communist.

Fall, Bernard B. (ed.), *Ho Chi Minh on Revolution* (New York: Praeger, 1967) contains many of Ho's key formulations.

Frederick, William H., 'Alexandre Varenne and Politics in Indochina, 1925-6', in W. F. Vella (ed.), *Aspects of Vietnamese History* (Honolulu: University of Hawaii Asian Studies, 1973) pp. 96-159, discusses the failure of a socialist party governor-general to institute reforms.

Hémery, Daniel, 'Aux origines des guerres d'indépendance Vietnamiennes: pouvoir colonial et phénomène communiste en Indochine avant la Seconde Guerre mondiale', *le Mouvement Social*, 101 (Oct.–Dec. 1977) pp. 3–35, looks at French policy options in the 1930s.

Ho Chi Minh, *Selected Works*, 4 vols. (Hanoi: FLPH, 1960–2) will reward dedicated readers.

Lacouture, Jean, *Ho Chi Minh: A Political Biography* (New York: Random House, 1968) is the most serviceable biography pending a more scholarly study that taps the growing Vietnamese language sources.

Langlois, Walter G., *André Malraux: The Indochina Adventure* (New York: Praeger, 1966) treats the 1920s from the perspective of a soon-to-be famous author who dabbled in colonial politics.

Our President Ho Chi Minh (Hanoi: FLPH, 1976) is the official Vietnamese biography.

Osborne, Milton E., 'Continuity and Motivation in the Vietnamese Revolution', *PA*, **XLVII**, 1 (Spring 1974) pp. 37–55, provides a measured overview of the 1930–1 confrontation between the French and Vietnamese communism.

An Outline History of the Viet Nam Workers' Party, 1930–70 (Hanoi: FLPH, 1970) summarises the official view of communist history in Vietnam.

Pike, Douglas, *History of Vietnamese Communism, 1925–76* (Stanford: Hoover Institute Press, 1978) is the most disastrous of many treatments of the Indochinese Communist Party.

Sainteny, Jean, *Ho Chi Minh and His Vietnam* (Chicago: Cowles Book Co., 1972) tells us as much about the author as it does about Ho.

Thompson, Virginia, *French Indochina* (London: Allen and Unwin, 1937) is still essential reading in the absence of a rigorous analysis of French policy and performance.

Turner, Robert F., *Vietnamese Communism: Its Origins and Development* (Stanford: Hoover Institute Press, 1975) is very superficial on the pre-1951 period.

4. THE AUGUST 1945 REVOLUTION

Chen, King C., *Vietnam and China, 1938–54* (PUP, 1969) is valuable for the author's access to Kuomintang leaders involved in Vietnam affairs.

Chinh, Truong, *Primer for Revolt* (New York: Praeger, 1963) includes the ICP secretary-general's overall assessment in 1947.

Giap, Vo Nguyen, *Unforgettable Days* (Hanoi: FLPH, 1975) concentrates on diplomatic manoeuvres, 1945–6.

History of the August Revolution (Hanoi: FLPH, 1972) summarises ICP and Viet Minh activities, 1941–5.

Khanh, Huynh Kim, 'The Vietnamese August Revolution Reinterpreted', *JAS*, **XXX**, 4 (Aug. 1971) pp. 761–82, looks closely at Vietnamese sources.

——, *Vietnamese Communism: The Pre-Power Phase, 1925–45* (Ann Arbor: University Microfilms, 1972) offers a wealth of detail.

McAlister, John T., Jr and Mus, Paul, *The Vietnamese and their Revolution* (New York: Harper, 1970). Events from the perspective of a distinguished French scholar of Buddhism, Paul Mus, who became directly involved in the conflict, 1945–7

McAlister, John T., Jr, *Viet Nam: The Origins of Revolution* (New York: Knopf, 1969) is useful mainly because the author had access to classified French army documents of the 1940s.

Smith, Ralph B., 'The Japanese Period in Indochina and the Coup of 9 March 1945', *JSEAS*, **IX**, 2 (Sept. 1978) pp. 268–301, includes data from Tokyo files seized by American occupation forces.

Tan, Chu Van, *Reminiscences on the Army for National Salvation* (Ithaca: Cornell SEAP, 1974) recalls guerrilla operations prior to August 1945.

5. THE FIRST INDOCHINA WAR

Cameron, Allan W. (ed.), *Viet-Nam Crisis: A Documentary History*, vol. 1, 1940–56 (Ithaca: Cor UP, 1971) contains most of the key diplomatic pronouncements.

Duncanson, Dennis J., *Government and Revolution in Vietnam* (London: OUP, 1968). A stern Tory interpretation.

Fall, Bernard B., *The Viet-Minh Regime* (Ithaca: Cornell SEAP, 1956) tries to fathom the nature of people's war in a Vietnamese context. No other Western author has had a better grasp of the Franco-Vietnamese military equation.

——, *Street without Joy* (Harrisburg; Stackpole, 1961) vividly describes the French inability to pin down the Viet Minh.

——, *Hell in a Very Small Place* (New York: Vintage Press, 1968) recounts the battle of Dien Bien Phu and the overall picture, 1953–4.

Giap, Vo Nguyen, *Dien Bien Phu* (Hanoi: FLPH, 1954). Compare this with Fall's account.

Hammer, Ellen J., *The Struggle for Indochina, 1940–55* (Stanford: Stanford UP, 1955) remains the best general account in English.

Lancaster, Donald, *The Emancipation of French Indochina* (London: OUP, 1961) benefits from the author having been a British diplomat in Vietnam.

O'Ballance, Edgar, *The Indo-China War, 1945–54* (London: Faber & Faber, 1964).

6. THE GENEVA CONFERENCE AND AFTER

Elliott, David W. P., *Revolutionary Re-integration: A Comparison of the Foundation of Post-Liberation Political Systems in North Vietnam and China* (Ann Arbor: University Microfilms, 1976) analyses developments above the 17th parallel during the late 1950s.

Lacouture, Jean and Devillers, Philippe, *End of a War* (New York: Praeger, 1969) is the best study.

Lacouture, Jean, *Vietnam: Between Two Truces* (New York: Random House, 1966) discusses the failure of the Geneva formula.

Race, Jeffrey, *War Comes to Long An* (Berkeley: UCP, 1972) details the Diem government's repression and communist countermeasures in a Mekong-delta province.

Warner, Denis, *The Last Confucian* (New York: Macmillan, 1963) affords an insight into Ngo Dinh Diem, his family and the entire Saigon political system.

7. BIBLIOGRAPHIES

Cotter, Michael, *Vietnam: Guide to Reference Sources* (Boston: G. K. Hall, 1977) lists 1400 publications in English, French and Vietnamese.

Chau, Phan Thien, *Vietnamese Communism: A Research Bibliography* (Westport, Conn.: Greenwood Press, 1975) is of only limited use for the pre-1954 period.

6. MALAYA

1. HISTORICAL BACKGROUND

Bastin, J. and Winks, R. (eds.), *Malaysia: Selected Historical Readings* (Kuala Lumpur: OUP, 1966).

Bonney, R., *Kedah 1771-1821* (Kuala Lumpur: OUP, 1971). A study of Kedah's history by a Malaysian historian with a fresh perspective on the establishment of the British presence in Penang.

Chai Hon Chan, *The Development of British Malaya* (Kuala Lumpur: OUP, 1967) is based largely on colonial annual reports and deals broadly with changes introduced by the British.

Cowan, C. D., *Nineteenth Century Malaya: The Origins of British Political Control* (London and New York: OUP, 1961). Scholarly study of British intervention in the Malay states.

Emerson, R., *Malaysia: A Study in Direct and Indirect Rule* (New York: Macmillan, 1937 [reprinted in Kuala Lumpur: University of Malaya Press, 1964]). Regarded as a classic in the study of British and Dutch colonialism in the area.

Gullick, J. M., *Indigenous Political Systems of Western Malaya* (London: The Athlone Press, 1968). Useful for understanding the traditional political systems in Perak, Selangor, Negri Sembilan and Pahang.

Khoo Kay Kim, *The Western Malay States* (Kuala Lumpur: OUP, 1972). A study of early European economic interest and the extension of British control in the west coast states of Malaya.

Loh, Philip, *The Malay States 1877-1895* (Kuala Lumpur; OUP, 1969) pays attention to the leading administrators and their thinking.

Parkinson, C. N., *British Intervention in Malaya 1867-1877* (Singapore: University of Malaya Press, 1960).

Sadka, E., *The Protected Malay States, 1874-1895* (Kuala Lumpur: University of Malaya Press, 1968) studies the residential system of the four western Malay states.

Thio, Eunice, *British Policy in the Malay Peninsula 1880-1910*, Vol. 1 (Kuala Lumpur: University of Malaya Press, 1969) documents the extension of British influence to the other parts of Malaya.

Turnbull, C. M., *The Straits Settlements, 1826-67* (Kuala Lumpur: OUP, 1972). A study of Penang, Malacca and Singapore which together formed the Straits Settlements.

Winstedt, R. O., *A History of Malaya* (London: Luzak and Co., 1935). Though dated, this study, together with the volume on *The Malays* (below), are useful introductions by a former British official.

——, *The Malays: A Cultural History* (London: Routledge & Kegan Paul, 1935).

2. ECONOMY AND SOCIETY

Ali, S. Husin, *Malay Peasant Society and Leadership* (Kuala Lumpur: University of Malaya Press, 1975). Leadership and society in three rural areas by a local anthropologist.
Allen, G. C. and Donithorne, A., *Western Enterprise in Indonesia and Malaya* (London: George Allen & Unwin, 1957).
Arasaratnam, S., *Indians in Malaysia and Singapore* (Kuala Lumpur: OUP [revised edition] 1979). A useful survey.
Blythe, W., *The Impact of Chinese Secret Societies in Malaya* (London: OUP, 1969). Detailed study by a former Secretary for Chinese Affairs in Malaya who had access to police and other government records.
Drabble, J., *Rubber in Malaya 1876-1922* (Kuala Lumpur: OUP, 1973). The beginnings of the rubber industry.
Gamba, C., *The Origins of Trade Unionism in Malaya* (Singapore: Eastern Universities Press, 1962). One of the first books on the subject.
Jackson, J. C., *Planters and Speculators: Chinese and European Agricultural Enterprise in Malaya 1786-1921* (Kuala Lumpur: University of Malaya Press, 1968). A study of early commercial agriculture by a historical geographer.
Lim Chong Yah, *Economic Development of Modern Malaya* (New York: OUP, 1967). A good general account.
Lim Teck Ghee, *Peasants and Their Agricultural Economy in Colonial Malaya 1874-1941* (Kuala Lumpur: OUP, 1977). Examines the impact of colonial rule on the Malay peasantry.
Loh, Philip, *Seeds of Separatism: Educational Policy in Malaya* (Kuala Lumpur: OUP, 1975). The author attempts to show that the lack of racial integration can be traced to the development of different educational systems.
Parmer, J. M., *Colonial Labor Policy and Administration: A History of Labor in the Rubber Plantation Industry, 1910-1941* (New York: Association of Asian Studies, 1960).
Purcell, V., *The Chinese in Malaya* (First edition, 1948. Reprinted in Kuala Lumpur: OUP, 1967). Dated but still useful. The author once served as Protector of the Chinese in Malaya.
Puthucheary, J., *Ownership and Control in the Malayan Economy* (Singapore: Eastern Universities Press, 1960). A stimulating volume.
Puthucheary, M., *The Politics of Administration: The Malaysian Experience* (Kuala Lumpur: University of Malaya Press, 1978). Covers the development of the Malaysian bureaucracy.
Wong Lin Ken, *The Malayan Tin Industry to 1914* (Tucson: University of Arizona Press, 1965).

3. POLITICAL DEVELOPMENT

Allen, James de V., *The Malayan Union* (New Haven: Yale Monograph, 1968) provides a handy starting point.
Barber, N., *The War of the Running Dogs: The Malayan Emergency 1948-1960* (New York: Weybright and Talley, 1971) is intended for a popular audience.
Bedlington, S., *Malaysia and Singapore: The Building of New States* (Ithaca: Cor UP, 1978).
Cheah Boon Kheng *The Masked Comrades: A Study of the Communist United Front in Malaya, 1945-48* (Singapore: Times Books International, 1979) provides some new and interesting material.
Clutterbuck, R., *Riot and Revolution in Singapore and Malaya, 1945-1960*

(London: Faber & Faber, 1973). The MCP's use of the schools and trade unions as part of its urban strategy is looked into as well as the Emergency itself.

Gordon, B. K., *The Dimensions of Conflict in Southeast Asia* (New Jersey: Prentice-Hall, 1966). Southeast Asian international relations.

Hanna, W., *The Formation of Malaysia: New Factor in World Politics* (New York: American Universities Field Service, 1966). A collection of field reports.

Hanrahan, G. Z., *The Communist Struggle in Malaya* (New York: International Secretariat, Institute of Pacific Relations, 1954) is one of the first books on the subject.

Mackie, J. A. C., *Konfrontasi: The Indonesia-Malaysia Dispute 1963-1966* (Kuala Lumpur: OUP, 1974) examines the external factors as well as domestic politics that led to Confrontation.

Means, G., *Malaysian Politics* (London: Hodder & Stoughton [second edition], 1976) is regarded as a standard text.

Milne, R. S. and Mauzy, D., *Politics and Government in Malaysia* (Singapore: Federal Publications, 1978) examines both the institutions and processes of Malaysian politics.

Mohd. Noordin Sopiee, *From Malayan Union to Singapore Separation* (Kuala Lumpur: University of Malaya Press, 1974) recounts the attempts at political unification in the Malaysian area and their attendant difficulties.

Ongkili, J. P., *The Borneo Response to Malaysia, 1961-1963* (Singapore: Donald Moore, 1967) looks at the formation of Malaysia not from Kuala Lumpur but from the perspective of the three Borneo territories involved in the Malaysia negotiations.

Pye, L., *Guerilla Communism in Malaya* (Princeton: PUP, 1965). The author had the cooperation of the government and the book thus contains useful material.

Ratnam, K. J., *Communalism and the Political Process in Malaya* (Singapore: University of Malaya Press, 1965). One of the first published analyses of the racial factor in Malaysian politics.

Roff, W., *The Origins of Malay Nationalism* (Kuala Lumpur: University of Malaya Press, 1967). An invaluable study of the emergence of pre-war Malay political awareness.

Short, A., *The Communist Insurrection in Malaya, 1948-60* (London: Frederick Muller Ltd., 1975). Commissioned by the Malaysian Government and intended to be an official history of the Emergency, this book benefits from the access its author had to Government papers and captured documents.

Stenson, M. R., *Industrial Conflict in Malaya* (Kuala Lumpur: OUP, 1970). The growth of organised labour and the pre-war industrial unrests are examined in the context of the subsequent MCP revolt of 1948.

Stockwell, A. J., *British Policy and Malay Politics during the Malayan Union Experiment 1942-48* (Kuala Lumpur: Malaysian Branch of the Royal Asiatic Society Monograph, 1979). Discusses a crucial period in the development of Malay politics and is based largely on interviews and recently opened records.

Yeo Kim Wah, *Political Development in Singapore 1945-1955* (Singapore: University of Singapore Press, 1973). An account of Singapore at a time when it was an integral part of Malaysia's political history.

Wang Gungwu (ed), *Malaysia - A Survey* (New York: Frederick A. Praeger, 1964). Contributions by various scholars who examine Malaysia from the perspective of their respective disciplines.

4. WRITINGS BY POLITICAL PARTICIPANTS

Abdul Rahman, Tunku, *Looking Back* (Kuala Lumpur: Pustaka Antar, 1977). Reminiscence by the former Prime Minister which first appeared in a local newspaper.

Boestamam, A., *Carving the Path to the Summit* Athens: Ohio University Press, 1979). Translanted from Malay. Covers the early years of Boestamam's political career.

Ibrahim Yaacob, *Melihat Tanah Air* [Observations on the Motherland] (Kota Bharu: Matba'ah Al-Islamiah, 1941). Attempts to provide a nationalistic perspective of Malaysian history. Useful in providing some insight into Ibrahim Yaacob's political views and his early political involvements, the book awaits translation into English.

Lee Kuan Yew, *The Battle for Merger* (Singapore: Ministry of Culture, 1961). Collection of speeches.

Omraet, R., *Singapore: A Police Background* (London: Dorothy Crisp and Company, 1949). Written by a former senior police officer who for a period dealt with political affairs.

Tan Cheng, Lock, *Malayan Problems from a Chinese Point of View* (Singapore: Tannsco, 1947).

Tan Siew Sin, *Blueprint for Unity* (Kuala Lumpur: Malaysian Chinese Association H.Q., 1972). Speeches by a former President of the MCA.

Tan, T. H., *The Prince and I* (Singapore: Sam Boyd Enterprise and Mini Media, 1979). Anecdotal but useful.

Index

Numbers in bold-face type indicate a full Biographical Note.

Index

The Contributors

ROBIN JEFFREY is in the Department of Politics, Latrobe University, Melbourne, Australia. He is the author of *The Decline of Nayar Dominance* (1976) and editor of *People, Princes and Paramount Power* (1978).

LEE KAM HING is Deputy Dean, Faculty of Arts and Social Sciences, University of Malaya, Kuala Lumpur. He has published *Politics in Perak, 1969-74* (1977) and *A Socio-Economic History of Perak in the 1920s and 1930s* (1978) and has edited *The 1978 Malaysian General Elections* (1979).

D. A. LOW, Vice-Chancellor of the Australian National University, Canberra, is the author and editor of a number of studies of modern Africa and the editor of *Soundings in Modern South Asian History* (1967) and *Congress and the Raj: Facets of the Indian Struggle* (1977).

ALFRED W. McCOY lectures in the Department of History, University of New South Wales, Sydney. He is the author of *The Politics of Heroin in Southeast Asia* (1972) and *Drug Traffic: Narcotics and Organized Crime in Australia* (1980), and has edited *Southeast Asia under Japanese Occupation* (1980).

DAVID MARR is in the Research School of Pacific Studies, Australian National University, Canberra. He has written *Vietnamese Anticolonialism* (1971) and *Vietnamese Tradition on Trial* (1981) and has edited *Reflections from Captivity* (1978) and, with Anthony Reid, *Perceptions of the Past in Southeast Asia* (1980).

ANTHONY REID is in the Research School of Pacific Studies, Australian National University, Canberra. He is the author of *The Contest for North Sumatra* (1969), *The Indonesian National Revolution* (1974) and *The Blood of the People* (1979). He has edited *Pre-Colonial State Systems in Southeast Asia* (1975) with Lance Castles, and *Perceptions of the Past in Southeast Asia* (1980) with David Marr.